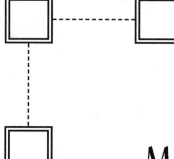

MULTICULTURAL TEACHING

A Handbook of Activities, Information, and Resources

SEVENTH EDITION

Pamela L. Tiedt
University of California, Berkeley

Iris M. Tiedt
Moorhead State University

PEARSON

Boston • New York • San Francisco
Mexico City • Montreal • Toronto • London • Madrid • Munich • Paris
Hong Kong • Singapore • Tokyo • Cape Town • Sydney

Series Editor: Traci Mueller
Series Editorial Assistant: James P. Neal, III
Marketing Manager: Krista Groshong
Production Editor: Patrick Cash-Peterson
Editorial Production Service: Walsh & Associates, Inc.
Composition Buyer: Linda Cox
Manufacturing Buyer: Andrew Turso
Electronic Composition: Omegatype Typography, Inc.
Cover Administrator: Joel Gendron

For related titles and support materials, visit our online catalog at www.ablongman.com.

Between the time website information is gathered and then published, it is not unusual for some sites to have closed. Also, the transcription of URLs can result in typographical errors. The publisher would appreciate notification where these errors occur so that they can be corrected in subsequent editions.

Library of Congress Cataloging-in-Publication Data

Tiedt, Pamela L.
    Multicultural teaching : a handbook of activities, information, and resources / Pamela L. Tiedt, Iris M. Tiedt. — 7th ed.
      p. cm.
    Includes bibliographical references and index.
    ISBN 0-205-45117-9
    1. Multicultural education—United States.   2. Cross-cultural orientation—United States. 3. Teaching—United States.   4. Education, Elementary—Activity programs—United States. 5. Teachers—Training of—United States. I. Tiedt, Iris M. II. Title.

LC1099.3.T54   2005
370.117'0973—dc22

                                    2005045800

Printed in the United States of America

10 9 8 7 6 5 4 3 2 1   09 08 07 06 05

C O N T E N T S

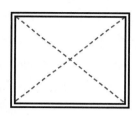

8   Teaching Multiculturally around the Year   247

TO THE READER

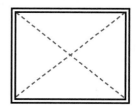

The seventh edition of *Multicultural Teaching* is dedicated once again to teachers who are now in K–8 classrooms as well as to students in teacher education programs who will be our future teachers. Our intent is not only to inform you but also to inspire you to become excellent teachers who care about children and involved citizens who care about our country and our world.

Multicultural education has long been an important concern. Each day we are inundated with new information about the needs of people in our multicultural world. The media present instantaneous reports of what is happening throughout our global village. We can't fail to be involved in multiculturalism.

Over the years since we wrote this first comprehensive book on multicultural education in 1979, we have seen shifting perspectives and controversy among Americans. We have noted the ongoing discussion of the separation of church and state, questions related to the role of the federal government versus that of the individual states in maintaining civil rights, and total reversals of thought as in the matter of bilingual education. Multicultural education is a subject that is constantly in flux.

In 2006, we present a revised edition of *Multicultural Teaching* that incorporates the strengths of previous editions yet also:

develops a powerful Esteem/Empathy/Equity Model featuring three major themes interwoven throughout the text.

clarifies the evolution of multicultural thinking from the founding of our country to current decision making as we go through the first decades of the twenty-first century.

integrates theory (the knowledge base) and practice (creative learning activities that cross the curriculum).

includes many activities and thematic studies designed to help teachers engage students with multicultural concerns.

engages future teachers with keeping a Reflective Teaching Portfolio and working with Cooperative Learning Groups as they learn to teach *multiculturally*.

We would like to thank the following reviewers of this edition for their time and input: Lacey S. Curtis, Ohio University Southern; Theresa Garfield, Palo Alto College; Younghee Kim, Southern Oregon University; and Gary Stiler, University of Southern Indiana.

We hope that you will join with us in reaching out to young learners who will be making crucial decisions as we move through this new century. They need our guidance as they look ahead to envision solutions to problems that we face today.

Pamela and Iris Tiedt

MULTICULTURAL TEACHING

Part I

A Framework for Multicultural Education

Concern for multicultural education affects all of us. The issues may vary from school to school, as each community experiences such challenges such as religious intolerance, achievement gaps, and diverse languages spoken in the classroom. In Part I we present the fundamentals of multicultural education as we see them: (1) what multicultural education means today and how it has become what it is, (2) what is to be taught under the umbrella of multicultural education, and (3) how we can best teach multiculturally.

In our efforts to meet these challenges, we can learn from the words of hope written by Rabindranath Tagore, a noted Hindu poet, philosopher, and Nobel laureate:

> Where the mind is without fear
>   And the head is held high,
> Where knowledge is free;
> Where the world has not been broken up
>   Into fragments by narrow domestic walls;
> Where words come out from the depth of truth;
> Where tireless striving stretches its arms towards perfection;
> Where the clear stream of reason has not lost its way
>   Into the dreary desert sand of dead habit;
> Where the mind is led forward by thee
>   Into ever-widening thought and action;
> Into that heaven of freedom, my Father,
> Let my country awake.

"Give me your tired,
your poor,
Your huddled masses
yearning to breathe free,
The wretched refuse of
your teeming shore,
Send these, the homeless,
tempest-tost to me,
I lift my lamp
beside the golden door!"

Emma Lazarus
"Mother of Exiles"

Educating Children in Our Unique Multiculture

Because our population is derived from many different nations throughout the world, over the years, the United States has become a giant multiculture, unique in its diversity. Physically, our citizens range in skin color from the very lightest to the very darkest. Philosophically, we represent those who follow the teachings of Buddha, those who follow the teachings of the Book (Christians, Jews, and Moslems), and many other variations in religious belief. As a nation, we recognize our individual differences, and we uphold our individual rights; yet we celebrate our commonality as citizens of a strong democracy.

How can such diverse people coexist? How did national thinking evolve toward our current approach to multiculturalism? As we begin this text, we focus on the many facets of multicultural education, including teaching and learning in a diverse society. In this chapter, we will talk about the concept of diversity, different definitions of multicultural education, the development of multicultural thinking, and the assumptions underlying our approach to multicultural education.

We build multicultural education on a shared goal: to create an educational system that will educate *all* children in our society, to permit them to develop to the greatest extent of their potential, so they can participate fully in what the world has to offer, to contribute to the world and to benefit from the best resources of the world. This has not always been the goal of education in the United States. In the past, the best education has been limited to a few, primarily white, English-speaking males. Membership in this elite group was usually conferred at birth, so there was little chance for others to break into this world. For most people, education was focused on attaining basic skills that prepared them to be interchangeable cogs in the burgeoning industrial workforce.

Throughout the twentieth century and into the twenty-first, we have begun to seek this more inclusive goal for education, to reach out to groups that have been historically underrepresented in positions of power, and to become concerned that all students achieve at their highest possible level. It would be terribly naïve to claim that we are even close to meeting this goal. However, the increasing attention paid to multicultural education in our schools is a sign of greater awareness of the importance of diversity and the need to provide education that is appropriate for individual students. We want to educate *all* children in our

3

society so they can learn to see themselves as worthwhile human beings, participate fully as citizens of the world, and achieve their dreams.

DIVERSITY IN THE UNITED STATES

When we talk about diversity in schools, we almost immediately think of race, ethnicity, or skin color, but diversity comes in many forms. Some differences are visible, such as age, height, or left-handedness. We are accustomed to categorizing people into distinct groups. As someone walks by, we may experience discomfort if we cannot immediately sort that person as "male" or "female." And if people dye their gray hair black or their brown hair blonde, we can conclude that the gray hair of aging or the dark hair associated with certain ancestries has negative value. However, this prestige norm can readily change. Sometimes curly hair is popular and straight-haired people have permanents to make their hair "better." Other times, straight hair is more highly valued and people go to the extremes of having their hair ironed in order to fit in. But diversity is more than a simple question of hair style or group identification. In the largest sense, *diversity* means our future as a society because diversity is the foundation of evolution. Unfortunately, the unpleasant reality is that social diversity becomes inextricably tied to the hierarchy of power as prestige value is associated with particular forms. "White"-skinned people are more often hired than equally qualified, or even more qualified, African Americans. Latinos are a majority in many regions, but the number of Latinos in politics doesn't reflect their percentage in the population. Women still earn less than men in the same jobs. Children from families with incomes below the poverty level are more likely to go to schools that are in disrepair and have less experienced teachers, whereas children from higher income families go to schools with more computers, enrichment opportunities in the arts, advanced placement classes, and support for a variety of sports.

The Unites States Has Always Been Diverse

Consider the population in the United States: From Alaska to Florida, from Hawaii to Maine, each region has been influenced by a variety of distinct racial, ethnic, linguistic, religious, and cultural groups. Each region has brought its diversity to the union of states. For example, look at the range of languages other than English spoken in the following states, given in order of percentage of population:

Alaska:	Inuit, Inupiaq, and Yupik (Eskimo/Aleut languages), Spanish, Tagalog
Florida:	Spanish (and Spanish Creole), French (and French Creole), German
Hawaii:	Native Hawaiian, other Pacific Island languages, Tagalog, Japanese, Chinese
Maine:	French, Spanish (and Spanish Creole), German, Italian, Chinese[1]

Some of these language speakers are recent immigrants; others have been residing there for many generations. As the United States grows in population and diversity, the question of how best to serve the interests of every group and how to protect the rights of the minorities and less powerful has brought increasing controversy.

Compared to other countries, the United States has always looked like a haven for diversity. In Europe and Asia, religious intolerance and lack of economic opportunities went hand in hand with a state religion and strict class system. Here there was room to practice one's religion in peace. One's parentage did not define how people treated you; rather one's own efforts determined one's worth. People from different cultures and speaking different languages were able to live together in relative harmony in cities such as New Orleans, in which speakers of English, French, and Spanish, African American slaves, and *gens de couleur libre* (free men of color) mingled with a French-educated aristocracy, American fur trappers, and a mixed-race social class.

But even in this land of freedom, there were substantial structural inequities. The Chinese Exclusion Act of 1882 is an example of the virulent anti-immigrant prejudice of the nineteenth century. Men controlled their wives' property while children labored as hard as adults or starved in the streets. Originally, only white men who held land could vote. Rich men's sons received schooling; women were often illiterate. The indigenous people were decimated by unfamiliar diseases, physically and culturally uprooted, and constantly betrayed by agreements they had made to share the land peacefully.

The first Africans probably came as to this country as indentured servants, like many Europeans, obligated to work off their debt to pay their passage. As the "Slave Triangle" expanded, traffic in human flesh became an opportunity to grow wealthy. In the three legs of the triangle, kidnapped Africans were picked up in West African ports and sold as slaves in the Indies and southern U.S. markets. The money bought goods such as rum and cotton, which were then taken to England to feed the manufacturing industries.

The history of the United States has been intimately intertwined with the history of African Americans and that "peculiar institution" of slavery since its very beginning. Even the framers of the new republic wrestled with the question of slavery. And each generation that followed has had to deal with slavery in its own way, often pushing much of the controversy under the carpet for future generations.

The American Multiculture

With increasing pressure due to immigrants from Europe and then Asia, refugees from Latin America and Africa, along with the African American and Native American populations already present, the United States have struggled to fulfill the welcome expressed on the Statue of Liberty. The *essence* of the country continues to be diverse, making it difficult to describe a single *American culture*. Unique among countries at the time, the United States was attempting to build a society that encompassed many diverse cultures. Therefore, we claim this identity as a MULTICULTURE. As the poet Ishmael Reed describes us, we are a place "where the cultures of the world crisscross." We use the concept of a *multiculture* as a recognition of the reality we live in as well as the goal toward which we strive. In a multiculture, there is more than one "normal" way to think, live, or practice, and the right to do so is protected by the most basic laws of the country.

Our discussion of the multiculture is predicated on an understanding of the meaning of *culture*. Look at the some of the different ways *culture* is defined in the dictionary:

1. Cultivation, tillage.
2. The act of developing the intellectual and moral faculties, especially by education.

3. Enlightenment and excellence of taste acquired by intellectual and aesthetic training.
4. The integrated pattern of human knowledge, belief, and behavior that depends upon the capacity for learning and transmitting knowledge to succeeding generations.[2]

In our discussion of culture, we will focus on its anthropological dimension, as in the following definition, from the same dictionary:

> Cultural anthropology is the study of mankind that deals with human culture, especially with respect to social structure, language, law, politics, religion, magic, art, and technology.

Some of the diverse cultures in the United States may be familiar, such as the Amish in Pennsylvania and Indiana, or the Puerto Ricans in New York, because we have seen pictures of them or they are labeled in the media as distinct groups. Other groups, such as Hassidic Jews and Sikhs, are highly visible groups in areas where they congregate because of their distinctive dress and appearance. Yet the cultures behind the turban (Sikh) and the beard (Hassidim) remain opaque to "mainstream" America. In addition, many ethnic groups or cultures may be invisible to us because they exist below the level of mainstream awareness.

"Deaf culture" is an example of this invisibility. Because deaf people are spread throughout the population, it is easy to neglect this unique culture until you see someone standing off to one side at a lecture, translating spoken language into sign for a small cluster of people. An example of another little-known group is the estimated 50,000 to 100,000 "little people" in the United States. Defined as anyone under 4'10", they are often called midgets, which is offensive, or dwarves, which is preferred.

These groups we have mentioned are only a few examples of the true diversity of human life, but they are the ones who are left out when we learn to consider certain beliefs and practices as "normal."

Who Is an American?

Professor Ronald Takaki, a noted historian and Asian American, tells of a cab ride in which the driver asks him where he is from. Not satisfied with Takaki's answer of "California," the driver wants to know where he is *really* from. Of course, Takaki understands that the driver wants to know his Asian country of origin. He has categorized this English-speaking gentleman as Asian or Asian American, but certainly not *American*. However, we must remember that we all came from somewhere else, and we carry our cultural heritage along with us into today's world.

Technically, any person who lives on the North or South American continents could be called an "American," but it has become acepted usage for citizens of the United States to allocate that term solely for themselves. Canadians and Mexicans also live in North America, but only the United States has the presumption to call itself America. In addition to the original colonists who were here in 1776 and those later granted citizenship through legislation—that is, former slaves and Native Americans—an American is a person born in the United States or a person who chooses to become a naturalized citizen of this country.

To define what it means to be an American today is complex, for our population is comprised of people from many different national and cultural backgrounds. The 2000 census reveals a total population of more than 283 million diverse people living in the United States; yet few families can be considered native to this land. Even the Indians "discovered" by Columbus are known to have migrated across the Bering Strait thousands of years ago. Many people first came to America on ships; today many arrive in airplanes as well. The Americans of tomorrow arrive for many of the same reasons as in the past. They come by choice, fleeing physical and economic threats, or looking for a refuge from religious intolerance. The United States is a country populated by immigrants.

In this book we propose **multicultural education** as the education appropriate for all Americans, regardless of ethnic, racial, religious, linguistic, or other distinct heritage. By studying the history and contributions of Asian Americans, therefore, we are not separating Americans of Asian heritage from being Americans. Nor is the study of African American history meant only for the benefit of African Americans. *E Pluribus Unum* ("Out of many, one"). We are unified as Americans and proud of our diversity as Americans.

"Positionality" and Power

We can talk about individual identity in terms of "position," the place one occupies at the table of power. A white man has a different position from which to view the world than a white woman. A black woman has a different perspective on society than a white woman. The differences in their positions constrain what they feel they can and cannot do. Each of us belongs to many different groups; therefore, we need to recognize the impact of membership on ourselves and others. Roles and power in the world are distributed unequally, with the white European male at the top of the heap. Look around you for evidence of these hierarchies: the staff of the local elementary school (are more minorities working the more menial jobs?), the faces you see on TV (what percentage of faces reflect the distribution of race/ethnicity in your community?), the expectations underlying the appeal of advertising (what kinds of families are shown in ads—are there any same-sex couples?). We can describe this situation by saying that in our society, "whiteness" is assumed unless otherwise specified, that "whiteness" is the privileged position.

The movements to establish university programs such as ethnic studies and women's studies have enlightened all of us to the power of the lens through which we view the world. This lens is made up of many different elements; for example, the culture in which we grew up—our personal experiences, our knowledge, skills, and attitudes—is unique to each individual. As a result, we understand that everyone is "biased"; that is, no one's lens can be considered the "standard" against which others are judged. We all need to become aware of the limitations of our lenses and the assumptions that they lead us to make about others as we divide the world into "us" and "them."

As society changes so rapidly, we look for new ways to think about ourselves. In Gloria Anzaldúa's landmark book *La Frontera/Borderlands,* she drew on her experience as a Latina, a lesbian, and a writer to introduce the concept of "the Borderlands." She defines it as follows:

> The Borderlands are physically present wherever two or more cultures edge each other, where people of different races occupy the same territory, where under-, lower-, middle- and upper-classes touch, where the space between two individuals shrinks with intimacy.[3]

Anzaldúa sees a new kind of America developing, an America in which people move freely among different cultures and different identities, an America of many possibilities. Perhaps this change is threatening to some who will hide behind their gated communities and ignore the reality around them. But evolution can't be stopped, even by strengthening border patrols and deporting illegal immigrants. Most of us experience the presence of the Borderlands as we go about our daily activities, in the faces and the voices that we interact with. However, the people who still live in a mentally "white" world need to be prepared for the coming changes.

A HISTORY OF MULTICULTURAL THINKING

When this book, *Multicultural Teaching,* was first published in 1979, multicultural education was a new idea. Similar concepts had been presented under the rubric of "intergroup relations" or "intercultural communication," but these had been small steps in recognizing the true breadth of what came to be called multicultural education. The next step was the development of Ethnic Studies as a discipline, led by such scholars as James Banks. Our book was one of the first to propose a more comprehensive, integrated approach better suited to teaching in the elementary and middle schools as well as an inclusive definition of multicultural education that brought in, for example, women, religious groups, the disabled, and English language learners. The process of bringing multicultural education and teaching multiculturally into the school curriculum had begun. Today, the need for multicultural education is recognized throughout the nation.

The Myth of the Melting Pot

As the United States was built on the promise of welcoming immigrants to its shores, so it was built on the promise of the melting pot as described by Israel Zangwill in his play *The Melting Pot* in 1909.

> America is God's Crucible, the great Melting Pot where all the races of Europe are melting and reforming! Here you stand, good folk, think I, when I see them at Ellis Island, here you stand in your fifty hatreds and rivalries, but you won't be long like that, brothers, for these are the fires of God. A fig for your feuds and vendettas! Germans and Frenchmen, Irishmen and Englishmen, Jews and Russians—into the Crucible with you all! God is making the American . . . The real American has not yet arrived. He is only in the Crucible, I tell you—he will be the fusion of all races, the coming superman.[4]

Zangwill coined the term *melting pot,* an image of American culture that continues to appeal to many people today. The picture he draws is striking—no more petty feuds, greater freedom for the individual, all national or ethnic identities transmuted into *Americanism.*

Although people still advocate the goal of the melting pot, or assimilation into the American culture, we hear the term through different ears. Newcomers should forget their native languages and learn to speak and write only English, the language of their *new* selves. Their children should be brought up in American schools where they will learn the shared American values and leave behind the antiquated thinking of the "Old Country."

Estee Lauder, a Jewish Hungarian immigrant who became a fabulously successful businesswoman, says that she was often repelled by the accents and folkways of her family. "I wanted desperately to be 100 percent American," she wrote in her autobiography. We hear the same dream in the voice of Hassan, a Bantu refugee from Somalia, who arrived here in 2004 after spending twelve years seeking freedom for his family: "We can live in peace. There is a law in America: nobody can take your life. That's what makes me believe in peace. I want my children to have a good education. I want to live like the people who live in America—only better. I want to work."

These immigrants thought that assimilation was the key to success. But we question today whether the *melting pot,* a metaphor with implications of total transformation, was ever an accurate description for living in America. Even the earliest immigrants settled into communities where they were near others who shared their culture and language. Many sent their children to special classes to ensure their heritage was preserved. People came together in congregations of shared religion and built community churches, temples, mosques, and synagogues. Urban communities sprouted newspapers and periodicals in different languages, maintaining traditions of reading and writing in the home language. In addition, thinking of the United States as a melting pot requires closing one's eyes to the many examples where assimilation was not possible, such as the treatment of African Americans, the internment of Japanese Americans (but not German Americans), and the abysmal conditions on the reservations where the Native Americans were forced to live.

We need to replace the melting pot metaphor of homogeneous America with a new description to reflect the preservation of diversity. The image we prefer is that of a *tossed salad.* People became part of this country in many different ways; they have combined what they brought into a fresh mixture, keeping one hand on the old (food, language, holiday traditions) while reaching with the other hand for the new (higher education, changing sex roles, different occupational goals.) The "tossed salad" metaphor is even more appropriate today as we welcome new immigrants without expecting them to leave essential parts of their true selves behind. With increasing social and economic mobility, diversity appears to be out in the open and not hidden away anymore.

Many people equate diversity with racial or ethnic groups. They don't believe that multicultural education applies to them because all the children in their classrooms are "white." But diversity is always present behind the facade of similar student faces. An apparently homogeneous classroom might include such children as:

- Thomas, who picked up the message not to talk about his two moms. He knows it's not safe to invite other kids over to play at his house.
- Kendra, who is the lightest colored one in her African American family. She cringes almost daily as unsuspecting people assume she is "white" or tell racist jokes in her presence.
- Larry, whose parents are divorced but share custody. One parent encourages him to study and do his homework while the other only watches TV. As a result, his performance in school is erratic.
- Katrina, whose parents speak English with an accent that she is ashamed of, so she doesn't invite them to come to school events.

America Is a Tossed Salad!

- Julie, who is dyslexic but is too embarrassed to ask for help and, anyway, she believes everybody who says she's just stupid or lazy.
- Joseph, whose parents are Jehovah's Witnesses. When other children talk in class about what they got for a birthday present, he feels his family must be really weird because they don't celebrate birthdays.
- Lily, whose attention in class is limited. After both parents lost their jobs, her family has been homeless, living in a car or a temporary shelter.
- Paul, with no books in the home. Although his parents are educated, they do not read books and certainly not to him because they have no time. When other students mention stories such as "Jack and the Beanstalk," "The Little Engine That Could," or "Goldilocks and the Three Bears," he has no idea what they are talking about.

These children remind us to look at diversity at the individual level. Becoming a multiculturally sensitive teacher requires more than learning about Asian American contributions or Jewish holidays.

New Voices, New Perspectives

The story of the United States has always been the history of *us*—the story of slaveowners and slaves, the story of women rich or poor, the story of the working class. But what most people have learned in U.S. history classes is the story of a *few.* When we see phrases such as *the pioneers and their families, Columbus "discovered" the New World, the push for the "Westward Expansion,"* and *"everybody" needs milk,* we are closing off the possibility of an entire range of differences in human experience. Women and children were pioneers, too. Columbus could "encounter" but not "discover" a land that was already well known to its inhabitants. Native Americans might prefer to think of the Westward movement as the "Invasion from the East." If "everybody" drank milk, many would become sick, since milk products are not processed well by a majority of the world's population (among them Asians, Indians, and East European Jews). When we study the travels of Lewis and Clark, we read the journals kept by them and other men of the company. Would that story seem different viewed through the eyes of York, Clark's black slave, or Sacajawea, who had a baby during the trip? How does the person who tells the tale affect our perspective of the event?

The fact that these voices have not usually been heard from is an example of racism— the assumption that whites represent the "norm" in thoughts and behavior—and sexism— the assumption that men can represent the experiences of the entire human race. In order to learn the new history, no longer the tale told just by the winners, we need to hear multiple voices and stories from different points of view in order to acknowledge that there are many legitimate perspectives. For example, we are reading more diaries and other primary sources to hear the "voices" of the people themselves, telling their own story instead of having it told for them by others. The new questions we must ask are:

- Whose story is worth telling?
- What kind of story will be told?
- How will the story be told?

The new stories that are told may make us uncomfortable because they are full of violence and pain. We have not always made good choices or been rewarded for our struggles. Our history is not a straightforward tale of progress and continued improvement.

A major consequence of this rethinking process was the breaking down of the canon's stranglehold on education. Suddenly people noticed that the reading lists for the required college classes typically known as "Intro to Western Civ" included only works by DWEMs (Dead White European Men). This implied that other cultural traditions were not as civilized (China, the Arab world) or had not produced work of intellectual value (Africans, women). Eliminating these gaping holes in the curriculum required a massive structural change that led to strong resistance and counter-resistance. However, in the years since the DWEMs were first identified, the chorus of diverse voices that was added under protest has proved to be enriching for students as well as for teachers. As more diverse voices show up on reading lists, we are able to participate in an ever-widening conversation among all humans, about the nature of all humanity.

The United States in the Twenty-First Century

The 2000 census data are still being analyzed but the portrait of change is clear. As of 2002 we are a nation of almost 3 million people, 49 percent male and 51 percent female. In addition, for the first time in a U.S. census, respondents were able to identify themselves as belonging to more than one racial group. Previously, in the 1990 census, only one ethnic or racial group could be checked. The new population figures give us a better picture of the racial distribution in the nation when people can indicate that they identify with more than one race or ethnicity. For example, 1,572,000 African Americans also checked another box in the section for race. A similar figure holds for the Asian Americans—1,528,000 checked more than one box. Our picture of the diversity of the U.S. population is becoming more complex. Adding to this complexity is the wide range of refugees steadily streaming in from many different countries. For example, between 1991 and 2001, the percentage of African refugees let into the United States rose from less than 5 percent to nearly 30 percent of the total refugee population.[5]

In 1964, 20.7 million African Americans comprised the largest minority group in the United States. The year 2002 found the 38.3 million black population outpaced by the 38.7 million Hispanics. In turn, the Hispanic population had gone up 58 percent from 1990 to 2000, while Hispanics weren't even counted in the 1980 census. This means that many communities have a "majority of minorities." However, an increase in population has not necessarily improved the position of minorities, or historically underrepresented groups. Since the Civil Rights Act of 1964, black median family income has increased from $18,859 to $44,634 in 2002. The poverty rate for blacks in 1966 was 41.8 percent and in 2002 it was 23.9 percent. However, it is still much higher than the 12 percent poverty rate for the general population in 2002.[6]

On the other hand, education is one area that has shown improvement. In 1964, only 26 percent of the African Americans aged 25 and older had at least a high school diploma. By 2003, the rate was 80 percent. In addition, in 1964 there were 306,000 black college students; by 2002 the number was 2.3 million. The number of African Americans elected to office also increased, from 1,469 in 1970 (the first year this information was collected) to 9,101 in 2001.[7]

> Our songs, our toil, our cheer…have been given to this nation in blood-brotherhood. Are not these gifts worth the giving? Would America have been America without her Negro people?
>
> *The Souls of Black Folk,* 1903 WEB DuBois

Public school students in preschool through grade 12 numbered 48.2 million in September 2004, an increase of about 135,000 over the previous year. A decade ago, the total enrollment was 44 million. Both the baby boom "echo" (25 percent increase in birthrate from 1970 to 1990) and immigration have affected the student population. By 2013, student enrollment is projected to become 49.7 million. Looking at the fourth grade in 2003, we find this distribution in the total public school enrollment:

White:	60.2 percent
Hispanic:	17 percent
African Americans:	17 percent
Asian origin:	4.1 percent
American Indian:	1.1 percent[8]

But in the same year, 47 percent of the African Americans and 51 percent of the Hispanics were in the poorest schools, defined as those schools where 75 percent of the students are eligible for free or reduced price school lunches. Obviously, preparing to become a teacher today will require increased awareness of these shifts and the skills to meet these challenges.

THE BUMPY ROAD TO HUMAN RIGHTS

Reluctantly, over the years, the growing United States began to acknowledge the right of various sectors of the population to exist and to be entitled to legal rights. Always, there was much opposition to overcome, and many steps backwards, but *slowly* a public concensus prevailed to grant freedom to African Americans, suffrage for women, and rights for new immigrants, among others. It was a bumpy road, indeed, and even concerted efforts to pass legislation or change public opinion did not immediately achieve the intended goals, as we shall see in the time line that follows.

African Americans Enslaved

From 1503 to the mid-1800s, the slave trade was a major part of the world economy. The first U.S. Census, commissioned by Congress in 1790, found 700,000 black slaves (out of a total population of nearly 4 million Americans, not including Native Americans). Over 90 percent were concentrated in the Southern states.

Between 1777 and 1784, six states made slavery illegal. However, arguments over the status of slavery in the new nation continued. The historian Joseph Ellis claims that "The Civil War . . . was a direct consequence of the decision to evade and delay the slavery question during the most vulnerable early years of the republic."[9]

An early crucial decision was the Dred Scott case in 1857. The U.S. Supreme Court ruled that Congress had no right to prohibit slavery in the territories, that the Missouri Compromise setting a boundary for slavery was illegal, and that Dred Scott, a former slave living in Minnesota, was still a slave with no legal rights. In effect, all former slaves, although living in free states, could be returned to their previous owners. In a fury at this decision, Abraham Lincoln risked his party's U.S. Senate nomination when he said: "A house divided against itself cannot stand. I believe this government cannot endure, permanently half *slave* and half *free*."

The Thirteenth Amendment abolished slavery, followed by the Fourteenth Amendment, which took a larger leap and guaranteed citizenship to anyone born in the United States or naturalized. Citizenship meant equal protection under the law and the privilege of due process of law. Nonetheless, another amendment, the Fifteenth, appeared necessary to reinforce the point. It affirmed that the federal or state governments could not deny citizens the right to vote on account of race, color, or previous condition of servitude. But another key legal case maintained the status of segregation in the South. In 1892, Homer Plessy deliberately challenged the "whites only" Separate Car Act (Louisiana law since 1890) by sitting in a *white* train car. When the case reached the U.S. Supreme Court in 1896, the *Plessy v. Ferguson* decision upheld segregation.

Education: The Key

Finally, in 1954, the U.S. Supreme Court ruled that segregated schools were unconstitutional because they violated the Fifth and Fourteenth Amendment guarantees of "equal protection." This *Brown v. Topeka* decision opened many doors. Southern states were recalcitrant, however, and the Court was forced to issue a second ruling in 1955, called Brown II, ordering desegregation "with all deliberate speed." After eight African American students, including Melba Beals, endured a year of hostility and violence in their attempt to attend Central High School in Little Rock, Arkansas, Governor Orville Faubus ordered the public schools closed as his way of avoiding desegregation.

A Landmark in Civil Rights

After many sit-ins at lunch counters and other demonstrations had taken place, President Johnson signed the Civil Rights Act in 1964. This landmark legislation outlawed racial discrimination and supported the army of activists who had been facing guns, dogs, and water hoses in their struggle to end segregation. The act made discrimination on the basis of race, color, religion, or national origin illegal in public places. It also made clear the voting rights of citizens. Myrlie Evers-Williams, whose first husband Medgar Evers was one of the civil rights workers who was killed, said the act "gave hope to the hopeless." One of the most prominent figures in the fight for African American civil rights was Dr. Martin Luther King, Jr. But he made it clear that this struggle was about larger social issues than just the right to vote. He spoke up on behalf of all people who experienced discrimination: Mexican American farmworkers, the working class, and women. The 1964 Act laid the groundwork for much needed additional legislation, including the Voting Rights Act of 1965. Subsequently, numerous lawsuits were filed, leading to the desegregation of previously all-white institutions, such as police and fire departments.

Immigrants Contributing to Building the Country

The building of the Transcontinental Railroad was a heroic effort by about 10,000 Chinese men working from the West and some 10,000 Irish, German, Dutch, Czech, and Civil War veterans working from the East. The project, finished in 1869, had taken six years and many 12-hour days. However, the Chinese Exclusion Act was passed in 1882 to cut off this source of cheap labor when the Chinese were blamed for a downturn in the economy. This Act remained on the books and limited immigration until it was repealed when China became an ally in WWII.

The Ellis Island Immigration station opened in 1892, processing about 12 million people before it was closed in 1954. Its counterpart on the Pacific Coast, Angel Island Immigration Station, near San Francisco and open for thirty years, was the port of entry for many nationalities. The Chinese, however, were the largest group and were treated differently from the rest. They were often held for days and interrogated in attempts to break their stories of joining relatives in the United States, their only hope of being allowed to enter this country. Both Ellis Island and Angel Island have websites where you can learn more about the individuals who passed through their doors.

Women's Suffrage

A group of women met in Seneca Falls, New York, in 1848, to write a Declaration of the Rights of Women and to begin the long struggle for women's suffrage. It would not be concluded until 1920, when the Nineteenth Amendment finally gave women the right to vote. But there were many accomplishments to be celebrated along the way. Belva Lockwood had the temerity to run for president in 1879 after she had been the first woman lawyer permitted to argue before the U.S. Supreme Court. In 1916, Jeanette Rankin was elected to the U.S. House of Representatives from Wyoming, becoming the first woman in Congress, despite the fact that women could not vote in national elections at the time. On the other hand, women continued to experience discrimination in many areas, such as property rights and working conditions. The passage of Title IX in 1972, an amendment to the Civil Rights Act of 1964, signaled a major leap forward as women's sports in school were put on a par with men's.

Bilingualism in the Schools

However, some ideas that were at first widely acclaimed were later rejected—for example, bilingual approaches to education. When Dade County, Florida, began its bilingual program for Cuban American children in 1963, bilingual approaches were widely heralded as forward-thinking. The most significant case related to multicultural/bilingual education was *Lau v. Nichols,* a Supreme Court case that required all school districts to provide for linguistic and cultural diversity. In 1974 it charged a school district as follows:

> The failure of the San Francisco school system to provide English language instruction to approximately 1,800 students of Chinese ancestry who do not speak English, or to provide them with other adequate instructional procedures, denies them a meaningful opportunity to participate in the public educational program and thus violates . . . the Civil Rights Act of 1964. . . .

This class-action suit against the San Francisco Unified School District led to a decision that school districts must provide education in languages that meet the needs of students who attend the school. Thus began plans to teach students in their native language, whether it be Yupik or Tagalog, and to provide English as a second language programs specifically designed for each group.[10] In 1999, however, the pendulum suddenly swung to the opposite side of the spectrum with bilingual methods and materials viewed as handicapping students and emphasis placed on learning English as soon as possible. This movement is aligned with earlier efforts to declare English the "official language" of the United States. Although a constitutional amendment failed in 1963, a number of states have voted to declare English as their "official state language."

The Full Range of Human Rights

Peruse the following chronology of the many events and shifts in thinking about human rights that led to multicultural education as it exists today.

A Chronology of Human Rights Events in the United States

1503–mid 1800s	Active slave trade. Approximately 60 million West Africans captured, sold as slaves. About 40 million died before reaching their destination.
1619	First twenty Africans arrived in the United States, probably as indentured servants.
1776	Declaration of Independence signed.
1777–1784	Vermont, New Hampshire, Pennsylvania, Massachusetts, Connecticut, and Rhode Island made slavery illegal.
1790	Quaker delegations to the Constitutional Convention proposed making slavery illegal in the United States.
1808	Louisiana Purchase added large French-speaking territory to the United States.
1820	Liberia created in Africa as a place to send free African Americans.
1820	Missouri Compromise outlawed slavery north of 36°30'N latitude.
1831	Nat Turner slave uprising. The most effective slave rebellion in U.S. history.
1835	Cherokees forced off their land.
1839	Amistad rebellion in which Africans overcame Spanish ship carrying them to slavery. They were picked up by United States and tried. Former President John Quincy Adams argued their case, and they were freed to return to Africa.
1848	Declaration of Women's Rights at Seneca Falls, New York.
1848	Treaty of Guadalupe-Hidalgo assured that Spanish and English would both be the official languages of California.
1850	Great Compromise. Utah and New Mexico were allowed to vote for or against slavery when they were admitted to the Union.
1852	*Uncle Tom's Cabin,* by Harriet Beecher Stowe, published.
1857	Dred Scott decision.
1858	Lincoln made "A house divided cannot stand" speech.
1859	John Brown led raid on Harper's Ferry, Virginia.
1861	Civil War began.
1862	Emancipation Proclamation signed, freed slaves in Confederate states only.
1864	First black daily newspaper, the *New Orleans Tribune,* was published.
1865	Slaves in Texas found out that they were free (Juneteenth).
1865	Civil War ended.
1865	Ku Klux Klan organized to resist perceived threats by Union occupation troops and Negroes.
1865	Thirteenth Amendment passed, abolished slavery.
1868	Fourteenth Amendment passed, granted U.S. citizens due process and equal protection under law.
1869	Fifteenth Amendment passed, affirmed that citizens cannot be denied right to vote.

1869	Wyoming was the first territory to permit women to vote.
1869	In the United Kingdom, unmarried women could vote in local elections (full suffrage in 1894).
1876	Sitting Bull defeated Custer at the Battle of Little Bighorn.
1876	Rutherford Hayes's compromise won him the election, having promised his Southern supporters he would not enforce the Fifteenth Amendment.
1879	Belva Ann Lockwood was the first woman admitted to argue before the U.S. Supreme Court.
1882	Chinese Exclusion Act passed, for the first time limited immigration by race or nation.
1884	Belva Ann Lockwood was the first woman to run for president of the United States.
1890	Massacre at Wounded Knee. Band of 350 women, children, and elderly Lakota killed while seeking refuge. This massacre became symbol of Native American genocide.
1892	Homer Plessy defied the law that segregated train transportation.
1892	Ellis Island Immigration station opened for East Coast.
1893	New Zealand gave women the right to vote.
1895	Booker T. Washington gave speech later known as the Atlanta Compromise.
1896	*Plessy v. Ferguson* upheld segregation.
1898	Philippine-American War began.
1900	Number of African Americans registered to vote dropped precipitously.
1903	President Theodore Roosevelt orchestrated coup in Colombia in order to create Panama Canal.
1909	National Association for the Advancement of Colored People founded, with W. E. B. DuBois its only black officer.
1910	Angel Island Immigration station opened for West Coast.
1916	Margaret Sanger opened first birth control clinics.
1917	Puerto Ricans became citizens of the United States, although they could not vote in national elections.
1918	World War I brought reactions against Germany and a resurgence of nationalistic feeling in the United States. Use of "English only" legislated in many states.
1920	Nineteenth Amendment gave women the right to vote.
1924	Native Americans made citizens and, therefore, had right to vote.
1925	Nellie Ross elected first woman governor, of Wyoming.
1932	Hattie Caraway elected first woman senator, from Arkansas.
1932	Franklin Delano Roosevelt elected president, hid his disability.
1932	African American "Scottsboro Boys" determined by U.S. Supreme Court to have received inadequate defense when tried for rape in Alabama. First support for due process applied to African Americans.
1941	Tuskegee Institute began training African American pilots for WWII after Eleanor Roosevelt photographed in airplane with African American pilot.

	992 African Americans received their wings and flew combat missions in North Africa, Italy, and Germany.
1942	Japanese American (and Canadian) internment ordered.
1943	Chinese Exclusion Act repealed.
1944	Port Chicago Mutiny. Massive explosion at Naval Shipyard killed mostly blacks because of segregation. Fifty African Americans refused to return to work, sentenced to 15 years in prison.
1946	National School Lunch Act established free lunch for poor children.
1948	U.S. Supreme Court ruled against racial discrimination in housing deeds.
1948	California Supreme Court in *Perez v. Sharp* decision declared interracial marriage legal, allowing Andrea Perez, a Latina, to marry Sylvester Davis, an African American.
1948	President Harry Truman integrated the U.S. military.
1950	Ralph Bunche was first African American to win the Nobel Peace Prize.
1954	Rosa Parks refused to give up her seat on a bus to a white man in Montgomery, Alabama.
1954	In *Brown v. Topeka,* U.S. Supreme Court ruled segregated schools were unconstitutional.
1954	Hydrogen bomb tested on Bikini Atoll, first of six. Largest nuclear bomb test ever.
1954	United States organized coup that overthrew democratically elected President Jacebo Arbenz of Guatemala, leading to civil war lasting 36 years and claiming about 200,000 lives.
1954	President Eisenhower added phrase "under God" to the Pledge of Allegiance.
1955	Brown II, U.S. Supreme Court ordered integration of schools with "all due deliberate speed."
1955	14-year-old African American Emmet Till was abducted, beaten, shot, and dumped in a river with a barbed wire noose around his neck for supposedly whistling at a white woman in a store in Mississippi. Two men were tried and acquitted but later admitted their guilt.
1957	U.S. Commission on Civil Rights established.
1958	Arkansas Governor Orville Faubus ordered closing of public schools to avoid integration.
1960	First lunch counter sit-in at Woolworth's in Greensboro, North Carolina, inspired wave of similar protests throughout the South.
1961	U.S. Supreme Court ended segregated interstate transport after two years of "freedom rides" organized by the Congress of Racial Equality (CORE).
1961	Musician Ray Charles was banned from his native state of Georgia for refusing to play a segregated concert.
1963	First bilingual school program begun in Miami/Dade County for children of Cuban immigrants.
1963	Dr. Martin Luther King, Jr., made his "I have a dream" speech, Washington, DC.
1963	U.S. Supreme Court abolished Bible reading in the public schools.

1964	President Lyndon Johnson signed the Civil Rights Act, guaranteed federal enforcement of voting rights, school integration, equal employment opportunities, and desegregation of public facilities.
1964	Headstart created to aid "disadvantaged" children.
1964	Three civil rights workers murdered in Mississippi, indictments against 19 suspects are dismissed in federal court.
1964	The Free Speech Movement began at UC Berkeley California as the nation's first major campus sit-in in a nonviolent protest.
1965	President Lyndon Johnson signed the Voting Rights Act.
1966	Kwanzaa created as a holiday to celebrate the heritage of African Americans.
1967	Thurgood Marshall became first African American U.S. Supreme Court judge.
1967	U.S. Supreme Court ruled that interracial marriage was legal. At the time, 16 states had laws against interracial marriage.
1967	Federal jury convicted seven men of murdering civil rights workers in 1964.
1968	Dr. Martin Luther King, Jr., assassinated.
1968	Bilingual Education Act: Title VII of ESEA promoted bilingual programs in schools.
1969	Riots after police action at Stonewall, a gay bar in Greenwich Village, New York City, signaled start of gay rights movement.
1969	"Indians of all tribes" occupied Alcatraz Island, former prison site in San Francisco Bay.
1971	Massachusetts Bilingual Education Act passed, first state to mandate bilingual education for "non-English-speaking" (NES) students.
1971	Switzerland gave women the right to vote.
1972	Title IX amendment to Civil Rights Act passed, added sex discrimination to civil rights coverage.
1973	Bilingual Education Reform Act updated 1968 law, mandated study of history and culture as well as language in bilingual education programs.
1974	U.S. Supreme Court *Lau v. Nichols* decision, "NES" had legal right to bilingual education as part of "equal educational opportunity."
1974	Aspira Consent Decree (New York City) class action suit provided for instruction in students' native languages.
1974	U.S. Supreme Court overturned school busing in Detroit, Michigan.
1977	U.S. Supreme Court ruled that Alan Bakke was denied equal opportunity when applying to the University of California Law School because he was not a minority applicant.
1979	Ray Charles was allowed to return to Georgia and his song "Georgia on My Mind" became the official state song.
1981	Senator Hayakawa introduced Constitutional Amendment to declare English the official language of the United States; it was defeated.
1983	Sandra Day O'Connor appointed first female U.S. Supreme Court judge.
1984–85	Illinois, Indiana, Kentucky, Nebraska, and Virginia passed resolutions declaring English as their official state language.

1988	U.S. government apologized for internment of Japanese Americans, offered monetary compensation.
1988	U.S. Senate supported Puerto Rico's right to self-determination.
1989	U.S. removed Noriega as leader of Panama.
1990	Americans with Disabilities Act prohibited discrimination against the disabled.
1992	Riots broke out when four Los Angeles white police officers found not guilty of beating Rodney King, an African American.
1997	Proposition 209 passed in California rescinding affirmative action.
1998	Puerto Rico held a referendum on whether to become a state, a commonwealth, or a country; none-of-the-above won over 50 percent of the vote.
1998	Matthew Shepard killed in Laramie, Wyoming, because he was gay.
1998	Canada formally apologized for past oppression of its indigenous peoples—Indians, Inuit, and Métis.
1998	Filipino Veterans Equity Act passed.
1999	Panama Canal passed from United States to Panamanian control, twenty-five years after U.S. Senate ratified treaty giving the Canal back to Panama.
1999	Proposition 227 passed in California eliminating bilingual education programs.
1999	Department of Agriculture class action suit settled in favor of black farmers.
1999	Same-sex relationships with benefits for partners recognized in Vermont.
2001	The Elementary and Secondary Education Act (ESEA) was reauthorized as "No Child Left Behind."
2002	Transgender teenager Gwen Araujo killed apparently because three men found out she was born male but identified female.
2002	California State Supreme Court ruled phrase "under God" unconstitutional, U.S. Supreme Court declined case.
2003	Qatar was the most recent country to give women the vote.
2003	Supreme Court ruled that the University of Michigan's point program for minority applicants was an unconstitutional quota, but found the admissions program of the University of Michigan Law School legitimate in its "indeterminate weighting of race as one of many factors ensuring diversity."
2004	Anti-gay marriage constitutional amendment defeated in the U.S. Senate.
2004	Anti-gay marriage ballot initiatives in many states.
2004	*Williams v. California* required state to provide additional funding for poverty-ridden schools.
2004	Massachusetts legalized same-sex marriages.
2004	Trial began in Georgia over whether a sticker attached to biology textbooks warning that evolution is "a theory, not a fact" violated the separation of church and state.
2004	U.S. Congress passed a resolution calling the violence in the Sudan "genocide."

THE BEST EDUCATION FOR ALL

The underlying goal of multicultural education is to provide the best education to all students, regardless of their race, gender, language, and so on. We must develop our awareness of the way "white" norms are unconsciously enforced, identify sources of bias, and consider the different kinds of power present in the classroom. Instead of sweeping differences under the table, we bring them to the forefront, acknowledging that all students are different from one another and that a variety of approaches are required to reach every student. In order to achieve our goal of including all students, we must learn how to treat these differences as strengths. In this section, we present the concept of *inclusion* as the hallmark of multicultural education, the stamp by which you can recognize its authenticity.

Creating an Inclusive Classroom Culture

What does an inclusive multicultural classroom look and feel like when you walk in? The first aspect you would notice is that everyone is engaged in some way. There are no students hanging out passively in the back. The teacher may be working with a small group of students or walking around the room checking in with each student. There is a steady buzz of conversation as students talk with each other and ask each other questions. The seating is organized so that it can be changed depending on the activity. The students seem proud of their accomplishments and examples of student work cover the classroom walls.

Planning for such an inclusive classroom culture must take into account many elements, for example:

- Rules—Each class must draw up and agree upon rules for respectful language and behavior, as well as the consequences for failing to uphold these rules.
- Community—Each class will build shared experiences through reading books together and participating in discussions that create a common background to draw on.
- Organization—The power to make others do something must be shared among all, not just a few, and rotated. Everyone gets a turn, not just the student who is always the first one to raise a hand.
- Values—Each class has the responsibility to discuss the difference between helping each other and stealing someone else's work and passing it off as your own.
- Evaluation—The students will be encouraged to measure success by their own improvement rather than by always competing to be the top student.

A community exists when people share activities and values, when the people feel that everyone is on the same side, reaching for the same goals, and everyone knows that all of them depend on each other. In order for every student to succeed, we need to tap the diversity in each one, because each student is unique. Because everyone will have something to contribute to the class knowledge and welfare at all times, students will feel supported in their efforts by the inclusive classroom culture.

Definitions and Appropriate Terminology

As we strive to define multicultural education, it is important to agree on the meanings of the terms we use. We start with *race,* one of the most explosive topics today.

IDEAS IN ACTION!

The Right to Vote

People of various ages stand in the early morning daylight, single file. What are they waiting for so patiently? They are waiting for the polls to open. It's only the third all-race election in the history of South Africa, so they want to be sure they get to vote. "This is what people died for, so we could achieve this day," said a woman waiting in line. Long lines snake around the polling stations, and some will stay open late to accommodate everyone. Whites wait next to blacks. The ordinariness of the election shows just how far the country has come, said Desmond Tutu, Nobel laureate and archbishop. Until 1994, only the 10 percent white minority could vote. The South Africans have not forgotten their history; they are still grateful for the precious right to vote.

In the United States, the attitude toward voting is different. People argue over whether their vote makes any difference, or they are skeptical of any politician's promises. Talk about voting with your students. Do they know that people died for the right to vote in this country as well? When did women get the right to vote? How old do you have to be to vote? What measures were used to prevent African Americans from voting in Southern states? How can we avoid taking our right to vote for granted? Challenge students to plan a campaign to increase the number of people voting in their community in the next election.

Race

The human population is divided into five principal groups corresponding to the major geographical areas of the world: Africa, Europe, Asia, Melanesia, and the Americas. Ninety-five percent of our genetic makeup is the same; the small differences in the DNA that distinguish us are due to the relatively recent dispersal of humanity from its African homeland. What we usually call *race,* however, is a social construct. This means that in the United States, a person with even the smallest amount of African American ancestry, for example, is labeled African American. Many African Americans have at least some Caucasian blood, especially dating back to the days when rape was a common fact of life for slaves. However, our society assigns racial categories based on stereotyped physical appearance, such as slanted eyes (Asian) or broad lips (African). This stereotyping is slowly changing as more and more people recognize their racial diversity and identify themselves as being of "mixed race."

Social Class

We say that the United States is a classless society because of our value system that says anyone can grow up to be president or to achieve great wealth. However, the social mobility taken for granted here cannot hide the fact that there are distinct social classes, that is, groups separated from one another by income, occupation, and relative prestige. There is still a difference between blue-collar workers and white-collar workers (as well as pink-collar workers). Teachers, for example, despite earning less than a factory worker, may enjoy higher prestige as members of the middle class.

Ethnicity

Ethnicity is related to nationality. An American whose family came from Germany, Ireland, and Scotland would be of German-Irish-Scots ethnicity. Natives of a country such as the former Czechoslovakia, which had incorporated former nations, might retain that identity by referring to themselves as ethnic Czechs or Slovaks.

Immigrant populations of Chinese found in Vietnam or South Africa, for example, are called ethnic Chinese. *Hispanic* refers to an ethnic group, not a race, though many people use it to make racial distinctions. Hispanics can be of any race, including white.

Minority Group

As our population shifts, this term becomes more symbolic than numerically accurate. When we use the term *minority group,* we are referring to people who have been historically underrepresented. These groups have been subject to prejudice and treated as less-than-equal members of society. Whites may be "in the minority" in many areas but they are not considered a "minority group."

Group Names

It is most respectful to use the label that a group chooses to identify itself when speaking of that group. However, group names have changed over time and sometimes there are political messages attached to the use of particular group names. The population familiarly known as *Gypsies,* for example, considers that a derogatory name. They call themselves, and prefer to be called by others, the *Roma. Eskimo* is another label that is outdated. To the indigenous people of northern Alaska, Canada, and Greenland, *Eskimo* is not a positive label. They prefer to be known as the *Inuit.*

- *African Americans:* Different terms have been acceptable at different times. We use the label that was appropriate at that period, such as Negro, but otherwise prefer to use African American, referring to an American of African heritage. Afro-American or black is also used by many. The n-word is not acceptable, of course, despite its occasional use in literature. The fact that we all know what word the n-word stands for is evidence that this derogatory term is still a part of our language.
- *Asian Americans: Asian* has replaced *Oriental* as the preferred term for this group. Ideally, a more specific term would be used, such as Cambodian Americans or Japanese Americans, to represent the diversity of this large category.
- *European Americans:* Europeans, or whites, tend to think of others as belonging to an ethnic or racial group but not themselves. This pattern of thought is an example of the assumption of skin privilege, or making whiteness the norm against which all other groups are judged. Many "white" students wonder where they fit in. "That's the million dollar question. It's come up among people who think about a truly multicultural society and what that looks like," says Anthony Lising Antonio, associate professor of education at Stanford University. "The fact is we still don't understand

what 'whiteness' is," he continues. "It's been such a norm that we haven't defined it, and I think white students might feel like they're in a cultural vacuum, whereas other folks—the Asians and the Latinos, for example—have something tangible to call their culture."[11]

- *Latinos or Hispanic Americans:* We prefer the term *Latino* but *Hispanic* is also used, especially in population statistics. Latinos are not a racial group but may be white, black, Indian, or any mix of these. Their culture and customs also vary according to the country they come from so we prefer to specify Puerto Rican (a U.S. citizen), Cuban, or Guyanian. *Chicano* is used to refer to Mexican Americans.
- *Native Americans:* Although the term *Indian* is sometimes used, we prefer the name of specific tribes, for example, Lakota, Navajo, or Pomo.
- *LGBT:* This acronym stands for Lesbian/Gay/Bisexual/Transgender and is a label intended to include the broad range of people who do not fit into normative social categories of heterosexual male and female. Young people who are questioning their gender identity require a lot of sensitive support in today's society.
- *People of color:* This is one of many candidates to replace *minority group* as a collective label. In this case, color is meant as a sociopolitical construct, not a reference to actual skin tones. If one is not a person of color, one is white.

Comparing Models of Multicultural Education

Although most multicultural educators would agree upon a general definition, there remain differences of opinion about the relationship between theory and practice. Sleeter and Grant identified five discrete theoretical approaches to multicultural education: assimilation, human relations, focused group studies, integrated studies within the total curriculum, and social reconstructionism.[12] They critiqued each in turn, concluding that social reconstructionism was the only desirable model for multicultural education because it was based on critical pedagogy. In this text, we acknowledge and incorporate the positive contributions of each of these theories as we develop our inclusive definition of multicultural education. Rather than the mutually exclusive typology of programs argued by Sleeter and Grant, we believe that each theory offers something to a fully realized multicultural curriculum. We also add a sixth approach, that is, the influence of global and international studies.

Assimilation

Assimilation theory, which dominated the thinking of the early United States, assumes that all persons living in the United States should be acculturated to become *Americans*. According to this view, everyone should be culturally similar as in the "melting-pot" metaphor discussed previously. This theory lies behind the contemporary "English only" movement and is inherent in many of the questions related to immigration. The problem is that those who espouse assimilation may equate *difference* with *deficiency*. This stance can scarcely be termed multicultural, but it is a viewpoint that still appears in newspapers and is clearly lodged in the minds of many Americans who were educated to perceive assimilation and the melting-pot concept positively.

Aspects of assimilation theory that we continue to support, however, are related to work with English as a Second Language programs. We want to express value for knowing more than one language in today's world. However, we encourage students to learn English as a means for entering the privileged mainstream culture and preparing for a future career. It would be unrealistic for any teacher to pretend that learning standard English and cultural literacy, prestige knowledge, is not a desirable goal for any child in U.S. schools today.[13]

Human Relations and Ethnic Studies

The concern for human rights that characterized the civil rights movement of the 1960s led directly into the human relations movement in education with its emphasis on valuing the individual, nurturing individual self-esteem, and helping everyone succeed. In 1972, for example, the American Association of Colleges for Teacher Education (AACTE), defined multicultural education as follows:

> Education which values cultural pluralism. Multicultural education rejects the view that schools should seek to melt away cultural differences or the view that schools should merely tolerate cultural pluralism. Instead, multicultural education affirms that schools should be oriented toward the cultural enrichment of all children and youth through programs rooted in the presentation and extension of cultural alternatives. Multicultural education recognizes cultural diversity as a fact of life in American society, and it affirms that this cultural diversity is a valuable resource that should be preserved and extended. It affirms that major education institutions should strive to preserve and enhance cultural pluralism. Multicultural education programs for teachers are more than special courses or special learning experiences grafted onto the standard program. The commitment to cultural pluralism must permeate all areas of the educational experience provided for prospective teachers.[14]

At the same time, many states began incorporating elements of this widely accepted statement into teacher education requirements. By now, most states have similar requirements.

Note that part of this "human relations" requirement even then was—and still is—focused on studies of ethnic groups. Many universities created Black Studies or Chicano Studies programs at that time. Following this period into the 1980s, James Banks and others wrote books advocating ethnic studies and presenting methods for teaching ethnic studies, particularly at high school and university levels. Such focused ethnic studies courses emphasized pride in one's heritage, which is still an important goal of multicultural education. These programs also stressed interpersonal communication skills. Human relations programs remain an important tool for teaching how to get along in a culturally diverse society.

Integrated Multicultural Education

The broader term *multicultural education* was not widely used in educational literature until the late 1970s. It appeared for the first time in *Education Index* in 1978. In 1977, however, the National Council of Accreditation of Teacher Education rewrote its standards to include one on multicultural education. This text, *Multicultural Teaching,* which appeared in 1979, was the first comprehensive textbook to address multicultural education in the schools. In 1980, AACTE published *Multicultural Education: An Annotated Bibliography of Selected Resources* "to stimulate discussion, study, and experimentation of multicultural education among educators."[15]

Because the K–12 curriculum often lags behind current theory, however, it was not until 1988 that Minnesota's Board of Education adopted a ruling directing all school districts to develop and deliver a curriculum plan that emphasized: (1) the cultural diversity of the United States and the contributions made by diverse ethnic groups to the country's development, (2) the historical and contemporary contributions of both women and men to society, and (3) the historical and contemporary contributions to society by disabled (at that time termed *handicapped*) persons. The curriculum that is now being implemented is expected to be gender-fair and sensitive to the needs of the disabled.

Concern for the needs of all people now extends to include newly recognized groups, for example, the elderly, homosexuals, working women, people with AIDS, and disabled persons. Efforts to teach multicultural concepts and processes as an integral aspect of every subject area reach into all levels of education, including the preschool years. Multicultural education covers broad, inclusive themes touching on human relations, morality, values, and ethics; and it draws heavily on the study of pedagogy, for example, in its recognition of differing learning styles and individualization of instruction.

Global and International Education

Defined more broadly, thus, multicultural education connects the study of other countries, the concept of the world as a global village, and recognition of the need for everyone on this planet to collaborate to ensure clean air and preserve our resources. Focus on international studies brings an awareness of the shared concerns of nations around the world. It leads to a greater understanding of other people and the universal issues human beings face. Ecologically and economically, we will always be interdependent. Such studies engage us in reading the literature and becoming familiar with the cultures of specific groups around the world that may speak the same language or share a religious belief, thus helping to broaden studies across the total curriculum in the United States.

Social Activism

Active efforts to bring about a change in thinking and behavior have always been integral to our society—from the behavior of the eighteenth-century revolutionaries to contemporary efforts to challenge established views on such issues as abortion and the right to control one's own death. Activism, involvement rather than passive acceptance, is perhaps the newest approach to multicultural education. Refusing to be victimized, we all have a responsibility to speak out against injustice, discrimination, and prejudice and to work to ensure that human rights are upheld for all. Individual involvement in this social reconstructivism will vary, but increasingly, educated Americans are intervening when unthinking individuals tell stories that insult certain ethnic groups or use insensitive language. Others join groups that work actively to achieve and maintain civil rights for specific groups. It is important to take a stance and to make our viewpoints known. Teachers have a special responsibility to manage classroom procedures and to plan the multicultural curriculum appropriately.

In *Multicultural Teaching,* we define multicultural education as:

> An inclusive teaching/learning process that engages all students in (1) developing a strong sense of *self-esteem,* (2) discovering *empathy* for persons of diverse cultural backgrounds, and (3) experiencing *equitable* opportunities to achieve to their fullest potential.

Accordingly, multicultural education is fundamental to all learning. It is an integral aspect of the discussion about fair behavior on the playground that might concern primary students. It underlies the conflicts and concerns that intermediate students face as they develop as individuals. And it explains why recognizing the existence of racism is a significant part of the middle school learning experience. Multicultural education belongs in science, history, mathematics, language arts, social studies, and the arts. Teaching multiculturally requires the efforts of committed professionals and community members at all levels of education.

Our Assumptions

Many multicultural programs have been derided for their "heroes and holidays" approach. True multicultural education must aim at a larger goal, beyond superficial activities that only foster appreciation of one another's culture. Borrowing from the early women's movement, which also aimed to change people's awareness at a fundamental level, we suggest that multicultural education be thought of as "consciousness-raising" education. Multicultural education is for and about everyone. It must promote an anti-victim consciousness in historically oppressed groups as well as increase understanding in those who belong to the dominant groups of the extent of the privileges they accrue just by being born to that group. We believe multicultural teaching, in order to be effective, must be based on the following premises:

- Multicultural education is fundamental in order for all students to participate fully in today's world.
- Multicultural education exposes the cultural bias already inherent in all education.
- Multicultural education must be infused throughout the curriculum.
- Multicultural education includes affective as well as cognitive goals.
- A diverse student population leads to the best learning for all students.
- Children learn to read best through their primary (oral) language.
- English language learners should learn content as they learn English.
- Children must feel welcome to bring their identity and their culture to the classroom.
- Multicultural teaching needs to be flexible because no one method fits all students.
- Multicultural teaching is student centered, not lecture based.
- Multicultural education provides all students with the best education possible.
- Multicultural education is based on a foundation of *Esteem, Empathy,* and *Equity.*

These assumptions will be developed further in the following chapters.

CONNECTIONS

You will notice that each chapter in this book begins with a quote, presented as a poster that you can enlarge and use in your classroom to stimulate discussion, debate, and different topics for writing. In addition, each chapter concludes with several special sections. In Connections, we summarize the ideas of the chapter and tie them to other chapters throughout the book with the result that the chapters can be read in any order. This introductory chapter summarizes the evolution of multiculturalism in the United States and the changing ways of thinking that impact directly on the schools. It is essential that we teachers recognize our own ethnicity and cultural background as we learn to address the needs of our students. We begin with our own stories and then reach out to take in the stories of the students with whom we work. In this book we define multicultural education inclusively to take in the concerns of all of the diverse people that populate the United States.

A major focus in *Multicultural Teaching* also is education that provides *esteem, empathy,* and *equity* for all students. Educators need to lead the way in breaking down the stereotyped thinking that leads to dissension and violence. A humane approach to education threaded throughout the total curriculum presented in home and school over twelve or more years should prepare students to live peaceably in a democratic society and a diverse, interconnected world. The next two chapters explore in greater detail how to achieve this goal through both presenting multicultural content (Chapter 2) and teaching multiculturally (Chapter 3).

FOLLOW-THROUGH

In this section of each chapter we intend to assist you and your colleagues in addressing multicultural education in varied ways. After reading the chapter, you will engage in follow-through activities designed to guide you toward becoming a knowledgeable teacher, well prepared to promote the learning of your diverse students. As explained below, you will first work on your own Reflective Teaching Portfolio (RTP) and then you will interact with other students in a Cooperative Learning Group (CLG).

Creating Your Reflective Teaching Portfolio (RTP)

Purchase a large three-ringed notebook in which to begin your Reflective Teaching Portfolio (RTP). This portfolio will summarize multicultural education and its impact on you as an individual, a teacher. To begin your portfolio, mark dividers to begin organizing the record of your progress toward becoming a multiculturally competent teacher. Include dividers for Learning Log, Information, Teaching Ideas, and Resources. Later, you may need to add other dividers. As the first entry in your portfolio, write several sentences about each of the assumptions listed in the section titled "Our Assumptions." These comments will provide a benchmark, summarizing your present position regarding multicultural education. Date this sheet and place it in your Learning Log.

In addition to this notebook, you will need to begin a larger resource file (perhaps a heavy cardboard box with a lid) in which you can collect printed materials, including books, pictures, charts, and realia (artifacts representing different cultures). Purchase a packet of manila folders in which to store such resources as clippings, pictures, and book lists. Your portfolio can be stored at the front of your resource file.

Beginning to Work with a Cooperative Learning Group (CLG)

Form cooperative learning groups (CLGs) to work on activities presented throughout this text. Groups of four to six people with similar interest in a grade level or subject area can work together to plan lessons. CLGs can be reformed to suit different needs and to increase interaction among diverse students. Findings of groups can be shared with the entire class.

1. Select a song to learn, such as "John Henry" or "Swing Low, Sweet Chariot" (you can recite it as a poem if you are uncertain about your musical ability) and investigate the origins of the song you choose—an Appalachian ballad, an African American spiritual, an Irish jig.
2. Take two pieces of paper. Fold one piece into quarters. In each section, write one factor that affects your lens. Take the second sheet and draw a large circle. Divide the circle into sections representing how important each of these four factors is in your life. Share with your CLG.

GROWING A PROFESSIONAL LIBRARY

In this section, we suggest some readings to follow up on topics presented in the chapter. The books mentioned are ones that we consider essential to your professional development as lifelong learners, and you might consider buying them as you build your own Multicultural Education Library. We consider it important for you to read fiction as well as nonfiction in order to be able to get inside the heads of others. Some of the ideas in these books may be controversial because they are intended to stimulate further thought and critical discussion. Additional readings and sources of information are available in the Instructor's Manual.

Gloria Anzaldúa. *La Frontera/Borderlands,* 2nd ed. Aunt Lute Books, 1999.

Lisa Delpit. *Other People's Children.* The New Press, 1996.

Richard Rodriguez. *Brown: The Last Discovery of America.* Penguin, 2003.

Ronald Takaki. *A Different Mirror: A History of Multicultural America.* Little, Brown, 1994.

ENDNOTES

1. U.S. Bureau of the Census Public Information Office. *USA Statistics in Brief,* 2004. Accessed from www.census.gov
2. *Merriam-Webster's Collegiate Dictionary* (11th ed.), Merriam-Webster, 2004.
3. Gloria Anzaldúa, *La Frontera/Borderlands.* Aunt Lute Books, 1999.
4. Israel Zangwill, *The Melting Pot* (play), 1909. Reprinted by Ayer Company Publishers, 1994.
5. U.S. Bureau of the Census Public Information Office. *USA Statistics in Brief,* 2004. Accessed from www.census.gov
6. Ibid.
7. Ibid.
8. *Statistical Abstracts of the United States,* op. cit.
9. Joseph Ellis, *Founding Brothers: The Revolutionary Generation.* Random House, 2003, p. 12.
10. *Information Please Almanac.* Houghton Mifflin, 2001.
11. Jose Antonio Vargas, "In a World of Racial Diversity, What Is 'White'?" *San Francisco Chronicle,* December 8, 2003.
12. Christine Sleeter and Carl Grant, *Making Choices for Multicultural Education: Five Approaches to Race, Class, and Gender.* Merrill, 1988.
13. *American Association of Colleges for Teacher Education Newsletter,* 21(9) (1972): 3–15.
14. *Multicultural Education: An Annotated Bibliography of Selected Resources.* AACTE, 1982.
15. Ibid.

There've been times
that I've thought I
couldn't last for long
But now I think
I'm able to carry on
It's been a long time
coming
But I know a change
is gonna come

Sam Cooke

C H A P T E R

Organizing for Learning in Multicultural Education

In a classroom, the curriculum and the teaching are indivisible. It's not possible to have teaching without a curriculum behind it, or a curriculum without knowing how it is going to be implemented through teaching. However, in order to examine these fundamental aspects of multicultural education in greater detail, we have separated curriculum and instruction into two distinct chapters. After pulling apart the content and process of multicultural education, Part II will illustrate how we put all of this back together again in the classroom setting.

In this chapter we first identify outcomes that we might expect to achieve through implementing a multicultural program. These outcomes provide a framework for the curriculum we will develop. We also make it clear just how multicultural outcomes and objectives become an integral aspect of the total curriculum designed for a specific subject area. Then, we discuss examples of well-planned multicultural curricula as well as what is often called "the hidden curriculum," the unplanned, yet influential, learning that occurs in any classroom. Finally, we offer several sample units that illustrate multicultural thematic teaching across the curriculum.

DEFINING A MULTICULTURAL CURRICULUM

It's easier to talk about what multicultural education is *not* than to pinpoint what it *is*. Multicultural education is:

- *not* facts and figures
- *not* an add-on to the regular content areas
- *not* a set of skills
- *not* easily assessed
- *not* one approach that fits all students

31

It is important to be precise when we use the term *curriculum* because it can be used to mean a number of different concepts. The definition of curriculum can range from the broadest level, such as the state standards linked to high-stakes testing, to the more local level, which includes commercial programs, teaching units, and classroom materials. All of these aspects need to be considered when we discuss the multicultural curriculum. In addition, our multicultural curriculum will include developing changes in attitudes, reworking lessons to allow for diverse points of view, and balancing large differences among students in background and interests.

Presenting the Model: Esteem/Empathy/Equity (EEE)

We present the EEE model shown in Figure 2.1 as the foundation for multicultural education because we believe that the three elements—*Esteem, Empathy,* and *Equity*—are central to working with students to achieve multicultural goals. When we teach multiculturally, we will use the EEE model to ensure that the following basic objectives are met:

1. Develop students' identities as individuals of worth so that they can contribute to the class and have the motivation to persevere after making mistakes.
2. Value differences of opinion and understand how these differences enhance students' ability to make decisions at different times.
3. Understand different perspectives and what factors influence one's perspective.
4. Learn about one's heritage and that of others without stigmatizing others.
5. Promote global ways of thinking and understand the interdependence of humanity.
6. Recognize and accept the responsibilities of a citizen in a multicultural society.

All of these objectives need to considered when dealing with each instructional area.

Our emphasis on the *Esteem, Empathy,* and *Equity* model for multicultural education begins in early childhood and continues throughout a student's development. Reinforcing these efforts through cooperative planning within a whole school promises to achieve significant results from preschool through junior high school and beyond. Multiculturalism is not a medicine with which we can inoculate children at one point in time. Rather, these understandings and attitudes must grow slowly as the result of small incidents, repeated acts of kindness, and carefully designed instruction over a period of years.

Teachers' attitudes toward students, their obvious caring, their respect for the students are quickly transmitted in casual encounters in the hall as well as in work together in a self-contained classroom. Moreover, it is extremely important that teachers in departmentalized middle schools recognize their role in promoting multicultural education within their daily lessons in a specific subject area. They, too, need to plan learning experiences that support individual self-esteem and promote cooperative activities that build empathy among students. And equity for all students must be a goal in every classroom. Multiculturalism must permeate the total curriculum.

Expected Outcomes

The multicultural curriculum emphasizes affective as well as cognitive goals. For example, as students explore and collect information about people living in a different time or place, they are also learning to value the differences and commonalities they discover.

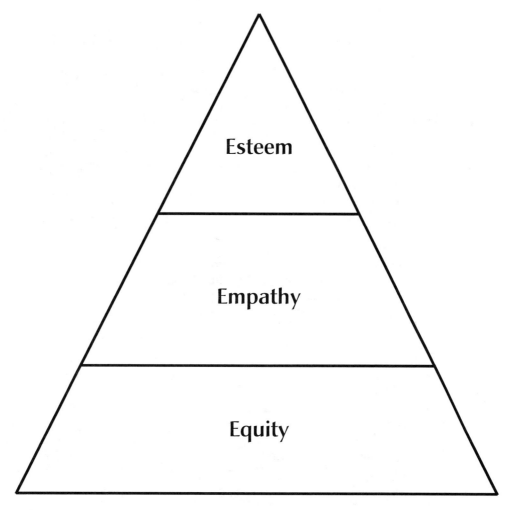

FIGURE 2.1   THE FOUNDATION OF MULTICULTURAL EDUCATION

What do we expect students to know and do as a result of experiencing the multicultural curriculum we plan? How will their attitudes be affected? Before we embark on specific learning activities, we need to identify multicultural outcomes that we expect from our instruction. For example, when students inquire multiculturally as they engage in broad thematic studies related to history, we might expect students to:

- Identify their own strengths and express the need and right of all other persons to similar feelings of self-esteem.
- List areas in which they need to grow.
- Describe their cultures of origin, recognizing the influences that have shaped their thinking and behavior.
- Identify racial, ethnic, and religious groups represented in our pluralistic society (e.g., African Americans, persons from Italian backgrounds, Jews).
- Express positive feelings for others.
- Review the history of immigration to the United States after its formation and the changing thinking about immigrants that evolved over the years.
- Categorize needs and concerns universal to people of all cultures (e.g., love, family, and health) and compare interesting cultural variations (e.g., food preparation, naming practices, or music).
- Analyze and compare literature by and about members of diverse cultures.
- Share folklore from different cultures, noting the common subjects and motifs that occur in folk literature.
- Give examples of special gender-related concerns (e.g., sexual abuse, job discrimination based on sex, or the socialization of children).
- Summarize the needs of persons with disabilities (e.g., mainstreaming in school, parking facilities, special equipment).
- Explain concepts about diverse people that are accurate and free of stereotypes and bias.
- Define key terms such as racism and sexism.
- Role play and empathize with the perspectives of different groups.
- Respect and interpret cultural diversity as a characteristic of the population of the United States and of the world.
- Work cooperatively with diverse others in small groups.
- Critique examples of stereotyped thinking and prejudice in real life and in literature.
- Inquire multiculturally as they engage in broad thematic studies related to any field (e.g., science, history, or health).

Education is an important element in the struggle for Human Rights. It is the means to help our children and our people rediscover their identity and thereby increase their self-respect. **Education is our passport to the future,** for tomorrow belongs to the people who prepare for it today.

Malcolm X

- Connect local community concerns with global issues such as violence, hunger, and pollution.
- Participate in community and school affairs as informed, empathetic young citizens who know and care about other people and recognize the enriching effect of having many cultures represented in our population.
- Continue to learn about cultural diversity as part of lifelong learning.

Such outcomes can be assessed through students' speaking or writing performances as well as observed in their body language or behavior. Students should discuss a list of expected outcomes for any study they undertake before the work begins. The outcomes listed above can be adapted for inclusion in the outcomes for a particular unit of study in any subject area, as we will discuss in the chapters that follow.

Planning a scope and sequence for a multicultural program begins with the outcomes that we expect all students to perform. Working toward achieving these outcomes will take time—a semester, a year, or more. Any list of outcomes that you use as a basis for planning should, of course, be shared with students so that they, too, know your expectations for them.

IDEAS IN ACTION!

Learning Is a Kid Thing

When Barack Obama, a young black lawyer politician from Illinois, addressed the Democratic National Convention in 2004, he noted the problem that children of color face, saying:

> Go into any inner-city neighborhood and folks will tell you that government alone can't teach kids to learn. They know that parents have to parent, that children can't achieve unless we raise their expectations and eradicate the slander that says a black youth with a book is *acting white.*

We need to send the message to all students that "education is not a black thing or a white thing. It's a kid thing. It's the way to get ahead in life." Until poor black students, especially boys who may prefer to be on the street, understand and accept this motto, we won't conquer the achievement gap.

Begin a campaign in your school to adopt the following motto: LEARNING IS A KID THING! Talk to other teachers about the reasoning behind your idea for this particular school motto. Read Obama's words to them. Suggest that teachers talk with their students about the importance of education to them, why "learning is a kid thing." Then, plan together to initiate a schoolwide contest for creating posters to illustrate the motto. Have all posters displayed in the school library or halls where students can vote on the top ten. Have an assembly at which prizes are awarded to the winners and invite the local media to attend. Arrange for the posters to be duplicated and posted in public places where they can be seen by everyone in the community.

Ongoing assessment, then, refers back to these outcomes as we observe student performance and guide students to improve their progress toward achieving a specific outcome.

Multicultural Objectives

Involving all faculty members in identifying competencies for the multicultural program will ensure that each person assumes responsibility for the success of the program. Objectives must not only cross the total curriculum but also permeate deeply into the very practices that we use as we teach.

Objectives should be written in active terms that engage students in performing thinking tasks, for example:

acting out	deciding	inquiring	retelling
analyzing	defining	listing	solving
applying	describing	observing	stating
arguing	explaining	recalling	visualizing
comparing	identifying	reciting	writing

The process of discussing and identifying the essential competencies to be developed throughout the elementary and middle school is a critical step for all members of the staff in building a multicultural curriculum. Those who are engaged from the beginning will be committed to carrying out the program they plan together. We need to identify outcomes for each curriculum area—reading, oral and written language, mathematics, social studies, science, and so on. In teaching science, a teacher, for example, might include the following objectives for a study of animals:

Students will:

- Learn about people from different countries and the animals that live with them (expands horizons).
- Keep a learning log summarizing what they learn each day (reinforces learning; individualized).
- Identify stereotypes that we associate with specific animals (introduces multicultural concept in nonthreatening context).
- Compile information to support or disprove one specific stereotype (the scientific method).
- Define stereotyped thinking in general (transfer of knowledge).
- Demonstrate how to support generalizations with scientific facts (inquiry method; thinking skills).
- Explore the roles animals play in different cultures (cultural diversity).

Teaching about Prejudice and Racism

Many teachers would prefer *not* to talk about prejudice and racism in the classroom, assuming perhaps that young children are not aware of it or that the subject is too controversial to discuss with older students. Nobody is born a bigot, after all. However, even preschool-age children have been affected by the attitudes of the society in which they live. For example, one study of a racially diverse daycare center for children aged 3 to 6 found that the children were deliberately using racially hurtful words expressing prejudiced attitudes.[1] We need to listen to what our students are saying to each other, especially when they think we are not paying attention, in order to prevent the acceptance of biased speech and racially hostile attitudes.

Begin this discussion with your students by sharing a book such as the following:

For primary students:

Louise Erdrich. *The Birchbark House.* Hyperion, 1999. A young Ojibwa girl grows up on an island in Lake Superior in the mid-1800s.

Michelle Edwards. *Pa Lia's First Day.* Harcourt, 1999. A second-grade Hmong girl's first day in a new school.

For intermediate readers:

Jon Hassler. *Jemmy.* Fawcett, 2000. Jemmy is half-Chippewa and half-white and has conflicts over her family responsibilities.

Avi and Rachel Vail. *Never Mind! A Twin Novel.* HarperCollins, 2004. Meg is ashamed of her twin Edward and is terrified her friends will find out about him.

As you discuss the book, bring up and define the key terms of *prejudice, racism,* and *stereotyping.*

Prejudice: A negative opinion or judgment of someone or something formed beforehand, not based on experience or evidence.

Racism: The belief that one's own ethnic or racial group is superior to all others.

Stereotyping: Having a fixed idea about a person or a group without allowing for individual differences.

Have students cite examples of each of these from their own experience. Discuss how to recognize prejudice, possible responses to racist remarks, and the harmful effect these have on everyone involved. Students can complete the following sentences individually or in groups.

Prejudice means _____.

I don't like it when someone calls me a _____.

People assume I am _____.

Racist attitudes hurt because _____.

The "Hidden Curriculum"

We need to remember that curriculum consists of more than consciously, carefully planned messages presented through lectures and in textbooks. Children also learn concepts and attitudes through the hidden or covert curriculum that may not be recognized and is almost never assessed. Consider what students are learning from the speech and behavior of these teachers:

Motherly Mrs. McIntyre loves children and loves to teach first-grade reading. She always brags to the principal about the wonderful readers in her Great Books group and has one of them read aloud when he visits the classroom. (How do the less able students feel? What knowledge and attitudes are they internalizing?)

Jim Melville loves to teach fourth-grade language arts. He reads aloud to his students and brings in piles of books from the library. He tells students that he always picks out books about boys because he knows boys hate stories about girls but girls enjoy the adventure stories about boys. (How might this practice affect the self-esteem of girls in this classroom? What are the boys and girls learning?)

Eighth-grade history teacher Donna Fosdick has regular celebrations for Martin Luther King's birthday and Cinco de Mayo. She comments that she can't afford more time from the curriculum for extra observances. (Is there more to understanding other cultures than just observing these few holidays? What do students learn from hearing this attitude expressed? What are they failing to learn?)

Children are very attentive to the hidden messages communicated by teacher behavior. We need to be aware of the stereotyped thinking that causes us to behave, for example, as if all children have the same advantages or disadvantages at home or that everyone in a class shares the same values. Beware of repeated evaluative statements such as "That's good" whenever students make a contribution. Students quickly learn to perform for teacher approval. We need to be aware of our role as the adult who not only chooses instructional content and strategies but also models respect and caring for students in the classroom.

In offering an inclusive educational program that serves the needs of all students, we want to refrain from:

- *Trivializing:* Organizing activities only around holidays or only around food; involving parents only for holiday or cooking activities.
- *Tokenism:* Displaying one black doll amidst many white dolls or having only one multicultural book among many others; any kind of minimal display in the classroom.
- *Disconnecting cultural diversity from daily classroom life:* Reading multicultural books only for special occasions or teaching one unit related to cultural diversity and never addressing the topic again; for example, featuring African Americans only during Black History Month in February or talking about Native Americans only in relationship to November's Thanksgiving celebration.
- *Marginalizing:* Presenting people of color only in the context of the past or as victims.
- *Misrepresenting American ethnic groups:* Using books about Mexico, Japan, or African countries to teach about contemporary cultural groups in the United States. (We may be confusing Mexican Americans with Mexicans.)

Mary Jalongo cautions that the teacher must:

1. Be aware that multiculturalism must begin with adults.
2. Know the students and their cultural backgrounds.
3. Expect conflict and model conflict resolution.
4. Bring the outside world into the classroom and help parents see the value of learning, including play, firsthand.

5. Present modern concepts of families and occupations.

6. Use literature to enrich children's learning and understandings about cultural pluralism.[2]

As a future teacher, consider how you can carry out this author's recommendations. We need to think of a multicultural curriculum as permeating the many disciplines that we teach. Goals, objectives, and expected outcomes in all subject areas should include both affective and cognitive aspects of learning and should result in active student performance. The subsequent grade multicultural curriculum introduces concepts, building on them at each level. The teacher plays a crucial role in selecting content and methods of instruction as well as modeling appropriate behaviors.

THEMATIC APPROACHES ACROSS THE CURRICULUM

Throughout this chapter you have seen how well multicultural education fits within the total curriculum. It is important that teachers plan together as a whole school to determine just how *Esteem, Empathy,* and *Equity* can best be promoted for each student through multicultural education. All teachers in self-contained classrooms will find it easy to include multicultural objectives in all areas of the curriculum. Teachers in departmentalized schools will need to agree on regular inclusion of multicultural concepts each week in their individual teaching plans. Through such efforts, student understandings and attitudes will be constantly reinforced over the entire school year.

The thematic approach to organizing learning activities is particularly appropriate for studies that cross the curriculum. Within a self-contained classroom the teacher can readily guide students through a study based on general themes, for example, "Survival," which engages students in developing literacy skills as they learn information related to science and social studies and apply mathematical concepts. Art and music also become integral aspects of such studies.

Humanities approaches to the curriculum in the middle school offer an opportunity for this kind of thematic study. Core class arrangments often bring the social science and language arts together in large blocks of time that facilitate thematic studies. Core teachers can reach out to include other subject areas, for example, science and math as well as the fine arts. Planning together pays off in terms of helping students see how knowledge comes together from many fields as they learn to "write like scientists" and enhance their sharing of findings through artistic displays or dramatic interpretations.

Planning for Thematic Study

The planning sheet shown in Figure 2.2 is designed to assist one teacher or a team of teachers in developing a thematic study that crosses the entire curriculum. This sheet can be used in varied ways. For instance, a group of teachers might sit around a table brainstorming together the possibilities for developing a theme, perhaps, "Celebrations." Each person can have a copy of this planning sheet, or you may want to create a larger version on a big sheet of butcher paper attached to the wall.

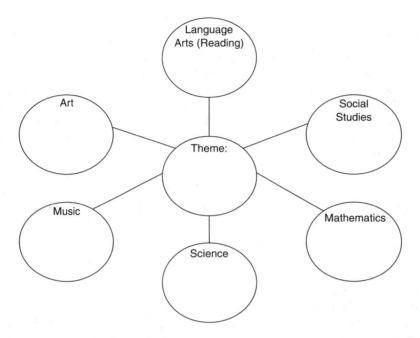

FIGURE 2.2   THEMATIC PLANNING SHEET

Students, too, can use this kind of planning sheet as they develop thematic studies with the teacher or in cooperative learning groups (CLG). For students you might choose to change the headings to reflect skills or specific subject matter instead of courses, for example, reading, writing, history, geography, art, music, biology, and math. If each CLG selects a theme it wants to explore, this sheet will encourage members of the CLG to consider how different subject areas contribute to the development of the theme. Or, if the whole class is working with one theme, an enlarged planning sheet will provide a *work wall* that will guide individual and small group projects as students integrate their work into the total study. Of course, the planning sheet will expand as students discover different avenues for exploration. Scheduled class meetings can help the group to assess just where they are in the study and to plan for further investigation.

Thematic studies offer many interesting opportunities for students. Ideally, ideas open up as information is gathered and new possibilities become apparent. Therefore, it is not necessary, or even desirable, for the total study to be prescribed with precise expectations defined before you begin. Letting other teachers and your students help to develop the theme pays off in terms of "ownership" of the project. If you try to control the total operation, there will be considerably less enthusiasm for participating, and you will be exhausted.

The important thing, as you begin, is to see that the planned study offers sufficient breadth to permit all students to be involved and that resources be available for beginning activities. The following sections outline how a thematic study might be organized.

Selection of an Appropriate Theme

Focusing units of study on broad themes is perhaps the best way of providing for individual abilities and different interests. Thematic studies enable teachers to integrate the learning of factual knowledge with the kinds of multicultural understandings that we intend to promote through a multicultural program. Integrated studies include opportunities for students to contribute to the total knowledge gathered by all class members and also to work together on common tasks, thus learning from each other.

Plan a thematic study around any curriculum topic or theme that seems timely and useful. The best topics from a multicultural viewpoint will be sufficiently broad so as to include a wide spectrum of peoples from different cultures, for example:

courage	food around the world
familes	overcoming obstacles
friendship	persecution
growing up	sports around the world

Introduction of the Theme

The purpose of the introduction is to engage student interest in the theme you plan to undertake. You might choose an approach that begins with:

- Reading a novel aloud (*The Sign of the Beaver; Sounder*).
- Discussing a current news event (conflict in Indonesia; Native American rights).
- Displaying a picture (poverty in the United States; the plight of the elderly in your community).
- Sharing picture books (*Don't You Know There's a War On?; The Butter Battle Book*).
- Interviewing a guest (a Japanese American; a rabbi; a woman politician).

To introduce the theme, Persecution, for example, read Lois Lowry's Newbery Award–winning *Number the Stars,* a novel set in Copenhagen in 1943, when Nazi soldiers were rounding up Danish Jews. Follow up by inviting students to list all the ideas that were presented in the book.

Write the words and phrases quickly on the chalkboard, linking those that are related. Notice how the ideas develop into clusters, as shown in Figure 2.3.

Reading the novel may lead to a broader study of Jewish beliefs, the wholesale persecution of Jews during World War II by the Nazis, or the life of Jews in the United States today. A novel motivates students to become involved with the characters and the action described. They will want to know why the German soldiers behaved as they did and why the Jews in particular were threatened. They can depict scenes on a large floor map as they follow events in the story. Small groups can research the history and geography related to this novel. Through this study, students should gain insight into the plight of the Jewish people during the Holocaust and the historical significance of World War II. This thematic study is an excellent example of how to align an international focus with ethnic studies in the United States.

Students may also be stimulated to read other fiction and nonfiction about Jewish people and the horrors they have experienced as they have tried to survive, for example, *Letters from Rifka* by Karen Hesse or *Memories of Anne Frank* by Alison Leslie Gold.

FIGURE 2.3   CLUSTERING IDEAS PRESENTED IN A BOOK

Working Together

The purpose of planning at this stage is for students to identify the tasks they need to undertake. They should identify, for example:

What We Know
What We Need to Find Out

Students can work in small groups to assess this kind of information. Using Cooperative Learning Groups encourages greater participation by all students and provides the opportunity to get acquainted with individual students. Working as part of a team also gives students a sense of belonging that supports their self-esteem. After making lists, the class will work together to create a Wall of Information that can stay up while the study is ongoing.

The tasks listed under "What We Need to Find Out" will be assigned, perhaps by a drawing, to each of the learning groups. Group planning will then address the next stage of development of the study—locating resources. Later, they will need to plan how they will share the information gained.

Enlist the aid of the librarians in your area. They will be happy to supply a collection of materials related to the study plan. Students can visit a library as a class or in their learning groups to find information specific to their portion of the assigned task. The librarian can help them locate books, newspapers, articles in magazines and journals, and other print material. Libraries will also be a source of multimedia materials such as videotapes, audio presentations, and computer software.

Schedule the computer lab for several periods where all students can use pertinent software and visit the Internet. Students should also use other means of finding information, for example, the telephone, personal interviews, and writing letters, faxes, or email.

Note that, periodically, you will need to plan lessons on specific skills, for example, notetaking, interviewing, and accessing the Internet.

Students will plan again to decide how they can share what they have learned through this study. If they have been actively involved, they will consider what they have learned as valuable information that everyone should know and they will want to communicate the information to others. Have students brainstorm methods they might use, for example:

- Creating a class book to put in the library.
- Producing a schoolwide assembly.
- Inviting another class to visit them to see what they have accomplished.
- Preparing a multimedia presentation.

Following is an example of a multicultural thematic study.

LEARNING ABOUT LATINOS: THEMATIC STUDY I

As more data are analyzed from the 2000 census, a better picture can be built of this major group in the United States. The Hispanic (or Latino) population has increased 58 percent since 1990 and reached 35.4 million, or 12.8 percent of the population, in 2000. Many claim

TABLE 2.1   COUNTRY OF ORIGIN– POPULATION IN MILLIONS (2000)

Mexico	20.6
Puerto Rican (U.S.)	3.4
Cuban	1.2
Dominican Republic	2.4
Central and South American countries, others	10

Source: U.S. Bureau of the Census Public Information Office.
USA Statistics in Brief, 2004. Accessed from www.census.gov

Latinos are still being undercounted. This growth makes the Latino population almost comparable to the black population of 36.4 million. However, the Latino population remains diverse. Have students look at Table 2.1. In general, Mexican Americans have the lowest income and education, while Cubans show the highest income and education.

Latinos are linked by an identity that includes many diverse factors, such as religion, language, customs, food, and immigration concerns. It is important, however, to remember not to stereotype Latinos. Not all Latinos speak Spanish, belong to the Catholic Church, or are farmworkers. Many Latinos have lived in the United States for several generations, prefer to speak English, or are highly educated.

In this sample unit, students will have an opportunity to:

- Learn more about Latinos and their culture.
- Explore Latino influences on the United States.
- Discuss differences among Latinos and the implications for social change.

The following activities are examples of how you might incorporate Learning about Latinos into your curriculum.

Setting up a Spanish Language Center

Prepare a chart such as Table 2.2 to show common names in Spanish and English. Make a point of pronouncing the Spanish names correctly. You might ask Spanish-speaking students to help you.

Bring books in Spanish into the classroom. Students will enjoy exploring bilingual books, where they can compare stories in Spanish and English, as well as books in Spanish alone. Perhaps children who read Spanish can tell the other students about these books. Show students that knowing another language, such as Spanish, can be an asset.

Francisco Alarcón. *Laughing Tomatoes and Other Spring Poems/Jitomates risueños y otras poemas de primavera.* Illustrated by Maya Christina Gonzales. Children's Book Press, 1997. Twenty poems in Spanish and English in a colorful book for intermediate students.

Julia Alvarez. *A Cafecito Story/El Cuento del Cafecito.* Illustrated by Belkis Ramirez. Chelsea Green, 2004.

TABLE 2.2   NAMES IN SPANISH AND ENGLISH

Pedro—Peter	María-Mary
Juan—John	Juana-Jane
Esteban—Stephen	Esperanza—Hope
Luís—Louis	Margarita—Margaret
Carlos—Charles	Josefina—Josephine
José—Joseph	Teresa—Theresa
Ricardo—Richard	Elena—Helen
Roberto—Robert	Susanna—Susan
Jacinto—James	Beatríz—Beatrice
Arturo—Arthur	Carlota—Charlotte
Eduardo—Edward	Emilia—Emily
Jorge—George	Estrellita—Stella
Enrique—Henry	Anna—Ann
Alejandro—Alexander	Rosa—Rose
Guillermo—William	Luísa—Louise

George Ancona. *Somo Latinos/We Are Latinos.* Children's Book Press, 2004. This six-book bilingual series includes titles such as *Mi Casa/My House, Mi Barrio/My Neighborhood,* and *Mis Amigos/My Friends.*

Gloria Anzaldúa. *Prietita and the Ghost Woman/Prietita y la llorona.* Illustrated by Christina Gonzalez. Children's Book Press, 1996. A fanciful journey of a young girl with the ghost woman on the King Ranch in Texas.

Lucha Corpi. *Where Fireflies Dance/Ahí, donde bailan las luciernagas.* Illustrated by Mira Reisberg. Children's Book Press, 1997. Memories of growing up in Mexico.

Lois Ehlert. *Cuckoo/Cucú: A Mexican Folktale/Un cuento folklórico mexicano.* Harcourt, 1997. A bilingual tale illustrated with examples from Mexican folk art.

Juan Felipe Herrera. *The Upside Down Boy/El Niño de Cabeza.* Children's Book Press, 1999. Memories of poet's childhood.

Tish Hinojosa. *Cada Niño/Every Child: A Bilingual Songbook for Kids.* Illustrated by Lucia Angela Perez. Cinco Puntos, 2002.

Bobbi Salinas. *Three Pigs/Los tres cerdos: Nacho, Tito Y Miguel.* Children's Book Press, 1999. Bilingual story, not the usual tale of the wolf and the three little pigs.

Nancy Tabor. *El Gusto del Mercado Mexicano/A Taste of the Mexican Market.* Charlesbridge, 1996. Readers learn counting skills and information about the Mexican culture.

A Spanish color wheel is helpful to show students the names for colors they know. Make a large poster to display on the wall like that shown in Figure 2.4. This idea can be

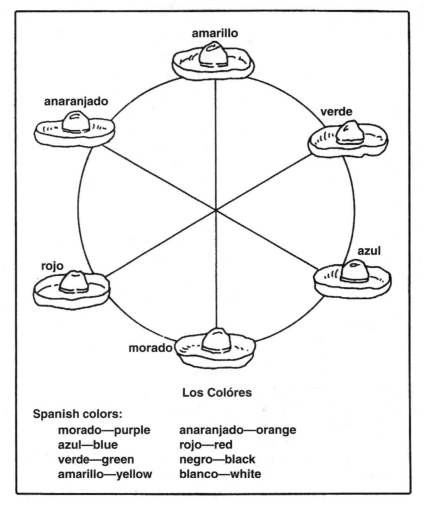

Los Colóres

Spanish colors:

morado—purple	anaranjado—orange
azul—blue	rojo—red
verde—green	negro—black
amarillo—yellow	blanco—white

FIGURE 2.4   SPANISH COLORS

easily adapted for use with any language spoken by students in the class. Prepare a variety of displays similar to the color wheel showing basic vocabulary. Include numbers, days of the week, and words used in the classroom.

Help students practice Spanish vocabulary they have learned or seen by preparing review charts (see Figure 2.5). Construct a slip chart with common Spanish words written on the front. Students read the Spanish, say it aloud, give the English equivalent, and check their response by pulling the tab that shows the English word below each Spanish example. These are especially useful for practicing limited sets of words such as numbers and days of the week.

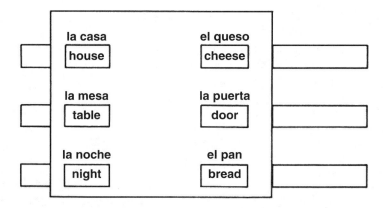

FIGURE 2.5   SLIP CHART

Spanish Is All around Us

Students may be surprised to see how many Spanish words they know. If Spanish is frequently used in the community, students should have no trouble recalling words seen on signs and heard in conversations. Have students list words they know as you write them on the board. Do they know what the words mean? They might suggest the following words:

amigos   fiesta   siesta
adiós   tortilla   piñata

Do any stores in the community have signs in Spanish? Where do the children hear Spanish spoken? What does "Aquí se habla español" mean? ("Spanish is spoken here.") Are there any Spanish place names or street names in the community?

English has borrowed extensively from Spanish, particularly in the Southwest. List examples of borrowings on the board. Do students know what these words mean? What kinds of words have been borrowed? Discuss why borrowings might take place. The following are examples of borrowings from Spanish:

arroyo   burro   avocado   plaza
bronco   canyon   vanilla   stampede
rodeo   lasso   adobe   mesa
sombrero   chili   mustang   sierra

Many words borrowed into English from Spanish come originally from the native languages of Latin America. *Chocolate* was borrowed from Nahuatl, the Aztec language, into Mexican Spanish and then into English. As students research Spanish borrowings, have them notice examples of Native American words. The following are examples of words borrowed from Guaraní, a language spoken in Paraguay, into English: *tapioca, maracas, jaguar, jacaranda, tapir,* and *toucan.* The Spanish spoken in the United States is developing differently from the rest of Latin American Spanish because it has continued to borrow from the Native American languages, and it has also been influenced by English.

All students can appreciate the following books about Spanish culture, holidays, and other celebrations.

George Ancona. *The Piñata Maker/El piñatero.* Harcourt Brace, 1994. Shows a dedicated craftsman in Mexico at work on a piñata, step by step.

Arthur Dorros. *Tonight Is Carnaval.* Dutton, 1990. Describes the preparations for the festival in Peru. Features local crafts, culture.

Francisco Jimenez. *The Christmas Gift/El Regalo de Navidad.* Illustrated by Claire Cotts. Chronicle Books, 2000. Bilingual picture book tells a story from the author's life as a migrant farm worker, as explained in *The Circuit: Stories from the Life of a Migrant Child.*

Nancy Luenn. *A Gift for Abuelita: Celebrating the Day of the Dead/Un Regalo para Abuelita: En Celebración del Día de los Muertos.* Rising Moon/Northland, 1998. A bilingual story explains the importance of the Day of the Dead.

Jose-Luis Orozco, comp. *Fiestas: Holiday Songs from Latin America.* Illustrated by Elisa Kleven. Dutton, 2002.

Students will become more aware of the Spanish influence in the United States when they explore place names on a map. Project a copy of a U.S. map on the wall so that all the students can see the names marked on the map. Have students find examples of Spanish place names. Talk about how you can tell whether a name is Spanish or not. If the first word is *San* or *Santa* the name is probably a Spanish saint name. What would these names be in English? (San Francisco/Saint Francis, San Antonio/Saint Anthony, for example.)

Look at different areas of the country separately. Students will notice that more Spanish names occur in certain areas. Which areas have more Spanish names, and why?

As students search for Spanish names, they will notice other groups of foreign names. There are a number of French names in Louisiana, for example. Why? Ask students if they can think why the names used on the map might reflect the history of a region. Does the presence of Spanish names in an area necessarily mean that there are Spanish-speaking people living there?

Celebrating Latino Culture and Heritage

As you select books, look for ones that include culturally specific details and promote respect for the diversity of Latinos. The following books introduce students to the lives of young people in Latin America, along with information about their culture and language.

George Ancona. *Charro: The Mexican Cowboy.* Harcourt, 1999. Photographs depict life of typical charro.

Nancy Andrews-Goebel. *The Pot That Juan Built.* Illustrated by David Diaz. Lee & Low, 2002. This book for all ages shows the world-famous Mexican potter Juan Quezada at work.

Ann Cameron. *Colibrí.* Farrar, 2003. A Mayan girl is forced to beg in rural Guatemala. Story shows conflict between traditional beliefs and modern issues.

Omar Castañeda. *Among the Volcanoes.* Lodestar, 1991. A Mayan girl, living in a village in Guatemala, has to take care of her sick mother. She wants to become a teacher.

Rachel Crandell. *Hands of the Maya: Villagers at Work and Play.* Holt, 2002. Shows everyday tasks performed by people in Belize.

Carlos Cumpián. *Latino Rainbow: Poems about Latin America.* Illustrated by Richard Leonard. Children's Press, 1994. Includes history and biographies.

Campbell Geeslin. *Elena's Secret.* Simon & Schuster, 2004. Story about glassblowers in Monterrey.

Eric Kimmel. *Montezuma and the Fall of the Aztecs.* Holiday, 2000.

Peter Laufer. *Made in Mexico.* National Geographic, 2000. Illustrated by Susan Roth. Life in a small Mexican village where great guitars are made.

Trish Marx. *Reaching for the Sun: Kids in Cuba.* Millbrook, 2003. A children's arts group flies from Los Angeles to Cuba to perform a play along with Cuban children.

Pat Mora. *A Library for Juana: The World of Sor Juana Inés.* Illustrated by Beatriz Vidal. Knopf, 2002. Story of the noted seventeenth-century poet and scholar.

Jonah Winter. *Frida.* Illustrated by Ana Juan. Scholastic, 2002. Biography of Mexican painter Frida Kahlo. Also available in Spanish.

As you assemble information about different countries in Latin America, you might have students record their findings on a timeline like that in Figure 2.6.

Latino students need to see books that reflect their own lives and cultural experiences, just as children from any cultural background do. Choose books that represent a variety of regions and backgrounds, from Puerto Rico to Mexican Americans in the Southwest. These examples include rich cultural information and Spanish language in context.

Elisa Amado. *Cousins.* Groundwood, 2004. A young Latina girl has two grandmothers.

Lulu Delacre. *Salsa Stories.* Scholastic, 1999. Carmen receives a blank notebook in which she begins to write family stories.

Kristyn Estes. *Manuela's Gift.* Illustrated by Claire Cotts. Chronicle Books, 1999. Manuela wants a new dress for her birthday and is disappointed to receive a hand-me-down.

Carmen Lomas Garza. *Family Pictures/Cuadros de familia.* Children's Book Press, 1990. The life of a young Mexican American girl who lives in south Texas. Excellent for details about Latino culture in the region.

Cruz Martel. *Yagua Days.* Dial, 1996. On his first visit to Puerto Rico, a boy learns how children use the large yagua leaves to slide down a hill after a rainstorm.

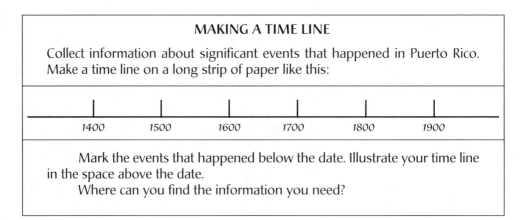

MAKING A TIME LINE

Collect information about significant events that happened in Puerto Rico. Make a time line on a long strip of paper like this:

| | | | | | |
1400   1500   1600   1700   1800   1900

Mark the events that happened below the date. Illustrate your time line in the space above the date.
Where can you find the information you need?

FIGURE 2.6   SAMPLE TASK CARD

Victor Martinez. *Parrot in the Oven.* Harper, 1998. Novel about a Mexican teenager who lives in the projects.

Jane Medina. *My Name Is Jorge: On Both Sides of the River.* Boyds Mills, 1999. Twenty-four poems in English and Spanish chronicle the school days of Jorge, a Mexican boy.

Pat Mora. *This Big Sky.* Illustrated by Steve Jenkins. Scholastic, 1998. Poems about the landscape of the Southwest by noted Latina writer.

Yoland Nava. *It's All in the Frijoles: 100 Famous Latinos Share Real-Life Stories, Time-Tested Dichos, Favorite Folktales and Inspiring Words of Wisdom.* Turtleback, 2000.

Gary Soto. *Baseball in April.* Harcourt Brace Jovanovich, 1990. Short stories of growing up Chicano in central California, each featuring a different Mexican American child.

Muriel Stanek. *I Speak English for My Mom.* Whitman, 1989. Reflects a common experience for many children. Lupe's mother works in a factory, but she begins taking English classes to get a better job.

Valerie Tripp. *Meet Josefina: An American Girl.* Illustrated by Jean Paul Tibbles. Pleasant, 1997. Life in New Mexico on a rancho in 1824.

An important aspect of studying Latino language and culture is Latino folklore. This folklore reflects Spanish, English, African American, and Indian influences and is an important part of the American experience. Folklore includes stories (cuentos), sayings (dichos), songs, music, legends (leyendas), and drama. Special types of songs are *corridos, mañanitas,* and *rancheros.* Many legends center around *La Bruja* (the Witch) and *La Curandera* (the Healer).

Provide examples of different kinds of folklore and discuss the ritualized characteristics of each form. Encourage students to research more examples. Because all of the stories and songs are short, they are particularly suitable for presenting in front of the class. Several students can take turns telling stories that are spooky or humorous. You can also obtain records of traditional ballads and songs to play.

Alma Flor Ada. *The Three Golden Oranges.* Illustrated by Reg Cartwright. Atheneum, 1999. Traditional tale of Blancaflor, about the value of working together.

Pura Belpré. *Perez and Martina.* Viking, 1991. From the Puerto Rican storyteller, the tale of Perez the mouse and Martina the cockroach.

Gerald McDermott. *Papagayo the Mischief Maker.* Harcourt Brace Jovanovich, 1992. Papagayo the parrot is the traditional trickster hero of the Amazon rain forest.

The Pura Belpré Award, established in 1996, is given by REFORMA and the ALA to honor Latino writers and illustrators whose work best portrays, affirms, and celebrates Latino culture and heritage in books for children. This award is named for Pura Belpré, the first Latina librarian at the New York Public Library. As a children's librarian, storyteller, and author, she enriched the lives of Puerto Rican children in the United States through her pioneering work of preserving and disseminating Puerto Rican folklore. The awards are given biennially.

In 2004, the winners were:

Julia Alvarez. *Before We Were Free.* Knopf, 2002. Twelve-year-old Anita lives in fear because of the violence around her in the Dominican Republic.

Kathleen Krull. *Harvesting Hope: The Story of César Chávez.* Illustrated by Yuyi Morales. Harcourt, 2003. Describes the life of the Chicano labor leader.

Yuyi Morales. *Just a Minute: A Trickster Tale and Counting Book.* Chronicle Books, 2003. Expresses the essence of Mexican culture through illustrations.

Nancy Osa. *Cuba 15.* Delacorte Press, 2003. Violet Paz prepares for her quinceañero and comes to understand her Cuban heritage.

Amada Irma Pérez. *My Diary from Here to There/ Mi Diario de Aquí Hasta Allá.* Children's Book Press, 2004. Family emigrates from Mexico to California.

L. King Pérez. *First Day in Grapes.* Illustrated by Robert Casilla. Lee & Low, 2002. About a child of migrant farmworkers.

Other Pura Belpré award winners are:

Alma Flor Ada, author and illustrator. *Under the Royal Palms: A Childhood in Cuba.* Memories of her life, sequel to *Where the Flame Trees Bloom.* Harcourt Brace, 1998.

Francisco X. Alarcón. *From the Bellybutton of the Moon and Other Summer Poems/Del Ombligo de la Luna y Otros Poemas de Verano.* Children's Book Press, 1998. Poems inspired by author's childhood summers in Mexico.

George Ancona, author and illustrator. *Barrio: José's Neighborhood.* Harcourt Brace, 1998. Descriptions of 8-year-old José's life in the Mission District, San Francisco, California.

Amelia Lau Carling, author and illustrator. *Mama & Papa Have a Store.* Dial, 1998. Young Chinese girl describes her parents' store in Guatamala City.

Carmen Lomas Garza. *Magic Windows/Ventanas Magicas.* Children's Book Press, 1999. Author tells about family's Mexican heritage while introducing readers to the art of *papel picado,* cut paper.

Juan Felipe Herrera. *Laughing Out Loud, I Fly: A Carcajadas Yo Vuelo.* HarperCollins, 1999. Poems of sound and rhythm reflect author's Latino heritage.

Joseph Slate. *The Secret Stars.* Illustrated by Felipe Davalós. Cavendish, 1998. In New Mexico, Grandmother comforts Pepe and Sila, who worry that the three kings won't be able to find their way to deliver the children's presents.

Gary Soto. *Chato and the Party Animals.* Illustrated by Susan Guevara. Scholastic, 2002. Another story about Chato, the bilingual cat.

Students can collect what they have learned and develop a book to share with other classes and schools. A model for this activity is *Kids Explore America's Hispanic Heritage* from the Westridge Young Writers Workshop. This book, written by students, includes information about and examples of dances, food, games, history, art, songs, and people.

A NATION OF IMMIGRANTS: THEMATIC STUDY II

Almost all of the people who now live in the United States are immigrants or children of immigrants. Native Americans were the only ones here to greet Christopher Columbus, and even they emigrated earlier from Asia. (While African Americans did not emigrate, they did come from other countries.) Immigration is a particularly timely topic as issues at state and national levels are receiving media attention. This thematic study might be developed following these steps.

Introduction

Reading a book about an immigrant is a good way to engage students with the human as well as political and social issues that are involved in a discussion of immigration. For example, *Grandfather's Journey,* Allen Say's Caldecott Award–winning picture book, tells how the author's grandfather, a Japanese man, came to the New World, which he learned to love. He married a Japanese woman and brought her to California where they had a baby daughter, Allen's mother. His grandfather was happy in the United States, but he missed his homeland so much that he and his family returned to Japan to live. His mother remained in Japan and married there, so Allen was born in Japan. Later, he, too, emigrated to California where he learned to understand his grandfather's love for both countries.

This sensitive cross-cultural account may provide insight into the feelings that immigrants share as they become naturalized citizens and pledge allegiance to their new country, the United States, saying:

> . . . I will support and defend the Constitution and laws
> of the United States of America against all enemies,
> foreign and domestic . . .
>> Oath of Allegiance required of Naturalized Citizens

Other picture books that support this theme include:

Amy Hest. *When Jessica Came across the Sea.* Candlewick Press, 1997.

Liz Rosenberg. *Grandmother and the Runaway Shadow.* Harcourt, 1996.

Planning an Integrated Study

Talk about the three generations represented in *Grandfather's Journey.* Discuss the conflicting feelings they had about Japan and the United States and how difficult the decision must have been to leave one country for the other. Use the world map to point out the great distance between the two countries. Ask if students know anyone who has immigrated from another country (perhaps the students themselves, their parents, or grandparents).

Then let students join with you in planning a study called A Nation of Immigrants. You might begin an information wall on which to collect facts related to the topic. Label sections on which to place information in various categories, for example:

- Where Our Ancestors Came From (make a big map)
- Who Lives in Our Community
- What We'd Like to Find Out:
  1. How do you become a citizen?
  2. What is the INS? Where is its nearest office?

Brainstorm for a while, but expect to keep adding information to this wall. Then, form CLGs to begin locating information on different aspects of this study, for instance:

- Emigrating to the New World.
- Laws regarding immigration.
- What immigrants contribute to life in this country.
- The question of language differences.

Locating Resources to Share

Take students to the school library and then to the local public library for a Treasure Hunt. The librarian can suggest various ways of searching for information: the card catalog, books on the shelves, the computer, and so on. Have students make a card for each discovery, which will go in a class Resource File. Include such books as the following:

Elisa Bartone. *American Too.* Lothrop, 1996. Rosina sails into New York Harbor just after World War I. She wants to be American, but everyone she knows is Italian.

Eve Bunting. *How Many Days to America? A Thanksgiving Story.* Clarion, 1988. Refugees are welcomed to a holiday celebration.

Anne Galicich. *The German Americans.* Chelsea House, 1992. This book is one in an excellent series of more than fifty books, *The Peoples of North America.*

Mary Hoffman. *The Color of Home.* Penguin, 2002. Hassan, from Somalia, is newly arrived and homesick. In school he paints a picture of home and why he left.

Dorothy Hoobler and Thomas Hoobler. *We Are Americans: Voices of the Immigrant Experience.* Scholastic, 2003.

Jim Murphy. *Across America on an Emigrant Train.* Clarion Books, 1994. The story of immigrants who migrated west.

Claire A. Nivola. *Elisabeth.* HarperCollins, 1997. A Jewish child's memories of the flight from Nazi Germany.

Pegi Deitz Shea. *Tangled Threads: A Hmong Girl's Story.* Clarion, 2004. After years in a refugee camp, a young girl and her grandmother reach their family in Rhode Island. Each has trouble adjusting to the new culture.

John Son. *Finding My Hat.* Scholastic, 2004. As his family moves around the United States, a young Korean boy becomes "American."

Jeanette Winter. *Keana's New World.* Knopf, 1992. A Swedish girl emigrates from Sweden to Minnesota in the 1800s.

Connecting across the Curriculum

Help students plan ways of sharing what they have learned with each other first and then with other classes, or perhaps the whole school. Following are a few suggestions:

- *Teaching a Lesson.* Each CLG can prepare a lesson to present to other members of their class. One teaching team might, for example, engage students in role-playing situations that occur as diverse people interact: What Would You Do?
- *A Readers' Theater Presentation.* The whole class could plan a presentation to be given before one or more classes of their peers. The readings could vary from a short play to poetry or a series of quotations. The presentation should follow a clear theme, for example, Coming to a New Home.
- *A School Assembly.* The class could plan an assembly, perhaps titled New Citizens. This presentation could also be given at a PTA meeting as a way of spreading this information throughout the community.

ASSESSING STUDENT PROGRESS

All methods of assessment are being critiqued on the basis of equity. To provide for diverse learning styles, students need to experience varied methods of assessing mastery. A new assessment strategy that is receiving much attention is portfolio assessment, a method that is highly individualized.

The American Association for Higher Education (1 Dupont Circle, Washington, DC 20036) has published the following excellent summary of assessment practices, "Principles of Good Practice for Assessing Student Learning":

1. *The assessment of student learning begins with educational values.*

   Assessment is not an end in itself but a vehicle for educational improvement. Its effective practice, then, begins with and enacts a vision of the kinds of learning we most value for students and strive to help them achieve. Educational values should drive not only *what* we choose to assess but also *how* we do so. Where questions about educational mission and values are skipped over, assessment threatens to be an exercise in measuring what's easy, rather than a process of improving what we really care about.

2. *Assessment is most effective when it reflects an understanding of learning as multi-dimensional, integrated, and revealed in performance over time.*

   Learning is a complex process. It entails not only what students know but what they can do with what they know; it involves not only knowledge and abilities but values, attitudes, and habits of mind that affect both academic success and performance beyond the classroom. Assessment should reflect these understandings by employing a diverse array of methods, including those that call for actual performance, using them over time so as to reveal change, growth, and increasing degrees of integration. Such an approach aims for a more complete and accurate picture of learning, and therefore a firmer basis for improving our students' educational experience.

3. *Assessment works best when the programs it seeks to improve have clear, explicitly stated purposes.*

   Assessment is a goal-oriented process. It entails comparing educational performance with educational purposes and expectations—these derived from the institution's mission, from faculty intentions in program and course design, and from knowledge of students' own goals. Where program purposes lack specificity or agreement, assessment as a process pushes a campus toward clarity about where to aim and what standards to apply; assessment also prompts attention to where and how program goals will be taught and learned. Clear, shared, implementable goals are the cornerstone for assessment that is focused and useful.

4. *Assessment requires attention to outcomes but also and equally to the experiences that lead to those outcomes.*

   Information about outcomes is of high importance; where students "end up" matters greatly. But to improve outcomes, we need to know about student experience along the way—about the curricula, teaching, and kind of student effort that lead to particular outcomes. Assessment can help us understand which students learn best under what conditions; with such knowledge comes the capacity to improve the whole of their learning.

5. *Assessment works best when it is ongoing, not episodic.*

   Assessment is a process whose power is cumulative. Though isolated, "one-shot" assessment can be better than none, improvement is best fostered when assessment entails a linked series of activities undertaken over time. This may mean tracking the progress of individual students, or of cohorts of students; it may mean collecting the same examples of student performance or using the same instrument semester after semester. The point is to monitor progress toward intended goals in a spirit of continuous improvement. Along the way, the assessment process itself should be evaluated and refined in light of emerging insights.

6. *Assessment fosters wider improvement when representatives from across the educational community are involved.*

Student learning is a campus-wide responsibility, and assessment is a way of enacting that responsibility. Thus, while assessment efforts may start small, the aim over time is to involve people from across the educational community. Faculty play an especially important role, but assessment's questions can't be fully addressed without participation by student-affairs educators, librarians, administrators, and students. Assessment may also involve individuals from beyond the campus (alumni/ae, trustees, employers) whose experience can enrich the sense of appropriate aims and standards for learning. Thus understood, assessment is not a task for small groups of experts but a collaborative activity; its aim is wider, better-informed attention to student learning by all parties with a stake in its improvement.

7. *Assessment makes a difference when it begins with issues of use and illuminates questions that people really care about.*

Assessment recognizes the value of information in the process of improvement. But to be useful, information must be connected to issues or questions that people really care about. This implies assessment approaches that produce evidence that relevant parties will find credible, suggestive, and applicable to decisions that need to be made. It means thinking in advance about how the information will be used, and by whom. The point of assessment is not to gather data and return "results"; it is a process that starts with the questions of decision makers, that involves them in the gathering and interpreting of data, and that informs and helps guide continuous improvement.

8. *Assessment is most likely to lead to improvement when it is part of a larger set of conditions that promote change.*

Assessment alone changes little. Its greatest contribution comes on campuses where the quality of teaching and learning is visibly valued and worked at. On such campuses, the push to improve educational performance is a visible and primary goal of leadership; improving the quality of undergraduate education is central to the institution's planning, budgeting, and personnel decisions. On such campuses, information about learning outcomes is seen as an integral part of decision making and is avidly sought.

As we plan a multicultural program, it is essential to use practices that stand out as exemplary. Across the country, teachers and school districts are making sincere efforts to reach multicultural goals from different perspectives. Grounded in the principle of achieving self-esteem for all students and leading to understanding of others, these programs may address the needs of preschool children or adolescent at-risk students; they may be directed toward preparing the teacher; or they may deal directly with selection of content or methods of delivering the curriculum.

CONNECTIONS

Multicultural education requires a teacher who is committed to the welfare of all students. It requires a teacher who is willing to accept a challenge. The rewards lie in seeing students succeed and enjoy school.

Teaching for multicultural understanding begins with a well-planned curriculum based on expected outcomes. The teacher's role in delivering this curriculum is to guide student inquiries and to serve as facilitator and resource person. The student learner also plays an active part in initiating avenues of inquiry in conjunction with a group of fellow researchers. The best of methodologies and resources must be selected as we develop an integrated humanistic study that furthers multicultural understanding.

A sound multicultural education program depends on careful planning across levels and across subject areas. The major quality indicators of an effective program include:

- Teachers who recognize the need for multicultural education, who are involved in the planning, and who are willing to learn with their students.
- Students who are self-motivated learners concerned about their own rights as well as the rights of others.
- Content that makes interdisciplinary and multicultural connections.

When we successfully bring these three components together, we will have an outstanding multicultural education program. All children will learn.

FOLLOW-THROUGH

Expanding Your RTP

1. Label a section of your portfolio "My Ethnic and Cultural Identity." Find out where your parents and grandparents were born and how you happened to come to live in your present community. How did your parents meet? Think about what values are important to your family, how you celebrate rituals or holidays, and what kinds of foods you enjoy together. Discuss your findings with others in your Cooperative Learning Group. You might bring pictures to show each other or plan to share some foods. List the objectives involved in this kind of sharing and how you might help young students engage in this type of sharing, too.

2. Elizabeth Fitzgerald Howard wrote a picture book, *Virgie Goes to School with Us Boys,* which is illustrated beautifully by E. B. Lewis. This author tells the touching story of a little African American girl who passionately wants to accompany her older brothers to a Quaker school that they attend.

   In an Afterword this African American author relates the historical background for this tale, noting "Repression of their natural desire to learn was perhaps the cruelest punishment endured by slaves before the Civil War." Slaves were prohibited from learning to read and write, a theme that appears in many other contemporary books about that period in our history. See *Silent Thunder: A Civil War Story* by Andrea Davis Pinkney, a novel about a brother and sister, slaves who also longed to read.

When you were young, did you ever wish you didn't have to attend school? Did you ever grumble about having to read a book in school? In your portfolio write about how you would feel, if you were *forbidden* to go to school. How would you feel if you were told you *could not* read a book?

Working with Your CLG

1. Choose one country or group of people to investigate as you develop a thematic unit of study with other CLGs on "New Americans." Begin by examining children's books you can use. For example, if your group focuses on the Vietnamese as a subject, you might locate the following:

   Alexandra Bandon. *Vietnamese Americans.* New Discovery Books, 1994.
   Tricia Brown. *Lee Ann: The Story of a Vietnamese Girl.* Putnam, 1991.
   Sherry Garland. *Shadow of the Dragon.* Harcourt, 1993.
   Jeremy Schmidt and Ted Wood. *Two Lands, One Heart: An American Boy's Journey to His Mother's Vietnam.* Walker, 1995.
   Andrea Warren. *Escape from Saigon: How a Vietnamese War Orphan Became an American Boy.* Farrar, 2004.

   Read these books as a starting point to supply basic information and to suggest other avenues of research. Don't forget the local community as a resource.

2. Choose one state to study in detail. Think chiefly about the people who now live in that part of our country. Find out their backgrounds and how they came to settle there.

   If you choose Hawaii, for example, you might list the following:

   Georgia Gulack. *Luka's Quilt.* Greenwillow, 1994. This intergenerational story focuses on tradition and the importance of communicating.
   Graham Salisbury. *Under the Blood-Red Sun.* Yearling, 1994. A Japanese American teenager in Hawaii in 1941.
   Ruth Tabrah. *Hawaii: A Bicentennial History.* Norton, 1980. Written for the bicentennial, here is a good overview of Hawaiian history.

GROWING A PROFESSIONAL LIBRARY

Jonathan Kozol. *Savage Inequalities: Children in America's Schools.* Crown, 1991.

Gary Marcuse. *The Mind of a Child: Working with Children Affected by Poverty, Racism, and War.* Face-to-Face Media, 1995. (Video)

Theresa Perry and James Fraser, eds. *Freedom's Plow: Teaching in the Multicultural Classroom.* Routledge, 1993.

ENDNOTES

1. Mary Jalongo in Edwina B. Vold, *Multicultural Education in Early Childhood Classrooms.* National Education Association, 1992, pp. 56–62.
2. Ibid.
3. Debra Van Ausdale, *The First R: How Children Learn Race and Racism.* Basic, 2000.

Tell me,
I forget.

Show me,
I remember.

Involve me,
I understand

Chinese Proverb

Individualizing Instruction for Multicultural Education

With an emphasis on learning processes, multicultural teaching attempts to facilitate the learning of every child, assisting each one to reach his or her highest potential. We need to plan instruction that accommodates individual differences and use teaching strategies that ensure successful learning for children with diverse abilities. No matter what race or culture a student comes from, he or she requires teaching that is flexible and adapted to his or her individual strengths and weaknesses. Implementing the *Esteem, Empathy, Equity* Model should help you assess the needs of the student, plan an appropriate multicultural program, and deliver this curriculum, having selected the best methods and materials.

Research findings support our conviction that effective multicultural teaching is student centered rather than teacher dominated. The teacher does not abdicate his or her position but rather plans quality learning activities that engage students in active, hands-on experiences and builds on success to develop students' self-esteem. The teacher models appreciation for diversity by building on students' prior knowledge and setting clear, realistic expectations for each student's abilities. Learning experiences are designed to promote student interaction and to generate inquiry and thinking through both talking and writing. Such approaches benefit all students, but they are especially recommended for those who come from cultures that are very different from the school culture or are learning English as an additional language.

EFFECTIVE MULTICULTURAL TEACHING

"Good teachers make all the difference," says Deborah Stipek, Dean of Stanford University's School of Education. In such states as California, for example, too few students have access to qualified teachers and the poorer the school, the less qualified the teacher. If we want our children to succeed, we have to pay attention to preparing teachers well before and after they enter the classroom.

Hiring and retaining effective teachers has become an increasingly serious problem across the nation. Educated young men and women are choosing jobs in industry where they can command excellent salaries that may include greater opportunities for career advancement. Teacher salaries have consistently lagged far behind those in industry, leaving teachers unable to live in the communities in which they work. Gradually, school districts and state leaders are adopting strategies to make teaching more attractive for those who do choose to teach.

At the same time, in an effort to improve public school education, state leaders are trying to limit the size of classes, particularly in the primary grades. Thus, the total number of teachers needed has increased. Therefore, school districts are often forced to hire inexperienced teachers and those who are not fully credentialed. Here, too, educators are trying to offset this problem by offering more support for beginning teachers in the form of mentorship and professional development.

Improving the Quality of Teachers

Kenneth Zeichner, in his study *Educating Teachers for Cultural Diversity,* deplores the widening gap between classroom teachers and the children they teach as "teachers become increasingly different from the students they teach. Furthermore, the number of persons of color entering the teaching field is much too small to overcome the discrepancy between the teacher's cultural background and that of the culturally diverse group of students in most classrooms.[1]

It is essential, therefore, that all teachers acquire the appropriate attitudes, knowledge, and disposition needed to work effectively with students who come from varied cultural or class backgrounds. It is important to recognize, too, that not only will teacher and student be different, but also that in many classrooms students will also differ from one another. Multicultural education requires that teachers plan an inclusive classroom in which children learn about each other and learn to respect each other.

Hopkins and Stem synthesized the findings of a worldwide study of excellent teaching by The Organization for Economic Cooperation and Development (OECD) sponsored by the Centre for Educational Research and Innovation (CERI). Selected excellent teachers were studied in a number of different countries; each teacher was observed and interviewed for approximately twenty hours each. The most important characteristics of excellent teachers included:

- A passionate commitment to doing the very best for their students.
- A love of children enacted in warm, caring relationships.
- Pedagogical content knowledge, e.g., knowing how to identify, present, and explain key concepts.
- Use of a variety of models of teaching and learning.
- A collaborative working style with other teachers to plan, observe, and discuss each other's work.
- A constant questioning of, reflecting on, and modifying of their own practice.[2]

According to Zeichner, university students who intend to become teachers today must have the following key characteristics to be effective as culturally sensitive teachers:

- A clear sense of their own ethnic and cultural identity.
- High expectations for student success.

- The expectation that all students can succeed and that they can help them succeed.
- Commitment to achieving equity for all students and knowledge about accommodating different learning styles and abilities.
- The ability to bond with students; genuine caring about young people and their welfare.
- A strong multicultural knowledge base that includes both depth and breadth regarding ethnic studies, gender concerns, and sensitivity to persons with special needs.[3]

Strategies and skills that the effective teacher needs to be able to use include:

- Planning meaningful learning tasks based on the curriculum.
- Engaging students in interactive and collaborative learning tasks.
- Challenging students to develop higher-level thinking skills.
- Providing scaffolding (support) for students to ensure that they can succeed.
- Building on students' prior knowledge.
- Communicating to students the expectation that they can succeed and that you, the teacher, will help them.
- Explaining the culture of the school to students.
- Maintaining students' sense of ethnocultural pride and identity.
- Involving parents in their children's education.

You can reduce the gap between school culture and the home environment by informing parents of the goals you expect to achieve and learning outcomes students are working toward in their classrooms. Engage parents as partners directly involved in their children's learning, providing encouraging connections for school-initiated learning. Suggest ways, too, that parents can support their children's learning of content and skills. A

IDEAS IN ACTION!

An Urban Odyssey

It was called an Urban Odyssey, a trip through four of New York City's boroughs for twenty teachers from all over the country and from every kind of school. The purpose of this expedition was to make them better teachers by motivating them to examine their beliefs and biases. Sleeping on the floor in community centers, they were immersed in the life of the neighborhood, often for fifteen hours a day, participating in activities as diverse as climbing a rope course, learning salsa dancing, visiting a Sikh temple, and handing out sandwiches to homeless people in a park. One participant commented "I was surprised to find out how much I had to learn, not only from the students I met, but also from working together with the other teachers to answer the challenges of the trip."

Present this challenge to your students: If you could invite twenty teachers from around the country to visit this community, what would you like to show them? What would surprise them about your area? What might be unfamiliar to someone from another part of the country? What knowledge and attitudes would you like them to take away from this visit?

short list of reasonable activities can be sent home, including taking children to the local library or just talking with their children and listening to their conversation with respect. Such practices support the child's development of self-esteem and a positive attitude toward learning.

A Student-Centered Approach

Effective multicultural education must be student centered if it is to be equitable. In learning to teach for diversity, we need to perceive students as individuals, being careful to avoid generalizations that lead to stereotyped thinking. Student-centered instruction recognizes student learning as the ultimate aim of education. We want students to be self-motivated learners, to inquire and to discover, and also to question established practices or assumptions. At the same time, students need to be aware of the responsibilities that are directly related to choice and decision making.

As we plan a multicultural program, we might begin by considering the rights of the students we teach. The *Bill of Rights for Children: An Education Charter for the Decade of the Child* was drafted by Thomas Sobol, Commissioner of Education in New York State. Note that these rights tie in closely with the aims of multicultural education.

All children have the right to:

- A healthy, secure, nurturing infancy and early childhood.
- A free, sound, basic education.
- An education appropriate for his or her needs.
- An education which respects each student's culture, race, socioeconomic background, and home language.
- Schools and educational programs which are effective.
- Educational programs that prepare them for jobs, for college, for family life, and for citizenship in a democracy.
- The resources needed to secure their educational rights.
- Education in school buildings which are clean, safe, and in good repair.
- Pursuance of their education without fear.
- An education which involves responsibilities as well as rights.[4]

Sonia Nieto, noted researcher and educator, adds a Puerto Rican perspective to the subject of multiculturalism. She sees "affirming diversity as a key to children's learning." In her book *Affirming Diversity: The Sociopolitical Context of Multicultural Education,* she stresses the need for acknowledging differences while also recognizing the strengths of each individual child. For example, rather than operating with the deficit model that labels a child as "non-English proficient," we need to retrain ourselves to think more positively: "Here is a child who knows how to speak Japanese" or "This boy has lived in Mexico and can read Spanish." As Nieto notes, there should never be a reason for students to feel bad about who they are.[5]

So, we encourage students to tell their stories. We let them share what they have to contribute whether it is through storytelling, writing poetry, or painting a picture. Each child should know that he or she is a valued member of the group.

All of us are members of many groups, yet each one of us remains a unique individual. Beginning with the accident of birth, we are shaped by the knowledge, experience, values, and attitudes that we encounter in the people with whom we live; we are socialized into a particular community, time, and place. However, out of all the diverse factors that influence our attitudes and values, each of us internalizes a unique self-identity from which we operate.

We teachers therefore need to remind ourselves constantly that the students who face us in a classroom are unique individuals. In our efforts to understand and to teach children from the many groups that make up our multiculture, we often seek to make generalizations about learners who are members of a specific culture. Understanding that respect for the family is a characteristic of the Latino culture justifies neither the assumption that all Latinos possess this characteristic nor the corollary that persons from other cultures do not. Likewise, in learning about Black English, we need to be aware that not all African Americans speak Black English; furthermore, many who can speak Black English readily may be bidialectal, easily switching from this highly informal form to standard English depending on the situation. Now we recognize the range of "families" that children experience, from those affected by divorce and remarriage to those formed by same-sex parents, adoption, and multiple generations. Teachers must plan carefully to accommodate individual characteristics, permitting children to remain different. We must consciously work to avoid stereotyped thinking about members of any one particular ethnic group; for example, the expectation that all Asian American children are mathematical whizzes. Such stereotyped expectations may exert undue pressure on children and be damaging to a young learner's self-esteem and true abilities.

Self Confidence Is Contagious

As teachers we model behaviors that we want students to emulate. We can make some of these behaviors explicit through discussion and activities designed to help students acquire new skills, different ways of thinking, and behaviors that facilitate getting along with others. If students have positive feelings of self-esteem, they will be self-confident. Talk with students about what self-confidence is and how it is demonstrated. Self-confidence shows in the way we walk and the way we talk. Have students show how a person might walk, if he or she were not self-confident compared to one who is self-confident. A person who has self-confidence will be able to handle a job interview successfully. He or she will be able to carry on a conversation with one or more other people. Have several students sit around a table at the front of the classroom in order to carry on a conversation for three to four minutes. Role-playing a given situation—for example, three neighbors having coffee together or three people sitting on a park bench—may help them be less self-conscious. Be aware that cultural differences may make such interactions more difficult for some children.

Students can learn self-confident behavior. Share this tip with your students: When you meet someone for the first time, look at the color of the person's eyes. That way you will really look at the person, and you will also make a good impression. Such behavior forces you to hold your head up with confidence and keeps you from looking at the floor instead of the person to whom you are talking. Here again some children have been trained not to look directly, particularly at an older person.

Note that different cultures may indicate respect for elders, for example, by *not* looking directly at another person. Such differences between "school culture" and "home culture" can be dealt with explicitly, in the same way you talk with students about when it is appropriate to use an "inside" voice and an "outside" one. As you discuss these differences, be careful to point out to students that it is OK to switch between the two codes of behavior.

Encourage students to discuss any related topics that come up. Younger students might talk about being kind to others, for example, making a newcomer welcome. Older students may be interested in how to dress when you go perhaps to the local grocery store to apply for a job.

Humanistic educators wrote of self-image and self-concept in the 1960s, and affective education became a goal for many teachers. Concern for the student as the center of the curriculum was expressed by such theoreticians as James Moffett in the first edition of *The Student-Centered Curriculum.*[6] Currently there is renewed interest in the student's role in the learning process. We talk of student self-esteem as the foundation for learning; we recognize that all students need a sense of worth—an "I can" attitude—if they are to strive to achieve. We are concerned about the classroom climate as we try to build an attitude of trust between student and teacher. We try to let students know that making mistakes is an essential part of real learning, so that they will dare to take risks as they brainstorm and solve problems together. We need citizens who have genuine self-esteem, for they are the people who can reach out confidently to others with empathy and caring.

Plan Multicultural Evaluation Strategies

We need to make certain that teachers and administrators are well-informed and that their knowledge is accurate and up-to-date. Teachers also need to know how to use the best of teaching strategies—questioning, cooperative learning, engaging students in active hands-on learning activities. They need to select methods and materials that will involve students in thinking about real issues that affect their daily lives. Study after study reveals that the teacher is the key to the success or failure of any program, so what you do in your own classroom every day is of primary importance. From the moment students enter the classroom they begin learning. The climate of the room, the way you treat students, the language you speak all serve as models for student behavior. Fair evaluation, recognition of individual needs, a clear sense of liking projected to students as you work with them will demonstrate what you want to teach.

Teachers who respect students select teaching methods that treat students equitably. For example, good teachers do not need to use sarcasm as a way of putting students down nor do they overuse "teasing," which is often misunderstood by young people. Respect for students is shown in the acceptance of their needs as growing young people. Evaluation of student performance is a particularly sensitive aspect of teaching. As we consider "putting grades on report cards," we should be aware that students see us as "putting grades on them," which can be very threatening, indeed. As we plan for evaluation, keep the following alternative factors in mind:

1. *Grading.* Don't put grades on everything a student does. Have many short writing and speaking activities that are not graded, but shared with other students or perhaps placed in a class collection that students can read at their leisure.

2. *Writing in all subject areas.* Never grade the first draft of a student's writing. Periodically have students revise a selection that will be published in some way (on the bulletin board, in a class book, in the school newspaper). Tell the students that you will put a grade on this work after they have revised it to their satisfaction.

3. *Establishing criteria.* Always make your criteria clear for grades you give. What does a student have to do to receive an *A, B,* or *C*? Talk with students about the characteristics of outstanding work, average work, and poor work as you make a specific assignment, and show them examples.

4. *Self-evaluation.* As much as possible, have students check their own work. Provide answer sheets so they can discover mistakes immediately. Stress reading items over again as needed, and correcting errors. If you eliminate yourself from this kind of "grading," you cease to be the ogre who has all the "right" answers.

5. *Individual conferences.* Have a short conference, a conversation, with each student once a week, if possible. Five minutes of individual attention does a lot for children who need support. This is a good time for examining children's writing or talking about the library book they are currently reading. Focus on supporting the student's efforts, not "correcting errors" at this time.

6. *Send a commendation to parents.* Several times during the year, send a letter to each parent commending at least one thing his or her child has accomplished. Children will be glad to take a Good Work Letter home. Make an effort to write this letter in the language of the home, even if you have to prepare translations into several different languages.

7. *Accentuate the positive!* Focus on what students accomplish, not what they fail to achieve or the mistakes they make. Compare the difference in impact on student self-esteem in the following two sentences:
   • Wow, you spelled thirteen words out of fifteen correctly!
   • Too bad, you missed two words out of fifteen today.

The Important Early Years

We have long known that attitudes and values are firmly rooted in what is learned during a child's early years. What is not learned at this time, furthermore, constitutes a great loss that may never be overcome. Although we now recognize and can work to correct it, children who do not have good learning opportunities during these early years may enter kindergarten and first grade several steps behind.

Early childhood intervention instruction for children may alleviate many of these gaps. Such projects as Head Start and other organized preschool programs strive to build a strong experiential and knowledge base before children enter the formal school system, so that children are better prepared for success in formal schooling from the outset.

As we are making special efforts to prepare children to enter school, we are also rethinking the concept of "readiness." Rather than making the student "ready" for literacy instruction, for example, we are now considering how the school can better meet the needs of each individual child. This means investigating a child's early literacy behaviors, such as picking up a book, holding it right side up and turning the pages from right to left. Such "emergent literacy" skills are often found before a child is actually taught to read. As a result, we focus on building early reading instruction on what the child already knows about literacy.

The ungraded primary is not a new idea, but it is being used in many contemporary schools that recognize the importance of individualizing instruction. In an ungraded structure, the emphasis is on achieving specific outcomes rather than moving through the grades. We know that some children require more time (and some less) to achieve the basic foundation for learning on which upper-grade teachers can build. Giving children more time without branding them "failures" by "holding them back" increases children's success rate and their sense of self-esteem. Thus, they have a much better chance of success throughout their elementary school years.

Vivian Paley, an experienced kindergarten teacher in New Orleans, New York City, and Chicago's Laboratory School, focused on the ethics of play with young children. To avoid exclusionary attitudes and behaviors, she established this rule: "You can't say you can't play." Children quickly learned to accept the rule as fair, although many discussions ensued related to its implications. Paley notes that in her early years of teaching she tried to ignore children's unfairness, hoping it would work itself out. It was only when she was almost 60 years old that she undertook to assume a more active leadership role as a teacher. She has written a number of books about her experiences, including *You Can't Say You Can't Play* (Harvard University Press, 1992). As she states optimistically, "If every kindergarten in the country were to promote this idea and it would continue year by year by year, in twenty years, when everybody got out of college, we would have a nicer world."[7]

What happens in school and in the home has a significant effect on the development of this natural potentiality to learn. School experience, peer attitudes, and teacher expectations directly influence children's performance. A six-year study of 1000 children from low-income and middle-class homes by Virginia Shipman and others investigated "how home and school work together to influence the child's development." Findings revealed that:

1. "Disadvantaged" and middle-class children enter school with the same average level of self-esteem and as broad a range of abilities.
2. After three years of schooling, children from low-income homes experience a significant drop in level of self-esteem compared to children from middle-class homes.
3. Although there is a loss of self-confidence, children from low-income homes still feel positive at this stage rather than negative about their ability to take care of themselves.
4. Children who come from low-income homes experience the same range of positive and negative influences on learning as do middle-class children.[8]

These findings should help teachers rid themselves of the misconception that low socioeconomic status automatically means little family value for learning. They also point up the need for viewing each child as an individual. The implications of this study support caring, accepting classroom processes. Shipman notes, "It gets down to what happens in the classroom between the teacher and the child—how much encouragement that child is given, how much stimulation and warmth."

Children who experience failure and frustration in their schooling may perceive themselves as having limited ability or little chance of success and may not even try a task before saying "I can't." Our task is not easy even if we begin working with a young child at the age of 4 or 5; it becomes increasingly difficult as the child grows older. The earlier we begin planning for multicultural teaching, the better chance we have of counteracting negative influences.

DEVELOPING MULTICULTURAL LESSON PLANS

In planning any lesson it is important to think through the entire process. First of all, what are your objectives for teaching the lesson? What do you want students to be able to do? Remember that objectives can, and should, be both affective and cognitive.

Next, you begin thinking about how you can reach these outcomes. What procedures will you use? What materials—videos, books, pictures, software, objects—will help you stimulate student learning? Then determine what students will do in response to the stimulus. Plan an active, hands-on experience—something all students *can* do (realistic expectations). Next comes the follow-up. What do students do after participating in the learning activity? How do they share the results? Finally, how will you know they have met the objectives you specified? Evaluation techniques may range from acting out to telling to writing, some performance by the student.

By following the model of the Thinking + Lesson Plan Form in Figure 3.1, you will plan a theoretically sound learning experience for children.

Here is a lesson developed to show you how the lesson plan works.

A SAMPLE LESSON FOLLOWING THE MODEL

Thinking + Lesson 1: A Biographical Sketch

Level of Difficulty: Grades 6–8

Expected Outcomes
Learner will:

1. Read a short biographical sketch of a minority author.
2. Analyze the quality of the writing.
3. Identify the features of a biographical sketch.
4. Compose a biographical sketch following the model.
5. Expand knowledge about diverse authors and their writings.

Teaching/Learning Strategies
Resources Needed
This lesson should be developed over a period of several days. Duplicate copies of the following biographical sketch of Alex Haley:

Introducing Alex Haley   Alex Palmer Haley is the well-known author of *Roots: The Saga of an American Family,* which was published in 1976 and made into a stirring film that was presented on television to millions of Americans. Born August 11, 1921, in Ithaca, New York, Alex Haley was the son of a professor.

(continued)

Thinking + Lesson Plan Form

Title of Lesson: _____

Expected Outcomes. The learner will:

1. _____

2. _____

3. _____

Teaching/Learning Strategy

Resources Needed

Directions

Step 1:

Step 2:

Step 3:

Performance Assessment

1.

2.

FIGURE 3.1   THINKING + LESSON PLAN FORM

Alex Haley served as a journalist in the U.S. Coast Guard. He tells of writing love letters for his fellow seamen who weren't particularly good at writing. He won their admiration and gratitude (and earned considerable money, too) by creating romantic letters that ensured that the men's sweethearts were waiting when they returned to port.

Haley soon decided that he wanted to concentrate on writing full-time. After struggling for a number of years to earn a living as a writer, he finally succeeded by collaborating with Malcolm X, writing *The Autobiography of Malcolm X*, which appeared in 1965.

But it was *Roots* that brought Haley real acclaim. Recognizing this unique contribution to American literature, the noted author James Baldwin writes:

> *Roots* is a study of continuities, of consequence, of how a people perpetuate themselves, how each generation helps to doom, or helps to liberate, the coming one—the action of love, or the absence of love, in time. It suggests, with great power, how each of us, however unconsciously, can't but be the vehicle of history which has produced us. Well, we can perish in this vehicle, children, or we can move on up the road.

After twelve years of painstaking genealogical research, Haley collected the life story of seven generations of his family in the United States and several more generations in a village on the Gambia River in West Africa. He presents these facts in a fictionalized story, a form he calls "faction," a delicate combination of fact and fiction that allows him to flesh out these ancestral characters, to include their thoughts and emotions. The resulting novel has touched the lives of millions of readers in a way that a scholarly report would never have achieved. As Haley knows, "When you start talking about family, about lineage and ancestry, you are talking about every person on earth." Alex Haley died in 1992.

Directions

Step 1: Have students read the sketch of Haley's life. Tell the students this form of writing is called a biographical sketch. Ask students to note and then discuss particular words they find interesting. Identify collectively and list on the board the features of a well-written biographical sketch, for example:

Tells where and when the person was born.
Makes clear why the person is known.
Uses a quotation about the person's work.

Tell students that they are going to write a biographical sketch about any minority (broadly interpreted) writer whose work they have read or want to read. (You may brainstorm a list of recommended authors on the board, such as Laurence Yep, Virginia Hamilton, Isaac B. Singer, Richard Wright, or Richard Rodriguez.) They may begin with an encyclopedia entry, but they are to use other resources, too. You may wish to specify that they locate at least two sources other than the encyclopedia.

(continued)

Step 2:   Take students to the library where they can locate the encyclopedias, check out books by the author selected, use the computer, and locate other sources of information. Point out *Current Biography* and *Contemporary Authors*. Students should take notes from resources they cannot check out. For homework, they are to begin the first draft of the biographical sketch to present in class on the following day.

Performance Assessment

Assessment 1.   On the next day review the features of a biographical sketch and make any additions recommended. Then have students work in pairs as they read the first drafts of the sketches and check their writing together against the list of features. The partners should work cooperatively to suggest revisions that will strengthen each paper.

Assessment 2.   The aim is to communicate to an audience with clear expository prose that is interesting to read. Students can evaluate the finished products as Grabs Me! (5 points), So-So (3 points), and Not So Hot (1 point). Students should be permitted to improve their writing in order to gain more points. Cooperative learning techniques used in groups can assist each student in achieving the top score. Note that this teaching strategy aims to develop self-esteem by facilitating success. All students are learning to collaborate to reach a goal.

The polished biographical sketches are published in a class book entitled "Authors We Have Known." Students may refer to this book when they are selecting books to read. The collection can be further developed by including book reviews (see Chapter 3). Note that students are learning about the contributions of members of diverse cultures to what we call "American literature." They learn about these authors as people, and they are introduced to literature they may be motivated to read based on a classmate's recommendation.

Developing Multicultural Learning Centers

Let students help to develop a center that seems to be called for as a result of ongoing study in the classroom. Have students suggest a name for the center that they can print on a large sign above the space allocated for this learning center. You may have several centers operating at any one time.

Use your ingenuity to create a suitable place in which to focus activities. A reading table can be used to collect materials together. You may have students construct a kind of cubicle with the bottom and sides of a large carton, placed on a table, forming the back of the center. Varied shapes and sizes of tables are appropriate. Feature information pertinent to the study. A corner of the room is easily transformed into a center focusing on Alaska as shown in Figure 3.2. In this case you might include a map of Alaska.

Invite students to participate in locating pertinent information and materials that might be useful—clothing, postcards, magazine articles. Brainstorm possible activities, people to contact, and places to visit as you develop the study together. Provide paper, pen-

A Cozy Corner

FIGURE 3.2   MULTICULTURAL LEARNING CENTER

cils, and other materials that may be needed as students engage in work at the center. Depending on the type of study being developed, you might consider the following materials and equipment:

- Tape recorders
- Pens and pencils
- Staplers
- Scissors
- Rulers

- Various papers: lined and unlined, drawing paper, colored construction paper, cardboard, posterboard, and corrugated cardboard for construction
- Computers

In addition to pictures and information displayed to make the center attractive and inviting, there should be a variety of individualized activities. Planned activities should range from easy to more difficult as well as involve using varied skills—listening, speaking, reading, and writing. Include, too, activities that draw from different subject areas and those that stimulate student creativity in music and art.

Using the Learning Center

As you and your students create one or more learning centers, you need to talk about using them. Discuss how many students can work at each center at any one time. The number of seats provided is a good way to indicate how many can work at a center. As a seat is vacated, someone else may come to the center. Students may need to sign up for a particular center.

A good way to begin work at learning centers is to post a schedule giving each student a specific assignment for the day. You can prepare the schedule for a week, two weeks, or a month, depending on how long the study will take and how many centers are available. Working in the library could be one center activity that would accommodate a number of students. Your schedule for ten days might look like that shown in Table 3.1.

Enlarging specific centers to provide more activities and seating space will permit additional students to participate. Sometimes, activities can be completed at the student's desk.

Keeping track of materials at each center is another important part of planning. Here are several tips that may help you.

1. Package all the parts of a game in one large envelope. Label the envelope in big print (see Figure 3.3).
2. Color-code everything that belongs at one center. If the center on France is blue, then mark games, task cards, modules, and so on, with a blue felt pen. Students soon learn to replace task cards or games at the appropriate center.
3. Hang activities in envelopes or plastic bags on the wall where they are visible. Pegboard is ideal for this purpose, but you can improvise with cork bulletin boards or strips of wood on which hooks can be placed. If you have a specially marked hook for each item, you can quickly tell when something is missing at the end of the day.

Whenever there are problems regarding classroom operations, have a class meeting to thrash out the problems and possible solutions. If students decide on the solution, their decision is more likely to carry weight; and they will enforce it, not you!

As teacher, your role in working with learning centers is to help students organize their work toward a goal and specific objectives. You facilitate and guide the learning experiences and serve as a resource, a person to be consulted when help is needed. You guide the students in assessing their own growth and learning as well as in checking their own work. Avoid playing the undesirable role of corrector or grader. Instead, use your talents and expertise to respond to student needs, to plan strategies for stimulating further learning, and to explore new resources and materials that come your way.

TABLE 3.1   LEARNING CENTER SCHEDULE

Name	M	T	W	TH	F	M	T	W	TH	F
Felipe	1	1	2	2	L	3	3	4	4	L
James	1	1	2	2	L	3	3	4	4	L
Kentu	1	1	2	2	L	3	3	4	4	L
Sandra	2	2	L	3	3	4	4	L	1	1
Hope	2	2	L	3	3	4	4	L	1	1
Harold	2	2	L	3	3	4	4	L	1	1
Marisa	3	3	4	4	L	1	1	2	2	L

Making Task Cards

The task card is one of the most useful and versatile forms of presenting learning activities. Developing sets of cards is well worth the time invested, for the cards can be used repeat-

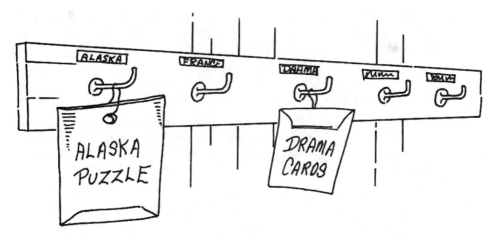

FIGURE 3.3   LEARNING CENTER MATERIALS

edly and in various ways. Task cards are sometimes called job cards or activity cards. They come in various sizes, from small (about 3" × 5") to large (about 8½" × 11"). The size you choose depends on the age of the students who will use the cards (young children can handle large cards more easily) and on your instructional purpose.

Small Cards.   Small cards work well for "idea files" to which older students refer individually, for example:

- *Acting Out.*   On each card a problem situation is described that calls for role-playing. Activities could be for small groups.
- *Books to Read.*   Each card lists the title and author of a book as well as a short synopsis of the story. Students use this file as they are searching for a book to read about Egypt, living in New York City, or any other topic you want to include.

Have students themselves develop these sets of cards. Each person can prepare a card, for example, about the book he or she has read. This activity serves a dual purpose—the students have a purpose for reading, and they create a set of cards about books other students will find interesting. Preparing "acting out" situations gives students a purpose for writing a short paragraph.

Large Cards.   Large cards are usually constructed of sturdy poster board, so they are stiff and durable. These cards are used to present an activity that one or more students will undertake at different times. Directions must be clear if students are to work independently.

A task card for upper-grade students that focuses on the money used in various countries is presented in Chapter 6. When material is prepared for you like this, simply enlarge the material presented. You can also use larger type sizes on the computer to facilitate reading. If directions are short, printing with a felt pen is effective. Throughout this book you will find informative material and activities that can be presented in similar fashion on task cards.

Make these cards more durable by covering them with clear contact paper or by laminating them. This kind of coating makes it possible to have students write on a card with a grease pencil. The writing can later be wiped off.

Sample Learning Center

Traveling to France. Focus a learning center on France (see Figure 3.4). In the 2000 census, 8.3 million Americans claimed French descent.[9] Americans of French origin were the ninth largest group in the United States. You might develop task cards that involve students in the following activities (see Figure 3.5):

- Draw a map of France. Identify its capital, cities, and waterways.
- Reproduce France's flag on paper or cloth.
- Write letters or visit the Web to obtain information about such places of interest as Brittany, the D Day landing beaches, the horses of the Camargue.
- Make a poster featuring facts about France.
- Read a book set in some part of France.

Provide a variety of books for students to investigate.

> Kate Banks. *The Cat Who Walked across France.* Illustrated by Georg Hallensleben. Farrar, 2004. The cat's travels take him past most famous sights.
>
> Julie Andrews Edwards. *Little Bo in France: The Further Adventures of Bonnie Boadicea.* Illustrated by Henry Cole. Hyperion, 2002. Billy and his cat Little Bo look for work in Paris.

FIGURE 3.4   LEARNING CENTER ON FRANCE

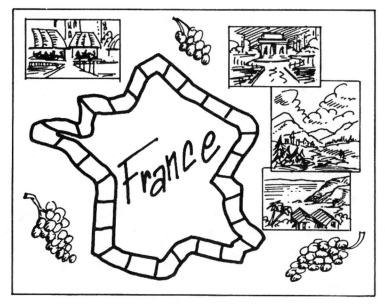

FIGURE 3.5   SAMPLE TASK CARD

Catherine Stock. *A Spree in Paree.* Holiday, 2004. A group of animals join a farmer for a wild trip to the big city, Paris.

Monica Wellington. *Crepes by Suzette.* Dutton, 2004. Suzette sells crepes from her cart on the streets of Paris. Her customers resemble famous works of art.

A study of French-speaking Americans or those who have French backgrounds could also include a Louisiana learning center. Include such books as the following:

Sharon Arms Doucet. *Alligator Sue.* Illustrated by Anne Wilsdorf. Farrar, 2003. A girl from the swamp is raised by the gator family that adopts her.

Candace Fleming. *Gator Gumbo.* Illustrated by Sally Anne Lambert. Farrar, 2003. The Little Red Hen story, told Cajun-style with informal language and occasional French words.

Gini Holland. *Louis Armstrong.* World Almanac, 2004. Biography of Louisiana-born musician from the Trailblazers of the Modern World Series.

Elaine Pascoe, ed. *In Wild Louisiana.* Blackbirch, 2003. Join naturalist Jeff Corwin and explore the swamps and bayou country.

Another center might focus on French in our language—the many English words borrowed from French (ballet, adroit), place names that are French, or French expressions that we use (R.S.V.P.). In this truly interdisciplinary approach to teaching, students study concepts from social studies, mathematics, and literature and develop such skills as reading, writing, painting, and singing. Of course, the ideas presented for this center can be adapted for a study of another country or ethnic group.

Learning centers offer a versatile method for engaging students in varied activities focusing on studies that cross the curriculum. Students enjoy the change from the more common textbook approach to instruction, including the opportunity to move around the classroom. Because students proceed at their own speed, individual differences are more readily accommodated. Gifted students should have challenges that extend the study in new directions. These students might design a new learning center that others in the class could use.

MULTICULTURAL TEACHING STRATEGIES

Sometimes we think of reading aloud as strictly for little children. However, nothing is more effective in establishing a pleasant classroom climate than sharing literature together. Reading aloud is an outstanding method to use with students of all ages and abilities. It helps create a nice rapport between the teacher and class members. It also cements a sense of community as children laugh together or even share a moment of grief. And it gives you yet another opportunity to bring in literature about different people and their experiences. In addition, of course, students are learning through listening.

Picture Books as Launching Pads

Illustrated books have much to offer teachers as launching pads for learning at all levels. They present fine examples of folklore from countries around the world, and they offer a way of sharing our heritage of Mother Goose rhymes and nursery tales that many students may not know.

During a study of African Americans and their contributions to the development of the United States, you might make a point of bringing in picture books written and/or illustrated by African American authors and illustrators. One outstanding author is Andrea Davis Pinkney, who wrote a wonderful collection of stories about the accomplishments of ten Black American women. *Let It Shine: Stories of Black Women Freedom Fighters* (Harcourt, 2000) is illustrated handsomely with full-page paintings by Stephen Alcorn. In the foreword to this book, Pinkney states:

> I hope their lives reflect something in each of us—the courage to fight for what we believe is right, the willingness to stand up under fire and disadvantage, the serenity to carry on when self-doubt, weariness, and the ignorance of others stand in the way of progress, and the fortitude to keep one's eyes on those prizes that will lead to a better world.

Other African American authors and illustrators to look for include:

Authors	Artists
Jacqueline Woodson	Bryan Collier
Elizabeth F. Howard	Brian Pinkney
Angela Johnson	E. B. Lewis
Virginia Hamilton	Jerry Pinkney
James Haskin	Christopher Myers

Learn about the illustrators Leo and Diane Dillon in "Talking with Leo and Diane Dillon," Anne Davies, *Booklinks,* January 2005. An excellent resource for discovering more names to add to this list is available on the Internet under the Coretta Scott King Award. This award is given annually to an outstanding children's book authored by an African American, as well as to an outstanding African American artist who has illustrated a picture book. Honor Books are also listed for each award. Books are listed back into the 1970s. See the updated list at *<www.ala.org/srrt/csking/cskawin.html>*.

Learning through Listening

Reading aloud to students is an outstanding method of assuring that even less able readers have an opportunity to know good literature. Begin by presenting the book, short story, article, or poetry as writing done by another human being with whom students can enter into a transaction. The aim of the transaction is to construct meaning collaboratively. All we have are the words before us that an author wrote and our own ideas, so encourage students to ask questions about what the author might be saying and also about their responses to these ideas. (Avoid being the teacher who has all the "right" answers that you expect students to know.)

Use reading aloud as a method of engaging students at all levels and in all subject areas with the ideas presented in books. As you read a novel by Gary Soto, a picture book by Paul Goble, or the poetry of June Jordan, students are learning:

1. *What book language sounds like.* Remember that written language is different from the spoken language familiar to your students. More formal, usually representing the standard English dialect, book language is what they will gradually learn to write. Before they can be expected to produce this written form, they need to hear it, to begin acquiring the structures and conventions of English in much the same manner that they earlier acquired the ability to speak their home language.
2. *Forms that writing can take.* As students listen to language or read it, they also gain knowledge of the forms (genres) through which they can express their ideas. Through listening to novels or short stories, for example, students are developing a "sense of story." They are learning how an author engages characters in dialogue and how character traits are revealed through behavior. They are introduced to such concepts as theme, setting, and plot development. Sharing other forms—haiku, song lyrics, an editorial, a letter of complaint—helps students learn how to write those forms.
3. *Grammatical structures.* As students listen to good writing, they hear a variety of sentence structures. They hear sentences composed of varied combinations of clauses, phrases, and strings of words, adding to and reinforcing their knowledge of English grammar. Listen to the opening sentences that William Saroyan wrote for *The Human Comedy:*

The little boy named Ulysses Macauley one day stood over the new gopher hole in the backyard of his house on Santa Clara Avenue in Ithaca, California. The gopher of this hole pushed up fresh moist dirt and peeked out at the boy, who was certainly a stranger but perhaps not an enemy. Before this miracle had been fully enjoyed by the boy, one of the birds of Ithaca flew into the old walnut tree in the backyard and after settling itself on a branch broke into rapture, moving the boy's fascination from the earth to the tree.

4. *Feelings, ideas, content.* A good book presents interesting content, vicarious experiences, and ideas that students can talk and write about. The characters share emotions with which they can identify. Students gain insight into the lives of others and begin to understand the concepts of diversity and universality applied to the people with whom they inhabit the earth.

5. *The sound of fluent reading—intonation.* As you read, students hear what fluent reading sounds like. They hear the accents and pauses, the intonation that a good reader uses automatically. They can talk about the meaning that intonation adds to language.

6. *The joy of reading; what books have to offer.* Less able readers may be hearing a book that they could not read independently whereas able readers are often motivated to read for themselves a book that you have shared. All enjoy the experience of sharing an exciting story or laughing together. They are learning to enjoy reading and talking about good books together. The students are developing positive attitudes toward reading through your enthusiastic sharing.

Working with Cooperative Learning Groups

The interaction that students experience while working together in groups has much to offer in developing empathy. Students talk to people that they might ordinarily have little to do with. They get to know each other as they share stories or work together toward a common goal.

Teach students how to work more successfully in their cooperative learning groups. Talk with the class about what makes a good group leader, for example:

- Give everyone a chance to talk.
- Listen to each person who is talking.
- Give other people a chance to lead the discussion.

Also discuss the qualities of a good contributing member of the group. Each student needs to recognize the responsibility of each person for how well the group functions. Civility will play a role here, too.

Literature-Based Instruction

A developing trend is the use of literature or trade books to support instruction in all subject areas. The use of library books instead of the usual textbook humanizes the curriculum and lends a vitality to learning that has not heretofore been present. Studies point out that the usual history textbook, for example, presents a sterile summary of events compared to a well-written trade book.[10] Furthermore, literature (including nonfiction, narrative prose, and poetry) sets historical events in a rich context that may more effectively engage student interest in learning. Students who read Scott O'Dell's novel *Sarah Bishop,* for example, will have an affective knowledge of the War for Independence that is not produced by the prose of most history textbooks for young adults.

Use of literature presumes that we will dismiss the necessity to "cover a textbook" in favor of guiding students to choose selections that provide different perspectives of the same period of history or the geography of a country. This method also presupposes a different way of teaching—employing discovery methods that lead students to question and to think as they analyze, evaluate, and reflect. This approach presupposes, too, a confident teacher who can facilitate student learning and who does not need to lean on textbooks that provide questions at the end of each chapter and an answer key to ease the task of grading. We need a way of teaching that leads students to construct their own meaning based on knowledge gathered from varied sources. Literature study offers such a way, a way that also engages students in a humanistic experience that may lead to the empathy we are attempting to achieve through multicultural education.

Whole-language instruction, one theory of teaching in the elementary school, uses literature for instruction and the development of literacy skills. A whole-language program encourages students to use both oral and written language, real language for real purposes. This approach includes listening to many stories read aloud and also reading many books. As they write and read, children also learn to connect sounds (phonemes) and symbols (graphemes), popularly termed "phonics," as they work with words in context. They respond to the stories they hear through active discussions, acting out, retelling; through literature they learn varied content about many interesting topics. They also begin to author books themselves, putting their books on the shelf beside those of other writers. Above all, they should learn to enjoy reading and writing.

Writing "Thinking"

Focus on the writing process, as advocated by National Writing Project consultant-teachers across the country for the past decade, is closely tied to the development of thinking skills. Thinking leads to writing as one way of expressing ideas, and the process of writing these ideas extends thinking. Thus, the writing of "thinking" is a generative process that engages students in dealing with real issues and concerns. Students who have self-esteem express their ideas confidently, and their successful writing supports the growth of self-esteem, another interlocking learning process that should be in any classroom.

Other Supportive Strategies

Multicultural teaching calls for supporting students as they engage in a learning activity. Support can take many forms, for example, methods that break a task into manageable parts. Following are recommended strategies that support successful student learning: brainstorming and SUCCESS FOR ALL.

Brainstorming Ideas about a Problem or Topic

Brainstorming is a good way of engaging all students in developing solutions to a problem. Make it clear that everyone's contribution is equally acceptable.

1. Ideas are suggested and listed without evaluation, critical analysis, or even comment.
2. Usually even wild ideas can be expected in the spontaneity that evolves when you suspend judgment. Practical considerations are not important at this point. The brainstorming process should stimulate creativity.
3. At this stage, the quantity of ideas counts, not quality. All ideas should be expressed, not screened out by any individual. The greater quantity of ideas will increase the likelihood of generating outstanding ones.

4. Encourage piggybacking, building on the ideas of other group members, whenever appropriate, thus pooling creativity. Students should be free to adapt ideas or to make interesting combinations of various suggestions.
5. Focus on a single problem or issue. Break a complex problem into parts or stages.
6. Establish a congenial, relaxed, cooperative climate.
7. Make sure that all members, no matter how shy and reluctant to contribute, get their ideas heard.
8. Record *all* ideas.

Write ideas on a chalkboard or large sheets of paper. After numerous ideas are generated, follow these procedures:

1. Review the list of ideas, selecting the top five or ten (any appropriate number) to discuss further in terms of practicality. Have small groups discuss each one in detail. Have each group present the pros and cons of that idea for consideration.
2. Then vote on the top two or three ideas to try. Place them in order of priority according to your purpose or need.
3. Begin implementing the ideas in order.

Multicultural topics lend themselves to such brainstorming techniques. Invite students to suggest alternative solutions or ideas about such questions as:

1. How might we help a student who is having trouble getting along with other students in school?
2. Why should we be concerned about what is happening in Israel or Somalia?
3. How have African Americans contributed to the development of the United States?
4. What would be appropriate behavior if someone called you an insulting name?
5. What might you do if you witnessed such behavior?

Brainstorming techniques can be used with groups or can be done individually before beginning to write or planning a presentation.

SUCCESS FOR ALL—A Structural Support Program for Literacy Learning

Led by Robert Slavin, the research team at the Center for Research on Elementary and Middle Schools (CREMS) attempts to provide support for children during the crucial preschool and primary grade years when the "die for failure is cast" for many children. Support is provided for children at risk through the use of certified teachers who serve as reading tutors. A tutor spends twenty minutes a day working one-on-one with a child during nonreading class time. Assessment of performance is ongoing so that support is given only when need for help is indicated.

"Working one-on-one is a uniquely different situation from group teaching," reports Slavin. "There are no problems with student motivation; no management problems—you put your arm around a child and teach that child what he or she needs to know."[11] As Frank Smith phrases it, "You respond to what the child is trying to do."[12]

In SUCCESS FOR ALL the focus is on story. In larger groups children may listen to the teacher read an interesting book, for example, the fine translation of *The Crane*

Wife by Katherine Paterson or John Steptoe's beautifully illustrated African tale *Mufaro's Beautiful Daughters.* The children talk about the story, retelling especially interesting parts. Discussion includes questions and speculation about possible answers, thus stimulating thinking abilities. On subsequent days acting out activities are included with children playing roles and providing dialogue that fits the performance. The teacher may have cards on which paragraphs from the story are printed so that children can rearrange the cards to sequence events appropriately. As they handle the cards, children are rethinking and rereading the story. Thus, the story is told and retold in many ways without exhausting the children's interest. Throughout these activities, teachers are expanding children's language so that all children are immersed in new words used in context. Gradually, children move into structured literacy activities with greater emphasis on reading literature and responding in writing. In individual tutorials a child may read this same text so that he or she receives help, as needed, and is assisted in participating in followup activities.

ENGAGE STUDENTS WITH COMPUTER-BASED LEARNING

As we move into the twenty-first century, much of our lives revolves around computers. Computer skills are essential in almost any line of work. We use the computer to locate a book in the library, our groceries are checked out by computerized pricing, and we use computers to write a report. Education, too, is fast moving toward greater use of the computer as whole schools are wired, equipment is acquired, and teachers learn how best to utilize computers in their classrooms and in laboratories.

Computers have much to offer to multicultural teaching. In this section we first address general techniques for using the computer with special multicultural applications, and then we list a number of Internet connections that fit with a multicultural program.

Word Processing

The most common use of computers is for all forms of writing. Encourage students to use computers to produce writing—for example, poetry, book reviews, reports. The computer facilitates revision thus encouraging students to write more, and the printer permits students to create an attractive copy of what they have written.

CD-ROM Programs

Computers enable students to use a wide range of interesting multimedia programs presented on CD-ROMs that support integrated reading, social studies, and science lessons. Virtual field trips provide sound, pictures, and text, integrating reading with geography and history knowledge and engaging students in challenging activities that stimulate thinking. One of the first to be published was *The Oregon Trail* (MECC), which takes students along the route of Lewis and Clark, led by Sacajawea, including encounters with Native American tribes. They have to solve problems and make decisions as they meet the challenges of the trail.

Tips for Using Computers Effectively

Following are a few suggestions that you may find helpful:

1. If you have only one computer in your classroom, maximize its use by providing a signup sheet where students can "make appointments" for 15- to 30-minute blocks of time. Encourage collaborative groups of 2 to 3 to gather around the computer to suggest ideas as members of the group take turns looking for or recording information for a study they are undertaking.
2. Teach a specific skill that students may find helpful each time students begin individual work in the computer lab. You might, for example, show them how to center a title or introduce them to spell-check. Don't be afraid to ask for help in teaching these skills from another teacher or even your students.
3. Give each student (or have them purchase) an initialized disk on which they can work using whatever program you have available. After students print their names on the disks, they can be filed alphabetically in a box in the classroom ready for use when needed.

Using the Internet

Now available in many schools and libraries, access to the Internet (the World Wide Web, or Web for short) has opened up many possibilities to add content and interest to multicultural studies. Students can obtain up-to-date information about people and events, participate directly in the exchange of ideas and expression of their opinions with others around the world, and plan research to follow up on individual interests. Here are a few Internet sites that support the aims of multicultural education: namely, (1) developing empathy for others and (2) exploring the world.

Developing Empathy for Others

1. Abraham Lincoln Research Site: Discovering the Man, the President. <*www.members.aol.com/RVSNorton/Lincoln2.html*>. A retired U.S. history teacher hosts this collection of material about Lincoln and his life. Includes information about Mary Todd Lincoln and links to other sites with information about Lincoln. He will also answer questions by email.
2. Edison National Historic Site. <*www.nps.gov/edis/home.htm*>. Site run by the National Park Service has a special section for students called "Edifun." The site also offers virtual tours of Edison's home and Edison's laboratory.
3. Faith Ringgold Teacher Resource File. <*www.falcon.jmu.edu/~ramseyil/ringgold.htm*>. This site, sponsored by the Internet School Library Media Center, offers links to interviews and biographical information about this inspirational artist and author as well as a variety of lessons tied to her children's books.
4. The World of Ben Franklin. <*www.fi.edu/franklin/*>. The Franklin Institute Online offers teachers science lessons and links to other inventors such as the Wright brothers.

Exploring the World

1. Global Schoolhouse Project. *<www.globalschoolnet.org/index.html>*. This group has supported international online education since 1984. Check its list to find out more about its projects around the world, such as Friendship through Education, the American Forum for Global Education, and International Youth Exchange Programs.
2. Time for Kids. *<www.timeforkids.com>*. Organized to supplement *Time for Kids,* a special edition of *Time Magazine,* this site offers news and current events for the United States and the world.
3. Congress for Kids. *<www.congressforkids.net>*. Designed for grades 4–12, this site uses the character of "Uncle Sam" and interactive methods to help students learn the basics of the U.S. government. See also *<www.whitehousekids.gov>*.
4. The New West. *<www.pbs.org/weta/the_west/index_cont.htm>*. This site expands on the material available through the PBS program *The New West.* For example, there are special sections on topics such as the transcontinental railroad and Mark Twain. Lesson plans, provided for grades 6–12, can be modified for younger students. Look for other PBS sites that accompany their television productions.

Web Smarts for Teachers and Students

1. A URL is a web address. If you type a URL into your browser, it will take you directly to that site. Pay attention to the ends of site URLs, the part that follows the period (.), called a dot. Some common ones are *.edu,* which means the site is sponsored by an educational institution such as a university; *.org,* which identifies the site as belonging to an nonprofit organization; *.gov,* for sites hosted by the government; and *.com,* for commercial sites.
2. A browser or search engine such as Internet Explorer, Safari, Yahoo, or Google gives you the power to look for sites by subject. Unless you use the special features under "Advanced Search," you are likely to end up with more possible sites than you can handle. The more you can limit your search, the more you will come up with useful suggestions.
3. Even if you have found the URL on a list of approved sites, be careful and check each site before letting the students loose on it. An acceptable site may still have links that transfer the users to unsavory sites without their being aware of it.
4. Teach the students to question the reliability of all material that they see posted on the Web. Government (.gov) or educational (.edu) sites are usually dependable, but students can learn to confirm all information by checking several other sites.
5. Explain to students the importance of not giving out personal information on the Web. If a site asks for their name or other information in order to access a special section, they should exit that area because such a request is inappropriate, and they need to let you know about it.
6. At the end of a website you should be able to find a date indicating when the site was last updated. This can be crucial information as not all sites are updated regularly and their information may not be reliable.

CONNECTIONS

Individualized instruction challenges students of all ages to progress as quickly as possible at their own individual ability levels. Your guidance will assure each student that he or she is on the right track as that student moves ahead. Learning centers, broad thematic units of study, and focused multicultural learning modules offer variety to the usual classroom learning activities based on a single textbook.

Bringing in resources suitable for students with different abilities will make certain that all children can participate in any study. Support groups will assist students who need special help with some of the activities. Gifted students, on the other hand, can be guided to extend their research beyond the minimal expectation. These flexible individualized approaches to teaching are especially appropriate for integrating multicultural concepts across the curriculum. As we plan a multicultural program, it is essential to use practices that stand out as exemplary. Across the country, teachers and school districts are making sincere efforts to reach multicultural goals from different perspectives. Grounded in the principle of achieving self-esteem for all students and leading to understanding of others, these programs may address the needs of preschool children or adolescent at-risk students; they may be directed toward preparing the teacher; or they may deal directly with selection of content or methods of delivering the curriculum.

FOLLOW-THROUGH

Expanding Your RTP

1. Write a short paragraph about just what "individualization of instruction" means to you at this stage of your training. What is the teacher's role in presenting individualized instruction? Then, begin a list of ways that you could provide support for slower students who might need an extra boost. Make another list of strategies for engaging gifted and talented students in more challenging investigations or projects that will extend their thinking. You can continue adding to these lists as you learn more and also by discussing this topic with your classmates.
2. In your RTP, respond to the following questions:
   a. What is the difference between equality and equity?
   b. How might you introduce the subject of racism to children of different age levels?
   c. What can you do to create a climate of acceptance that supports each student's self-esteem?

Working with Your CLG

1. Develop a learning center about one of the lesser known cultural groups in the United States. Begin by discovering as many books and other forms of literature as you can. You might, for example, initiate your exploration of Appalachia and the people who have lived in that region by searching for picture books by Cynthia Rylant, who comes from West Virginia. Look for:

When I Was Young in the Mountains. Harcourt, 1983.

Appalachia: The Voices of Sleeping Birds. Harcourt, 1991.

Best Wishes. Owen, 1992.

Silver Packages. An Appalachian Christmas. Orchard, 1997.

   2. Each CLG can select a book appropriate for middle school students. Discuss the multicultural concepts presented and how you might develop a class study based on reading this book aloud together. You might consider such titles as:

Michael Dorris. *Guests.* Hyperion, 1994. Moss, a Native American boy, resents his father's inviting the "strange white men" to join their harvest feast.

Sharon Arms Doucet. *Fiddle Fever.* Houghton, 2000. A 14-year-old boy in Louisiana wants to learn to play the fiddle like his 'Nonc Adolphe. Set in a small town in 1914.

Brent Hartinger. *Geography Club.* Harper, 2003. A boy keeps his being gay a secret until he finds others like him. They create the "Geography Club" as a cover for their meetings.

Claudia Mills. *Dinah for President.* New York: Macmillan, 1992. A middle school girl runs for president of the sixth grade; humorous.

Mitali Perkins. *Monsoon Summer.* Delacorte, 2004. A girl reluctantly travels with her family to India to work in the orphanage where her mother lived as a child.

   Keep a journal as you read the book selected, recording questions, teachable moments, and so on. Compare your notes with those of others in your CLG.

   3. Work with a group of fellow students to plan lessons for the primary grades. Locate appropriate books to use as stimuli for exciting learning activities. You might begin with these that focus on intergenerational understanding:

Tomie de Paola. *Nana Upstairs & Nana Downstairs.* Putnam, 1998. Rev. ed. A child learns about death.

Mem Fox. *Wilfrid Gordon McDonald Partridge.* Kane/Miller, 1985. A boy looks for his friend's missing memory.

Cynthia Rylant. *The Old Woman Who Named Things.* Harcourt, 1996. This Appalachian woman names only things she will outlive until she falls in love with a shy little dog, whom she names Lucky.

GROWING A PROFESSIONAL LIBRARY

Abby Goodenough. *Ms. Moffett's First Year: Becoming a Teacher in America.* Public Affairs, 2004.

Kathryn M. Pierce, ed. *Adventuring with Books: A Booklist for Pre-K–Grade 6.* National Council of Teachers of English, 2000.

Iris Tiedt. *Teaching with Picture Books in the Middle School.* International Reading Association, 2000.

Joyce Carol Thomas, ed. *Linda Brown, You Are Not Alone: The Brown v. Board of Education Decision.* Jump at the Sun, 2003. Well-known children's authors reflect on their life before and after the *Brown* decision.

ENDNOTES

1. Kenneth Zeichner, *Educating Teachers for Cultural Diversity.* Michigan State University, National Center for Research on Teacher Learning, 1993.
2. Graham Nuthall, "Raising Classroom Teaching to Student Learning: A Critical Analysis of Why Research Has Failed to Bridge the Theory-Practice Gap," *Harvard Educational Review* 74 (3) (Fall, 2004): 273–274.
3. Kenneth Zeichner, op.cit.
4. Thomas Sobol, *The Bill of Rights for Children: An Education Charter for the Decade of the Child.* New York State Department of Education, n.d.
5. Mary M. Kitagawa, "The Light in Her Eyes: An Interview with Sonia Nieto." *Language Arts* 76 (2) (November 2000): 158–164.
6. James Moffett and Betty Jean Wagner, *The Student-Centered Language Arts and Reading Curriculm.* Houghton, 1996.
7. Mary Beth Marklein, "Learning to Play by the Rules: Teacher Adds Ethics of Play to Preschool Curriculum." *National Retired Teachers Association Bulletin* (September 1993): 24.
8. Virginia Shipman et al., *Young Children and Their First School Experiences.* Educational Testing Service, 1976.
9. U.S. Bureau of the Census Public Information Office. *USA Statistics in Brief,* 2004. Accessed from www.census.gov
10. Paul Gagnon, "Why Study History?" *Atlantic Monthly* (November 1988).
11. Robert Slavin, Wisconsin Center for Education Research. *WCER Highlights* 3 (1) (Fall 1990): 1–2.
12. Frank Smith, *Understanding Reading.* Holt, 1973.

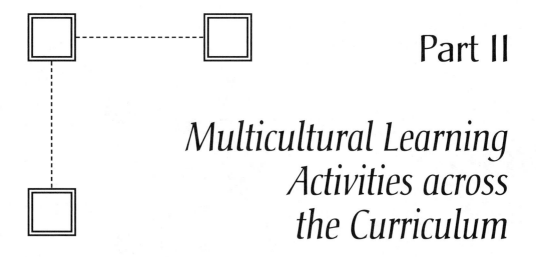

Part II

Multicultural Learning Activities across the Curriculum

As spelled out in the first three chapters, we recognize that multicultural education permeates the entire curriculum presented in K–8 classrooms. It is essential, however, that all teachers teach multiculturally, consciously and with careful forethought. In Chapters 4, 5, 6, 7, and 8, we focus on teaching strategies and learning activities that are specific to different areas of the curriculum, yet with the clear objective of helping students make multicultural connections across the curriculum.

As we teach, we will constantly remember that we are teaching the diverse children who will be the adults of tomorrow, on whom we all must depend. We must continue to be proactive in dealing with multicultural education as urged by Senator Hillary Clinton in addressing the National Education Association, February 2004:

> The challenges of change are always hard. It is important that we begin to unpack those challenges that confront our nation and realize that we each have a role that requires us to change and become more responsible for shaping our future.

FRIENDSHIP FOREVER

Teaching Language Arts and Reading Multiculturally

As we consider how the language arts and reading curricula can be presented with greater sensitivity for the needs of all students, we are impressed at how important the language skills are to all of learning. The language arts curriculum not only covers the skillful use of listening, speaking, thinking, reading, and writing as we express ideas but it also includes the studies of language and literature. Being literate in any language is truly foundational to all of learning.

In this chapter, we first discuss learning activities that focus directly on the development of language and literacy skills. We present instructional strategies that are highly recommended for language arts and reading, and we then examine sample lessons planned according to research-based methods of instruction. In the second part of the chapter, we consider ways of infusing language arts and reading instruction into teaching and learning throughout the curriculum. Several thematic studies that integrate language and literacy with content from other curricular studies are also described. Our aim here is to assist teachers in making effective multicultural teaching a reality at any grade level.

FOCUSING ON LANGUAGE ARTS AND READING INSTRUCTION DIRECTLY

In this section we describe briefly a number of techniques that teachers have found successful in engaging K–8 students in developing oral and written language skills and thinking, as well as reading and writing. Notice that these suggestions are flexible and can be adapted for different ability levels.

Effective Language Arts and Reading Instructional Strategies

Learning experiences that are truly effective engage all students in an activity they can accomplish at their different levels of ability. Following are a few examples of student-centered strategies that are also multicultural in nature.

Conducting Meaningful Discussions

We often allude to discussion as part of classroom instruction. However, studies show that what is called discussion is often teacher dominated; that is, the teacher asks questions to which students respond one by one. The percentage of student involvement revealing real thinking remains very low.[1]

Focusing on multicultural understanding offers an opportunity to deal with meaty concerns, matters of consequence. Introducing controversial topics that are presented in fiction is a safe way to open up what we identify as "philosophical discussions," the kind of talk in which informed adults frequently engage. Depending on the content of a particular book, a worthwhile discussion might involve students in talking about "experiences all children have had, such as being embarrassed by not knowing an answer. By discussing what happens to the characters in a novel, they can talk about things in the third person: Somebody else is the one involved."[2] An excellent selection to share in grades 4 to 6 is *The New One* by Jacqueline Turner, a novel about Jury, an African American boy, and his friends, that introduces issues of racism and prejudice.

Reading Aloud

Reading books aloud to a class has many benefits. This strategy is discussed in detail in Chapter 3. Select multicultural titles by talented authors, for example, Virginia Hamilton, a prolific African American writer. Her book *Cousins* is a complex realistic novel that provides many interesting multicultural topics to discuss and to write about, such as the elderly, relations with family, and personal responsibility. Other books that present multicultural themes include:

Primary:

Ashley Bryan. *Beautiful Blackbird.* Atheneum, 2004.

Janet S. Wong. *Buzz.* Illustrated by Margaret Chodos-Irvine. Harcourt, 2000.

Elementary:

Christopher Paul Curtis. *Bud, Not Buddy.* Random, 2002.

Patricia C. and Frederick L. McKissack. *Days of Jubilee: The End of Slavery in the United States.* Scholastic, 2004.

Middle School:

Sharon M. Draper. *The Battle of Jericho.* Atheneum, 2004.

Sharon G. Flake. *Money Hungry.* Hyperion, 2003.

International Pen Pals

Your students might like to write a letter to the editor of a major newspaper in a city such as Buenos Aires, Prague, London, and so on. Research on the Internet will produce addresses for newspapers around the world. Here is a real letter that appeared in the San Jose (California) *Mercury News*.

> Dear Editor:
>
> We are children who live in Israel and we like to collect stamps and trade stamps with people around the world. We really like stamps with animal pictures. When we get stamps from different places, we learn about your country, and we learn about you.
>
> We are a girl and a boy, ages 13 and 10. If you print this letter, maybe people will send us stamps and we will send them our stamps. Our address is 9 Lotham Street, Efrat, Israel.
>
> Thank you,
>
> Rivka Bedein
> Elchanan Bedein

Your class might begin by writing letters to the editor of some of the newspapers your research has produced. The Internet is also a great source of pen pal contacts with whom you can often correspond via email.

IDEAS IN ACTION!

Choosing Your Favorite Poem

The thirty-ninth U.S. Poet Laureate, Robert Pinsky, developed a wonderful nationwide poetry project. He invited people across the country to choose their favorite poem and to read it aloud to a group. A number of these presentations were presented on Public Television, several as features on "The News Report." It was amazing to hear ordinary people—a housewife, a carpenter, a fireman—reading a poem that has meant a lot to them.

Robert Pinksky and his staff also developed directions for carrying out a "Favorite Poem Reading" in any community. These directions are available at: <*www.favoritepoem.org*>.

Plan with a group of teachers and other community members to have a Favorite Poem Night at your school. Invite people to sign up to read their poems and perhaps to tell the audience why they consider these poems special. Repeat the program if it proves especially popular.

You can also hold a Favorite Poem Assembly in your school, inviting students to share their favorites. You may have to repeat this program, too, more than once in order to accommodate all of the interested persons.

Role-Playing

Role-playing is a versatile oral activity that allows students to express their opinions in a realistic situation. They can literally stand in someone else's shoes as they speak in the role they have assumed. Ideas for role-playing come from all areas of the curriculum, for instance:

- A group of parents discussing a city problem.
- Children greeting a new student from Vietnam.
- A Japanese American family talking after they arrive at an internment camp.
- The Abenaki tribe holding a feast in 1700.

Role-playing may be performed by a group of three to five students as the others observe and take notes. After the performance, class discussion focuses on the strengths and weaknesses of the performance, for example, the language used and the appropriateness of the topics discussed. After this analysis, another group can perform with the same roles and situation.

At other times, the whole class can role-play a situation, such as plantation life in 1800. Before beginning this activity, of course, students need to study to determine what the various roles would be. Group activities in specific areas of the room might focus on the slave quarters, the barn where horses are shod, or a group of runaways in the woods. Simple costuming lends interest to this dramatic play.

Role-playing can lead to formal debate as students discuss the pros and cons of an issue. After arguing informally in role-play, students may be stimulated to search out more information to be presented in a panel discussion or debate. These oral activities lend interest to learning, and they provide a firm foundation for writing to express opinions. They also teach advanced thinking skills. Role-playing is discussed further in Chapter 3.

Libraries

President of the International Reading Association in 2003, Jerry Johns, presented a powerful message on the importance of libraries in promoting students' reading abilities. He notes that "Reading for pleasure begins with access to books and time to read them." To support access to books the International Reading Association advocates the importance of having classroom libraries with at least seven books per student and staffed school libraries with at least twenty books per student in the school. Although most educators support the presence of school libraries in all schools, with funding problems such libraries, particularly in elementary schools, are often eliminated. For this reason Johns recommends working closely with our partners, the public libraries.[3] Students can also conduct a campaign to collect books in their neighborhood, making posters, door-to-door canvassing, and writing letters to the newspaper.

What can you do to help strengthen funding for libraries? Johns suggests the following tactics:

1. Request appropriate numbers of books for classrooms, school libraries, and public libraries.
2. Inform parents and policy makers of the importance of access to books.
3. Remind state and local policy makers of the need to allot funding for books.

Sample Multicultural Language Arts and Reading Lesson Plans

In addition to the above strategies, here are two lesson plans developed in more detail to demonstrate just how a multicultural language arts and reading lesson is presented. Notice that the first lesson can be designed appropriately for any grade level by adjusting the material used to fit the ability levels of the students involved. The second lesson is suitable for use with middle school (or high school) students. Notice that these plans follow the Thinking + design presented in Chapter 3.

A THINKING + LESSON PLAN

The Universal Need for Friendship

Grades 5–7

Expected Outcomes
Learners will:

1. Discuss the need for friends.
2. Identify problems that occur between friends.
3. Suggest solutions to problems that arise.

Teaching/Learning Strategies

Resources Needed
After listening to the teacher's reading of *Always and Forever Friends* by C. S. Adler (Houghton Mifflin, 1988), students discuss Wendy's search for a friend. Through discussion they identify the need for friendship as a universal need that they share with all other human beings. In small groups they discuss problems that can arise between friends and possible solutions.

Directions
Obtain a copy of *Always and Forever Friends* about a friendship between a white girl and a black girl.* Read the story aloud to the whole class, chapter by chapter, over a two-week period. Give students a chance to talk about the events depicted in each chapter following the reading. This lesson is designed to follow the completion of the whole book. It requires at least two class periods.

Step 1:
Present the following quotation from the book on a transparency:

*See also Joyce Hansen's *The Gift-Giver* (Clarion, 1997) about two fifth-graders in the Bronx. Another charming book is *Amelia and Eleanor Go for a Ride* by Pam Muñoz Ryan and illustrated by Brian Selznick (Scholastic, 1999). This true story is about friends Eleanor Roosevelt and Amelia Earhart. For grades 1–4 try: *All Kinds of Friends, Even Green*, written and photographed by Ellen Senisi (Woodbine, 2002), which tells of 7-year-old Moses, who has spina bifida.

(continued)

"The way I look at it," Honor continued earnestly, "you don't wind yourself around a friend like a strangler vine, and you don't expect friendship to be always and forever."

"But Honor, if it doesn't last, what good is it?"

"I didn't say it *wouldn't* last. All I'm saying is, we shouldn't expect it to because life's sure to change us, you and me. In high school, we'll be different people, and boys will come in the picture—for you anyway. I don't know if I'll have time for them if I'm going to be a lawyer. And if boys don't do us in, then after high school we'll go our separate ways, and that'll make it hard."

Ask students to state Wendy's view of friendship. Then ask someone to restate what Honor is saying.

Step 2:
Have students number off from 1 to 6 to form six cooperative learning groups. (Adjust these numbers to produce groups of four to six students.) Assign a Leader and a Recorder for each group, and give everyone copies of the following questions. Give the recorder an extra copy.

1. Could you live without having friends?
2. Can boys and girls be friends?
3. What are the problems that make finding friends difficult?
4. What problems might break up a friendship?
5. What can we do to make a friendship last?

Take a few minutes for each person to read the questions and to write at least one response to each question.

Then discuss each question in turn. Each person should read one answer to the first question. Talk about the answers that were shared and agree on a response for the whole group. After the Recorder has written the group answer on the Group Answer Sheet, go to question 2, and so on.

Step 3:
Working with the full class, have one person share the group response to each question in turn. After ideas have been shared, have each student write a paragraph about the importance of friendship in his or her life.

Performance Assessment
Have students meet in the same groups to share their paragraphs. After the group listens to a student's paragraph, group members in turn will identify one aspect of the writing they especially like. Then each student will make one suggestion for improving the writing of the paragraph.

Students will then rewrite their first drafts. The revised copies will be placed in a three-ringed notebook entitled *Friendship Forever*. You might use the art on p. 90 for the cover. After class members have had ample time to read it, place this class publication in the school library.

A THINKING + LESSON PLAN

Writing a Book Review

Grades 5–8

Expected Outcomes
Learners will:

1. Read a book review.
2. Identify characteristic features of this form.
3. Write a book review that includes these features.

Teaching/Learning Strategies

Resources Needed
Locate the review of a book that you would like students to know or perhaps an author you would like to introduce. Duplicate a class set of copies of the review. (You can write one yourself following the model presented here.) This lesson requires at least two class periods.

Directions
Step 1: *Read the Book Review:* Where the Red Fern Grows
Wilson Rawls was a country boy from the Ozarks. He spent much of his time roaming the hills with a blue tick hound, hunting and fishing, enjoying the out of doors.

It was natural, then, for him to write a book about a boy who wanted hunting hounds, a boy who also roamed the hills and river bottoms of the Cherokee country so familiar to Rawls. He describes the setting, thus:

> Our home was in a beautiful valley far back in the rugged Ozarks. The country was new and sparsely settled. The land we lived on was Cherokee land, allotted to my mother because of the Cherokee blood that flowed in her veins. It lay in a strip from the foothills of the mountains to the banks of the Illinois River in northwestern Oklahoma.

Where the Red Fern Grows is a story of love for family, for animals, and for this country. It is also a story of adventure as Billy achieves his greatest dreams.

Ten-year-old Billy wanted a pair of coon dogs, but hounds cost more money than the family could possibly afford. Determined, Billy began saving his money, storing it in an old K. C. Baking Powder can. After almost two years, he had fifty dollars, enough to buy the two redbone coon hound pups that would change his entire existence.

Billy, Dan, and Little Ann spent their lives together from the time he brought them home. As he said:

(continued)

It was wonderful indeed how I could have heart-to-heart talks with my dogs and they always seemed to understand. Each question I asked was answered in their own doggish way.

Although they couldn't talk in my terms, they had a language of their own that was easy to understand. Sometimes I would see the answer in their eyes, and again it would be in the friendly wagging of their tails. Other times I could hear the answer in a low whine or feel it in the soft caress of a warm flicking tongue. In some way, they would always answer. (p. 68)

The high point of the book is Billy's winning the gold championship cup in the annual coon-hunting contest. With the cup came a large cash prize that answered his mother's prayers for a new house.

Billy continued to hunt with his dogs until one night they met the "devil cat of the Ozarks, the mountain lion." His brave little dogs tried to save Billy from the lion whose "yellow slitted eyes burned with hate." Although Billy finally killed the huge animal with an ax, the dogs were badly wounded. Old Dan died from his injuries, and Little Ann soon died, too, of heartbreak at losing her hunting companion. Billy sadly buried the two dogs in a beautiful spot on the hillside.

As the family was leaving the Ozarks the following spring, Billy ran to this grave for one last farewell. It was then that he saw the beautiful red fern that had sprung up above the graves of the little dogs. He remembered the old Indian legend that "only an angel could plant the seeds of a red fern, and that they never died; where one grew, that spot was sacred." As they drove away, the family could see the red fern "in all its wild beauty, a waving red banner in a carpet of green."

Fast action, human interest, and believable characters make this a book for readers of all ages. A master storyteller, Wilson Rawls has shared a piece of himself.

Step 2: *Stimulus (Prewriting)*

Give students copies of the book review you have selected. Read the book review aloud slowly as students read their copies. (This is especially helpful for less able readers and ESL students, and it helps keep the class together for the purposes of the lesson.) Then have students return to the beginning of the review and direct them to identify the kinds of information the author included in the review.

Features of a Book Review
1. Includes quotations from the book.
2. Comments about the content presented by the author.
3. Tells something about the author, biography.
4. Expresses personal reaction to the book.
5. Includes the title and author of the book.

Direct the students to bring a book that they have already read to class the next day.

Step 3: *Activity (Writing)*
See that each student has a book to review. Display the Features of a Book Review list that the class compiled. Go through the features one by one with the class as students take notes based on the books they are reviewing. Tell students to complete the first draft of the new book review they have begun as homework.

Step 4: *Followup (Postwriting)*
On the next day students should have the first drafts of their book reviews and copies of the book to be reviewed. Have students work in cooperative learning groups of three to five students. Each student is to read his or her book review aloud as the others listen to see if all features on the list have been included. After listening to a review, each member of the group should answer the following two questions for that writer:

1. What one aspect of this review was especially well written?
2. What one recommendation would help improve the writing?

The next day revised versions of the book reviews can again be shared in the same editing groups. Each writer should point out exactly what changes were made from the first draft. Any further changes should be made, as needed.

Performance Assessment
Before completing the final draft of the book reviews, students should work as a class to determine just how these reviews will be evaluated, for example:

A Simple Rubric or Standard (some recognition for excellence)

10 Uses excellent detailed description.
     Shows clear personal involvement.
     Includes important biographical information.
     Speaks clearly to the audience.
     Includes all features listed, very well presented.

 5 Presents all features adequately.
     Needs further revision.

 2 Presents most features, very weak writing.
     Needs extensive revision.

Students who are involved in determining evaluation measures for their own work are assuming responsibility for their work, and they can help each other so that potentially everyone in each group can get the top score. Students learn much about writing by reading and evaluating each other's writing.

When book reviews are fully revised, they can be published instantly in a three-ringed notebook that bears the title Books We Recommend. Have someone decorate the cover. This collection, containing something by everyone in the class, should be available for reading in the classroom and, later, in the library.

INFUSING MULTICULTURAL LANGUAGE ARTS AND READING INSTRUCTION ACROSS THE CURRICULUM

As you make lesson plans for a month or more, consider just how you can teach the various language skills through learning activities that also connect with another curriculum area. Middle school and elementary school teachers might like to plan together.

Engaging Students in All Language Processes across the Curriculum

How can you teach students how to listen while learning history content? Or, how about developing critical thinking skills while learning something about biology? Keep the objectives for the multicultural curriculum listed in Chapter 2 in mind as you plan these activities. Following are suggestions that should trigger ideas:

Listening:
- Retell a folktale the teacher has read aloud, for example, "Clever Gretel."
- Act out an Indian trickster tale after hearing it at the Listening Center, for example, "Raven the Trickster."
- Summarize the life of a writer after listening to *The Lives of Writers* (Audio Bookshelf, 1995).

Speaking:
- Discuss the problems that Karana faced in *Island of the Blue Dolphins* by Scott O'Dell.
- Tell a "flannel board story" to younger children, for example, *John Henry.*

Reading:
- Read a poem by Langston Hughes aloud as part of a class presentation on poetry.
- Review a book about someone who lives in another country, for example, *Winding Valley Farm: Annie's Story* (Poland).

Writing:
- Keep a process journal while reading a book about the Japanese American internment, for example, *Journey to Topaz* by Yoshiko Uchida.
- Use mapping to outline the life of a famous woman leader, such as Indira Gandhi or Mother Teresa.
- Write "memory stories" after reading *I Was So Silly* by Marci Curtis.

Thinking:
- Compare your life with that of Lisa in *Lisa and Her Soundless World* by Edna Levine (deafness).
- Write questions to ask Katherine Paterson after reading *Come, Sing, Jimmy Jo* (Appalachia).

Developing Extensive Multicultural Thematic Studies

Focusing instruction on the study of a broad theme is especially recommended because it permits making connections among all the subject areas taught in a self-contained class-

---

IDEAS IN ACTION!

Storytelling

A STORY, A STORY! As you already know, storytelling is an enjoyable way of sharing ideas with others. We all engage in storytelling with our friends and family. Storytelling is especially effective in the classroom. Unlike the informal stories we related to our friends, however, telling a story to a class may take a little practice. Follow these steps to get started.

1. Choose a story to tell that you know very well, perhaps "The Three Billy Goats Gruff" or "Goldilocks and the Three Bears."
2. Reread the story you select. Make a simple outline of the events, something like this:
   - Introduction—setting, characters.
   - Little goat crosses bridge; Troll speaks.
   - Middle-sized goat crosses bridge; Troll speaks.
   - Big goat crosses bridge; Troll speaks.
   - Big goat attacks the Troll.
   - Ending.
3. Tell the story aloud in your bedroom standing before the mirror.
4. Then, tell the story to your class. If they know the story, they will join in as you say, "Trip-trap; trip-trap" or the Troll yells, "Who's that tramping across my bridge?"

Move into telling the children other folktales. A wonderful collection of stories is included in *A Pride of African Tales* by Donna L. Washington and illustrated beautifully by James Ransome, HarperCollins, 2004. The author provides tips for storytelling, and she has deliberately chosen varied folktale forms, for example, the pourquoi tale, trickster tales, a fable, and so on. As you gain skill as a storyteller, you will also want to help your students develop their storytelling abilities—a wonderful teaching/learning experience!

---

room. Each individual student can contribute to the findings amassed through a group effort, so there is opportunity for success for everyone. Thematic studies also work well in middle schools organized around core curriculums that encourage a humanities approach to learning.

Here we introduce three studies that focus on broad themes: (1) Community, (2) Naming, and (3) Women. The first study explores a basic multicultural component while the second suggests a study of diversity that is more personal. The third study is a multicultural focus on a group in our society, that is, women who are searching today for equity in the work world and in life in general; this study can be expanded to cover all gender issues. Included for each theme are activities and resources designed to help you begin developing a unit of study that might last from two weeks to two months.

Thematic Study 1: Community

Discuss the meaning of community with your students. This study offers an excellent opportunity to begin creating a classroom community that will enable students later to reach out into the larger community in which they live. This theme would be an excellent choice for the beginning of a school year as all students share a feeling of belonging to an inclusive classroom community.

In order to create a community in your classroom, it is important to make sure that all of the students feel included. The following activities will enable you to make sure that every student's voice is heard and that students are comfortable bringing their familiar cultures into the classroom.

Welcoming Students.   Challenge a group of older students to organize a "Welcome Club" that would assume responsibility for personally welcoming newcomers to the school. Students of all levels could be part of this team effort. Encourage students to brainstorm possibilities for making students feel at home in their new surroundings. They might ask themselves, "What would make me feel good about coming to a new school?" Here are some ideas.

- Introduce the student to several children who live near him or her.
- Meet the child at the principal's office to express a welcome and to introduce him or her to the classroom teacher.
- Give the newcomer a small gift, such as a welcome card made by students or a flower to pin on (if everyone knows this symbol, they can be encouraged to smile their own welcome or to say hello).
- Assign a buddy in the class to help the newcomer with classroom routines.
- Enlarge the poster in Figure 4.1 to display in your room.

Getting to Know Each Other.   An activity for the beginning of the year is to ask each student to write ten things about himself or herself. Students can list anything, for example:

Alice Hafoka
I get up at 5:30 each morning to deliver papers.
I make breakfast for my brothers and sisters.
I live next to Julio and Uriel.
My favorite food is groundnut stew.

Students can exchange their lists. Working in small groups, each person then introduces the student whose paper he or she received. The student introducing Alice might say:

I'd like you to meet Alice Hafoka. She gets up at 5:30 every morning and makes breakfast for her brothers and sisters. I'm impressed—my mother won't let me cook anything on the stove. Her favorite food is groundnut stew. That's an African dish. Groundnuts are also called peanuts. She lives next to Julio and Uriel.

A Class Directory.   Type a list of the students' names to give to the children in your room. You may include their addresses, birthdays, or other information that might interest the children as they become acquainted. They will be highly motivated to read this directory even though names of students and streets may be difficult.

Welcome

Bienvenidos

Hawn txais tos

Chào Qúy Vị

ԲԱՐԻ ԳԱԼՈՒՍՏ

歡迎

សូមស្វាគមន៍

Maligayang Pagdating

어서오십시요

ຍິນດີຕ້ອນຮັບ

Bem Vindos

ПРИВЕТСТВИЕ

FIGURE 4.1 WELCOME POSTER

Have students introduce themselves according to this listing. They may simply say, "I am Takasoto Watanabe. I live on Fairglen Avenue." Or they might add other information, such as what they like to do on Saturdays or where they were born. Ask the students what they would like to know about each other and what each is willing to share.

If you ask students to include information about their hobbies and what they like to do in their free time, they can identify other students who might share their interests. This is an easy way to break down barriers and help students become friends with people from different groups.

Provide a special container, such as a large box with a slit in the top, for students to use in writing letters or cards to each other. Once a week, one student can be the designated letter carrier and deliver the letters to students. You can have students make envelopes for their letters and design stamps, as well. Students also enjoy the simplicity of a postcard because the message can be short.

Cooperation.   Talk about ways we depend on other people. What would we do without people in the helping professions—firefighters, police, nurses, doctors? Bring an article from the newspaper about people helping one another to share with the class.

The importance of cooperation is well established in the folklore of many countries. Some students may have heard the story of the little red hen, who asks for help making bread. The other animals refuse. But they are eager to pitch in when it is time to eat the bread and then she refuses. Even students who are not familiar with the story will appreciate the moral. Share a version such as the following with students:

Mary Finch, reteller. *The Little Red Hen and the Ear of Wheat.* Barefoot Books, 1999.

Have students retell the story in their own words. Do they know other stories that make the same point? What is the message of this tale?

Older students will be interested in comparing two versions of a Russian folktale, about the value of teamwork—what one person cannot do alone may be accomplished by many people pulling together. Consider whether both stories illustrate the same moral.

Aleksei Tolstoy. *The Gigantic Turnip.* Illustrated by Niamh Sharkey. Barefoot Books, 1999. An old man is not able to pull a turnip out of his garden by himself.

Vladimir V. Vagin. *The Enormous Carrot.* Scholastic, 1998. Similar situation, with animals in modern dress.

Students also help each other. Discuss the importance of assisting other people in school or at home. Have students answer the following questions:

- How do you help your family?
- How do your family and neighbors help each other?
- How does a friend help you?
- How can students help each other at school?

Differences in answers may reveal some of the cultural diversity in what is considered *acceptable* helping behavior. Sometimes, "helping" someone can get you into trouble, like helping with the answers on a test. Students can discuss these differences and develop a list of acceptable helping behaviors for the classroom. Using the information on the list, prepare a chart for the classroom so that all students understand the rules and new students will be able to fit in easily.

Understanding Others.　Show middle school students a number of large pictures of people. Ask them to look at each picture in turn and to write several sentences about the person they are viewing, for example:

> This man is very happy.
> He is tall and handsome.
> He has a good job and earns a lot of money.

Compare what different students have written about several of the people. Discuss the fact that we often make assumptions about people that we see in the street or even about other students in the classroom. Someone could be feeling terrible, and we don't necessarily know. Pass out copies of the following poem, saying, "Here is a poem about a man who everyone thought was happy. Read it, and see what you think."

RICHARD CORY

> Whenever Richard Cory went downtown,
> We people on the pavement looked at him:
> He was a gentleman from sole to crown,
> Clean favored, and imperially slim.
>
> And he was always quietly arrayed,
> And he was always human when he talked;
> But still he fluttered pulses when he said,
> "Good morning," and he glittered when he walked.
>
> And he was rich—yes, richer than a king—
> And admirably schooled in every grace:
> In fine, we thought he was everything
> To make us wish that we were in his place.
>
> So on we worked, and waited for the light,
> And went without the meat, and cursed the bread;
> And Richard Cory, one calm summer night,
> Went home and put a bullet through his head.
> 　　　　　　　　—Edwin Arlington Robinson

Ask several students to locate the Simon and Garfunkel song that they wrote about this poem, "Richard Corey." They can compare the two versions of this brief story of a man's life. Have students write in their journals about what they have learned through this learning activity.

Who Needs Friends?　What is a friend? Do we need friends? Read a poem or two to students from the collection by Paul Janeczko, *Very Best (Almost) Friends: Poems of Friendship,* illustrated by Christine Davenier, to initiate a class discussion of friendship. The various poets included in this collection give us diverse perspectives on the joys and problems of being a friend. Provide opportunities for students to reflect on what friendship means to them by writing a story, creating a poem, describing a friend, or drawing a picture. Publish their efforts in a class book called *Friendship Is . . .* This book can be shared with other classes. Older students can read selections to students in the primary grades.

Other books that encourage discussion of the need for friends include:

Carolyn Crimi. *Don't Need Friends.* Illustrated by Lynn Munsinger. Doubleday, 1999. After his friend dies, a rat will have nothing to do with the other animals in the junkyard, until a new dog gets sick and needs his help.

Marilyn Helmer. *Mr. McGratt and the Ornery Cat.* Illustrated by Martine Gourbault. Kids Can Press, 1999. The old man and the stray cat both take a risk by caring for each other.

The Unlikeliest of Friends.   How does it come about that friends can make us feel better about ourselves, just by being there? Discuss what students look for in a friend. Do we expect our friends to be just like us? Can we be friends with someone who has very different beliefs or comes from a different background? Is it possible for boys and girls to be friends? In the following books, characters face similar questions.

Kimberly Willis Holt. *When Zachary Beaver Came to Town.* Holt, 1999. Two boys gradually befriend Zachary, the circus sideshow freak.

Susie Morgenstern. *Secret Letters from 0–10.* Puffin, 2000. Lonely boy finds his world turned upside down when he meets a girl from a family with thirteen brothers.

Friendship   Explore the ethical and moral dimensions of friendship through books that talk about how far we should go for the sake of our friends, or books honoring friendships that cross boundaries such as race, sex, or age. See the lesson plan titled "The Universal Need for Friendship" on page 95.

Lucille Clifton. *Everett Anderson's Friend.* Holt, 1976. Everett is disappointed in his new neighbor because she's a girl. But it turns out all right when he finds she can run and play ball.

Bruce Coville. *Jeremy Thatcher, Dragon Hatcher.* Harcourt Brace Jovanovich, 1991. At first, Jeremy is embarrassed that Mary Lou is the only one who understands him.

Kevin Henkes. *Words of Stone.* Greenwillow, 1992. Two motherless children, Blaze and Joselle, find comfort in each other.

Dirlie Herlihy. *Ludie's Song.* Puffin, 1990. In Georgia in the 1950s, Marty goes against community prejudice by making friends with a black family.

Jean Little. *Different Dragons.* Viking, 1986. This story by a Canadian writer features a boy who has a secret fear. When he makes friends with a neighborhood girl, he learns that everyone has different dragons to overcome.

Judith Nigna. *Black like Kyra, White like Me.* Whitman, 1996. Two little girls learn firsthand about prejudice.

Patricia Polacco. *Chicken Sunday.* Philomel, 1992. Two African American boys and a friend (the author as a girl) try to earn enough money to buy the boy's grandmother an Easter hat from a Jewish shopkeeper.

Marcia Savin. *The Moon Bridge.* Scholastic, 1992. The friendship of two fifth-grade girls survives the hatred and prejudice of World War II, even when Mitzi Fujimoto, a Japanese American, is sent to an internment camp.

Jerry Spinelli. *Maniac Magee.* Scholastic, 1990. An extraordinary boy brings racially divided communities together.

Additional Resources:

Jan Irving and Robin Currie. *From the Heart: Books and Activities about Friends.* Teacher Ideas Press, 1993. Includes literature-based programs and units, games, and speaking and writing activities for friendship-related themes in the primary grades. Books featured include *The Wednesday Surprise, Chester's Way, Frog and Toad Are Friends, Jessica, Won't Somebody Play with Me?* and *Henry and Mudge.*

Thematic Study 2: Naming

Naming practices around the world are interesting to all of us. How are names chosen? What do different names mean? This theme, too, provides an engaging topic that will involve all students as they begin a new school year. Students' names are key elements of their identity, especially their first names. Last names are also significant because they represent students' ties with their cultural heritage and family history. Provide opportunities for students to explore their names and how they feel about them as well as to investigate names in other cultures.

Choosing Names.   Ask children about their first names. How do they feel about their names? Are they named after someone, perhaps an aunt or grandfather? Perhaps they have a family name, like Jamison, or an invented name composed of both parents' names, such as Rayella. Have them write on one of these topics:

- My parents named me _____ because _____.
- I like my first name because _____.
- I wish I could change my first name because _____.
- If I could choose a name for myself, it would be _____ because _____.
- If I had a child, I would name the baby _____ because _____.

Read aloud *Chrysanthemum* by Kevin Henkes, the story of a young mouse who loves her unusual name until she starts school. Then the others make fun of her, saying her name is too long and not appropriate for a mouse. But one of her teachers helps her learn that her name is as special as she is.

Explore naming customs in different cultures. Catholic children choose a saint's name when they are confirmed. What does this mean? Jewish children are named after relatives but never living ones. Alex Haley begins his classic work *Roots* with a moving description of an African naming ceremony. Chinese children are given a "milk" name as babies to confuse evil spirits. Do students know of other naming customs?

What's Your Name? From Ariel to Zoe by Eve Sanders presents history and stories about names from many cultures. Many websites provide information about child names, such as *<www.parentsoup.com/babynames/finder>*.

My Name Design.   Help students see their names from a different perspective by having them make designs based on their first names (see Figure 4.2). Follow these instructions: Fold a piece of paper in half lengthwise. With the fold on the bottom, write the name, making sure that each letter touches the fold. Letters that extend below the line can be raised so they fit on the same level. Now hold the folded paper up to the light and trace the name in reverse on the other side. Open up the paper to find an abstract design. This can be colored in or decorated to make an imaginary figure. Display these on the bulletin board or use them to make covers for collections of student writing.

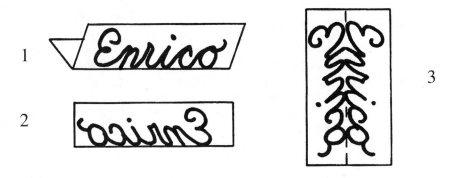

FIGURE 4.2   FIRST NAME DESIGNS

Name Acrostic.   Use your students' names often in puzzles or wordplay. A creative activity is to develop an acrostic based on a name. Students write their name vertically down the left side of a page. Then they fill in the acrostic with adjectives (or phrases) describing themselves, beginning with each letter of their name.

K ind
H elpful
A miable
L ight-hearted
I ntelligent
D aring

You can make the task easier by allowing students to start to the left of their letter. This increases the number of words they can use.

```
    b L ack
      A mbitious
    a M azing
   pr E tty
      L ively
friend L y
  hon E st
```

Students with short names can include their middle or last name to make the acrostic more interesting. Students with long names can choose a short version. You may want to award points for the number of letters to the right of the name, or for the most unusual words chosen.

Encourage students to check the dictionary to find creative word choices and to expand their vocabulary. They can explain their selections to the class.

Popular Names.   Some first names become fashionable and show up in packs in elementary classrooms for years before going out of fashion. Table 4.1 shows changes in the most popular names for babies.

For girls, the lists are completely different. For boys, Michael is still the most popular and Daniel has dropped below the top ten. Does your class roster look like this list? Or is it full of names like Marklon, Donte, Tanisha, T'Keyah, Hakeem? Or Lourdes, Felizardo, Cristeta, Amarnath, Ceizhar, and Keila? Discuss why this might be true. Do students want names like other people or ones no one else has?

Have students study the distribution of first names in the school or in one grade. Depending on their math skills, they can list the ten most common names and the ten least common, or they can calculate the percentage of frequency. Compare the list for your school to the national list of baby names given in Table 4.1.

TABLE 4.1   POPULAR FIRST NAMES

Girls		Boys	
1991	*2000*	*1991*	*2000*
Ashley	Hannah	Michael	Michael
Amanda	Emily	Christopher	Jacob
Jessica	Madison	Matthew	Matthew
Samantha	Elizabeth	Joseph	Joseph
Stephanie	Alexis	Daniel	Christopher

How to Translate Your Name.   Students will be interested, also, to discover that the same name is used in many languages. Table 4.2 illustrates the name John, which can be found in a variety of languages:

TABLE 4.2   TRANSLATIONS OF THE NAME JOHN

Yohanna (Arabic)	Jannis (Greek)	Johan (Norwegian)
Iban (Basque)	Yohanan (Hebrew)	Ivan (Russian)
John (English)	Sean (Irish)	Ian (Scots)
Jean (French)	Shane (Irish)	Juan (Spanish)
Hans (German)	Giovanni (Italian)	Evan (Welsh)
Johannes (German)	Jan (Northern European, Dutch)	

Many English names can be translated into Spanish and vice versa. See if the students can discover the equivalent in other languages of such names as Peter, James, David, William, Mary, Rose, and Helen. What names do not translate easily?

Family Names.   Whether Greek (Stephanopoulos), Belgian (Van Der Mensbrugghe), Georgian (Shalikashvili), Laotian (Khammoungkhoune), or Indian (Umamaheswaran), many U.S. family names are megasyllabic—and people are learning to spell and pronounce a greater diversity of names. Discuss family names (surnames). Why do we need them? Where do they come from? Have children state their surnames as you write them on the chalkboard. Observe the variety of names in the classroom. Some have only one syllable (Wong) and others contain several syllables (Asakura, Rodríguez, Anderson).

Use surnames in classroom learning experiences. Have students line up alphabetically for lunch. Younger students can line up according to the first letter only, while older students can check the second and third letters as needed for more precise order.

Discuss the characteristics of surnames. "Mc" and "Mac" names that originated in Ireland and Scotland, for example. Let students make generalizations about the names represented in their classroom:

- We have many Spanish names: Castañeda, Chávez, Feliciano, Vásquez.
- Chinese names are short: Wang, Lee, Ching.
- Many Vietnamese people have the same last name, but aren't related: Nguyen, Ng, Huynh.

Family Names in Different Cultures.   Different cultures have different rules for family names, or last names. In English-speaking countries, most children take the last name of the father. Some countries use both the mother's and father's names. In other countries, parents give different forms of the father's first and last names to male and female children.

In Spanish, for example, a person's surname consists of the father's family name followed by the mother's family name.

Teresa	Pérez	Gutiérrez	Carlos	Chávez	Martínez
	(father)	(mother)		(father)	(mother)

Sometimes the word *y* (and) is inserted between the surnames of the father and mother, for example: Juan López y Benavente. Juan would be called Señor López, however, and his name would be under L in the telephone directory. Likewise, Teresa and Carlos would be listed as follows:

> Pérez Gutiérrez, Teresa
> Chávez Martínez, Carlos

Russian names include a "patronymic" (this word means *father + name*) in the middle. In addition, the *-a* is added to the last name for women. For example:

> Tanya Ivanovna Kuznetsova (daughter of Ivan)
> Sasha Ivanovitch Kuznetsov (son of Ivan)

In traditional Vietnamese style, the last name is given first. When reading a Vietnamese name, to avoid confusion it is important to determine which order is being used.

Many children today have hyphenated names, to include the last names of both parents. School records can become confused, as when Rachel Vogel-Abrams is listed sometimes under V, sometimes under A.

Other students carry the last name of their father only and not the mother's, such as Matthew Peterson, son of Keith Peterson and Catherine McDonald. Children in "blended" families (formed by divorce and remarriage) may have surnames different from either parent, further complicating school records. As the teacher, you can't necessarily predict child–adult relationships by surnames.

Origins of Names.   Family names become more interesting to children when they discover the meanings that lie behind them. They can easily see that those names that have *-son* or *-sen* at the end carry the meaning "son of," for example, Andersen and Williamson. One of the most common names in English is Johnson, son of John. Endings that mean *son of* in other languages include *-ez* or *-es* (Spanish), *-tse* (Chinese), *-wicz* (Polish), and *-ov* (Russian and other Slavic languages).

Up through the early Middle Ages, only first names were used in England. After that time, family names began to be used to distinguish people from others with the same first name.

Many last names were associated with a person's line of work; for instance, Carpenter, Smith, and Cooper. Challenge students: What does a smith do? What does a cooper do? Characteristics of a person often led to other names, such as Young, White, and Little. Another source for last names was the place where someone lived: Hall, Street, Wood.

Surnames can also represent a painful history. Africans brought to the United States as slaves were taken away from their families and their names. Slaves had no last name of their own; instead, they were given their owner's family name. When we talk about surnames indicating pride in one's heritage, it is also important to recognize that African American surnames can preserve the memory of slavery. Leaders such as Malcolm Little chose to cast off these humiliating reminders and replace them with *X* for *unknown*.

For names of different origins, try a dictionary for each language. Set out on a discovery trip in which all can participate as they help each other find the origins of their family names.

Study of Names

Students might want to begin a more extensive study of names. This topic is called *onomastics.* Look for books such as the following that provide information about the meanings of common names and their origins:

Elza Dinwiddie-Boyd. *Proud Heritage: 11,001 Names for Your African-American Baby.* Avon Books, 1994.

Cleveland Kent Evans. *Unusual and Most Popular Baby Names.* Publications International, 1996.

Patrick Hanks and Flavia Hodges. *A Dictionary of First Names.* Oxford University Press, 1990.

Holly Ingraham. *People's Names: A Cross-Cultural Reference Guide to the Proper Use of over 40,000 Personal and Familial Names in over 100 Cultures.* McFarland & Co., 1997.

Justin Kaplan and Anne Bernays. *The Language of Names.* Simon and Schuster, 1997.

Women: Searching for Equity

What does it mean to think of women and men as part of the study of multiculturalism? In the classroom, verbal interaction between teachers and students and students and students may contribute to an atmosphere in which girls are less visible, less heard than boys. In the teaching materials used in the classroom, the language and the selection of content may portray a world in which women are insignificant or ignored. Both boys and girls suffer from the low expectations for female achievement and the sex-role-linked stereotypes that limit their full human potential.

A multicultural perspective reminds us that we must see all students, girls as well as boys, as problem solvers and risk takers, capable of active contributions to knowledge and able to overcome obstacles and to persevere. As you plan your teaching, consider how you can enable students to move beyond the recognition of prejudice and discrimination and toward a positive understanding of what changes need to take place.

Beginning a Unit on Sex Equity.   Begin a study of gender issues with an assessment of what students know. Ask students to make a list of ten famous men and ten famous women, not including people from television, movies, or popular music. After allowing time for students to complete the task, discuss what they have learned from the experience. Was it more difficult to think of famous women? Could everyone come up with ten names? Write on the board some of the women's names that students thought of. Are the same few women repeated many times? Ask students to come up with possible explanations for these results. What gaps in student knowledge of women's accomplishments show up in this exercise? Use this discussion to stimulate further study as students themselves identify areas they need to explore. Save these lists for comparison at the end of this unit.

Sex-Role Stereotypes.   Ask students to make individual lists of characteristics of men and women. After each has had time to write a number of items, ask each one to contribute something to add to a class compilation of these characteristics. The list may include items like this:

Men can	*Women can*
play sports	cook dinner
fix things around the house	go shopping
go to work	wear makeup
be firemen	be nurses

Discuss the items on each list. Do women play sports, too? Can men cook dinner, too? Have students respond from their experience.

To encourage them to expand their ideas of possible roles for men and women, turn their examples into sentences such as:

- Men can play sports, and women can too.
- Women can cook dinner, and men can too.

What's a "Woman's Job"?   Many students remain convinced that all doctors are men and nursing is a woman's job, even if their own experience provides examples to the contrary. These sex-role expectations are *stereotypes* because they artificially limit students' choice of occupation. Talk about job stereotyping with students and discuss what skills are necessary for success in different fields. Both girls and boys need to think about career choices in order to be able to support themselves. Help students overcome these stereotypes by featuring books about women in all kinds of jobs.

Nic Bishop. *Digging for Bird-Dinosaurs: An Expedition to Madagascar.* Houghton Mifflin, 2000. Photos of paleontologist Cathy Forster at work in the field.

Carole Ann Camp. *Sally Ride.* Enslow, 1997. *People to Know* series. Biography of first female astronaut from the United States.

Penny Colman. *Rosie the Riveter: Working Women on the Home Front in WWII.* Crown, 1997. Nonfiction account of women in nontraditional jobs, for middle school students.

Kathryn Lasky. *The Most Beautiful Roof in the World: Exploring the Rainforest Canopy.* Photos by Christopher G. Knight. Harcourt Brace, 1997. The story of field scientist Meg Lowman who works in Belize, Central America.

Virginia Meachum. *Jane Goodall.* Enslow, 1997. Biography of influential scientist famous for her ground-breaking work studying chimpanzees.

Elizabeth Partridge. *Restless Spirit: The Life and Work of Dorothea Lange.* Viking, 1998. Puts a face on this talented photographer who became known for her powerful images of people during the Depression.

Laurence Pringle. *Elephant Woman: Cynthia Moss Explores the World of Elephants.* Photos by Cynthia Moss. Atheneum, 1997. Book shows biologist's work with elephants.

Corinne Szabo. *Sky Pioneer.* National Geographic, 1997. A photobiography of Amelia Earhart, pioneer aviator, who was brought up to be "inventive, independent, and imaginative."

Comparing Accounts.   There are often several biographies available about a few famous women and yet no two books are alike. Encourage students to explore this opportunity to question the construction of history, the importance of primary sources, and the difference between fact and opinion by comparing several books about the same person. One person who continues to attract interest is Sojourner Truth, born a slave, who grew up to speak for blacks, women, and their rights. Offer students examples of differing accounts of Sojourner Truth such as the following:

Anne Rockwell. *Only Passing Through: The Story of Sojourner Truth.* Illustrated by R. Gregory Christie. Knopf, 2000.

Patricia and Frederick McKissack. *Sojourner Truth: Ain't I a Woman?* Scholastic, 1992.

Patricia and Frederick McKissack. *Sojourner Truth: A Voice for Freedom.* Enslow, 1992.

As students read these books to compare and contrast their coverage, have them consider the following questions:

- Do these books agree on the facts of the person's life?
- What does each book focus on as the motivation for achievement?
- If the books are written for different levels, how is the material adapted?
- Does the author include information on the sources of this material?

Younger students can compare two picture books about the same person, such as:

Laurence Anholt. *Stone Girl, Bone Girl.* Illustrated by Sheila Moxley. Orchard, 1999. Mary Anning accompanies her father to search for "curiosities" in the English cliffs.

Jeannine Atkins. *Mary Anning and the Sea Dragon.* Illustrated by Michael Dooling. Farrar, Straus & Giroux, 1999. Mary is fascinated by fossils at a young age and becomes a paleontologist.

Take Our Daughters to Work Day.   Since April 28, 1993, many companies have participated in a program (sponsored by the Ms. Foundation) to introduce girls aged 9 to 15 to opportunities for women in the workplace. In your classroom, support these efforts to build girls' self-esteem by planning to expose them to a greater variety of careers. Contact companies associated with your school and invite women who hold different positions to speak to the class. Survey parents and friends for suggestions of women who have interesting jobs. Feature photographs, news articles, and biographies of diverse women with a variety of careers.

Use students' stereotypes as starting points for discussion. They probably know that women can be secretaries, but do they know that women can be financial planners? Extend their awareness of the possibilities. Is baseball only for boys? Pose questions that connect careers with early education and training. What skills do you need to be a maintenance supervisor? Both boys and girls can benefit from increased awareness of career possibilities. Plan to use this day to discuss opportunities for men and women. Contact the Ms. Foundation on the Web to find out what others are planning in your area: <*www.ms. foundation.org*>.

A Female Perspective on History.   Too often, ordinary people, especially women and girls, have been left out of history. Instead of presenting the typical DWEM (Dead White European Males) history, look for resources that provide a look at daily life from the inside. The following books make excellent supplemental reading for a study of a particular period and stimulate student discussion of the differences from their own lives.

Eleanor Ramrath Garner. *Eleanor's Story: An American Girl in Hitler's Germany.* Peachtree, 1998. Due to unfortunate circumstances, Eleanor's family is trapped in Germany through the war. Describes the horrible conditions faced by everyone.

Judith Heide Gilliland. *Steamboat! The Story of Captain Blanche Leathers.* Illustrated by Holly Meade. DK Ink, 2000. Life on the Mississippi River as seen by a girl who grows up to be the first female steamboat captain.

Dorothy and Thomas Hoobler, eds. *Real American Girls Tell Their Own Stories.* Atheneum, 1999. Diary entries bring people in the past to life.

Andrea Warren. *Pioneer Girl: Growing up on the Prairie.* Morrow, 1998. A woman's memories, as told to her daughter, of the gritty details of early pioneer life in Nebraska.

Karen B. Winnick. *Sybil's Night Ride.* BoydsMills, 2000. Sybil risked her life on a dangerous ride to warn the Patriots of the British in the Revolutionary War.

Women Put Their Stamp on History.   Ask if students have noticed the images featured on postage stamps. Stamps are issued to commemorate many things, including famous people. Women who have been honored with a stamp for their achievements are as diverse as Ruth Benedict (anthropology), Virginia Apgar (medicine), and Maria Mitchell (astronomy). In 2001 the U.S. Post Office issued a stamp recognizing Frida Kahlo (artist), the first Latina woman to be honored. Bring in examples of stamps to show students or display the poster, *Putting Our Stamp on America* (available from National Women's History Project, 7738 Bell Road, Windsor CA 95492-8518, (707) 838-6000, or *<www.nwhp.org>*), which features forty-seven women who have been on stamps. Do students recognize any of these names? Challenge students to discover why these women were selected. Where would they look to find out more information about these people? Offer books such as:

Deborah Hopkinson. *Maria's Comet.* Illustrated by Deborah Lanino. Atheneum, 1999. Loosely based on childhood of Maria Mitchell, the first woman astronomer in the United States.

Mike Venezia. *Frida Kahlo.* Children's Press, 1999. Part of *Getting to Know the World's Artists* series; for primary students.

Women's Hall of Fame.   Women have been left out of most accounts of history. They are rarely seen as developers of ideas, initiators of events, or inventors of technology. The National Women's Hall of Fame, located in Seneca Falls, New York (76 Fall Street, Seneca NY 13148) conducted a survey of more than 300 historians and scholars to determine who were considered the most influential U.S. women of the twentieth century. The following are the top ten names. How many of these women are familiar to students?

1. Eleanor Roosevelt
2. Jane Addams
3. Rosa Parks
4. Margaret Sanger
5. Margaret Mead
6. Charlotte Perkins Gilman
7. Betty Friedan
8. Barbara Jordan
9. Helen Keller
10. Alice Paul

Use this list as a starting point for a discussion of women's achievements. Groups of students can research each woman's life and accomplishments to determine why she was voted into the Women's Hall of Fame.

Trailblazers and Freedom Fighters.   Stimulate students to investigate the lives of influential women, past and present. Have students select an individual by drawing a name out of a hat. They can prepare a report on that person's life and present it to the class so that all students learn more about these people. Students can write a diary entry for a significant day in the person's life. They can prepare artifacts or appropriate objects to accompany their presentation, such as eye goggles, a compass, and a map for Amelia Earhart. The following names provide a representative selection of different ethnic groups with which to start. You can also add names of local community interest.

Marian Anderson	Katherine Dunham	Wilma Mankiller
Maya Angelou	Amelia Earhart	Golda Meir
Joan Baez	Indira Gandhi	Toni Morrison
Mary McLeod Bethune	Althea Gibson	Georgia O'Keeffe
Elizabeth Blackwell	Ruth Bader Ginsburg	Sally Ride
Bonnie Blair	Zora Neale Hurston	Faith Ringgold
Gwendolyn Brooks	Judith Jamison	Wilma Rudolph
Susan Butcher	Florence Griffith Joyner	Maria Tallchief
Hillary Clinton	Frida Kahlo	Amy Tan
Bessie Coleman	Olga Korbut	Margaret Thatcher
Rita Dove	Nancy Lopez	Kristi Yamaguchi

These books will help students begin their study:

Don Brown. *Uncommon Traveler: Mary Kingsley in Africa.* Houghton Mifflin, 2000. Although born to a conventional English family in 1862, Kingsley became an adventurer and traveled through West Africa, collecting botanical specimens.

Shana Corey. *You Forgot Your Skirt, Amelia Bloomer.* Illustrated by Chesley McLaren. Scholastic, 2000. She thought "proper" clothing for ladies was silly and took action.

Shiobhan Donohue. *Kristi Yamaguchi: Artist on Ice.* Lerner, 1994. Description of skater's life and career with photos; for intermediate to middle school students.

Russell Freedman. *Eleanor Roosevelt: A Life of Discovery.* Clarion, 1993. Shows how Roosevelt overcame lack of support from her family, who considered her an ugly duckling, and her own shyness to create a new role as First Lady. She established herself as an individual, not just a politician's wife, and continued to make significant contributions after her husband's death.

Barbara Kramer. *Amy Tan: Author of the Joy Luck Club.* Enslow, 1996. One in a series of biographies for older students, this book looks at the Chinese American author's childhood and her struggle to get published.

Kathleen Krull. *Lives of Extraordinary Women: Rulers, Rebels, and What the Neighbors Thought.* Illustrated by Kathryn Hewitt. Holt, 2000. Covers a wider range than the usual collection, reaching as far as Cleopatra and Rigoberta Menchú.

Kathleen Krull. *Wilma Unlimited: How Wilma Rudolph Became the World's Fastest Woman.* Illustrated by David Díaz. Harcourt Brace, 1996. A biography of an African American athlete who overcame physical disabilities. (primary grades)

Reeve Lindbergh. *Nobody Owns the Sky.* Illustrated by Pamela Paparone. Candlewick Press, 1996. A picture book biography of Bessie Coleman, first licensed African American aviator.

Tom L. Matthews. *Light Shining through the Mist: A Photobiography of Dian Fossey.* Morrow, 1998. Primatologist Fossey followed her passion to study and protect the gorillas of Rwanda.

Yona Zeldis McDonough. *Sisters in Strength: American Women Who Made a Difference.* Illustrated by Malcah Zeldis. Holt, 2000. Eleven sketches of women who faced varied obstacles, from Pocahantas to Clara Barton.

Ann Whitford Paul. *All by Herself.* Illustrated by Michael Steirnagle. Harcourt Brace, 1999. True stories in verse about fourteen young heroines, from the well-known to the everyday.

Andrea Davis Pinkney. *Let It Shine: Stories of Black Women Freedom Fighters.* Illustrated by Stephen Alcorn. Harcourt Brace, 2000. Short pieces about women, both legendary and little known.

Maria Tallchief with Rosemary Wells. *Tallchief: America's Prima Ballerina.* Illustrated by Gary Kelley. Viking, 1999. With support from her family, Tallchief overcame objections from her tribe and social barriers to follow her love for dance.

Sports: Women in a Man's World.   For many years only men's sports received publicity and funding. Amateur or professional, few women were able to attract the same kind of audience. Women athletes had many obstacles to overcome in order to compete as they wished. With the advent of Title IX, however, girls' sports are receiving equal funding and girls are being attracted to athletics in greater numbers. Offer them encouragement, and show the boys that men are not the only ones who can set records.

David A. Adler. *America's Champion Swimmer: Gertrude Ederle.* Illustrated by Terry Widener. Harcourt, 2000. Biography of woman who swam the English Channel.

Russell Freedman. *Babe Didrikson Zaharias: The Making of a Champion.* Clarion, 1999. Noted historian describes multitalented athlete.

Sue Macy. *Winning Ways.* Holt, 1996. This black-and-white photohistory shows how U.S. women have changed the men-only status of sports, from bicycling in 1870 to baseball in 1990.

Sue Macy and Jane Gottesman, eds. *Play Like a Girl: A Celebration of Women in Sport.* Holt, 1999. Inspirational quotes and images.

Doreen Rappaport and Lyndall Callan. *Dirt on Their Skirts: The Story of the Young Women Who Won the World Championship.* Illustrated by E. B. Lewis. Dial, 2000. A baseball game in 1946.

Women's Suffrage.   When did women get the right to vote? Not until 1920, after black men, but before Native Americans. Why did it take so long? Investigate the struggle for women's rights from "suffrage" to the Equal Rights Amendment. Begin with these books.

Jean Fritz. *You Want Women to Vote, Lizzie Stanton?* Putnam, 1995. For intermediate students, an account by a noted writer.

Gwenyth Swain. *The Road to Seneca Falls: A Story about Elizabeth Cady Stanton.* Carolrhoda, 1996. How Stanton and Lucretia Mott organized the women's rights convention in 1848.

Women in Folklore.   Positive models and stories of successful women can help us persevere, overcoming obstacles and others' lack of faith. Folktales, a traditional source of community wisdom, often reflect stereotypical roles for men and women. However, alternative models do exist. Present tales of strong women to counteract popular folklore images, such as Cinderella and Sleeping Beauty, of passive women who need a man to rescue them. As you read stories with the class, talk about the stereotypes you encounter.

Suzanne I. Barchers. *Wise Women: Folk and Fairy Tales from around the World.* Teacher Ideas Press, 1990. Collection of stories and teaching ideas.

Virginia Hamilton. *Her Stories: African American Folktales, Fairy Tales, and True Tales.* Illustrated by Leo and Diane Dillon. Scholastic, 1995. This collection of nineteen tales includes captivating stories and legends.

Anne Isaacs. *Swamp Angel.* Illustrated by Paul Zelinsky. Dutton, 1994. Tall tale about the feats of Angelica Longrider, the greatest woodswoman of Tennessee and a female Paul Bunyan.

Uma Krishnaswami, retold. *Shower of Gold: Girls and Women in the Stories of India.* Illustrated by Maniam Selven. Linnet, 1999. Includes Hindu and Buddhist mythology, set in the context of cultural traditions.

Marianna Mayer. *Women Warriors: Myths and Legends of Heroic Women.* Illustrated by Julek Heller. Morrow, 1999. Twelve traditional tales from around the world.

Burleigh Mutén, sel. *Grandmothers' Stories: Wise Woman Tales from Many Cultures.* Illustrated by Sian Bailey. Barefoot Books, 1999. Perfect for reading aloud or storytelling.

Robert San Souci. *Cut from the Same Cloth: American Women of Myth, Legend and Tall Tale.* Illustrated by Brian Pinkney. Philomel, 1993. Less well-known tales of strong and determined women, including African and Native American traditions.

Jane Yolen. *Not One Damsel in Distress: World Folktales for Strong Girls.* Illustrated by Susan Guevara. Harcourt Brace, 2000. Thirteen examples of positive female role models by noted writer and storyteller.

Featuring Women Artists.   Show students that making "art" is not the sole property of men, although it has been dominated by them. The following books will broaden students' ideas about the nature of art, give students a cultural perspective on artistic achievement, and may inspire some to follow in the footsteps of these famous women.

Shaun Hunter. *Women in Profile: Visual and Performing Artists.* Crabtree, 1999. Eighteen sketches of performers and artists, from Madonna to Natalia Makarova, Georgia O'Keefe to Emily Carr.

Linda Lowery. *Georgia O'Keeffe.* Carolrhoda, 1996. Biography of artist known for her paintings of American Southwest.

Leslie Sills. *Visions: Stories about Women Artists.* Whitman, 1993. This collection features Mary Cassatt, Leonora Carrington, Betye Saar, and Mary Frank. Although they came from different backgrounds and lived at different times, they all had to overcome similar obstacles to pursue their careers as artists.

Robyn Montana Turner. *Frida Kahlo.* Little, Brown, 1993. From the series Portraits of Women Artists for Children. Other books in the series include *Rosa Bonheur, Georgia O'Keeffe, Mary Cassatt,* and *Faith Ringgold.*

Noted artists who are women that have been honored with U.S. postage stamps include Georgia O'Keefe, Louise Nevelson, and Frida Kahlo.

Invite students to respond to this quote about the meaning of art:

> I found I could say things with color and shapes that I couldn't say in any other way—things I had no words for.
> —Georgia O'Keeffe

For more information on women artists, contact The National Museum of Women in the Arts, 1250 New York Ave, NW, Washington DC 20005-3920.

Countering Sex Stereotypes in Children's Literature.   Frequently, you will encounter examples of stereotyped thinking and behavior in books that you use with students in the classroom. Over 75 percent of the characters in children's books are male. In addition, the male characters tend to take action, while the female characters stand on the sidelines. Stereotypes weaken the value of these books because they result in cardboard characters and predictable plots. However, you cannot eliminate all examples of stereotyping. Instead, help students practice critical thinking skills by identifying stereotypes and evaluating sexism in the books they read.

One example of such stereotyping in an older book is *Sylvester and the Magic Pebble* by William Steig. Although the characters are drawn as donkeys, they conform to stereotyped sex roles. The mother donkey wears an apron and acts "helpless." The father donkey sits smoking his pipe and reading the newspaper while his wife sweeps under his feet. Discuss with students the message communicated by these illustrations and accompanying text.

Even the Harry Potter books by J. K. Rowling, currently popular with girls and boys, have been criticized for a lack of positive female role models. Have students name examples of female characters from the series such as the teachers Minerva McGonagall and Sybill Trelawny, or students Ginny and Hermione. Students can list adjectives to describe these characters and discuss the roles they play in the story. Which characters would students like to emulate?

Select a well-known children's book such as Maurice Sendak's *Where the Wild Things Are*. Have students retell the story, changing the main character Max into Maxine. Can Maxine have the same adventures as Max? Discuss the changes with students. An alternative is to tell the story from another character's point of view.

Traditional folktales can be revised to reflect a different attitude toward men and women. For example, in *Rumpelstiltskin's Daughter*, by Diane Stanley, the miller's daughter refuses to marry the king as expected and instead chooses Rumpelstiltskin. Students can write their own versions of familiar tales, changing the characters or changing the endings.

Analyzing Sexism in Books and Other Media.   Students can begin to look critically at the material that they read in light of class discussion of sex-role stereotypes. Involve them in analyzing and collecting data. Students can count the number of male and female characters in books and categorize what kinds of activities these characters participate in. What do the characters say? Do they comment negatively on the abilities of boys or girls? Students can also look closely at the illustrations. How are the characters pictured? What effect does this have on the reader?

Have students assemble their data and prepare a report of what they have found. What conclusions do they draw based on their results? They can share this with other classes in the school or send it to the local newspaper.

Positive Models in Books for Children.   We know that books transmit values to children, particularly when the messages are subtle. As much as possible, consciously select books that portray males and females in nonstereotyped roles and in multicultural settings and explain to students why you are doing so. Share with students old favorites such as *Madeline* by Ludwig Bemelmans and *Pippi Longstocking* by Astrid Lindgren. Here are some more recent books that you will enjoy.

Picture Books

James Howe. *Horace and Morris but Mostly Dolores*. Illustrated by Amy Walrod. Atheneum, 1999. Three rats explore whether boys and girls can be friends.

Emily Arnold McCully. *Mirette on the High Wire*. Putnam, 1992. After Mirette learns tightrope walking, she helps her teacher conquer his fears.

Gerdine Nolan. *Raising Dragons*. Illustrated by Elise Primaverg. Silverwhistle, 1998. A young girl raises a dragon who then does favors for the family.

Allen Say. *Emma's Rug*. Houghton Mifflin, 1996. Portrays the creative process from a little girl's point of view.

Carole Lexa Schaefer. *The Squiggle.* Illustrated by Pierr Morgan. Crown, 1996. Story of the importance of imagination; illustrations feature a Chinese girl.

Camille Yarbrough. *The Shimmershine Queens.* Putnam, 1989. Self-esteem and achievement counter the negative images of sexism and racism that face black girls.

Books for Independent Readers

Elizabeth Levy. *Seventh Grade Tango.* Hyperion, 2000. Two friends, a boy and a girl, are paired up in their school's dance class.

Marilyn Levy. *Run for Your Life.* Houghton Mifflin, 1996. Based on the true story of the Oakland (CA) Acorn Track Team, shows how teamwork changed the lives of poor black girls.

Tryntje Van Ness Seymour. *The Gift of Changing Woman.* Holt, 1993. When an Apache girl comes of age, there is a special ceremony to teach her the story of creation and her place in the world.

Jerry Spinelli. *There's a Girl in My Hammerlock.* Simon & Schuster, 1991. Maisie faces opposition from her family and friends when she chooses wrestling as a sport.

Sources of Additional Information for Teaching about Women: Searching for Equity

Judy Alter. *Extraordinary Women of the American West.* Children's Press, 1998. Includes over fifty women and covers a range of races, occupations, and historical periods.

Tonya Bolden. *And Not Afraid to Dare: Stories of 10 African American Women.* Scholastic, 1998. Includes women from Ellen Craft to Toni Morrison.

Penny Colman. *Girls: A History of Growing Up Female in America.* Scholastic, 2000. True stories of ordinary girls illustrate their resilience and determination throughout history.

Emma Hahn. *16 Extraordinary American Women.* J. Weston Walch, 1996. Two-page biographies of famous women, including Cherokee leader Wilma Mankiller, black singer Ella Fitzgerald, Hawaiian Princess Ka'iulani, black Congressperson Barbara Jordan, and black poet Nikki Giovanni. For intermediate students, includes comprehension questions.

Kathleen Krull. *Lives of Athletes: Thrills, Spills, and What the Neighbors Thought.* Harcourt, 1997. Short biographies of famous athletes, women as well as men.

Myself and Women Heroes in My World; Women at Work, Home and School; Women as Members of Groups; and *Women as Members of Communities.* These integrated social studies/language arts elementary curriculum units are available from National Women's History Project, 7738 Bell Road, Windsor, CA 95492–8518. They include both famous (Harriet Tubman) and not-so-famous (Dolores Huerta) women of the past and the present.

National Women's History Project. *Women's History Resources.* Updated regularly. This book contains state and national lists of information, people, and publishers as well as annotated lists of resources for Native American, Asian, Hispanic, and African American women. Also see <*www.nwhp.org*>.

Profiles of Women Past and Present: Women's History Monologues for Group Presentations. Thousand Oaks Branch of the American Association of University Women, PO Box 4223, Thousand Oaks, CA 91359-1223. 1996. Monologues based on the lives of fifteen famous American women. One set is for primary grades, another for intermediate students, along with instructions for performing them.

Darleene Stille. *Extraordinary Women Scientists.* Children's Press, 1995. Fifty short biographies, from Marie Curie to Rosalind Franklin. Intermediate to middle school students.

CONNECTIONS

Language arts and reading instruction permeates the entire curriculum. So also does multicultural education. The teacher's task is to integrate these two important aspects of the K–8 curriculum as students develop literacy skills while learning essential multicultural concepts. Thus, students of all ages create a solid foundation for their education.

FOLLOW-THROUGH

Expanding Your RTP

1. In your journal write a response to the following quotation:

    In spite of everything, I still believe that people are really good at heart.
    —Anne Frank

    Who is Anne Frank? Given her circumstances, would you consider her sensible or naïve to make such a statement? Do your experiences support her remark?

    How might you use this quotation in teaching lessons to students at different grade levels? How does it fit with the studies of friendship and getting along presented in this chapter?

2. We are probably more conversant with the ill effects of stereotypes when we consider how they affect us. What groups do you belong to—athlete, sorority, blonde, Asian? Are there positive or negative stereotypes associated with these groups?

    In your RTP describe a stereotype that you believe has been applied to you. Describe an incident where this occurred and the effect it had on you. Were you consciously aware of the stereotype that was affecting someone else's judgment? Did you speak out? Why or why not? How do you feel now that you look back on this episode?

Working with Your CLG

1. Obtain multiple copies of *Bud, Not Buddy* by Christopher Paul Curtis. Read this book and discuss it in your group. Imagine that you are reading this book aloud chapter by chapter to a class. Brainstorm learning activities that you could develop based on the shared reading experience. Consider thinking, listening, speaking, writing, and additional reading activities.

2. See how many biographies about contemporary women you can locate in your public library to share with your group. Use the list in the section titled Trailblazers and Freedom Fighters in this chapter to suggest possible subject names to look for in the children's section under 920.

GROWING A PROFESSIONAL LIBRARY

Sharon Murphy and Curt Dudley-Marling, eds. *Literacy through Language Arts: Teaching and Learning in Context.* National Council of Teachers of English, 2003. Noted authors discuss best strategies for teaching reading, writing, and oral literacy.

Timothy V. Radinski. *The Fluent Reader.* Scholastic, 2005. Practical ideas for interactive oral reading that supports slow readers or those learning English.

Iris McClellan Tiedt. *Tiger Lilies, Toadstools, and Thunderbolts: Engaging K–8 Students with Poetry.* International Reading Association, 2002. Includes many multicultural ideas.

ENDNOTES

1. Paul Gagnon, "Why Study History?" *Atlantic Monthly* (November 1988): 43.
2. Ibid., p. 64.
3. Jerry Johns, "Libraries: Powerful Partners for Reading." *Reading Today* (December 2002/ January 2003): 6–7.

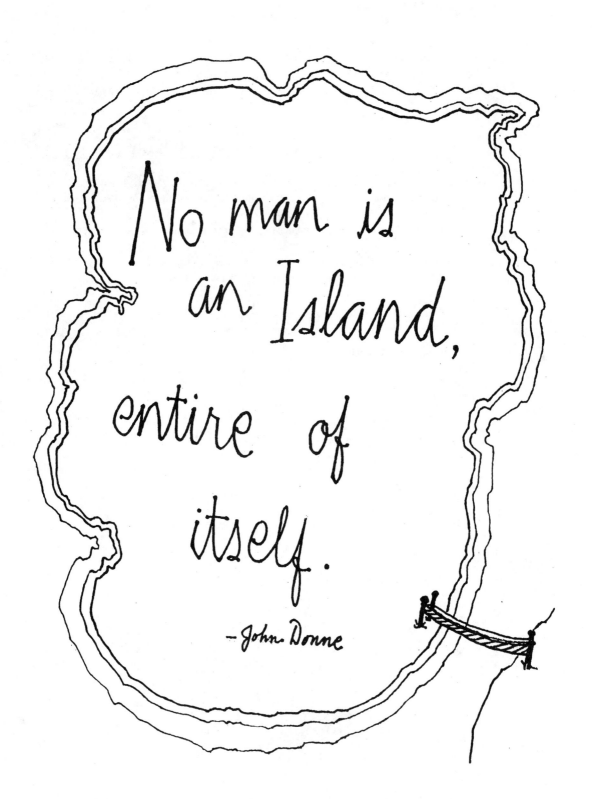

Teaching Social Studies Multiculturally

As we plan for teaching social studies at any level, we need to think specifically about meeting the needs of all of the students in each classroom. We recognize social studies as being especially important as we prepare students to become effective, active citizens in a democracy. Furthermore, students need to know the history and development of the United States with particular attention to the population's growing diversity and the demand for civil rights legislation as it has expanded over the years. Social studies instruction is designed to inform students and to educate them to question and discuss issues and concerns that face our nation every day. They need to gain experience in critiquing, analyzing, comparing, and evaluating events that occur in their world, decisions that are made, policies that are determined at the state and national levels.

In this chapter we include instructional strategies that suggest content from the broad areas included in the field of social studies, for example, history, geography, sociology, economics, and psychology. We first describe instructional strategies that lend themselves particularly to the teaching of the social studies, and we present sample lesson plans that suggest the type of instruction that we recommend. In the last half of the chapter, we consider ways of infusing multicultural social studies concepts across the curriculum with special emphasis on thematic studies. Our goal in this chapter is to help you open doors as you endeavor to design a multicultural social studies curriculum that you can teach *multiculturally*.

FOCUSING ON SOCIAL STUDIES INSTRUCTION DIRECTLY

Let us first examine several teaching strategies that are especially adaptable to the social science curriculum as K–8 students explore history and geography. Notice that instruction in social science, as noted in the preceding chapter on Language Arts and Reading, will engage students in developing thinking, speaking, listening, reading, and writing skills plus content from the social studies as well as from multicultural education. You might find it helpful to browse through Chapter 4 again as you plan for teaching social studies.

Effective Social Studies Instructional Strategies

Remembering that the most effective teaching allows for the individual differences that are in every class, we choose strategies that are inclusive. We also ensure that we provide a wide variety of resources to accommodate the needs of diverse students.

Discussion Topics

Children can study and discuss topics like the following: Why do we use the term *global village* today? Why has the history of the Middle East been full of conflict? Middle-grade students might read the novel, *The Boy from Over There* by Tamar Bergman (translation from the Hebrew by Hillel Halkin).

Contemporary history suggests the following topics related to learning to get along with the diverse people in the world:

1. Democracy's solutions for war-related problems at home and abroad and the strains on democracy produced by them.
2. The breakup of the U.S.S.R.
3. Problems faced by South Africa following democracy.

Mapping the Origins of the Members of the Class

Create a large outline map of the world by enlarging a map from a text. Have students interview their parents to ascertain general information about where grandparents and earlier ancestors came from. Students can then locate these places and outline the trail of their individual origins on the map with colored pens. Each student can then tell his or her story and show the trail on the map. Answer these questions: Which students have come the farthest? How many students were born outside the United States? How many were born in a different state? Where have students traveled? Have any of them visited other countries?

What languages do the students speak? If you include the languages their parents speak, how many languages are represented in the classroom? Consider ways to use these differences as assets. Have students teach others a few words in another language. Ask students to tell the class about life in a different region. Was the weather different? Did they play different games? Ask newcomers what they found particularly different or hard to get used to in their new environment.

Social Studies Themes in Literature

Social studies concepts can scarcely be separated from literature study. Choose books for reading aloud that include a clear multicultural theme like the following:

Kathleen Allan-Meyer. *I Have a New Friend.* Barron's, 1995. A Japanese friend.

Diana Cohn. *¡Si, Se Puede!/Yes, we can! Janitor Strike in L.A.* Cinco Printos, 2002.

Paula Fox. *The Moonlight Man.* Bradbury, 1986. Nova Scotia.

Jan Gilchrist. *Indigo and Moonlight Gold.* Black Butterfly Children's Books, 1993. African American mother and child.

L. King Perez. *First Day in Grapes.* Lee & Low, 2002. Migrant workers.

Patricia Polacco. *Pink and Say.* Philomel, 1994. Interracial friendship; Civil War.

Gary Soto. *The Pool Party.* Dell, 1993. Social class tensions; Latino.

Yoko Kawashima Watkins. *So Far from the Bamboo Grove.* Lothrop, 1986. Korea; autobiographical.

Have students work in CLGs to act out parts of a book they have read together as a way of sharing information and encouraging other students to read the book presented.

Reviewing Nonfiction about Multicultural History

Many fine books written for young people explain topics that are related to both multicultural education and social studies, for example:

S. Beth Atkin. *Voices from the Fields: Children of Migrant Farmworkers Tell Their Stories.* Little, 1993.

Richard Sobol. *One More Elephant: The Fight to Save Wildlife in Uganda.* Cobblehill, 1995.

Ted Wood with Wambli Numpa Afraid of Hawk. *A Boy Becomes a Man at Wounded Knee.* Walker, 1992.

Have students write book reviews of nonfiction they have read. Share the reviews orally, and publish them so other students can read them.

Reading about Real People: Life Lines

Both autobiography and biography provide information about history in action. Students will enjoy reading books about the lives of people who have clearly influenced world history, for example:

Linda Atkinson. *In Kindling Flame: The Story of Hannah Senesh, 1921–1944.* Lothrop, 1985. Hungary.

Carol Greene. *Mary McLeod Bethune: Champion for Education.* Children's Press, 1993. United States.

William Sanford. *Chief Joseph: Nez Percé Warrior.* Enslow, 1994. United States.

Anne Schraff. *Women of Peace: Nobel Peace Prize Winners.* Enslow, 1994. International.

Have students make time lines for the lives of such people they read about. Display the charts and have each student tell about the person featured in his or her time line.

Analyzing and Comparing: Using the Venn Diagram

The Venn diagram is used in mathematics to compare two sets. This method can be used to compare two concepts or books in an effective social studies lesson. After each student has read a novel about young people living in another land, ask each one to complete a Venn diagram that compares his or her life with that of the book character, for example:

Barbara Cohen. *Seven Daughters and Seven Sons.* Harper, 1994. This book is based on an Iraqi folktale that demonstrates the worth of daughters. Buran disguises herself as a man to help her family, and all kinds of adventures follow. It's really an exciting story.

In sections 1 and 2 of the Venn diagram unique characteristics are listed for each person. In section 3, the student lists adjectives that describe both, showing how they are alike (see Figure 5.1). After completing the Venn diagram, each student writes a five-paragraph essay following this pattern:

Paragraph 1: Introduction
Paragraph 2: Description of herself or himself
Paragraph 3: Description of the book character
Paragraph 4: Summary of how the two are alike
Paragraph 5: Concluding paragraph

This exercise may lead students to observe that people are more alike than different, particularly when they consider their personal characteristics and problems. Once students know how to use this diagram, they can use it to guide comparisons of more complex topics, for example, two ethnic groups, two religions, or two forms of government.

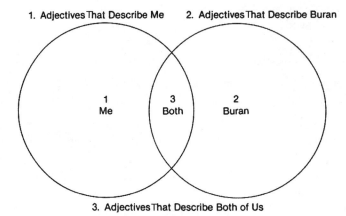

1. Adjectives That Describe Me   2. Adjectives That Describe Buran

1
Me

3
Both

2
Buran

3. Adjectives That Describe Both of Us

FIGURE 5.1   VENN DIAGRAM

Computers and Social Studies

Have students conduct a Treasure Hunt on the Internet to see what they can find. Working with the Internet opens doors to a great variety of social studies information. Many fine software programs are available that engage students in simulations and problem solving. Here are more ideas to add to your list of resources:

Educating for Peace. <*www.global-ed.org/e4p/resource*>

National Council of Social Studies "Trade Books for Reducing Violence." www.ness.org/
resources/moments.610506.shtm/

Order the following resources for your library:

U.S. Geography: An Overview. CD-ROM for Windows and Macintosh. This program presents more than geography, focusing also on history and people. Recommended for
grades 5 through 12, the program gives students a multicultural overview of U.S. history.
It includes complete U.S. census data, a concise encyclopedia, and an index as well as
audiotapes from famous speeches.

Where in the WORLD, USA, EUROPE Is Carmen Sandiego? Software Series, 3 packages;
Macintosh and Windows. Recommended for grades 4 through 9, this series is supported
with *Carmen Sandiego Day Kit; Carmen Sandiego Party Packet;* tapes; and lab packs
(including *Teacher's Guide, World Almanac, Fodor's USA Travel Guide, Rand McNally's
Concise Atlas of Europe*). This software is available in French.

Eco East Africa. CD-ROM for Windows; IVI Publishing, 1995, edited by Lee Barnes and
Christopher Thompson. Recommended for the advanced student, this program enables
players to experience some of the variables of overseas employment, e.g., as a game warden. The software focuses on issues of managing Ethemba, a game park in Tanzania.

Up to the Himalayas: Kingdoms in the Clouds. CD-ROM, Macintosh and Windows,
DNA Multimedia, 1997. Recommended for grades 5 through 12, this outstanding pro-
gram takes students on an interactive fieldtrip to Sikkim, India, and its capital city,
Gantok.

California Mission Series. Lerner Publications, 1996. Organized regionally into six volumes, this series provides a balanced account of the establishment of the missions, their
impact on existing cultures, and their influence on the growth and development of the
state of California. Recommended for grades 4 through 7, the books contain full-color
and black-and-white photographs, illustrations, maps, charts, and time lines.

*Gumshoe Geography: Exploring the Cultural, Physical, Sociological, and Biological
Characteristics of Our Planet* by Richard Jones. Zephyr Press, 1997. This text will in-
trigue advanced students with a game format that encourages them to learn more about
our planet. 176 reproducible activities send students on missions to gather information
about other cultures and places in the world. Teacher's Guide with each activity.

Readers' Theater

Readers' Theater should involve students in reading various kinds of multicultural literature that is related to a selected social studies theme. Several weeks are required for planning, searching for material, and giving the presentation to an audience. Follow these
steps:

Planning.   Talk with students about the idea of a reader's theater presentation. Explain that the presentation is read, not acted out. The presenters sit on stools or chairs and read their assigned parts. Discuss the kinds of materials that might be used, for example:

- Short stories (fables, myths, etc.) and excerpts from novels
- Sayings, proverbs, quotations, poetry, song lyrics
- Factual statements

Searching for Material.   Plan a visit to the library as the groups search for material related to the selected theme. If you notify the librarian ahead of time, she or he will be able to locate appropriate sources for class use. The material does not have to be written in play form for this kind of presentation, as you will see in the next step.

Preparing the Script.   Duplicate copies of folktales or poems that students plan to use. These copies can then be marked and revised as the group deems appropriate. There may be three or four roles to read plus one or more narrators who read the descriptive passages. Students can supply dialogue to add interest and to develop a character.

Rehearsing.   One student should be the director to signal the group when to stand and to sit. This person listens during rehearsals, ensures that students read clearly and effectively, makes suggestions for timing, and so on. Poetry and nonfiction can be divided in various sections or verses. One or more persons may read to provide variety.

The Presentation.   Select an audience for whom to perform the finished production. The audience may be the rest of the class, another class that is studying the same topic, or the whole school in an assembly. A Reader's Theater presentation can be given to the Parent Teachers' Association meeting to show parents what students are studying. A study of Japanese Americans and contemporary Japan might culminate with a Reader's Theater presentation based on selections from books such as the following:

Nancy Luenn. *The Dragon Kite.* Harcourt, 1982.

Toshi Maruki. *Hiroshima No Pika.* Lothrop, 1982.

Yoshiko Uchida. *The Dancing Kettle and Other Japanese Folktales.* Scribners, 1972.

Sumiko Yagawa (translated by Katherine Paterson). *The Crane Wife.* Morrow, 1981.

Plan a Readers' Theater presentation following the directions in the Thinking + box. Be aware that there are various methods of working with Readers' Theater; we have selected one that engages students in thinking as well as in improving their reading skills. To enhance a presentation for their audience, students could add songs or dances. Pictures could be displayed with original student haiku. A sharing time for both adults and children might be planned for May 5th, Children's Day in Japan.

A Readers' Theater Presentation—
Remembering the Japanese American Internment

Grades 4–7

Expected Outcomes
Learners will:

1. Read a story about the Japanese American internment.
2. Discuss the implications of this governmental act.
3. Plan and present a program celebrating the contributions of Japanese Americans to the United States.

Teaching/Learning Strategies

Resources Needed
Obtain a class set of *Journey to Topaz* by Yoshiko Uchida. (If a set is not available, plan to read the book aloud, chapter by chapter.) Students will discuss events in the book. They will then plan a Readers' Theater presentation to share with other classes.

Directions
Step 1:   Introduce students to the author, Yoshiko Uchida. Read the first chapter of *Journey to Topaz* aloud to the class. Discuss the beginning of the story, summarizing what has happened and what students think will happen next. Have students begin a log that they will keep during this project, writing in it at the end of each chapter of the book.

Step 2:   Students will continue reading the book, chapter by chapter, and writing in their logs as homework. Classtime will focus on discussion of what has happened in the story. As students express empathy for these displaced persons, suggest the preparation of a program that will show appreciation for what the Japanese Americans have contributed to their country—the United States.

Performance Assessment
Discuss with students appropriate criteria for rating the logs they are keeping, for example:

3   Outstanding writing: Clear, free from error, at least one page per chapter.

2   Good writing: Interesting comments, just a few errors, more than ½ page per chapter.

1   Acceptable writing: Appropriate comments, a number of errors, less than ½ page for more than one chapter.

0   Unacceptable writing: Missing or very short entries.

Evaluation for the Readers' Theater presentation will be Credit/No Credit based on participation with a group.

INFUSING MULTICULTURAL SOCIAL STUDIES INSTRUCTION ACROSS THE CURRICULUM

How do concepts from the various social studies areas connect with other areas of the curriculum that you teach? Thinking about the answer to this question will enable you to help students make these connections as they engage in multicultural social studies learning activities that relate to reading and writing instruction as well as art, music, technology, and science. Discuss the possibilities for integrating social studies instruction in this way with other teachers in your school.

Engaging Students

How might you direct students to make connections between social studies and the activities they are experiencing in other subject areas? For one thing, it helps to be aware of what is going on in other classrooms. Teachers will also find it profitable to plan together so that they, as well as students, make these important connections. Let's consider ways for linking such skill development as reading and writing, as well as artistic endeavors, with learning specific to the social studies curriculum.

Reading Fiction and Nonfiction

Social studies often focuses on the significant contributions that men and women have made to our welfare. Encouraging students to read autobiographical material and biographies that tell us about the lives of such people is an important way of linking the development of content reading skills with the study of history. Excellent historical fiction is also available in picture book format for younger students and in books written for young adults. Look for some of the following:

Tonya Bolden. *Portraits of African-American Heroes.* Illustrated by Ansel Pitcairn. Dutton, 2003. Profiles in "fortitude, sacrifice, and vision" capture the spirit of twenty African American men and women who have left a legacy for our country; includes large paintings of each person.

May-Lee Chai and Winberg Chai. *The Girl from Purple Mountain: Love, Honor, War, and One Family's Journey from China to America.* St. Martin's, 2001.

Patricia Reilly Giff. *Maggie's Door.* Random, 2003. When the potato famine hits Ireland, Nory Ryan and her family head for the ships to America with very little in their knapsacks.

Writing

Many forms of writing lend themselves to learning activities related to history and geography. Here are suggestions for engaging students in writing specific genres as they explore social science topics:

- Diaries: Each student keeps an imaginary diary as they travel with Columbus or Lewis and Clark. In order to compose plausible diary entries, the student will need to research information about the journey in question.
- Letters: Two students can work together to create a series of letters written by two historical figures, for example, Eleanor Roosevelt and her friend Amelia Earhart.
- Essays: Students write short persuasive essays in support of something they believe in strongly. Provide a simple outline that they can follow like this one:

> Paragraph 1: I believe that our state should _____.
> Give three reasons to support your belief. Restate your belief in fifth sentence. (Five sentences in all.)
>
> Paragraph 2: The first reason that we should _____ is that _____.
> Write two or three sentences to support this reason.
>
> Paragraph 3: The second reason that we should _____ is that _____.
> Write two or three sentences to support this reason.
>
> Paragraph 4: The third reason that we should _____ is that _____.
> Write two or three sentences to support this reason.
>
> Paragraph 5. Summarize the argument you have made in the first four paragraphs. End with a sentence that restates your position.

Art

Enhance social studies learning by engaging students in various kinds of multicultural art activities, for example:

- Collage: Have students create collages about topics they are studying. Students cut words and pictures from magazines and newspapers to present on a large sheet of paper as a way of presenting a complex topic, for example: Women's Rights, the State of Georgia, or the Civil War. Students can include small realia to provide a 3-D effect, or they can add original art to supply information they want to include but can't find in publications they have access to. Display these collages on the wall in the school hallway so that other students can examine them.
- Covers for Reports: After each student has completed a research report, typed it on the computer, and printed it out, findings can be presented formally in booklet form. Creating an attractive cover on a large sheet of 17" × 18" construction paper will enhance each student's presentation, which can be placed in the school library for other students to read. Show students how to create colorful covers by first dropping enamel paint on water in a cookie baking sheet with ½" sides and then laying their paper over the paint floating on the water. The result is a very attractive marbleized design that will dry overnight. The folded sheet provides a suitable front and back cover for a report printed on 8½" × 11" paper.

A THINKING + LESSON PLAN

Reading and Writing Haiku

Grades 3–8

Expected Outcomes
Learners will:

1. Read examples of haiku poetry.
2. Identify the characteristics of haiku.
3. Write original haiku.
4. Publish a collection of haiku.

Teaching/Learning Strategies

Resources Needed
Collect books of poetry related to social studies to read aloud to students. Students will write haiku poems about selected social studies topics. They will then contribute their best haiku to a class publication.

Directions
Poetry is especially suitable for enhancing a social studies lesson. Your own enthusiasm will be contagious as students listen to you read (or recite) a favorite poem related to the current study. A wonderful collection of poems about people in history is *The Book of Americans* by Rosemary and Stephen Vincent Benet. *Bronzeville Boys and Girls* is a collection by Pulitzer Prizewinner Gwendolyn Brooks. Sample the work of black poet Langston Hughes; the composer of outstanding free verse, Carl Sandburg; and the well-polished haiku written by Japanese poets of the thirteenth century. Give students a sheet on which you have typed three to eight examples of classic haiku. Have them identify the characteristics of these poems before they try writing their own haiku.

Step 1:
Writing poetry is a way for students to express their ideas and feelings. Have students write haiku as part of a study of Japan. Here are two examples of haiku translated from the original Japanese:

First cold showers fall.	All sky disappears
Even little monkey wants	The earth's land has gone away;
A wee coat of straw	Still the snowflakes fall.
—Bashō	*—Hashin*

An excellent source of information for the teacher who wants to know more about haiku is *An Introduction to Haiku* by Harold Anderson. Children are most successful with this brief verse form if emphasis is rightly placed on the thoughts they are expressing rather than on the confining form, for example:

The sun shines brightly.
With its glowing flames shooting
It goes down at night.

    –Ricky

The old cypress tree,
So beautiful by the rocks,
Has been there for years.

    –Marjorie

After first thinking about an idea they wish to express, the students are encouraged to write it on paper. They can then examine their own written thought to determine how it can be divided into three parts. Experimentation with word arrangement, imagery, changing the order of the lines, and choice of words used should be encouraged as the poem is developed.

Step 2:
Print out haiku written by a class with a computer using two long columns so that the folded sheets will produce two long, slim pages. Cut the sheets to form pages of an attractive booklet and make a decorative cover, as shown in Figure 5.2.

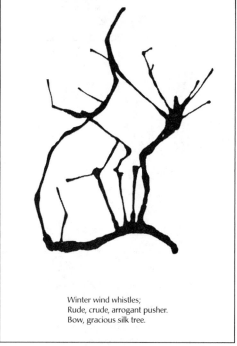

Winter wind whistles;
Rude, crude, arrogant pusher.
Bow, gracious silk tree.

FIGURE 5.2   HAIKU BOOKLET

(continued)

Step 3:

A rewarding art experience that correlates well with the writing of haiku is blowing ink with a straw. Washable black ink is applied in a swath near the bottom of an unlined file card (or any nonabsorbent paper). The wet ink is then blown with a straw to direct the ink in the desired direction. Blowing across the ink causes it to branch attractively. When the ink is dry, tiny dabs of bright tempera may be applied with a toothpick to add spring blossoms to the bare branch. The student then writes a haiku on the card below the flowering branch, and the card is used for display or as a gift for parents.

For an authentic presentation of haiku use rice paper (or thin onion skin or tissue paper) mounted inside colored paper. The poem is written (a felt pen will write on thin paper) along with a Japanese design—reeds, moon over water, flowering branch—and the author's name. The cover is folded so that the front flaps overlap slightly, as in the sketch. A ribbon is then tied around the folder, which is ready for presentation as a gift (see Figure 5.3).

Performance Assessment

Students will receive grades of Credit/No Credit based on their completing at least one haiku. Each student should have one haiku included in a class publication.

Folded slightly overlapping . . .
. . . tied with ribbon

FIGURE 5.3   HAIKU GIFT

Developing Extensive Multicultural Thematic Studies

Consider the possibilities for using these strategies to enhance your social studies curriculum as you develop thematic studies: Here, again, planning with other teachers will enable you all to plan a better outline for the study and to locate suitable resources.

Review the directions for developing thematic studies included in Chapter 3. Be sure that students are included in planning any unit of study from the beginning. Ownership for such studies is essential to engaging learners in delving into a topic with enthusiasm. In this chapter we present information that will assist you in beginning a study of three themes: (1) Families, (2) The Neighborhood, and (3) Native Americans.

Theme: Families

Families today come in a variety of shapes and sizes. At the same time, the family group is one of the most important factors affecting the development of a student's identity. From their relationships with siblings to the different roles they may be expected to take on, students need to know that many different kinds of families will be accepted in the classroom.

As students begin to look at who they are, they also begin to discover where they came from. Learning about their family history and customs can help them find their place in the world. They can learn that everyone has a family but families can be very different.

A Family Tree.   Begin a discussion with primary students by talking about the "family tree." Who are the members of their family? What relatives do they have? Students can draw a tree and write names or draw pictures in circles around the tree (see Figure 5.4).

What Is Genealogy?   Introduce the big word *genealogy* (notice the spelling), which means the study of lineage, family history. Many people trace their family history as a matter of pride. Today there are many resources available to help you.

Older students can ask their families about family history and write the information on a chart. They can interview their parents and any other relatives to assemble as much information as possible.

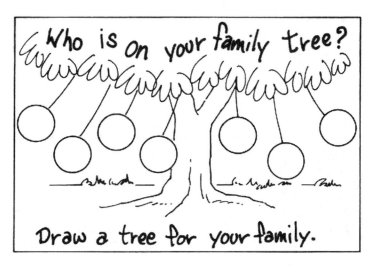

FIGURE 5.4   FAMILY TREE

Approach this potentially sensitive subject with caution, as parents my be concerned about an invasion of privacy. Professional genealogists make distinctions based on "blood," adoption, illegitimacy, and so on, but we are using "family" in the broadest sense, including family of choice. It is important to discuss the project in the classroom first so that children have a clear sense of your intent, namely, developing *pride in the family,* the importance of remembering our ancestors, our *roots.* You might, for example, tell the group something of your own origins.

Books to help students explore their family roots are:

E. Barrie Kavason. *A Student's Guide to Native American Genealogy.* Oryx, 1996. (Oryx *Family Tree* series)

Lila Perl. *The Great Ancestor Hunt.* Clarion, 1989.

Maureen Taylor. *Through the Eyes of Your Ancestors.* Houghton Mifflin, 1999.

Younger students will enjoy *Rosy Cole Discovers America!* by Sheila Greenwald in which Rosy, disappointed in her ordinary immigrant ancestors, invents a royal past for herself.

Older students can take advantage of the Internet resources to trace their family. Check out these sites to get started:

Computerized Ancestor	*<www.montana.com/yates/>*
Gendex	*<www.gendex.com>*
Roots Web	*<www.rootsweb.com>*

Families Differ.   Discuss the topic: What is a "typical" family? Students will probably respond with the stereotyped perception of a family as a mother, father, and two children, even if their family is not like this.

Is this what families are really like? How many families represented in the classroom consist of two parents and two children? Do there have to be children to call it a family? What other arrangements do the children know about? List them on the board.

- Father Mother Child/Stepchild
- Father Mother More than Two Children
- Mother Child
- Grandmother Three Children
- Father Two Children
- Father Mother One Child Grandfather
- Two Mothers or Two Fathers Three Children
- Foster Parent Three Children (not related)

The point of this discussion is to show children that families differ. It also opens up an opportunity for students to talk about their own families, something about which they may have felt uncomfortable. It helps to know that other parents have been divorced or that someone else's parent has died.

Related topics that can be discussed without evaluation include the following:

- Some mothers work outside the home and some do not.
- Sometimes relatives live together.
- Some children have a mother, a father, a stepmother, and a stepfather.
- Some children have half-brothers and half-sisters, or stepbrothers and stepsisters.
- Some children are adopted.
- Some families are multiracial.

Defining a Family.   With so many different arrangements of families, how do we know what a family is? Invite students to offer their definition of a family. Is a family a group of people who live together? What about when parents are divorced and a child may have more than one home? If you are adopted, are you part of a family? When you raise these topics, it shows students that it is okay for them to wonder about such questions.

Cultural background also affects how we define family. Some students may think of a family as composed of parents and children, known as a "nuclear" family. Others' conception may include several generations, with aunts, uncles, and cousins as well. This is called an "extended" family. Have students draw a picture of their "family." They can explain their drawing to the class. Some students may include their pets.

Family Legacies.   Sometimes what holds a family together is the memory of a shared history, often symbolized by an object that represents a link with the past. Ask students if they have any family treasures to remind them of previous generations. Share *The Keeping Quilt* by Patricia Polacco, a story of one family that managed to preserve memories in a quilt. Many families that immigrated to the United States were able to bring only a few objects to remind them of home. And, refugees may not have had even that opportunity. Descendants of slaves may prefer not to have physical reminders of past generations. The following books will stimulate discussion of the value of family legacies:

Carole Lexa Schaefer. *The Copper Tin Cup.* Illustrated by Stan Fellows. Candlewick, 2000. The cup that Sammy Carl drinks from every day, marked S. C., is the same one that his mother, grandpa, and great-aunt (an immigrant) used.

Deborah Turney Zagwyn. *The Winter Gift.* Tricycle, 2000. Gramma is moving and must sell the old piano, a family heirloom.

Students can talk about the importance of these symbols to them and their family and then write a story about a family treasure.

Getting Along in a Family.   Some of the most important relationships in a child's life are formed at home. All children face similar issues in getting along with their parents (or other adults) and their siblings. Introduce these topics by sharing a book such as *Max,* by Bob Graham, in which Max, a quiet type, feels overshadowed by his superhero parents. Following are more books to stimulate student responses:

James R. Berry. *Isn't My Name Magical? Sister and Brother Poems.* Illustrated by Shelly Hehenberger. Simon & Schuster, 1999. Familiar activities with families and friends, African American family.

Pat Brisson. *Little Sister, Big Sister.* Illustrated by Diana Cain Bluthenthal. Holt, 1999. Several short stories about two sisters.

Ralph Fletcher. *Relatively Speaking: Poems about Family.* Illustrated by W. L. Krudop. Orchard, 1999. Everyday and special events in life of young boy.

Bob Morris. *Crispin the Terrible.* Illustrated by Dasha Ziborova. Callaway, 2000. Crispin the cat thinks his family takes advantage of him and complains that he never gets a day off.

Janet S. Wong. *The Rainbow Hand: Poems about Mothers and Children.* Illustrated by Janet Hewitson. McElderry, 1999. Different perspectives on roles of mothers and sons/ daughters.

Family Responsibilities.   In every family, different people have different jobs to do. Everyone has something to contribute to the family, even the smallest child. Ask students what they do to help out. They may set the table, fold the laundry, watch a baby brother or sister, prepare food, go shopping, or help a parent by translating something into English. If parents work at home, students may even participate in the family business. Discuss how each of these tasks is important to the family. Point out how necessary even these small chores are in order for everyone to be able to live.

The following books show that in families, everyone is important.

Eve Bunting. *The Wednesday Surprise.* Clarion, 1989. A young girl secretly teaches her grandmother to read.

Kristine L. Franklin. *Dove Song.* Candlewick, 1999. In this novel, a brother and sister take on too many responsibilities when their father is gone and their mother becomes depressed.

Diane Hoyt-Goldsmith. *Arctic Hunter.* Holiday, 1992. The photographs in this book show how much is expected of each family member, including 10-year-old Reggie, when they go to their fishing camp each spring.

Ruth Yaffe Radin. *All Joseph Wanted.* Macmillan, 1991. Joseph loves his mother, but her illiteracy is hard on him. Finally, Joseph convinces his mother to go to an adult literacy class.

Marilyn Singer. *Josie to the Rescue.* Scholastic, 1999. Josie is eager to contribute to the family finances but none of her efforts turn out as planned.

Muriel Stanek. *I Speak English for My Mom.* Whitman, 1989. Lupe has to help her mother who doesn't speak English.

Family Routines.   All families have different daily routines and special rituals for marking celebrations. Students can compare their routine for waking up and preparing for the day with that of the girl in Jan Ormerod's *Sunshine.* Use student examples to practice sequencing skills. What do you do first? What happens next? What do you do last?

Share Byrd Baylor's classic *The Way to Start a Day,* illustrated by Peter Parnall, to stimulate discussion of different ways to greet the dawn. Students can add more examples to this exploration of how different cultures celebrate the sun. Have them describe how they would plan to celebrate the sun's rising. How would they celebrate the sunset?

Kate Banks. *The Night Worker.* Illustrated by Georg Hallensleben. Farrar, Straus & Giroux, 1999. A father shows his son what it's like to work the night shift on the construction site.

Eileen Spinelli. *Night Shift Daddy.* Illustrated by Melissa Iwai. Hyperion, 1999. A girl says goodnight to her daddy when he comes in from his night shift as she gets up in the morning.

Janet Wong. *Buzz.* Illustrated by Margaret Chodos-Irvine. Harcourt, 2000. A boy's morning routine shows a busy and buzzing world.

Two Mothers or Two Fathers.   Most discussions of families presume the existence of a mother and a father, even when only one parent lives at home. However, there are children whose family consists of two "Moms" or two "Dads." These children go to school like any other children. In addition, students may be related to or know of such families in the community. Classroom discussion of families headed by same-sex partners requires considerable sensitivity, yet open and careful discussion will allow children to feel more comfortable without exposing them to public humiliation and thoughtless ridicule by other children.

In your discussion, you can help students move from the stereotype that everyone lives in a nuclear family to the concept that a family can be built in many different ways and is held together by bonds of love and responsibility. *Homophobia,* the fear of people because of their sexual orientation, is based on intolerance for differences and prejudice. And just as with racism, sexism, or anti-Semitism, the fear of differences correlates closely with labeling others inferior or disgusting, and making them a target for violence. Your goal is for children to learn how to treat each other with respect, regardless of what beliefs they bring to school. Hateful behavior may only become a serious problem with students in high school and older but these attitudes start early and need to be addressed in elementary and middle school classrooms as part of teaching tolerance.

A book such as Christina Salat's *Living in Secret,* written for intermediate students, is useful for raising these issues in class. It presents the story of a girl who has to lie about her life with her mother and her mother's "girlfriend" and the effects that this concealment has on her.

Other books that present aspects of this sensitive situation are:

Rosamund Elwin and Michele Paulse. *Asha's Mums.* Illustrated by Dawn Lee. Women's Press, 1990. Asha's teacher doesn't understand about her two mums so they visit the class. Shows a diverse classroom in Toronto.

Keith Elliot Greenberg. *Zack's Story: Growing Up with Same-Sex Parents.* Lerner, 1996. For primary students, a family with two moms.

Leslea Newman. *Saturday Is Pattyday.* Illustrated by Annette Hegel. New Victoria Publishers, 1993. When lesbian mothers separate, Frannie is worried about losing a mom.

Johnny Valentine. *One Dad, Two Dads, Brown Dad, Blue Dads.* Illustrated by Melody Sarecky. Alyson Publishers, 1994. Lou has to answer questions about his dads. His friends discover that blue dads are like other dads.

Michael Willhoite. *Daddy's Roommate.* Alyson, 1990. When his parents divorce, a boy learns that his father is gay. Being gay means another way to love someone.

Jacqueline Woodson. *From the Notebooks of Melanin Sun.* Scholastic, 1995. A 13-year-old African American boy is upset when he finds out his mother is in love with a white woman.

Books about Different Family Arrangements.   Children's books are especially helpful in exposing students to a variety of different family arrangements. All children can benefit from a broadened perspective of this institution as it is rapidly changing in our society. Here are a few titles that you might keep for your library to read aloud or recommend to students when questions arise:

Picture Books

Roslyn Banish. *A Forever Family.* HarperCollins, 1992. Eight-year-old Jennifer is adopted after several foster homes. Shows multiracial families.

Catherine Bunin and Sherry Bunin. *Is That Your Sister? A True Story of Adoption.* Our Child Press, 1992. An adopted 6-year-old girl and her sister tell their story.

Lucille Clifton. *Everett Anderson's Nine Months Long.* Holt, 1987. Everett's mother has remarried and is going to have a baby. Look for other stories about Everett, an African American boy.

Karen Katz. *Over the Moon.* Holt, 1997. North Americans fly south of the border to pick up their adopted daughter.

David Kherdian. *A Song for Uncle Harry.* Illustrated by Nonny Hogrogian. Philomel, 1989. Set in the 1930s, this story describes the special relationship between Pete and Uncle Harry.

Rose Lewis. *I Love You Like Crazy Cakes.* Illustrated by Jane Dyer. Little, Brown, 2000. Mother's poignant tale of trip to China to adopt a baby girl.

Allen Say. *Allison.* Houghton Mifflin, 1997. Allison is angry because she looks like her Asian doll, not like her Caucasian parents. A story of the search for belonging.

Anne Herbert Scott. *Sam.* Illustrated by Symeon Shimin. Philomel, 1992. Reissue of an old favorite. Sam's family don't seem to want him around. Finally they realize he needs a job of his own.

Camille Yarbrough. *Cornrows.* Illustrated by Carole Byard. Sandcastles, 1991. As the girls have their hair braided into cornrows, Grammaw and Mama entertain them with stories of their African origins.

Books for Independent Readers

Candy Dawson Boyd. *Chevrolet Saturdays.* Macmillan, 1993. Joey, a fifth grader, can't accept his mother's remarriage, but his family understands him.

Melrose Cooper. *Life Riddles.* Holt, 1993. With Daddy gone and the family on welfare, mother tries to keep the family together.

Christopher Paul Curtis. *Bud, Not Buddy.* Delacorte, 1999. In the 1930s, Bud goes on the road to find his unknown dad.

Angela Johnson. *Heaven.* Simon & Schuster, 1998. Fourteen-year-old African American girl suddenly learns she is adopted and begins to question who she really is.

Patricia MacLachlan. *Journey.* Delacorte, 1991. Journey's mother leaves him when he is 11. He has to learn to accept her for what she is.

Susan Beth Pfeffer. *Make Believe.* Holt, 1993. Carrie and Jill's friendship is affected by Jill's parents' divorce.

Fred Rogers. *Let's Talk About It: Stepfamilies.* Photos by Jim Judkis. Putnam, 1997. A multiethnic cast talks about issues such as anger, difficulties to overcome, and step-sibling relations.

Marc Talbert. *The Purple Heart.* HarperCollins, 1992. Luke's picture of his dad as a war hero doesn't match the man who comes home.

When you read such stories as part of your regular time for reading aloud to the class, you help students feel comfortable knowing that there are other young people like themselves, and you provide a safe environment for discussing potentially difficult topics.

With the decline of neighborhood schools, students are less likely to be able to walk to school, live in the same area as the other students in their school, or see their classmates in other contexts besides school. In addition, teachers rarely live in the same neighborhood as their students and, consequently, are less familiar with students' daily lives. These factors contribute to a decline in the sense of a neighborhood community. In this section, we provide activities to enable students to explore the area that they live in and learn to pay attention to what they find around them.

Theme: The Neighborhood

Explore the concept of a neighborhood with your students. Does the area where your school is located have a name? Do all students live in the same neighborhood? Talk about the neighborhood. What are the most significant spots to students (church, school, park, ice cream store, etc.)? Bring a city map and have the students mark where they live. You can show students that a word such as *neighborhood* is a *concept,* an idea in people's minds, rather than a physical object, so that there may be more than one definition of the neighborhood.

Have students write a description of their neighborhood. How do they feel about it? What are some of the people and places in it? What sights, sounds, smells do they think of?

For another writing activity have students complete these sentences.

- My favorite place in the neighborhood is _____.
- I like it because _____.

- The most important thing that ever happened to me in the neighborhood was
_____.

- When I think of my neighborhood, I think of _____.

Students' responses to these prompts can be collected into an illustrated book entitled *Thoughts about Our Neighborhood.*

Have students compare their neighborhood to the one pictured in *A Street Called Home* by Aminah Brenda Lynn Robinson. This accordion-style, fold-out book portrays an African American neighborhood in Ohio in the 1940s. Students can use this book as a model to create their own books.

A Neighborhood Map.   Talk about maps with students. What are different kinds of maps? What goes into a map? What can maps be used for? In discussions about the neighborhood, students have talked about places and people of importance to them. Now each student can propose a list of elements to be included on a map of the neighborhood.

Construct a class map on a large sheet of butcher paper. Depending on the level of the students, you may decide to represent only one or two main streets, an interpretation of a larger area (not to scale), or a standard grid map with scale and/or cardinal directions. Students will enjoy developing symbols to use on the map (explained in the *key*) and illustrating or landscaping the map as much as they choose. A more elaborate project would be to create a relief map or three-dimensional model from clay, plaster, or similar material. Such a project will give students a different perspective of the place where all of them live.

Comparing Perspectives.   Maps can give you a different view of the world. Have students compare their own maps with maps prepared by other organizations. A street map of their neighborhood will show different relationships between areas. Aerial maps show features not visible from the ground. Many maps show political boundaries that are not physical features. Finally, all maps represent a particular perspective. Mapmakers tend to put themselves at the center and locate others based on that perspective. Students may be surprised to see that world maps published in other countries do not put North America at the center. See *Mapping the World* by Sylvia A. Johnson for more information on early maps and modern map-making technology.

Source for maps are:

State tourist offices, community Chambers of Commerce.

Federal government: Contact the Government Printing Office or the Superintendent of Documents, GPO, Washington, DC 20402.

U.S. Geological Survey, Earth Sciences Information Center, 507 National Center, Reston, VA 22092.

National Aeronautics and Space Administration (NASA), 400 Maryland Avenue SE, Washington, DC 20546.

Joel Makower, ed. *The Map Catalog.* Random House.

A Neighborhood Mural.   Have students make a mural to represent their neighborhood. They can do this individually or prepare a large class collage for a wall mural. Have them collect pictures and objects that portray their neighborhood. Think about:

- What do I see in my neighborhood?
- Who lives here?
- What do people do in the neighborhood?
- What kinds of buildings are found in the neighborhood?

Susan Meddaugh. *The Best Place.* Houghton Mifflin, 1999. Story about a wolf who loves his home but is persuaded to travel the world looking for someplace better. Moral: Being with friends is the best place of all.

A Place to Live.   One issue that has become critical in many neighborhoods is the increasing number of people, including families, who are living in cars or on the streets. Perhaps as many as 7 million Americans were homeless at some point in the late 1990s. Students may be aware of this problem through family and friends, or through the presence of people begging on the streets. Talk with students about the importance of having a place to live. All people, all living things need shelter.

A good introduction to the concept of shelter for primary-grade students is Mary Ann Hoberman's *A House Is a House for Me,* illustrated by Betty Fraser. This pattern book lists shelters for many animals in rhyme. The final line is "the earth is a house for us all."

Another book, *Houses and Homes* by Ann Morris, offers a global approach, with photographs of people and their homes from around the world. Also look at Michael Rosen's *Home: A Collaboration of 300 Distinguished Authors and Illustrators to Aid the Homeless,* which includes fifteen works that show the special meaning of home.

Enlist students in some form of action, to express their concerns about homelessness, such as writing to organizations that support better services, especially for homeless children. Share books such as Judith Berck's *No Place to Be: Voices of Homeless Children,* which includes quotations, photographs, and statistics about the causes and conditions of homelessness. Other books you can read with the class include the following:

Carol Fenner. *The King of Dragons.* McElderry, 1998. Boy and his father move into empty building and try to avoid discovery.

Paula Fox. *Monkey Island.* Orchard, 1991. Clay's mother has disappeared, leaving him in a welfare hotel. He takes to the streets, where he makes friends; but they're attacked, and Clay ends up in the hospital with pneumonia.

Monica Gunning. *A Shelter in Our Car.* Childrens's Book Press, 2004. A widowed mother and her daughter who have emigrated from Jamaica live in a car while the mother finds work.

Stephanie Tolan. *Sophie and the Sidewalk Man.* Four Winds, 1992. Sophie is saving money to buy a stuffed animal, but when she sees a homeless man sitting on the sidewalk, she decides to give him half of her savings.

A Community Guidebook.   What do students know about their community? How would they describe it to visitors? What do they think visitors might want to know about it?

Talk about the different elements that make up the community, such as people, services, places, history, and customs. Who might arrive in the community and need information? Have any students recently moved into the area? What did they have to find out? Talk about different types of visitors (including new arrivals), their reasons for coming, and the kind of information they would require. For example, if a family with young children moved into the area, they would want to know about schools, playgrounds, inexpensive family restaurants, and so on.

Decide what to include in your guidebook by determining who could benefit most from it. If there are other guidebooks to your area, examine them to discover what they have and have not included.

Divide students into small groups. Each group can take responsibility for a section of the book. They must decide among themselves how best to present their information (a list, description, story, illustration, etc.). Each student should have the opportunity to contribute something. Include other work done by students related to the community, such as the maps suggested in a previous activity.

When the groups have finished, their efforts can be assembled into a book that everyone will be proud of. You can have it duplicated for the parents, or even consider having it reproduced professionally and distributed by a group such as the local chamber of commerce.

Languages in Our Community.   Do students know what languages are spoken in their area? Begin with local names. What languages have influenced local names? Ask families. What languages are spoken in the students' families? Do students know people who speak different languages?

Make a map or chart of the area on which to record the information students find. Have them research local history to see what the earliest languages were. Were there any Native American groups living nearby? What language did they speak and what happened to them? What do names of local places mean in these languages? Ask who the first European settlers were and what languages they brought with them. Trace the language history down to the present time. Students should be able to discover what the major local language groups are and how long their speakers have been in the area.

Once the major languages are identified, they can become an important resource for further study. Plan lessons around examples from these languages. Bring in people who speak various languages so that students can hear what the languages sound like.

Community History.   Each community has its own history, reflecting the contributions of the various groups that comprise it. The history of the development of the community may reflect a mini-history of the state, or it may represent idiosyncratic development. In either case, students can learn a lot about the forces that formed this country by studying the example of their own community.

What is history? Talk about the idea of history. More than just a list of past presidents, history deals with events and their consequences, change, and the influence of the past on the present. Ask students why we would want to study history. Have them brainstorm a list of reasons and objectives for studying local history. What do they want to find out? The students might pose some of the following questions:

- Who was here first?
- What happened to them?
- Why did they come?
- What traces have they left behind?
- What did this area look like then?
- How did people live?
- Why is community important?

Share these books about the importance of maintaining the community:

DyAnne DiSalvo-Ryan. *Grandpa's Corner Store.* HarperCollins, 2000.

Margaree King Mitchell. *Uncle Jed's Barbershop.* Illustrated by James Ransome. Simon & Schuster, 1993.

Next, talk about where the students would go to find the information they are seeking. Have students suggest as many different sources as possible. They might mention the following:

- Visit the local library.
- Interview people who have lived there a long time.
- Read old newspapers.
- Review city records (archives)—maybe old maps.
- Search the Internet.

The results of student research can be compiled in a booklet that is organized according to the questions the students asked and the answers they found. Share this information with the community.

If your students are interested in continuing their study, consult David Weitzman's *My Backyard History Book.* This classic book, written by kids and teachers, is full of practical and creative ways to learn about the past and other people.

Interviewing: An Oral History Project.   Investigating your community's history can turn into a yearlong project if students decide to find out more information by interviewing people about their past. As students define questions they would like to have answered, they can begin to create a list of people who might know the answers. Brainstorm a list of possible interviewees. Have students tell everyone they know about this oral history project in order to identify more people to interview. They might ask the following questions:

- How long have you lived here?
- What was this town like when you first came?
- Where did you live when you were a child about my age?
- What was school like for you at that time?

Discuss what an interview is. What does the interviewer do? What is the interviewee supposed to do? Decide what questions you want to ask. Decide how you will record the information (tape recorder, notes on paper?). Prepare an interview schedule.

The most important aspect of this activity is the process that students go through, so the task should be carefully adapted to suit the level of the students. Students will come into contact with a different group of people (older people) and they will learn about people who are similar to and yet different from themselves. Children not only gain information related to social studies through this technique, they also increase language abilities. Both oral and written skills are developed as they conduct the interview, report back to the class, and record the results for a class book.

An English teacher in an Appalachian community developed the study of oral history to such an extent that his students have published several collections of their writings, starting with *The Foxfire Book* in 1972. There are now nine Foxfire books, edited by Eliot Wigginton and published by Doubleday Anchor Books. Information about the Foxfire Teacher Networks is available from Foxfire Teacher Outreach, P.O. Box 541, Mountain City, GA 30562.

Other examples of oral history are *Cracked Corn and Snow Ice Cream: A Family Almanac,* by Nancy Willard—recollections of rural relatives in Iowa and Wisconsin—and *Osceola: Memories of a Sharecropper's Daughter,* collected and edited by Alan Govenar and illustrated by Shane W. Evans, the story of one person's life, born in 1909.

A Community Time Line.   A time line can help students organize the information they have discovered about their community. Make a list of all the various dates, events, and historical periods that are important to your study of the community. Transfer this list, in chronological order, to a line drawn across several sheets of butcher paper. This can become a class mural as students add to the time line and update it. You can also have students draw or cut out illustrations for significant historical events.

Personalizing History.   When students compare their own lives with the history of their community, they can begin to see the connections between historical events and what has happened to them. What was happening in the community when they were born? Have them ask their parents or other relatives what they remember from that time. Students also can look up the front page of the local newspaper for their birthdate to see what people were thinking and talking about. Then they can report to the class on the significant events of the day that was most significant to them.

What has happened in the community and the world since the students were born? Using the time line they developed for their community and researching important inventions and world events, they can construct a list of the most significant happenings of the past ten years, more or less. (Opinions on what to include may vary among the students.) Now have students discuss and write about how these events affected them and their family. How has the world changed since they were born? How is it the same?

Community Action.   Students are members of a community and the problems of that community affect them, too. What do they think are the major issues facing their particular community today? Some responses may be:

- Drugs
- Graffiti
- Gang violence
- Traffic

How do these issues affect them? Often the opinions of young people are ignored in discussions. What would students like to say? They can make their voices heard by writing a letter to the editor of the local newspaper. Have students compose a letter in their cooperative learning groups or as a whole class. Discuss the essential features of an effective letter.

The following book provides examples of the impact that students' actions may have.

Susan Campbell Bartoletti. *Kids on Strike!* Photos by Lewis Hine. Houghton Mifflin, 1999. Labor strikes by young people in the nineteenth and twentieth centuries led to changes in child labor laws and working conditions.

Theme: Native Americans

Too often Native Americans have been seen only through the distorting stereotyped images of the romantic nature-lover, the exotic savage, or the source of spiritual wisdom. And now, after many years of hiding it in shame, having some Indian heritage is suddenly something about which to boast. But neither extreme, from the highly romanticized historical picture of chiefs and princesses to the modern Indian of declining culture and casinos, is an accurate depiction of the complexity of the position of Native Americans in the history of this country. Native Americans, although nearly exterminated by the European invaders, are still practicing a living culture as they adapt to a changing world.

Planning Your Study.   Before beginning a study of Native Americans in the United States, use some means of assessing student information and attitudes. This will provide an interesting and instructive comparison at the end of the study. Try some of these ideas:

- Have each student draw a picture of a Native American engaged in some activity.
- Ask students to complete this sentence at least three times: A Native American . . .
- Ask students to list as many Native American tribes as they can.

Put these sheets away until the study is completed. After the study, you might have the students repeat the same activities. Then compare the results.

Native American Tribes.   Many people are confused about the best way to refer to *American Indians* or *Native Americans.* The best solution is to specify the tribe you are referring to, instead of using the aggregate label for an extremely diverse group of people.

Draw a large outline map of the United States on which to locate the various groups of Indian tribes. They can be grouped as follows according to similar modes of living:

- *Eastern Woodland Area:*   Algonquin, Delaware, Iroquois, Massachuset, Mohawk, Mohegan, Narraganset, Onandaga, Penobscot, Powhatan, Tuscarora, Passamaquoddy, Pawtuket, Tippecanoe, Wampanoag, Wyandot.

- *Great Lakes Woodland Area:* Chippewa/Ojibwa, Huron, Illinois, Kickapoo, Miami, Oneida, Ottawa, Potawatomi, Sac and Fox, Seneca, Shawnee, Winnebago.
- *Southeastern Area:* Catawba, Cherokee, Creek, Lumbi, Natchez, Seminole, Yuchi.
- *North Central Plains Area:* Arapaho, Arikara, Assiniboine, Blackfeet, Cheyenne, Cree, Crow, Gros Ventre, Mandan, Pawnee, Shoshone, Sioux/Dakota.
- *South Central Plains Area:* Caddo, Chickasaw, Choctaw, Comanche, Iowa, Kaw/Kansa, Kiowa, Omaha, Osage, Ponca, Quapaw.
- *Southwest Area:* Apache, Hopi, Maricopa, Navajo, Papago, Pima, Pueblo, Zuñi.
- *California Area:* Chumash, Hoopa, Maidu, Mission, Modoc, Mohave, Mono, Pit River, Pomo, Tule River, Wailaki, Yahi, Yokuts, Yuma, Yurok.
- *Northwestern Plateau Area:* Bannock, Cayuse, Coeur D'Alene, Colville, Flathead, Kalispel, Klamath, Kootenai, Nez Percé, Nisqually, Paiute, Puyallup, Spokane, Ute, Walla-walla, Wasco, Washoe, Yakima.
- *Northwest Pacific Coast Area:* Aleut, Eskimo (Inuit), Haida, Lummi, Makah, Muckleshoot, Nootka, Quinault, Salish, Shoalwater, Snohomish, Suquamish, Tlingit.

An excellent resource for information about Indian tribes with maps is Carl Waldman's *Atlas of the North American Indian,* rev. ed. (Facts On File, 2000).

Native Americans in the United States.   There are more than 500 Indian tribes recognized in the United States, with most of them living on reservations in Western states (see Table 5.1). Although a small percentage of the total U.S. population (0.6%), Indians continue efforts to maintain a living culture.

Native groups in Canada include Indians, Inuit, and Métis (people of mixed heritage). Tribes in Mexico include the Maya, Nahuatl, Huichol, Purepecha, Tarahumara, Mazateco, Zapoteco, Nahua, Cora, Tzeltal, Otomi, and Mixteco. Students can investigate historical and contemporary Native groups in Latin America.

English Words from Native American Languages.   Words borrowed into English show how much the first settlers owed the Native Americans they encountered. Although the inhabitants spoke hundreds of distinct and fully developed languages, most of these words come from the Algonquin family of languages, spoken along the East Coast. Can students guess the English equivalent? Older students can develop a chart to show the relationship.

chitmunk	(chipmunk)	pawcohiccora	(hickory)
aroughcoun	(raccoon)	paccan	(pecan)
squnk	(skunk)	pasimenan	(persimmon)
ochek	(woodchuck)	msickquatash	(succotash)
musquash	(muskrat)	askootasquash	(squash)
moos	(moose)	tamahak	(tomahawk)
aposoun	(opossum)	mohkussin	(moccasin)

National Museum of the American Indian.   In September 2004, the *Smithsonian*'s cover displayed a handsome picture of the "new center for the hemisphere's first people," a curving limestone building with the Capitol visible in the background. The National Museum of the American Indian (NMAI) houses some 800,000 artifacts and 125,000 histori-

TABLE 5.1   NATIVE AMERICAN POPULATION (1990)

Tribe	Population	Percent
Cherokee	369,035	19.0
Navaho	225,298	11.6
Sioux	107,321	5.5
Chippewa	105,988	5.5
Choctaw	86,231	4.5
Pueblo	55,330	2.9
Apache	53,330	2.8
Iroquois	52,557	2.7
Lumbee	50,888	2.6
Creek	45,872	2.4
Blackfoot	37,992	2.0
Canadian/Latin American	27,179	1.4
Chickasaw	21,522	1.1
Tohono O'odham	16,876	.9
Potowatomi	16,719	.9
Seminole	15,564	.8
Pima	15,074	.8
Tlingit	14,417	.7
Alaskan Athabascans	14,198	.7
Cheyenne	11,809	.6
Comanche	11,436	.6
Paiute	11,369	.6
Osage	10,430	.5
Puget Sound Salish	10,384	.5
Yaqui	9,838	.5
All	1,937,391	100.00

For more information about the federal/Indian reservations and trust areas, look at <*www.doc.gov/edu/html/indianres.htm*>

cal photographs selected to bear the message "We are still here." The art featured ranges from traditional beadwork to paintings by such modern artists as Rick Bartow, a Vietnam veteran and Yurok Indian from Oregon.

This beautiful museum in a prominent position on the Mall in Washington, DC, should help us all recognize the contributions of the many tribes who have lived in the Americas over the centuries, as well as help us see them more clearly as they exist today. As Ron His Horse is Thunder, President of Sitting Bull College on the Standing Rock Reservation in North Dakota, states:

Americans tend to clump us all together, not realizing there are vast differences between Indians of various geographic regions, as well as between Indian Tribes with those regions. Too often history books portray us as either savages that stood in the way of progress or as naturalists in tune with nature. But what they don't show is that we made contributions to the United States. They don't tell about how over 50 percent of the world's current food supply comes from plants that Native Americans cultivated. Rarely do they ever show that Native Americans practiced horticulture and we used science to do that. Another contribution is medicine. A good many current medicines in this world came from plants that Native Americans knew about and knew how to use to take care of certain ailments. And they shared that knowledge with the non-Indian world.

Gifts from the Native Americans.   Students will be interested in learning of the many things we gained from the Native Americans. They knew the best trails and ways of traveling across the country by canoe and by snowshoe. They invented hammocks. The Native Americans were the first, too, to grow and use tobacco and rubber. They introduced white settlers to the following foods that we use today:

corn	tomatoes	cranberries	maple sugar
potatoes	vanilla	chicle (for chewing gum)	artichokes
chilies	avocados	beans	hominy
pineapples	peanuts	chocolate	popcorn

Have several students prepare an illustrated chart of these foods. You may experiment with hominy or dishes that are easy to make in the classroom.

Of course, Native American contributions were not limited to food supplies. The following books suggest areas that advanced students can explore:

Jack Weatherford. *Indian Givers: How the Indians of the Americas Transformed the World.* Fawcett, 1989.

Jack Weatherford. *Native Roots: How the Indians Enriched America.* Fawcett, 1991.

Native American Place Names.   Many state names, such as Massachusetts, originated in Native American languages. Names of many rivers, such as the Ohio and Mississippi, and cities, such as Pontiac, Michigan, and Chicago, Illinois, also originated from Native American languages.

Look for evidence of specific tribes. For example, there are many Abenaki place names in Maine, Vermont, and New Hampshire.

Androscoggin	place where fish are cured
Connecticut	the long river
Katahdin	the principal mountain
Kennebec	long water without rapids
Merrimack	at the deep place
Nashua	between streams

For more information on where names come from, see *Indian Place Names of New England* by John C. Huden.

Prepare a map on which to locate Native American names. Include a chart to explain what the names mean and where they come from.

The "New World" in 1492.   What did the world of the Native Americans look like when the European explorers arrived, beginning with Columbus in 1492? Students may be surprised to learn that there were no horses (dogs and turkeys were the only domestic animals). But there were a number of complex cultures, based in different regions, and trading with others. We tend to think only of the great Aztec and Inca civilizations, but there may have been about 20 million Indians in North America around 1492. In the century following, the Indian population dropped by as much as 95 percent.

Dennis Fradin's historical biography *Hiawatha: Messenger of Peace* provides much background information about the Iroquois. Although Hiawatha lived 500 years ago, he made significant contributions to American history. As a leader in his tribe, he helped set up the Iroquois Confederacy, the most politically complex group in 1492. Iroquois customs and beliefs eventually influenced the development of the U.S. Constitution. Also see volumes on the Iroquois and the Mohawk in the Chelsea House series *Indians of North America* for historical data.

For more information on life in 1492, see the following:

Jean Fritz, Jamake Highwater, Margaret Mahy, Patricia and Fredrick McKissack, and Katherine Paterson. *The World in 1492.* Holt, 1992. Provides a detailed description of each part of the world—Africa, Asia, Europe, Australia, the Americas—and how the people there lived at that time.

What Happened to the Native Americans after 1492?   After setting the stage with a picture of the Native Americans before the European conquest, continue the story and explore how the Native Americans were affected by it. Several books deal with specific tribes in specific regions.

Eva Costabel. *The Early People of Florida.* Atheneum, 1993. Presents the history of tribal groups such as Calusa and Tequesta present in 1492. First the Spanish and the French fought over their lands, then the British came.

Louise Erdrich. *The Birchbark House.* Hyperion, 1999. Life of an Ojibwa girl on island in Lake Superior in 1847.

Russell Freedman. *An Indian Winter.* Paintings and drawings by Karl Bodmer. Holiday House, 1992. Journal of a German prince and scenes painted by a Swiss artist who spent a winter with the Mandans in 1833–1834 in today's North Dakota. Afterwards, the Mandan and Hidatsa were devastated by smallpox and their traditional way of life vanished. The detail of this text and pictures bring to life the vanished customs of the people.

Paul Goble. *Death of the Iron Horse.* Aladdin, 1993. This picture book tells the true story of the Cheyenne's struggle to preserve their way of life after soldiers and settlers invade their territory with the steam locomotive.

Beatrice O. Harrell. *Longwalker's Journey: A Novel of the Choctaw Trail of Tears.* Dial, 1999. Story based on author's family, how a boy survived a tragic journey.

Kathleen Kudlenski. *Night Bird: A Story of the Seminole Indians.* Illustrated by James Watling. Viking, 1993. Eleven-year-old Seminole girl must leave Florida Everglades in 1840 to move to Oklahoma.

S. D. Lang. *Gift Horse: A Lakota Story.* Abrams, 1999. A boy's rites of passage into manhood.

Albert Marrin. *Cowboys, Indians, and Gunfighters: The Story of the Cattle Kingdom.* Atheneum, 1993. Outlines the destruction of the Plains Indians' way of life, from 1521 when the first cattle arrived from Hispaniola to the killing off of the buffalo.

How Native Americans Live Today.   Balance historical information with contemporary accounts that show real people living in today's world. Bring your historical account of Native American life up to the present. Students may be surprised to realize there are modern Native American children like themselves, not just characters out of history. Young Native Americans face many of the same issues concerning growing up that all children face. In addition, they may struggle to learn more about their heritage and the history of their people. They may wonder why people are prejudiced against them or their people. And they face the question of how to maintain their culture in a hostile world. Look for a variety of children's books to show students what it feels like to be a Native American today.

George Ancona. *Powwow.* Harcourt Brace, 1993. The Montana Crow Fair is the largest powwow in the country. Photographs by the author.

Susan Braine. *Drumbeat . . . Heartbeat: A Celebration of the Powwow.* Lerner, 1995. Traditions from the Northern Cheyenne reservation in Montana. Photographs by the author.

Joseph Bruchac. *Eagle Song.* Dial, 1997. Fourth-grade Mohawk boy is teased for being Indian; his father tells class the real story of Hiawatha, the Iroquois leader who sought peace.

Robert Crum. *Eagle Drum: On the Powwow Trail with a Young Grass Dancer.* FourWinds, 1994. Shows 9-year-old Louis and his family. Photographs by the author.

Normee Ekoomiak. *Arctic Memories.* Holt, 1990. A picture book of an Inuit childhood in Quebec illustrates a way of life that is almost extinct. Text in Inuktitut and English.

Jean Craighead George. *Water Sky.* Harper, 1987. Lincoln Noah Stonewright goes from Boston to Barrow, Alaska, to stay with an Eskimo family and learn what happened to his uncle, who had wanted to stop the Eskimo whaling there.

Susan Hazen-Hammond. *Thunder Bear and Ko: The Buffalo Nation and Nambe Pueblo.* Dutton, 1999. Trying to preserve traditions in New Mexico.

Diane Hoyt-Goldsmith. *Apache Rodeo.* Holiday House, 1995. Ten-year-old Felicita, living in Arizona, reflects on her history and traditions as she prepares for the rodeo.

Diane Hoyt-Goldsmith. *Lacrosse: The National Game of the Iroquois.* Holiday, 1998. A fine photo-essay; photos by L. Migdale.

Marcia Keegan. *Pueblo Boy: Growing Up in Two Worlds.* Cobblehill, 1991. Tells of 10-year-old boy's life; many photos.

Russ Kendall. *Eskimo Boy: Life in an Inupiaq Village.* Scholastic, 1992. Photographs of 7-year-old Norman, who lives in a remote village off the northwest coast of Alaska.

Sandra King. *Shannon: An Ojibway Dancer.* Lerner, 1993. A 13-year-old girl's life combines tradition and modern customs as she prepares to dance in a powwow in Minnesota. Photographs by Catherine Whipple. From *We Are Still Here* series.

Barbara Mitchell. *Red Bird.* Illustrated by Todd Doney. Lothrop, 1996. Powwows of the Eastern Indians; notes multiracial aspects of tribes.

David Morrison and George-Hebert Germain. *The Inuit: Glimpses of an Arctic Past.* University of Washington Press, 1996. A young girl tells the history of the Copper Inuit culture.

Tryntje Van Seymour Ness. *The Gift of Changing Woman.* Holt, 1993. When an Apache girl comes of age, she goes through a ceremony to teach her the story of creation and her place in the world. Includes pictures by Apache artists and words of the Apache people.

Laurie O'Neill. *The Shawnees: People of the Eastern Woodlands.* Millbrook Press, 1995. Part of a series: *Native Americans;* see also *The Inuit: People of the Arctic.*

Gordon Regguinti. *The Sacred Harvest: Ojibway Wild Rice Gathering.* Lerner, 1992. Color photographs; informative text about processing the rice.

Monty Roessel. *Kinaaldá: A Navajo Girl Grows Up.* Lerner, 1993. In recent years, Navajos have adapted an ancient coming-of-age ceremony for 13-year-old girls to modern days. Photographs by the author.

Monty Roessel. *Songs from the Loom.* Lerner, 1996. Photo essay of a young girl learning to weave.

Cheryl Savageau. *Muskrat Will Be Swimming.* Harcourt, 1999. Illustrated by Robert Hynes. Girl learns a positive lesson about handling name-calling when her grandfather tells a Seneca tale about muskrat.

Cynthia L. Smith. *Jingle Dancer.* Morrow, 2000. Illustrated by Cornelius Van Wright and Ying Hwa-Hu. Describes the traditional dance of the Muscogee (Creek) Nation.

Virginia Driving Hawk Sneve. *The Hopis: A First Americans Book.* Holiday, 1995. Abundant pictures of traditional Hopi life.

Frank J. Staub. *Children of the Tlingit.* Carolrhoda, 1999. Many photos of different children from this Pacific Northwest Indian culture.

Craig Kee Strete. *The World in Grandfather's Hands.* Clarion, 1995. An 11-year-old Cherokee boy who loses his father and moves to the city feels uprooted.

Rina Swentzell. *Children of Clay: A Family of Pueblo Potters.* Lerner, 1992. Story of a Tewa family in New Mexico.

Linda Yamane. *Weaving a California Tradition.* Illustrated by Dugan Aguilar. Lerner, 1997. Follows 11-year-old Western Mono girl's life; shows full process of weaving a basket.

Native American Leaders. Not all Native American are chiefs or princesses. Combat the stereotyped ideas of Indians with examples of real individuals as they struggle with questions of identity.

Joseph Bruchac. *Sacajawea: The Story of Bird Woman and the Lewis and Clark Expedition.* Harcourt, 2000. Skillful writing techniques; alternating first person narrative by Sacajawea and William Clark.

Nancy Lobb. *Extraordinary Native Americans.* J. Weston Walch, 1997. Sixteen brief biographies.

Morgan Monceaux and Ruth Katcher. *My Heroes, My People.* Farrar, 1999. Brief biographies and thirty-seven striking portraits of Native Americans and African Americans important in settlement of the West; includes the well-known figures as well as lesser known.

Maria Tallchief and Rosemary Wells. *Tallchief: America's Prima Ballerina.* Viking, 1999. Illustrated by Gary Kelley. First-person narrative about Maria's struggle to become a famous dancer.

Native American Stories and Folktales.   Folklore from the various Native American tribes is an excellent source for learning more about culture and for storytelling activities. Older students can learn one of these tales to present to students in the primary grades. All of these stories adapt well to other modes of oral presentation, such as Reader's Theater. In addition, when you read one of the teaching stories to the class, students can respond to the moral by drawing a picture and discussing what it means to them.

When selecting folktales for use with students, consider carefully the image presented of the people in the group. Many authors have written versions of Native American tales without respect for their authentic cultural background. Contrast these with books by writers such as Paul Goble and Gerald McDermott, who are scrupulous in citing the sources of their stories and in presenting appropriate cultural context in their illustrations. Also look for books by Native American authors, which have become more available as individuals and tribal organizations promote culturally sensitive materials. For example, a booklist of recommended works is available from Oyate, 2702 Mathews Street, Berkeley, CA 94702.

Shonto Begay. *Ma'ii and Cousin Horned Toad.* Scholastic, 1992. This Navajo teaching tale includes text in Navajo. Coyote is hungry but is too lazy to get his own food.

John Bierhorst. *The People with 5 Fingers: A Native California Creation Tale.* Illustrated by Robert Parker. Marshall Cavendish, 2000. Told in the days when each valley was home to a different Indian Nation.

Joseph Bruchac. *Between Earth and Sky: Legends of Native American Sacred Places.* Illustrated by Thomas Locker. Harcourt, 1996. Describes the seven sacred directions that represent the unity of life and our oneness with the natural world, seen and unseen.

Edward Field. *Magic Words.* Harcourt, 1998. Illustrated by Stefano Vitale. Inuit tale from Greenland.

Mary-Joan Gerson. *People of Corn: A Mayan Story.* Illustrated by Carla Golembe. Little, 1995. A creation story.

Paul Goble. *Iktomi Loses His Eyes: A Plains Indian Story.* Orchard, 1999. One of many trickster tales about Iktomi.

C. Shana Greger, retold. *The Fifth and Final Sun.* Houghton, 1994. An Aztec story tells of the origin of the sun.

Leanne Hinton, trans. *Ishi's Tale of Lizard.* Farrar Straus Giroux, 1992. Recent translation of a Yahi tale. Ishi, the sole survivor of the Yahi people, emerged from hiding in 1911.

Bruce Hucko. *A Rainbow at Night: The World in Words and Pictures by Navajo Children.* Chronicle, 1997.

Michael Lacapa. *Antelope Woman: An Apache Folktale.* Northland, 1992.

Jonathan London with Lanny Pinola, retold. *Fire Race.* Illustrated by Sylvia Long. Chronicle Books, 1993. The tale of what happens when Coyote steals fire from yellow jackets.

Rafe Martin. *The Eagle's Gift.* Illustrated by Tatsuro Kiuchi. Putnam, 1997. In this Inuit tale, a boy brings joy to his people.

Gerald McDermott. *Raven: A Trickster Tale from the Pacific Northwest.* Harcourt Brace Jovanovich, 1993. How the raven steals the sun from the Sky Chief so that the people can have light.

Paul Morin. *Animal Dreaming: An Aboriginal Dreamtime Story.* Harcourt, 1998. Boy's first walkabout to the Australian outback; rites of passage.

Howard Norman. *The Girl Who Dreamed Only Geese and Other Tales of the Far North. . . .* Illustrated by Leo and Diane Dillon. Harcourt, 1997. The best of the oral tradition, taken directly from Inuit storytellers.

Jerrie Oughton. *How the Stars Fell into the Sky: A Navajo Legend.* Illustrated by Lisa Desimini. Houghton Mifflin, 1992.

Mary Helen Pelton and Jacqueline DiGennaro. *Images of a People: Tlingit Myths and Legends.* Illustrated by Jennifer Brady-Morales. Libraries Unlimited, 1994. Description of the culture accompanied by tales.

Tom Pohrt, retold. *Coyote Goes Walking.* Farrar, 1995. Four brief stories, including a creation myth.

Carol Purdy. *Nesuya's Basket.* Illustrated by Paulette Lambert. Roberts Rinehart, 1997. Based on Maidu (California) Indian culture, part of *The Council for Indian Affairs* series.

Michael J. Rosen. *The Dog Who Walked with God.* Illustrated by Stan Fellows. Candlewick, 1998. Creation myth.

Gayle Ross, retold. *How Turtle's Back Was Cracked: A Traditional Cherokee Tale.* Illustrated by Murv Jacob. Dial, 1995.

Margaret Shaw-MacKinnon. *Tiktala.* Illustrated by Liszlo Gal. Holiday House, 1996. Wonderful art; realistic portrayal of Inuit.

Janet Stevens, retold. *Coyote Steals the Blanket: A Ute Tale.* Holiday House, 1993.

Harriet Peck Taylor, retold. *Coyote and the Laughing Butterflies.* Macmillan, 1995. A tale from the Tewa Pueblo.

Clifford Trafzer, ed. *Blue Down, Red Earth.* Archer, 1996. New Native American storytellers.
Nancy Wood. *Sacred Fire.* Illustrated by Frank Howell. Doubleday, 1998. Pueblo chronicle.

When studying Native American folklore with students, encourage them to look for patterns. Can they find several examples of a "trickster" tale? Compare some Coyote tales with tales in other cultures, such as Anansi stories in African traditions. Are there several versions of one tale? How do the versions differ? In folklore, stories are transmitted orally, so several different written versions may all be authentic. What values do these stories teach?

Other teaching ideas can be found in this collection:

Michael Caduto and Joseph Bruchac. *Keepers of the Animals: Native American Stories and Wildlife Activities for Children.* Fulcrum, 1997. An audiocassette of this book was published in 1992. Look for other examples of Caduto and Bruchac reading and telling stories.

Making Navajo Fry Bread.   Create a learning center at which children can take turns making a semiauthentic version of fry bread (see Figure 5.5). (Teacher supervision is necessary for this activity.)

Directions

Fill the electric skillet half full of oil. Turn on high to heat.
Measure into bowl:

4 c. flour	1 tsp. salt
3 tsp. baking powder	1½ c. water

Gradually add the water as you stir.

FIGURE 5.5   FRY BREAD LEARNING CENTER

Knead the dough until it does not stick to your hands. Add a little more flour as needed. Divide the dough into small balls. Then flatten them until thin and make a hole in the center like a doughnut. Slide into hot oil. Fry on each side until light brown. Remove and drain on layer of paper towels. Eat while warm.

Games and Sports Originating with the Native Americans.   A number of books contain information about Indian children's games, for example:

Gail Farber and Michelle Lasagna. *Whispers from the First Californians: A Story of California's First People.* Magpie Publications, 1994.

Joy Miller. *American Indian Games.* Childrens Press, 1996.

Luther Standing Bear. *My Indian Boyhood.* University of Nebraska Press, 1959.

Many of the sports we know today originated in games the Native Americans first played. They played shinny, a game with a puck, similar to ice hockey. Native American children played such games as hide and seek, follow-the-leader, crack-the-whip, prisoner's base, and blindman's bluff. They also had games not unlike hopscotch, marbles, and jack straws.

For more information about Native American sports and how to play them, look for *Sports & Games the Indians Gave Us* by Alex Whitney. This author shows children how to make equipment for use in the games described. Stick dice are easy to make, for example. Use a stick about one-half inch wide and four inches long. With a knife round off the ends of the stick. Paint one side red and paint a multicolor design on the other side. With the red side counting as one point and the design as two, see who can get twenty points first (see Figure 5.6).

Studying Native American Masks.   Begin a study of masks by showing the excellent film *The Loon's Necklace* (Britannica Films, 11 minutes), a legend told by the artful filming of authentic masks from the Pacific Northwest. Have students explore fiction and

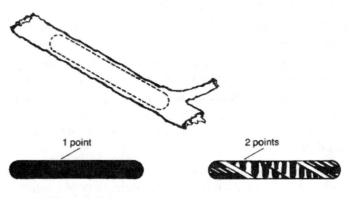

FIGURE 5.6   STICK DICE

IDEAS IN ACTION!

Wiping Away of Tears

In 1986, a small group of Lakota Indians were looking for a way to break the cycle of poverty and hopelessness found among Indians, especially on the reservations. They organized an event that would provide an opportunity to grieve, a symbolic journey from the site of Sitting Bull's death to that of the Wounded Knee massacre, culminating in a ceremony called the "Wiping Away of Tears."

In 1990, the 100th anniversary of Wounded Knee, the Lakota elders decided to make this an annual event and focus on teaching the future generations. It has continued every year since as the Future Generations Riders and has become an important coming-of-age ritual for the community.

"The grieving helps the children to accept who we are as a people and to grow from that. The hope is that these kids will someday become young leaders and help our nation to once again become whole," says Vina White Hawk, the only woman to participate in the original ride. However, "the ride is only the beginning. For 100 years, our young people have been taught that they needed to forget about being Indian to succeed. Today, we're trying to reverse that by letting them know that our culture is important and that being Indian is a *great* thing," says His Horse Is Thunder, president of Sitting Bull College in South Dakota, one of thirty-four tribal colleges on reservations across the country.

Research the history of Native Americans in your area. Interview representative members of local tribes. Share this information with others in your school.

---

nonfiction about Native Americans to learn about the importance of masks in Native cultures. Following are a few resources to use:

California Indian Arts. A full-color calendar of California Indian art. Heyday Books, Box 9145, Berkeley, CA 94709.

Indian Handicrafts Catalog. Southwest Indian Foundation, Box 86, Gallup, NM 87302-0001. A wide range of dolls, pottery, drums, and so on of interest to children and adults.

Yvonne Y. Merrill. *Hands on Alaska: Art Activities for All Ages.* K/ITS, 1994. (8115 Jewell Lake Road, Anchorage, AK 99502.) Beautiful book includes pictures of artifacts and instruction showing students how to replicate original Native American crafts. Highly recommended.

Students can create their own masks from heavy cardboard. Folding the cardboard in half makes it fit the child's face more closely. A piece of elastic holds it securely in place. The shape of the mask and the way the eyes are developed serve to suggest the person or animal. It is not necessary, however, to be overly realistic. Masks can then be used to tell folktales, perhaps pourquoi tales the children have written.

Native American Poetry.   Share Native American poems with the children in your room. Display the following poem so that students can read and discuss it together.

MAY I WALK

On the trail marked with pollen may I walk,
With grasshoppers about my feet may I walk,
With dew about my feet may I walk,
With beauty may I walk,
With beauty before me, may I walk,
With beauty behind me, may I walk,
With beauty above me, may I walk,
With beauty under me, may I walk,
With beauty all around me, may I walk,
In old age wandering on a trail of beauty, lively, may I walk,
In old age wandering on a trail of beauty, living again, may I walk,
It is finished in beauty.

—Navajo

Reading poetry written by people from another culture is an excellent way of learning about shared values and cultural differences. Feature examples from the following excellent collections.

Shonto Begay. *Navajo: Visions and Voices across the Mesa.* Scholastic, 1995. Art and poetry illustrate the struggle for balance and harmony in contemporary Native life.

Arlene Hirschfelder and Beverly Singer, eds. *Rising Voices: Writings of Young Native Americans.* Scribner's, 1992. Poems and short prose by middle and high school students represent a variety of tribes and regions. The poems were chosen to reflect concerns about identity, education, and harsh realities.

Hettie Jones. *The Trees Stand Shining: Poetry of the North American Indians.* Illustrated by Robert Andrew Parker. Dial, 1993. These oral tradition poems are really folk chants and songs, preserved for generations and only written down and translated in the nineteenth century. Each is short, identified by tribe, and grouped by similar topic.

Neil Philip, ed. *Songs Are Thoughts: Poems of the Inuit.* Illustrated by Maryclare Foa. Orchard, 1995. Originally collected by Danish ethnologist in 1920s, these poems are meant to be sung. Includes information on cultural context.

Brian Swann. *Touching the Distance: Native American Riddle Poems.* Harcourt, 1998. Illustrated by M. Rendon.

When the Rain Sings: Poems by Young Native Americans. National Museum of the American Indian. Smithsonian. Simon & Schuster, 1999.

After reading some of these examples, students can choose to write poems based on similar themes of nature or identity. Students can also write poems as a response to the unit on Native Americans, to show their reactions to what they have learned.

A Mural of Native American Life.   After students have gained information through reading and discussing topics related to Native American life, have them plan a large mural to which each one can contribute. The space of the mural might be considered similar to the map of the United States. Roughly, then, space could be allocated to activities associated with the Plains Indians, those of the Southwest, the Pacific Northwest, and so on. Sketch this plan on the board.

Bring in books with pictures that suggest scenes to be included. Crayons can be used for the figures, and the background can be painted in with pale brown or light green, as appropriate. When the mural is completed, display it in the school hall or a room where all can see it.

A Culminating All-School Assembly.   Plan a school assembly to share the results of your study. Let students discuss various ways they can present an informative and entertaining program. Consider some of the following activities:

- An introduction (the purpose of your study and some of the things you learned).
- Presentation of the mural with an explanation of the many Native American tribes in what is now the United States.
- Reader's Theater presentation of folklore from the tribe native to your area, which might include music.
- Demonstration of Native American sports, dances, and so on.
- Creative dramatization of a Native American story.
- An invitation to visit your room to see the things you have made.

CONNECTIONS

The social studies curriculum covers a broad range of multicultural topics. It offers particularly strong opportunities for infusing multicultural education across the entire program of study at any level. In the self-contained elementary classroom teachers find it easy to present a kind of humanities approach that includes the language arts and reading with the different performing arts in a thematic study that offers appropriate learning activities for all children. At the middle school level, this same approach works well with a two-hour core curriculum program which enables teachers to explore topics in some depth.

FOLLOW-THROUGH

Expanding Your RTP

l. Consider the following words written by Arthur Ashe in 1993:

When I think of the many horrors of slavery, the destruction of the family strikes me as probably the worst. We are still facing the consequences of that destruction.

Who is Arthur Ashe? What is the meaning of his words? How do you feel about this quotation?

2. Write several paragraphs about racism. What does it mean to you? Is racism still present in your community?

Working with your CLG

1. Choose a theme that you think would be especially useful as you begin teaching. Work together to collect resources and information to help you develop this study. Share your findings with the rest of the class. (If each group prepares copies of its thematic study to give to the whole group, each one of you will have a number of studies ready to go when you enter the classroom.)
2. Read one of the books suggested for a theme described in this chapter. Report to your CLG so that everyone will become acquainted with a number of the tradebooks listed.

GROWING A PROFESSIONAL LIBRARY

Thura Al-Windawi. *Thura's Diary.* Viking, 2004. The story of a young Iraqi girl in Baghdad.

Russell Freedman. *In Defense of Liberty: The Story of America's* Bill of Rights. Holiday, 2003.

Christine B. Moen. *Read Alouds and Performance Reading: A Handbook of Activities for the Middle School Classroom.* Christopher Gordon, 2004.

*A question is
a little lever
that opens up
inquiry*

*Naomi
Shihab Nye*

Teaching Science and Mathematics Multiculturally

Science and mathematics are interconnected as we learn more about our universe and how we can protect our planet, our bodies and how we can prevent disease, and how we can capture technology to improve our lives. Math and science have become increasingly important around the world.

In this chapter we will investigate the multicultural ramifications of these two fields of endeavor. As we become more aware of our interdependence, nations are uniting to address such problems as water and air pollution and others related to maintaining the Earth. Everyone is excited about the possibilities for exploring space and the new findings in astronomy.

The United States plays a leading role in both science and mathematical studies. It has lent its vocabulary to these fields so that, for example, Chinese and Italians alike use English in guiding air traffic or talking about computer technology. Mathematicians and scientists have developed universal languages that we share around the world.

TEACHING SCIENCE MULTICULTURALLY

Talk with students about what science is. Bring out the understanding that science is very important to life in the United States and in the world. Have them suggest appropriate activities to enlarge their knowledge about multiculturalism and science.

Science in the News

Have students bring in copies of the daily newspaper. Working in pairs, they can search out news about science around the world. This news may be in a special section; however, it may also be on the Home Page or in the Business section. Have each pair present one finding to the group until all have been covered. Comment on the different kinds of science represented. Note how our planet depends on science and how interdependent we all are.

Science and ESL Students

Judith Rosenthal's *Teaching Science to Language Minority Students* (Taylor & Francis, 1996) presents linguistically modified methods of science instruction. The author discusses such topics as diversity of learning styles among LEP students, the many cultures of the science classroom, and pedagogical issues. This book can be ordered from Multilingual Matters Ltd., 1900 Frost Road, #101, Bristol, PA 19007.

Women and Science

Considerable effort has been expended to increase girls' interest in science during the early years with the hope that they will continue with careers in science. Providing experience with science in industry and meeting women scientists who serve as role models are some of the methods used nationwide. The following filmed resources are recommended:

Discovering Women: Six Remarkable Women Scientists (VHS, color, six 1-hour videos). This outstanding series chronicles the stories of contemporary women scientists and their efforts to overcome prejudices in male-dominated fields. The scientists include a physicist, an archaeologist, a molecular biologist, a computational neuroscientist, a geophysicist, and a chemist. Encourage your library to order the set from Films for the Humanities and Sciences, Box 2053, Princeton, NJ 08543.

Jane Goodall: A Life in the Wild (VHS, color, 31 min.). Fascinating story of Goodall's life and work studying the chimpanzee. Films for the Humanities and Sciences, 1996, address above.

Evelyn Fox Keller: Science and Gender (VHS, color, 30 min.). Keller's life as a theoretical physicist working in mathematical biology and gender issues throughout the history of science. Films for the Humanities and Sciences, 1996, address above.

A Virtual Fieldtrip

The Africa Trail. (CD-ROM for Macintosh and Windows, Teacher's Guide with Educational Version) By the makers of *The Oregon Trail,* this complex simulation program takes students on a bike trek through Africa from Tunisia to South Africa. Although real problems (starvation, ethnic conflicts) and obstacles (rough roads) arise to be solved, the focus is on the people of the continent. The program presents the rich diversity of Africa today. Recommended for grades 6–12. Published by MECC, 1995. (See also *The Amazon Trail.*)

Virginia Walker suggests the following Book Connections:[1]

Nancy Farmer. *A Girl Named Disaster.* Orchard, 1996. Eleven-year-old Nhamo escapes from betrothal to a cruel old man by undertaking a dangerous trek across Mozambique and Zimbabwe.

Beverley Naidoo. *No Turning Back: A Novel of South Africa.* HarperCollins, 1997. A story of homeless young blacks struggling to live in post-apartheid Johannesburg.

Internet Connections

Kruger National Park. *<www.pix.za/Kruger_Park/>* The Park Warden takes you on a safari through the game reserve in South Africa.

South African National Gallery. *<www.gem.co.za/sang/index.html>* Touring the collections in this Capetown museum.

Categories

A vocabulary game that helps ESL students is the familiar "Categories." Most often used as a unit review, it consists of a word (the topic) written down the left side of a sheet and several categories across the top. Students fill in words under each category that begin with the letters of the topic word (see Table 6.1). For example, after discussing the subject of "space" for several days, give students this challenging exercise.

This game works best if there is more than one possible answer. If you want to make it more difficult, you can give points for each letter and reward students who have the longest entries.

TABLE 6.1   CATEGORIES

	Heavenly Bodies	*Colors*	*People/Professions*
S	Saturn	silver	scientist
P	Pluto	purple	pilot
A	Asteroid	azure	astronaut
C	Ceres	cocoa	chemist
E	Earth	emerald	engineer

Reading about Real Scientists

Autobiography and biography about scientists is becoming more available for students of all levels. Here are a few titles:

Steve Parker. *Marie Curie and Radium.* HarperCollins, 1992.

Andrea Davis Pinkney. *Dear Benjamin Baneker.* Gulliver Books, 1994.

Wendy Towle. *The Real McCoy: The Life of an African American Inventor.* Scholastic, 1993.

Ethlie Ann Vare. *Adventurous Spirit: A Story about Ellen Swallow Richards.* Carolrhoda, 1992.

Nonfiction about Science

Children's literature and that for young adults presents much informational material about science. Introduce students to the following:

Robert Cattoche. *Computers for the Disabled.* Watts, 1986.

Anne Ehrlich and Paul Ehrlich. *Earth.* Watts, 1987.

Maze Productions. *I Want to Be Series.* Harcourt, 2001.

Noel Simon. *Vanishing Habitats.* Gloucester, 1987.

Bernie Zubrowski. *Mirrors.* Morrow, 1992.

Science Themes in Fiction

Encourage students to explore the many novels that have science backgrounds, for example:

Richard Albert. *Alejandro's Gift.* Chronicle Books, 1994. Desert irrigation.

Midas Dekkers. *Arctic Adventure.* Orchard, 1987. Whales.

Jean G. Howard. *Bound by the Sea: A Summer Diary.* Tidal Press, 1986. Science diary.

Betsy James. *The Mud Family.* Putnam, 1994. Drought, rainfall, flood.

T. J. Steiner. *A Bug's Life: Classic Storybook.* Disney, 1998. Based on the film.

Suggest that students share what they are reading in small groups. Such sharing offers a splendid opportunity for peer recommendations that stimulate further student reading. As students read such novels, they learn science concepts that expand their knowledge and may lead to further investigation.

It is good to know that I shall live on even in the minds of many who do not know me and largely through association with things that are beautiful and lovely.

Rachel Carson
Silent Spring

A Multicultural Science Lesson Plan

A THINKING + LESSON PLAN

Dealing with Stereotyped Thinking

Grades 3–8

Expected Outcomes
Learners will:

1. Listen to a novel read aloud by the teacher.

2. Discuss the issues presented by the author.
3. Analyze the stereotyped thinking presented.
4. Discuss stereotyped thinking and how it can change.

Teaching/Learning Strategies

Resources Needed
Read *There's an Owl in the Shower* by Jean Craighead George to the class over a period of a week or two. This short novel introduces the topic of stereotyped thinking and how it can be changed. Students will investigate this topic.

Directions
Step 1: Read *There's an Owl in the Shower* to the class chapter by chapter. The plot can be summarized as follows:

> One day Borden finds a young owlet blown out of a tree by a gust of wind. Because the owlet is still white, Borden thinks he must be a barred owl, not the protected spotted owl that depends for its existence on the old growth forest in northern California. Loggers like Borden's father hate the spotted owls that prevent them from cutting the big trees. They display such bumper stickers as "I like spotted owls fried" or "The only good owl is a dead owl." The community is divided: loggers vs. environmentalists. At a community meeting there is a fistfight between Borden's father, Leon, and his science teacher, who is sympathetic to the plight of the spotted owls.
>
> Borden's father decides to care for the little owl Borden brings home to impress the judge when he appears for a hearing. He builds a box shelter and hunts mice to feed him, even cutting them up to feed this cute elfin baby, which they name Bardy. Feeding the funny little bird 9 to 10 mice a day, Leon gets hooked on Bardy, even making him a beautiful perch from a redwood sprout, and Bardy imprints on big Leon. The whole family comes to love Bardy, and then Borden notices the spots on Bardy's new feathers. Leon agrees to let Bardy go free when he realizes it is illegal to keep any endangered animal in captivity. He helps the other loggers realize that the owl has told them that they aren't managing the forests right. As Borden notes:
>
> > He came right into our midst and turned us all around. I'll never be able to look at an owl the same way again.

Jean George has presented a perfect example of how stereotyped thinking changes when we get to know an individual.

Step 2: Encourage students to discuss events as they occur in the book. After completing this story, guide students to analyze the thinking exemplified by the various characters created by Jean George. Introduce the concept of "stereotyped thinking." Invite students to identify examples of this kind of thinking that they may have observed.

(continued)

Ask students to complete the following phrases with the name of an animal:

as fast as a _____
as quiet as a _____
as busy as a _____
as sly as a _____

Point out that these phrases have been used so frequently that they have lost their freshness. They focus on only one characteristic of the animal rather than describing the animal in specific detail. Ask students what would happen if we did this to people.

Another theme in this book that could be developed is that of conflicting interests, in this case, logging as a source of jobs and company income versus the needs of an endangered species. Students could investigate similar situations that involve different issues.

Step 3: Have students work in groups to discover more about animals for which we have stereotyped ideas, for example, wolves, rats, and pigs. They can search out both fiction and nonfiction to provide greater insight into the characteristics of these animals. Each group will then give a class presentation, noting their conclusions about the animal studies. This lesson can also lead to a study of humans, for example, children around the world.

Performance Assessment
Students receive grades of Credit/No Credit based on their participation in a group study and presentation.

INFUSING MULTICULTURAL SCIENCE INSTRUCTION ACROSS THE CURRICULUM

One of the most effective ways of linking science to other subject areas in the curriculum is through a thematic study that has special science overtones. Refer to the directions for developing such a study in Chapter 3 as you plan a study of Nutrition. Consider how this topics brings in topics from the social studies and how students will be exercising their thinking, speaking, listening, reading, and writing skills. Following are a number of learning activities and information that suggest possible avenues of exploration.

A Thematic Study: Nutrition

Topics related to food can provide an appropriate theme for study across the curriculum at many different grade or student ability levels. A multicultural approach involves incorporating the diverse range of students' home experiences with food, exploring how modern solutions to the question of feeding ourselves vary across cultures, and learning about the varied origins of familiar food in our lives. Throughout, students can see the effects of cultural contact, illustrating the connections between the many cultures of the world. A multicultural unit on food will allow you to integrate science and math, social studies, language arts, and art activities in the classroom.

Favorite Foods

Ask students what their favorite foods are. List responses on the board. Have students write descriptions of their favorite foods and read them to the class. Do all students like the same foods? Or do some students' favorites inspire groans from others? Talk about these differences of opinion. Is it possible for different people to have different likes and dislikes?

Students will enjoy dipping into the following book:

James Solheim. *It's Disgusting—and We Ate It!: True Food Facts from around the World—and throughout History.* Illustrated by Eric Brace. Simon & Schuster, 1998. Truly a compendium of the gross and the curious, includes jokes and poems as well as facts and statistics.

Food Diary

Have students keep a log for one day of what they eat for breakfast, lunch, and dinner, including snacks. Ask them what they learned from this record. Are they surprised by the variety, the quantity, the specific items? Students can use this information to make a chart for the class showing the most common foods eaten and the least common. Challenge them to decide the best way to depict these results.

Discuss with students the influences on what they eat. Some influences they might suggest are:

- Convenience.
- Borrowed idea from a friend.
- Parent makes lunch.
- Parent does the food shopping.
- Cultural/ethnic background.
- Personal preferences.

The Science of Food

Food can be divided into three groups: proteins, carbohydrates, and fats. We need to eat food from each group in order to live. Prepare a large poster for each of these categories and have students decide where to place the foods they eat. They will have to do some research to determine what the foods are made of. Also, some foods will fit into more than one category.

Analyze Table 6.2 with students and point out the variety of foods we eat to satisfy our nutritional needs. Not everyone eats meat or fish. Some people eat tofu (soybean curd) as a source of protein. People eat many different kinds of beans, bread, fruits, and vegetables. Different groups use different kinds of fat for cooking, including lard, butter, and olive

TABLE 6.2   FOODS WE EAT

Protein	Carbohydrate (Includes starches, grains, fruits, and vegetables)	Fat
hamburger	bread	lard
tunafish	potato chips	butter
eggs	tortillas	peanuts
tofu	rice	olives
cheese	bok choy	oil
milk	eggplant	ice cream
yogurt	nopales	avocado

oil. While advertising promotes the slogan "everybody needs milk," people from many racial or ethnic groups (such as Native Americans, Asians, East European Jews) are allergic to dairy products and eat soy-based foods instead.

Table 6.2, produced from student experience, can provide a basis for comparison as students expand their study of food and nutrition around the world. The following books will extend their study.

Lizzy Rockwell. *Good Enough to Eat: A Kid's Guide to Food and Nutrition.* Harper-Collins, 1999. Includes recipes.

IDEAS IN ACTION!

The Edible School Yard

"Give me any kid. In six weeks, they'll be eating chard," says Alice Waters, founder of the pioneering Berkeley restaurant Chez Panisse. Her foundation, which funds community- and youth-oriented projects, has given the Berkeley Unified School District $3.8 million to write a curriculum incorporating food-related lessons in all content areas. Waters has already developed the Edible School Yard, turning a patch of asphalt into a garden at a local middle school.

Since then, every school in Berkeley has its own garden plot. Now Waters wants students to connect gardening with lunch and eating. A long-time promoter of organic, natural produce, she is hoping to make a difference in student consciousness that will lead to better eating habits.

Does your school have a garden? Maybe you could involve students and the community in creating an edible garden where students could learn food-related lessons in math and science and even enjoy the fruits of their labors.

Janice Pratt Van Cleave. *Janice Van Cleave's Food and Nutrition for Every Kid: Easy Activities That Make Learning Science Fun.* Wiley, 1999. For intermediate students.

Food around the World

Every culture around the world prepares some kind of bread, rice, pasta, or other starch. What kinds of bread do students eat? What other kinds of bread do students know? Provide students with a chance to generate questions about food in different cultures, based on their own interests. For example:

- Are the breads that people in India eat different from or similar to the bread familiar to our community?
- Where do bagels come from?
- How do you make sopaipillas?

In *Everybody Bakes Bread* by Norah Dooley, a girl explores her neighborhood and discovers how bread varies according to the country each family comes from. Recipes are included. Another resource is *Bread, Bread, Bread* by Ann Morris, which is a photographic tour of bread throughout the world's cultures. Students will enjoy selecting an unfamiliar type and experimenting with making and eating their own bread.

Sharing Food

Some of our most treasured moments may be of food shared with members of our family. Cultural heritage is passed down along with memories. Use the following books to stimulate student reflection, research, and writing about the meaning of food in their family.

Amy Córdova. *Abuelita's Heart.* Simon & Schuster, 1997. A grandmother passes on stories of her ancestors to a young girl as they prepare "la comida." Includes recipe.

Meredith Hooper. *A Cow, a Bee, a Cookie, and Me.* Kingfisher, 1997. Ben's grandmother teaches him how to make honey cookies and explains the origin of each ingredient. Includes recipe.

Class Recipe Book

Collect recipes to be duplicated and made into a collection for each student to take home. Students can bring in recipes for their favorite foods or a special dish from their family or culture. Each student can explain his or her recipe and talk about the preparation and ingredients. If possible, invite a parent or a member of the family to come to the class and show everyone how to make one of these dishes. (You might even ask students to bring in samples of their favorite foods.) Are there special foods that are specific to your region of the country?

Class work with recipes leads naturally to a study of measurement (weight, mass) and the mathematics of conversion. Students can practice measuring with different instruments and multiplying quantities for larger groups. Students may also want to investigate the scientific questions of cooking, for example, how food changes from raw to cooked.

Holiday Food

People in every culture celebrate special holidays and most holidays have special foods associated with them. Ask students what foods mean "holiday" to them. Perhaps latkes (potato pancakes) are a special treat for Hanukkah, or their grandmother prepares an elaborate traditional feast for Chinese New Year. Some may hold a family reunion where everyone brings food like corn on the cob and watermelon. What are students' favorite holiday foods? Food can also play a significant role in religious observances when people fast, as for Ramadan or Lent.

Read one of these books aloud to stimulate student sharing.

Gail Gibbons. *The Pumpkin Book.* Holiday House, 1999. Everything you would want to know about the pumpkin, from planting and drying the seeds to its role in the first Thanksgiving.

Jama Kim Rattizan. *Dumpling Soup.* Little, Brown, 1993. Multiracial family in Hawaii prepares special soup for New Year's.

Gina Macaluso Rodríguez. *Green Corn Tamales/Tamales de elote.* Hispanic Books Distributors, 1994. In this bilingual, predictable book, family prepares Labor Day meal.

Students can write a description of a holiday meal. Discuss what makes descriptive writing effective. Talk about specific words that appeal to the senses. Generate examples of adjectives and other vocabulary to make students' writing more powerful.

A Multicultural Menu

After studying food around the world, students can present what they have learned with a Multicultural Food Day. Groups of students can prepare examples to represent the range of food found across the continents of Europe, Asia, Africa, the Americas, and Oceania. Invite parents or other classes to share in your findings. Have students create posters to explain what each food is, who eats it, and where they live.

Food History

Ask students what food they consider typically "American." They might list pizza, hotdogs, hamburgers, tuna sandwiches, macaroni salad. Have them investigate the origins of these foods. What country did they come from? What foods come originally from the Americas? (tomato, potato, chocolate) Where did noodles come from? (China) What did Italians eat before they had what we think of as Italian food—tomato sauce and noodles? What foods did students' ancestors eat? Each student can choose a food to research and report back to the class.

Another area to investigate is regional food history. Are there foods that are particular to your area? Recipes for chili vary depending on the region. There are many foods found primarily in one region, such as grits or hush puppies in the South. Where do they come from? Students will be interested to discover that some foods they take for granted are unfamiliar in the rest of the country.

Eating Customs

How people eat varies along with what people eat. What implements do people eat with other than knife, fork, and spoon? Do any of your students eat with chopsticks? Bring chopsticks to class and have these students demonstrate how to pick up food. Some groups eat with their fingers. Hawaiians scoop up poi (a kind of mush) in their hands. Ethiopians use injera (bread) as a plate and tear off pieces to wrap up their food. When people with different eating customs meet, each may consider the other's habits awkward or impolite.

Ina Friedman. *How My Parents Learned to Eat.* Houghton, 1984. How two people, one from Japan and one from the United States, overcame this difference in customs.

Patricia Lauber. *What You Never Knew about Fingers, Forks, and Chopsticks.* Illustrated by John Manders. Simon & Schuster, 1999. A history of eating customs in different cultures.

Sources for Further Study

Dane Archer. *A World of Food: Tastes and Taboos in Different Cultures.* Video features interviews with people around the world to illustrate different ideas of food that is "normal" and food that is prohibited.

Deanna F. Cook. *The Kid's Multicultural Cookbook: Food and Fun Around the World.* Illustrated by Michael Kline. Williamson, 1996. Easy recipes from all six continents with illustrations and photographs of children.

Joan D'Amico and Karen Eich Drummond. *The Science Chef Travels around the World: Fun Food Experiments and Recipes for Kids.* Illustrated by Tina Cash-Walsh. Wiley, 1996. Includes fourteen countries.

Norah Dooley. *Everybody Cooks Rice.* Carolrhoda, 1991.

Linda Illsley. *A Taste of Mexico.* Thomas Learning, 1994. Food presented in context of history and geography.

Elaine Landau. *Apples.* Children's Press, 1999. (Other titles include: *Corn, Wheat, Bananas.*)

Patricia C. Marden and Suzanne I. Barchers. *Cooking Up World History: Multicultural Recipes and Resources.* Teacher Ideas Press, 1994. The book surveys cookery in more than twenty countries and regions, providing recipes and information to help students make the connection between culture, food, and history.

Virginia McLean. *Pastatively Italy.* Redbird, 1996.

Milton Meltzer. *The Amazing Potato.* HarperCollins, 1992. This book for young people tells the incredible history of the potato, weaving in stories of the Incas, European conquerors, wars, and immigrants.

Fran Osseo-Asare. *A Good Soup Attracts Chairs: A First African Cookbook for American Kids.* Pelican, 1993. Recipes from Ghana and West Africa, includes resources.

Catherine Paladino. *One Good Apple: Growing Our Food for the Sake of the Earth.* Houghton Mifflin, 1999. Organic farming and the effects of pesticides.

TEACHING MATHEMATICS MULTICULTURALLY

The use of numbers and mathematical concepts represents yet another universal language that we share around the globe. Students can study variations in applied mathematics in different countries, for example:

- Monetary systems—compare the worth of coins.
- The abacus and its use.
- Metric system compared with U.S. weights and measures.
- Computer use around the world.
- Calendars (see Chapter 8).
- Economic systems.

Help students make connections between mathematics and other subjects or areas of interest. For example, how does math relate to art and music? What are the many relationships between math and the sciences? How are mathematical concepts displayed in nature, for example, Fibonacci numbers (patterns in pine cones)?

Strategies for Teaching Mathematics Multiculturally

Recommended Resources

Material is constantly being published to help teachers connect math and multicultural education, for example:

The Multicultural Math Classroom: Bringing in the World by Claudia Zaslavsky (Heinemann, 1996). It presents a short history of mathematics, then suggests activities for grades K–8, beginning with finger counting and simple games and moving to geometry in architecture and art, data analysis, and probability theory.

Math across Cultures is a 50-page publication available from the San Francisco Exploratorium Order Department, 3601 Lyon Street, San Francisco, CA 94123 (Phone: 800-359-9899). Appropriate for grades 4 through 12, it includes many multicultural activities and resources. A small group of students might, for example, follow directions for unraveling and counting the Incan Quipu knots and then present a report and demonstration to the class. Another group could learn to play Madagascar solitaire, offering to teach others who were interested.

Cynthia Manthey's *Pre-K Math: Concepts from Global Sources* (Humanics Learning, ISBN 0-89334-240-8). Appropriate for ages 2 to 5, this 160-page book helps children learn to count in different languages and play number games. Sketches and detailed instructions help teachers share ideas from such countries as Brazil, Congo, Cuba, India, and Thailand.

A Mathematical Word Search

Have students prepare a display of terms appropriate to their level of mathematical understanding. Include the etymology of the terms. Students will be surprised to discover the ori-

> ### Relativity
>
> There once was a lady named Bright
> Who traveled much faster than light.
> She set out one day
> In a relative way
> And returned on the previous night.

gins of such words in math as *algebra* and *algorithm.* Discuss the contributions of the Arab civilization to modern math.

Women in Mathematics

Students can focus a special unit of study on the achievements of women in mathematics. Invite female mathematicians to visit your classroom. Discuss math anxiety and how students can overcome it. Have students search the Internet for information about women mathematicians. Teri Perl presents a summary of women's achievements in *Math Equals: Biographies of Women Mathematicians,* which students might update.

INVENTING TOMORROW

How to Invent the Year 2050!

Solve this problem:

Begin with the year 2050.
Subtract the current year.
Answer (years until 2050): _____

Now, add your age.
Answer (your age in 2050 A.D.): _____

IMAGINE! You are _____ years old. Look around you. What is life like at this time? Complete the following sentences:

1. In 2050, I will be living in:

   _____

   _____

(continued)

2. In 2050, I will be spending most of my time:

_____

_____

3. In 2050, my most significant relationship will be with:

_____

_____

4. In 2050, the newspapers will be featuring:

_____

_____

5. In 2050, our people's most serious problems are:

_____

_____

6. In 2050 the world's most serious problems are:

_____

_____

Have a small group of advanced students search for copies of Alvin Toffler's book *Future Shock*, which was very popular in the last decades of the twentieth century. See what he was predicting for the twenty-first century. Compare his ideas with those students are predicting for 2050.

Ask students to write on the following topic: Would you like to know exactly what is going to happen in the future? How would this be an advantage? How would it be a disadvantage?

A THINKING + LESSON PLAN

Money around the World

Grades 6–8

Expected Outcomes
Learners will:

1. Learn that different kinds of money are used in various countries.

2. Compare the value of money in other countries to the U.S. dollar.
3. Work at a learning center focusing on Money around the World.

Teaching/Learning Strategies

Resources Needed
Order a class set of newspapers from a major local paper. Be sure that it carries the daily business report and contains a chart of currency values. Set up a learning center—Money around the World—that includes laminated copies of the Task Card presented in Table 6.3. We suggest that you enlarge each part of the card, placing the questions on one side and the currency chart on the other. (See Chapter 3 for suggestions about creating a learning center.) Collect a few coins from different countries. Be aware that European countries began using the *euro* in 2002.

Directions
Step 1:
Distribute newspapers (at least one per two students). Ask the students to browse through the newspaper to see how many different uses of mathematics they can discover. List these on a large sheet of paper mounted on the wall. The stock prices (decimals) and foreign money values (percents) should be one of the items listed.

Step 2:
Point out the daily currency chart. Ask the students what this chart tells us (the value of world coins compared to the U.S. dollar). Show the students a few coins or bills from different countries, telling them the name of each—euro, peso, or krone. Ask them if they have traveled to other countries where they used different coins. Invite them to bring samples to show the class.

Ask students to tell you how many whole yen you would get for one U.S. dollar. Explain that when traveling in Tokyo, for example, you need to quickly translate a price into dollars, so that you know approximately how much you are paying for an item. If you saw a hat on sale for 24 yen, for instance, about how many dollars would you need to buy it? Show the students how to figure the amount exactly through long division.

Step 3:
Introduce the learning center you have set up entitled Money around the World. Explain the activities at the center, which they will visit in small groups as assigned. Post assigned times at the center.

Each day bring in the newspaper for this center so students can compare the changing values of certain coins, for example, Mexico's peso.

Notice that this math activity challenges student thinking and involves them in reading as well as the use of math processes. Students might make cardboard euros to use in role-playing purchases made in Paris or Berlin. Encourage students to use a few German or French words in their conversation, such as *Bonjour* or *Auf wiedersehn.*

(continued)

TABLE 6.3   MONEY AROUND THE WORLD TASK CARD

SIDE ONE
Money from Other Countries

Country	Currency	Worth in dollars*
Australia	dollar	1.2994
Austria	euro	.7664
Belgium	euro	.7664
Great Britain	pound	.5321
Canada	dollar	1.2244
China	yuan	8.2781
Denmark	krone	6.27
France	euro	.7664
Germany	euro	.7664
Hong Kong	dollar	7.7979
Israel	shekel	4.37
Italy	euro	.7664
Japan	yen	102.72
Mexico	peso	11.233
Netherlands	euro	.7664
Norway	krone	6.27
Russia	ruble	.00349
Sweden	krone	6.27
Switzerland	euro	.7664

*January 25, 2005.

SIDE TWO
Money around the World

Have you ever heard of a yuan?
In which country would you find this coin?
(Look at the chart on the other side of this card.)
How much is a yuan worth compared with our dollar?

Do other countries use dollars besides the United States?
Which countries use dollars?
Are these "dollars" worth the same amount?
Which "dollar" is worth the most?

Every day this list of currencies appears in the newspaper. See if you can find it in the financial or business section. Compare the values for each coin to see how it has changed since this list was published.
Why might values of coins or bills go up or down?
See if you can find information about what determines the value of a piece of currency.

Pretend you are traveling to several different countries. As you enter each country, you exchange $10 for the currency of that country.
How many euros would you get in Mexico?
How many francs would you get in France?
How many pounds would you get in Great Britain?

Find pictures of some of these coins. Perhaps someone you know has money from different countries.

Performance Assessment
Select several mathematically adept students to serve as consultants to assist students. The activity is graded Credit/No Credit based on a student's completing the questions on the Task Card (even with help). Students may receive extra credit by following the changing values of a specific coin for two weeks and reporting their findings to the class.

Using the Computer

Software can help engage students with math across cultures, too. *Maya Math,* for example, a CD-ROM program, was designed by Bank Street College of Education and published by Sunburst Communications (Box 100, Pleasantville, NY 10570; Phone: 800-321-7511). Appropriate for grades 4 through 8, it helps students discover the importance of place value and zero by deciphering the Mayan base-20 number system. They learn to convert Mayan dates to contemporary dates.

The above program has been integrated with social studies in *The Second Voyage of Mimi.* This program engages students in discovering a lost Mayan city.

INFUSING MATHEMATICS MULTICULTURALLY ACROSS THE CURRICULUM

As pointed out at the beginning of this section, mathematics is a universal language that peoples of all cultures can share. To assist students in realizing the importance of mathematics around the world plan a thematic study: The Global Village, that helps them relate math concepts with those from social studies, language arts, and reading. Encourage them to use art to enhance their presentations to members of their class or those from other classrooms.

A Global Village

The label "a global village" seems an increasingly accurate description of the way we live today. We can't isolate ourselves from the beliefs and actions of people who may be very different from us, whether they live nearby or far away, because all of us are interrelated. The activities in this section will enable students to appreciate the interesting diversity as well as the overriding commonalities of human experience.

This broad theme encompasses everything from communications to food to racial and ethnic backgrounds to religions and more. You might open up a discussion of what the concept "a global village" means by introducing the demographics shared by the United Nations, as shown in Figure 6.1.

You might present this information on a large poster so that the information could be readily available during the class study. Later, provide a copy for each student to place in his or her Learning Log, which will be kept throughout the study of the Global Village.

If we could, at this very moment, shrink the world's population to a village of exactly 100 people, and all existing human ratios remained the same, the people in the village would be:

57 Asians

21 Europeans

14 North, Central, and South Americans

8 Africans

Of those people:

70 would be non-Christians; 30 would be Christian.

6 people would hold 50% of the wealth of the village; these 6 people would all be from the United States.

70 of the people would be unable to read.

50 would suffer from malnutrition.

80 would live in substandard housing.

Only 1 person would have a university education.

United Nations, 1990

FIGURE 6.1   A VILLAGE OF 100

Read the information on the poster aloud to focus everyone's attention on the ideas presented and to see that they can all read the words. Ask students to think about why this information was shared with the public. What did the people who created this poster want to convey? Have several students record the answers students give on the chalkboard for later reference.

Then, lead a discussion about the information presented, beginning with the first section about population. What do these figures tell us? Then discuss the rest of the information item by item as each topic is summarized. Take plenty of time with this kind of discussion, probably at least forty-five minutes to cover the full poster. Be aware that this poster covers a wide breadth of major topics: total world population, religions, wealth and lifestyle, literacy, food, housing, and education.

This is an interesting way of beginning a study of what's going on with our planet and the people who live on it. This study could easily last a full year, if that much time were available. You can also see how readily the study crosses the full curriculum. The first math project would be to update the figures presented using data from the latest census.

One way to move forward with this study is to have students identify the general topics presented on the poster as you write each one on the chalkboard. Suggesting that the class needs to find out what lies behind each summarizing statement presented, ask students to sign up to investigate the topic that interests them the most. Limit the number of signups for each topic to the first five so that one study does not become overloaded. Students will then form cooperative learning groups and begin to brainstorm the questions they need to answer about each topic.

This study leads naturally to the computer and the Internet. A final class project might well be a multimedia presentation that the whole class can present to other groups of students as well as to parents.

Living in Other Countries

One of the best ways for students to experience what it is like to live in different countries is to read books about children of their own age who have traveled to a different country or who are growing up in another country. Here are some books you can suggest:

Maya Ajmera and Anna Rhesa Versola. *Children from Australia to Zimbabwe: A Photographic Journey around the World.* Charlesbridge, 2001. Shows the diversity of the world's children.

Caroline Binch. *Gregory Cool.* Dial, 1994. A boy visits his grandparents in Tobago and learns to adjust.

Carolyn Coman. *Many Stones.* Front Street, 2000. U.S. teenager goes to South Africa with her father to cope with the loss of her sister and to learn about truth and reconciliation.

Jean Fritz. *Homesick: My Own Story.* Paper Star, 1999. Fritz tells of her youth in China during the difficult years of the 1920s. She dreams of a homeland she has never seen.

Ineke Hotwijk. Wanda Goeke, trans. *Asphalt Angels.* Front Street, 1999. Thirteen-year-old Alex lives on the streets of Rio to escape abuse at home.

Alison Lester. *Ernie Dances to the Didgeridoo: For the Children of Gunbalanya.* Houghton Mifflin, 2001. Ernie spends a year on an aboriginal reserve in Australia. His postcards and snapshots show typical activities.

Naomi Shihab Nye. *Habibi.* Simon & Schuster, 1997. In this autobiographical novel, Liyana Abboud, 14, moves from St. Louis to Jerusalem and her unfamiliar Palestinian heritage.

Lyall Watson. *Warriors, Warthogs, and Wisdom: Growing up in Africa.* Illustrated by Keith West. Kingfisher, 1997. A white South African tells of growing up in the 1940s.

Amy Bronwen Zemser. *Beyond the Mango Tree.* Greenwillow, 1998. Sarina's family moves from Boston to Liberia and she discovers the world is very different from what she thought.

Making Sense out of Population Figures

How many people live in the world today? Have students guess and write their estimates on the board. Did anyone come close to 6 billion? Such a large number has virtually no meaning to most of us unless we can express it in familiar terms. Research some comparative figures. How many people live in your city? How many live in the state? What's the population of the United States?

Have students predict what country has the largest population and what country has the greatest land area. They may be surprised to learn that China has the largest population of any country in the world: over 1.2 billion inhabitants, 21 percent of the world's population.

India is second with 1.03 billion people: Its population is expected to reach 1.36 billion by 2025, and the population of China is projected to be 1.43 billion. The United States is next with a population of 293 million, followed by Indonesia, Brazil, Pakistan, Russia, Bangladesh, Nigeria, and Japan.[2] Russia has the largest land area, over 6.5 million square miles, followed by Canada, China, the United States, and Brazil. Students can research U.S. and world populations at <*www.prb.org*> where the Population Reference Bureau maintains an up-to-date data sheet.

Explore different strategies to represent the relative sizes of the population of the United States and the world. Students can make pie charts or block graphs. Another technique is to choose a small object such as a book, pencil, or apple to represent a fixed number (1000, for example). How many books would it take to show the population of your city, state, country, or the world? Demonstrations like this help students to understand and visualize large numbers and the relation between thousands, millions, and billions.

Studying Population: Demography

Ask students if they know what a demographer does. Can they figure it out on the basis of the roots *demo* and *graph?* (Think of other words that have these roots in them.) Reward the first student who uses the meanings of the roots to come up with a definition close to "one who measures population and its characteristics."

Challenge students to become *demographers* and find out how fast the population is growing. Has the rate of growth changed over time? Compare the growth rate in this century with the past century. What does this growth rate predict for the next ten years? Twenty years? Some areas are growing at different rates. How will the composition of the world change in the next ten years? Twenty years? What about age? How will the percentage of old and young people change over the next ten years? Why will this change? What effects might this have on all of us?

How do we count population figures? Is it really possible to count everyone living in the country on one day? What factors might affect the accuracy of this figure? Are there specific groups that might be "undercounted" or "overcounted"?

Dealing with Social Injustice and Global Conflict

As you talk with students about issues such as prejudice, racism, and the homeless, recognize their desire to take some action based on their beliefs. Although these large social questions will not be solved simply, do not discourage students from wanting to be involved. Despite their young age and lack of power in society, students have strong feelings about injustice. In discussing books and topics that raise troublesome questions, guide student responses into productive channels. What can students do? They can publicize problems, write letters, organize people, talk to others, invite people to speak, and publish their efforts. In *It's Our World, Too!* Phillip Hoose describes young activists who have taken a stand on sensitive issues such as sexism, racism, and the homeless and shows the power of people of any age to make a difference. Older students will appreciate *Finding Solutions to Hunger: Kids Can Make a Difference* by Stephanie Kempf. This book discusses both roots and solutions of hunger issues, from world famine to the working poor to colonialism.

One topic that concerns young people very much is war, or any violent conflict, and its impact on people. The following books will stimulate discussion of student fears and how these issues affect them:

Adam Bagdasarian. *The Forgotten Fire.* DK Ink, 1999. The 1915 Armenian genocide as seen through the eyes of a 12-year-old boy.

Eve Bunting. *Smokey Night.* Illustrated by David Diaz. Harcourt, 1995. Conflict sets a city afire; diverse people learn to get along.

Florence Heide. *Sami and the Time of the Troubles.* Clarion, 1992. A picture book about Sami, a 10-year-old Lebanese boy who spends his life in the basement bomb shelter hoping for peace.

Gaye Hicyilmaz. *Against the Storm.* Dell, 1993. This novel for older students is set in contemporary Turkey and focuses on the plight of displaced people and the strategies they use to survive.

Elena Kozhina. Vadim Mahmoudov, trans. *Through the Burning Steppe: A Wartime Memoir.* Putnam, 1999. How a young girl survived World War II in Russia.

Elizabeth Laird. *Kiss the Dust.* Dutton, 1992. Tara, 13, and her family are Kurds who are forced to flee Iraq during the 1984 war. They face a harsh existence in refugee camps.

Sonia Levitin. *Dream Freedom.* Harcourt, 1999. U.S. children join campaign against child slavery in the Sudan.

Marybeth Lorbiecki. *My Palace of Leaves in Sarajevo.* Dial, 1997. Girl's letters show the impact of ethnic conflict in Bosnia.

Yukio Tsuchiya. *Faithful Elephants: A True Story of Animals, People and War.* Tomoko Tsuchiya Dykes, trans. Illustrated by Ted Lewin. Houghton Mifflin, 1988. The story of what happened to the elephants in the Tokyo zoo at the end of World War II, when there was no more food. This story has been read aloud in Japan for twenty years to mark the anniversary of the end of the war and as a reminder of the uselessness of war.

Middle East

One area of the world that has experienced conflict over many centuries is the Middle East. Students can explore the historical roots of this conflict and learn how it feels to be living in the middle of it.

Laurie Dolphin. *Neve Shalom/Wahat Al-Salam: Oasis of Peace.* Scholastic, 1993. Describes a unique village near Jerusalem where Israeli Arabs and Jews choose to live and work together. Although the families maintain separate cultures, they meet in the bilingual, bicultural school setting.

Florence Parry Heide and Judith Heide Gilliland. *House of Wisdom.* Illustrated by Mary Grandpre. DK Publishing, 1999. Exceptional text and illustrations evoke the world of ninth-century Baghdad, when the House of Wisdom, a library, preserved important knowledge that had been lost in Europe.

Martin Hintz and Stephen Hintz. *Israel.* Children's Book Press, 1998. From *Enchantment of the World* series.

Jane Kurtz. *The Storyteller's Beads.* Harcourt Brace, 1998. Two girls from different backgrounds learn to overcome prejudice and trust each other in Jerusalem.

Ted Lewin. *The Storytellers.* Lothrop, Lee & Shepard, 1998. A boy and his grandfather in the marketplaces of Fez, Morocco.

Claire Sidhom Matze. *The Stars in My Geddoh's Sky.* Illustrated by Bill Farnsworth. Whitman, 1999. When his grandfather's visit is over, a boy is reassured to know that they can both look at the same sky.

Naomi Shihab Nye, sel. *The Space between Our Footsteps: Poems and Paintings from the Middle East.* Simon & Schuster, 1998. Over nineteen Middle Eastern countries are represented by a range of contributions, from humorous to thoughtful.

Varied Religions

Help your students recognize that there are many religions represented in the United States and the world (see Tables 6.4 and 6.5).

TABLE 6.4   DOMINANT NON–CHRISTIAN RELIGIONS IN THE UNITED STATES (PROJECTED FOR 2000)

Total:	41,054,000	14.8%
Atheists	925,000	.3
Baha'is	750,000	.3
Buddhists	2,000,000	.7
Chinese folk religions	70,000	.0
Hindus	950,000	.3
Jews	5,500,000	2.0
Muslims	3,950,000	1.4
(Black Muslims)	(1,650,000)	(.6)
New religionists	675,000	.2
Nonreligious	24,554,000	8.8
Sikhs	220,000	.1
Tribal religionist	350,000	.1
Other	1,110,000	.4

Source: Statistical Abstract of the United States, 1999.

Heather Forest. *Wisdom Tales from around the World: 50 Gems of Story and Wisdom from such Diverse Traditions as Sufi, Zen, Taoist, Christian, Jewish, Buddhist, African, and Native American.* August House, 1996. *World Storytelling* series.

Julius Lester. *When the Beginning Began: Stories about God, the Creatures, and Us.* Illustrated by Emily Lisker. Silver Whistle, 1999. Voice of a storyteller in tales of the "might have been."

TABLE 6.5 WORLD RELIGIONS

Christians (total)	1,943 million
Roman Catholic	1,026 million
Protestant	316 million
Orthodox	213 million
Anglican	63 million
other	373 million
Baha'i	6 million
Buddhist	353 million
Chinese folk religions	379 million
Confucians (Korea)	6 million
Hindus	761 million
Jain	3 million
Jew	14 million
Muslim	1,164 million
Sikh	22 million
Shinto	1 million

Source: *Statistical Abstract of the United States,* 1999.

What do students know about these religions? There are also less well-known religious groups, such as Quakers and Mormons, that have rich traditions of service to the community and support for equality of all peoples. Encourage students to become familiar with the diversity of religious belief. The following books will help:

Debbie Holsclaw Birdseye and Tom Birdseye. *What I Believe: Kids Talk about Faith.* Holiday, 1996. Six students talk about their religious beliefs, including Hindu, Buddhist, Jew, Christian, Muslim, and Native American.

Catherine Chambers. *Sikh.* Children's Press, 1996. This introduction includes beliefs, activities, and a glossary.

Demi. *Buddha.* Holt, 1996. A picture book about this religious figure.

Anita Ganeri. *What Do We Know about Hinduism?* Peter Bedrick, 1996. Shows how Hinduism affects people's daily lives.

William Jay Jacobs. *World Religions: Great Lives.* Atheneum, 1996. From the ancient world to the modern, profiles of religious leaders. Less familiar names are Baha'u'llah (founder of Baha'i), Ann Hutchinson (championed religious freedom in 1638), and Mary Baker Eddy (founder of Christian Science).

Betsy Maestro. *Story of Religion.* Illustrated by Giulio Maestro. Clarion, 1997. Basic introduction to Judaism, Christianity, Islam, Buddhism, Hinduism, and Chinese religions for young readers.

Susan Meredith. *Usborne Book of World Religions.* Usborne, 1996. Development, history, and practices of major religions.

Lisa Sita. *Worlds of Belief.* Black Birch, 1995. More in-depth coverage of major religions of the world, including leaders and rituals.

Jane Yolen. *O Jerusalem.* Illustrated by John Thompson. Blue Sky Press, 1996. This holy place for Jews, Christians, and Muslims is 3000 years old.

What Others Believe: Religions

Invite students to share with the class some of their religious beliefs, if any. Since stereotypes and prejudice are fed by ignorance, open discussion will aid in accepting and understanding different beliefs. Almost every Jewish child has seen a Christmas tree but how many non-Jewish children have seen a *dreidl*? Mormon children are sometimes taunted by those outside their faith because of misconceptions about Mormonism. Why do Muslims pray several times a day?

Invite guests to the classroom—a rabbi, a priest, a Protestant minister (a woman?)— to talk briefly about a specific religion. It may be difficult to find information about religions such as Voodoo, Santería, Native American, or charismatic Christianity, but these are important religions as well.

Sports and Games in Other Countries

Sports and games are of universal interest. Offer students the opportunity to learn about different games from other cultures. Students may already be aware of significant sports figures from other countries. In an Olympic year, plan activities related to the widespread interest in these sports and the countries represented.

Mary D. Lankford. *Jacks around the World.* Illustrated by Karen Dugan. Morrow, 1996. Fourteen variants of this favorite game. See also *Hopscotch around the World.*

Sarah Pooley. *Jump the World: Stories, Poems, and Things to Make and Do from around the World.* Dutton, 1997. A collection for ages 4–10.

Strategy Challenges. Collection 1: Around the World (includes Mancala, Nine Men's Morris, and Go-Moku). *Collection 2: In the Wild* (Surakarta [Java], Tablut [Lapland], and Jungle Chess), CD-ROM from Edmark, 1995. For ages 8 and up.

IDEAS IN ACTION!

A Picture Worth a Thousand Words

The Nature Conservancy, since 2001, has provided more than 220 people in 61 remote villages in China with inexpensive cameras with film included so that the Chinese villagers can capture pictures of their daily lives to share with the world. They talked with oral historians to record the stories that go with each picture. This project is called Photovoice.

ISN'T THIS A GREAT IDEA! You can do it, too. Watch for sales of these handy cameras so you can give them to your students. They can picture their lives by shooting scenes from their family life and activities to share with their classmates. The 24 or more pictures they take will provide a wealth of information about which they can talk and write for at least a semester. Of course, they will publish their work!

David Wallechinsky. *The Complete Book of the Summer Olympics: Sydney 2000 Edition* and *The Complete Book of the Winter Olympics* (1998 Edition). Overlook, 1998. History and statistics of the Olympic Games.

Older students can explore issues relating sports and politics. Many people believe that "sports" are about merit and, therefore, are not biased. Find a book such as the following to discuss this issue.

Susan D. Bachrach. *The Nazi Olympics: Berlin 1936.* Little, Brown, 1999. Shows how sports have been used for propaganda purposes.

Human Needs

Looking at other cultures can help students learn more about themselves and their culture. After you have been studying a particular group of people or reading tales from several cultures, ask students to list the most basic needs they think are common to all cultures. Focus on the fundamental human needs for love, food, and shelter. Relate these to students' lives. How are these provided for in their lives? How do different groups satisfy them?

Students can brainstorm examples of how different people respond to one need, such as *love.* Then they can write personal responses, completing the sentence "Love is . . . " and illustrating their ideas. As a class, students can prepare a collage for the bulletin board, showing how different needs are met in different cultures, based on their own illustrations or examples they have found.

For a graphic representation of the global family, see *Material World: A Global Family Portrait* by Peter Menzel. Thirty families, from countries such as Bosnia, Mali, Haiti, India, and Japan, were asked to display all their possessions and tell how they live. The striking disparities as well as similarities among the families will stimulate student interest and discussion.

Cultures of the World series from Marshall Cavendish. Includes countries such as Mongolia, Ghana, Barbados.

Enchantment of the World series from Children's Book Press. Includes countries such as Serbia, Japan, Colombia.

Beatrice Hollyer. *Wake Up, World! A Day in the Life of Children around the World.* Holt, 1999. Follow eight children from eight countries as they go through their daily routines.

Math in Thematic Studies

Mathematics will be part of any thematic study, as described in Chapter 3. Students can prepare different kinds of graphs to present their findings. They can report percentages of people involved and compare sizes in studies related to topography of the land. They can deal with time differences and mileages that affect travel plans. Students need to learn that math is very much a part of everyone's daily life and that it is far more than just 9×7 or $8 + 3$.

CONNECTIONS

Science and mathematics invite students to think in challenging ways. They invite inquiry. We need to encourage students to experiment and to consider different alternatives to problem solving. Both science and math are important to all cultures as they share information across national borders, providing a foundation for a new fund of knowledge in medicine and technology.

FOLLOW-THROUGH

Expanding Your RTP

1. Consider the following quotation:

   > Voyager, there are no bridges, one builds them as one walks.
   > —Gloria Anzaldúa

   Who is Gloria Anzaldúa? What do you think she meant by these words? Write a short paragraph about what her words suggest for your life.

2. Write a paragraph about how science and mathematics fit into your life. How can you encourage your students to enjoy delving into these subject areas?

Working with Your CLG

1. Work together to locate a number of biographies of men and women from diverse racial or cultural backgrounds who have made contributions in math and science. Discuss how you can use the books to encourage boys and girls to explore these fields for possible careers.

2. Make a display for a bulletin board that you could use as a way of sharing science and math information. Use the Internet as a source of ideas for the display.

GROWING A PROFESSIONAL LIBRARY

Deborah Ray. *The Flower Hunter.* Farrar, 2004. Biography of environmentalist William Bartram, who collected and named hundreds of American plants.

Greg Tang. *The Best of Times. Math Strategies That Multiply.* Scholastic, 2002. Ideas that encourage students to use intuition and understanding, not repetition and memorization.

Cora Wright. *More Hot Links: Linking Literature with the Middle School Curriculum.* Libraries Unlimited, 2002.

ENDNOTES

1. Virginia Walker, "Digital Connections." *Booklinks* (November 1997): 64.
2. "World Statistics," *Time Almanac 2005.* Pearson, 2004, p. 708.

"Of every hue and caste
am I, of every rank
and religion.

I resist any thing better
than my own diversity."

Walt Whitman
"Leaves of Grass"

Teaching the Performing Arts Multiculturally

Allowing for creativity in children's lives is an important aspect of education. Art, music, and other performance activities encourage students to express themselves in different ways. Thus, we allow for the development of diverse kinds of intelligences. Providing for variety in the curriculum also stimulates children's learning and provides a welcome change of pace during the school day.

The arts connect strongly with multicultural education as we explore how different cultures use these expressive means of communicating. Such exploration tends, furthermore, to enhance the curriculum and to guide students to be more observant and to personalize the literature they encounter.

FOCUSING ON TEACHING ART MULTICULTURALLY

Most students enjoy experimenting with various forms of art. In this section we present a potpourri of art activities that lend themselves to classroom learning.

Effective Multicultural Art Strategies

Illustrated Children's Literature

Children's books offer a special art form in the illustrations, which are commonly created by highly talented artists. The variety of the art presented is truly amazing. Look for the work of some of these artists, who represent different cultural groups within the United States. Have students analyze the work of such illustrators as the following:

Mitsumasa Anno. *Anno's U.S.A.* Japanese artist; many books.

Lulu Delacre. *Vezigante Masquerader.* Puerto Rican illustrator.

Carmen Lomas Garza. *Family Pictures: Cuadros De Familia.* Mexican American artist depicts family experiences in Texas.

Yumi Heo. *Father's Rubber Boots.* Korean story and artist.

Holly Keeler. *Grandfather's Dream.* Vietnamese story about saving the cranes.

Jacob Lawrence. *The Great Migration.* Noted African American artist depicts history.

Jerry Pinkney. *Talking Easter Eggs.* Popular African American illustrator.

Allen Say. *Stranger in the Mirror.* Japanese American author/illustrator.

Maurice Sendak. *Outside over There.* Jewish author/illustrator; this book won the Caldecott Medal in 1987.

Origami

Children will enjoy creating attractive folded-paper animals, for example, the popular crane, a turtle, or an elephant. This traditional Japanese art form is described in *Classic Origami* by P. D. Tuyen, which contains detailed instructions. Making origami fits well with writing such Japanese forms of poetry as haiku. (See the sample multicultural social studies lesson in Chapter 5.)

A touching Japanese story that all people can appreciate is *Sadako* by Eleanor Coerr and illustrated by Ed Young. According to Japanese legend, anyone who is ill will become well if they make one thousand origami cranes. Sadako died of leukemia, as a result of the bombing of Hiroshima, before completing the cranes. Every year on Hiroshima Day (August 6) children around the world make origami cranes in memory of Sadako.

Filmed Documentaries

The video, *Oaxaca: Valley of Myth and Magic* (Crizmac, 1995), recommended for grades 4 through 12, provides an overview of art in this region of Mexico. It includes historical background, a local myth, and a map-making activity as well as an introduction to the kind of weaving for which Oaxaca is famous. Check your school district catalog to determine what kinds of films about art they have to offer along this line.

ABC Books

The ABC or alphabet book continues to be used widely in primary grades. However, these illustrated books often present mature concepts and art that can provide interesting instructional ideas for older students, too. An ABC book that combines art and multicultural concepts is *Gathering the Sun: An Alphabet in Spanish and English* by Alma Flor Ada. On each page is a short poem presented in both English and Spanish. Illustrated by Simon Silva with a hot palette of bold gouache, the book literally "glows." He depicts farm produce with mouth-watering reality and farm laborers with strength and sympathy. The book is dedicated to César Chávez.

A second type of ABC book offers information about a specific topic. Tanis Jordan's *Amazon Alphabet* is an attractive example that connects art with science and social science. Illustrated by skilled artist Martin Jordan, the book includes illustrated letters in the glossary where information about each animal is presented. Such ABC books provide models for students who are creating their own original children's books on a multicultural theme.

Art as a Theme in Children's Fiction

Occasionally authors write fiction that includes art as a theme. In *In Summer Light,* for instance, Zibby Oneal writes about a girl who wants to be a painter. Newbury Award–winner *I, Juan de Pareja* by Elizabeth De Trevino is narrated by a slave in the household of Spanish painter Velasquez. In *Meiko and the Fifth Treasure* Eleanor Coerr tells of a 10-year-old artist whose hand was injured in the Nagasaki bombing and how she began to draw again. This book also presents attractive calligraphy by Cecil Uyehara. The beautiful Hmong stitchery in *The Whispering Cloth: A Refugee's Story* by Pegi Shea accompanies the story of Mai's life in a Thai refugee camp. See also the unit on quilting later in this chapter.

Reading about Real Artists

Students who are particularly interested in art may choose one of these autobiographies or biographies to review for a social studies report:

G. Everett. *Children of Promise.* Atheneum, 1992. Black artists.

Milton Meltzer. *Dorothea Lange: Life through the Camera.* Viking, 1985. Photography.

Philip Sendak. *In Grandpa's House.* Harper, 1985. Illustrated by Maurice Sendak, son of the author of this autobiography.

Kathleen Krull. *Lives of the Artists: Masterpieces, Messes (and What the Neighbors Thought).* Audio Bookshelf, 1996; 2 cassettes. An audio presentation suitable for grades 4–9. Read by John C. Brown and Melissa Hughes are minibiographies of 20 noted artists from da Vinci to Warhol. Students will enjoy the amusing, gossipy style that makes history and art come alive. Small groups of students could listen to these tapes at a Listening Center.

Check the index of this text for books about Native American, African American, Latino, and women artists.

Virtual Field Trip: Visiting Art Museums

For students in the United States, *The Louvre* (Windows and Macintosh), a CD-ROM for all ages, provides the experience of going to this famous museum in Paris and viewing more than 150 representations of the art displayed there. The program is user-friendly and includes games and activities to help reinforce learning. (See also *With Open Eyes,* a similar visit to Chicago's Art Institute.) Virginia Walker suggests the following Book Connections:[1]

Elaine Konigsburg's classic, *From the Mixed-up Files of Mrs. Basil E. Frankweiler.* Atheneum, 1967. Favorite story set in the Metropolitan Museum of Art.

Peggy Thomson. *The Nine-Ton Cat: Behind the Scenes at an Art Museum.* Houghton, 1997. Information about backstage work at the National Gallery of Art.

Internet connections include:

Fine Arts Museums of San Francisco. *<www.thinker.org/index.shtml>* Virtual visits to the DeYoung and the Legion of Honor; includes 60,000 item database.

WebMuseum. *<www.watt.emf.net/louvre//>* A stunning collection of famous paintings, including some items too fragile to be viewed in person.

Suggest artists that students might research, for example, Diego Rivera, Frida Kahlo, R. C. Gorman, Maya Lin, and Faith Ringgold. Also suggest questions to guide their research, for instance, Which women artists are included? or What kinds of art are presented?

Art in History

Art is an important aspect of our lives. Lead students to discover the role art has played throughout human development. Have them investigate the pictographs of the cave dwellers, the art of Native Americans, Chinese and Japanese calligraphy, American folk art, and modern art shown in galleries and museums today. The Internet will provide examples of all kinds of art.

Have students discuss the following quotation, which you can enlarge (use the computer to increase print size and to select an attractive style or font) for a poster to display in your classroom.

> Imagination and creativity are the wings
> Of one's mind.
> On these two wings, you will fly
> High and far.
> —Jean and Mou-Sien Tseng

The words of these two artists are quoted in *Wings of an Artist: Children's Book Illustrators Talk about Their Work* compiled by Julie Cummins (Abrams, 1999). Ask a librarian to help you locate books that contain their work. One example is the Chinese legend *Fa Mulan: The Story of a Woman Warrior,* text by Robert D. San Souci (Hyperion, 1998).

Artists' Work As Inspiration

These illustrators serve as role models and may inspire students to emulate their techniques. You might compare the work of two artists who present the same topic, for example, Las Posadas. Look for these books:

Tomie de Paolo. *The Night of Las Posadas.* Putnam, 1999.

Diane Hoyt-Goldsmith. Illustrated by Laurence Migdale. *Las Posadas: An Hispanic Christmas Celebration.* Photography. Holiday House, 1999.

Look for stories that have been retold and illustrated by different authors and illustrators, for example, *Cinderella* or *Sleeping Beauty.* Compare how each person handled the settings, the characterization, and the wording.

Planning Lessons

Following are several multicultural lessons that provide examples of the kind of activities that lend themselves to promoting multiculturalism in art.

A THINKING + LESSON PLAN

Cut Paper Art

Grades 1–8

Expected Outcomes
Learners will:

1. Examine examples of cut paper art.
2. Read and study books that use cut paper in the illustrations.
3. Make cut paper designs to decorate the classroom.

Teaching/Learning Strategies

Resources Needed
Ask the librarian to assist you in locating examples of cut paper art—Chinese, Mexican, Pennsylvania Dutch, and so on. An excellent resource is *Making Magic Windows: Creating Papel Picado/Cut-Paper Art with Carmen Lomas Garza* (Children's Press, 1999) in which the artist provides specific instructions for introducing students to both beginning and more advanced techniques. Collect the necessary materials for a beginning experience in paper cutting: scissors, paper (tissue and others), string, and glue. (Older, more expert students, might use an X-acto knife as Garza also describes.)

Directions
Step 1: This activity can be done at any time of year, but it is especially appropriate near November 2, *Dia de los Muertos* (Day of the Dead). Discuss the display of banners and cut tissue designs to honor the dead who, according to Mexican tradition, are permitted to return to earth to visit on this one day each year. Challenge students to investigate this holiday on the Internet. Many Mexican Americans observe the autumn holiday, which coincides with Halloween or All Saints Day.

Students can also research the topic: cut paper as an art form that is said to have begun in ancient China.

Step 2: Write the words *papel picado* on the chalkboard, saying: "Today we are going to make papel picado." Explain that *papel* means "paper" in Spanish and *picado* means "cut." Point out how in Spanish adjectives follow the noun described. In English adjectives precede the nouns. Spanish-speaking students might supply other examples of this grammatical feature.

Students will make cut paper hangings (papel picado) to decorate the room following the directions in Figure 7.1. Each can then take the decoration home to share with family members.

(continued)

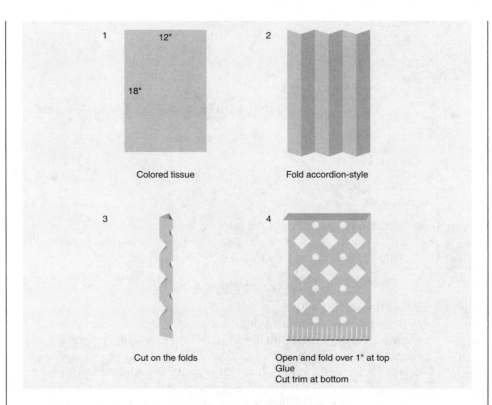

FIGURE 7.1   DIRECTIONS FOR CUTTING PAPER

Each hanging will be different, as shown in Figure 7.2:

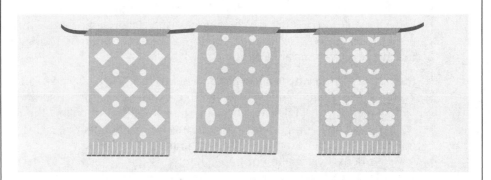

FIGURE 7.2   THREAD CUT PAPER ON HEAVY CORD

Step 3: Place the tissue paper decorations on a cord hung across the windows so that light can come through each individual creation. If there is air blowing anywhere in the classroom, the hangings will blow gently in the breeze.

Performance Assessment
Students receive credit for following directions and completing the task.

A THINKING + LESSON PLAN

Beautiful Writing

Grades 4–8

Expected Outcomes
Learners will:

1. Learn an interesting art form.
2. Select quotations from diverse cultures.
3. Create an attractive display.

Teaching/Learning Strategies

Resources Needed
Collect examples of quotations presented in calligraphy. Some are presented at the beginning of chapters in this text. Bring in books of quotations that students can use as resources.

Directions
Step 1: Show students examples of quotations presented in calligraphy. Explain the history of calligraphy. Teach students the rudiments of italic calligraphy, which is not unlike the manuscript or D'Nelian handwriting that they may have used in primary grades.

Step 2: Have students select and print a quotation or saying they like from a specific culture.

Step 3: Have each student frame the quotation. Framing can be done by mounting the quotation on a sheet of 9″ × 12″ red construction paper, or you may prefer to frame the quotations in simple black wooden frames that can be made or purchased. Older students may explore Chinese calligraphy following this experience.

Performance Assessment
Students should display their work in the classroom, the library, or another more public place where other students can view the art and the wise words depicted. No grades should be assigned for this project. Give credit or no credit for completing the task.

A THINKING + LESSON PLAN

Depicting Sports through Mixed Media

Grades 4–8

Expected Outcomes
Learners will:

1. Select one sport to research.
2. Collect information about this sport and the players.
3. Create a display depicting the sport.
4. Report on the sport and share your art.

Teaching/Learning Strategies

Resources Needed
Brainstorm a list of sports played around the world. Students will choose one sport to study, working individually or in groups of two to three students. All students will be encouraged to contribute information or clippings that other students can use. Representative players of different sports will be invited to the classroom to be interviewed by class members. Students will create collages and report on their study.

Directions
Step 1: Challenge students to see how many different sports they can name. Print their contributions on a large sheet of paper where they can remain for a few weeks. Tell students to talk with their parents or siblings about this list to see if they can suggest additional sports. You may need to define games versus sports.

Step 2: Have students choose one sport to research, for example, soccer, lacrosse, lawn bowling, or bocce ball. Students can work individually or in small groups, if several are interested in the same sport. Limit the number studying one sport to three so that more sports will receive attention. Students will visit the library to locate informative nonfiction or biographies, for example:

Crystal Bowman. *Ivan and the Dynamos*. Eerdmans Books, 1997. Fiction; hockey.

Stew Thornley. *Deion Sanders: Prime Time Player*. Lerner, 1997. Biography; football.

Kristin S. Fehr. *Monica Seles: Returning Champion*. Lerner, 1997. Biography; tennis.

Students can also invite high school or college players to come to the school for interviews and to demonstrate aspects of their sport. Have students bring in newspapers and magazines to use for information and to clip as they collect material for their collages. Criteria for making reports and creating an effective collage should be discussed in order for students to do a good job.

Step 3: A few at a time, students will present their studies and their collages to the class.

Performance Assessment
Reports and collages will be judged based on the criteria established. Five students can be selected as the judges to place ribbons on the collages: Blue for Outstanding; Red for Good; White for Incomplete. The class can select the best five collages to be displayed in the hall near the principal's office where they can be seen by parents and other students.

Infusing Multicultural Art Instruction across the Curriculum

Many images have been suggested to replace the "melting pot" as a more accurate picture of this multicultural country, such as a rainbow, tossed salad, or mosaic. We suggest that the quilt is a particularly apt metaphor to set against the melting pot because, in a quilt, many elements of different shapes and colors are pieced together to make larger patterns. No piece loses its identity but each piece contributes to the beauty of the whole. In addition, quilts have been a way of making use of discarded fabric, were often the result of a group effort, and connected people across many generations. Use quilts as the center of a thematic unit as you incorporate multicultural activities in the language arts, social studies, math and science, and the arts and physical education.

Teaching Multiculturally Around a Theme: Quilts

A quilt is often defined as a three-layer sandwich, composed of a top (created by piecing or appliqué), a filling or batting (for warmth), and a back (sometimes pieced as well). There are three distinct processes usually referred to by the term "quilting." *Patchwork* traditionally incorporates leftover scraps of material or pieces of old clothing. The scraps are "pieced" together into special patterns, often with attention to color and design, and then sewn together to make a block. These blocks may have colorful names, such as Rocky Road to Kansas or Jacob's Ladder. A special kind of patchwork is the crazy quilt. In this version, special pieces of fabric (often velvet or silk) are sewn together in a pleasing fashion but without a fixed pattern. In *appliqué*, a design (often floral) is cut out from material and sewn onto background fabric in blocks or for a whole quilt. *Quilting* itself refers to the stitching (done by hand or machine) that holds the three layers together. Sometimes the quilting stitches create a design in themselves. Quilts may also be held together by knots tied at intervals.

What are some of the names for patchwork patterns? Where do the names come from? Students can learn about the different patterns and investigate what they mean by reading Ann Whitford Paul's *Eight Hands Round: A Patchwork Alphabet,* illustrated by Jeanette Winter. This ABC book explains the origin of the interesting names for patterns (Flying Geese, Monkey Wrench), shows the different designs, and tells the story of the people behind the quilts.

Quilts in History.   Quilts kept log cabins warm, accompanied families in wagon trains, and preserved the memory of friends and relatives. Women (and men) used their needles to make quilts that reflected passages in their lives. Investigate the many books that tell stories of these early quilts and provide examples of quilt blocks.

Jane Bolton. *My Grandmother's Patchwork Quilt: A Book and Portfolio of Patchwork Pieces.* Doubleday, 1994.

Mary Cobb. *The Quilt Block History of Pioneer Days.* Millbrook Press, 1995. Examples of projects for children using paper and cut magazines.

Eleanor Coerr. *The Josefina Story Quilt.* Harper, 1989. When Faith's family sets out for California in 1850, she brings along the old hen Josefina. After Josefina rescues them from trouble, Faith sews a quilt to commemorate the trip. Also available in Spanish.

Valerie Flournoy. *The Patchwork Quilt.* Illustrated by Jerry Pinkney. Dial, 1985. When Tanya's grandmother gets too sick to work on her quilt, telling stories of family history, Tanya decides to help her finish it. African American family.

Ellen Howard. *The Log Cabin Quilt.* Holiday, 1996. Quilt scraps warm a family by providing chinking for their new cabin in Michigan.

Ann Whitford Paul. *The Seasons Sewn: A Year in Patchwork.* Harcourt, 1996.

Patricia Polacco. *The Keeping Quilt.* Simon & Schuster, 1988. Polacco traces her family's Jewish heritage through a quilt made from relatives' clothing and passed down through generations to celebrate births, marriages, and deaths. In each shape she can see the stories she's been told of her family.

Ask students if they have any quilts. Who made these quilts? What designs were used? What do these quilts mean to them? Share books with students that reflect how quilts can preserve people's heritage and help them make connections with others.

Underground Quilts.   Quilts may even have been used historically to carry secret information. In the same way that scraps of cloth were pieced together to keep memories alive, slaves may have sewn essential information into the quilts they made. Although it would be difficult to prove this actually took place, students can imagine how important it was to preserve knowledge when slaves couldn't read or write. These books give us a picture of what quilts might have meant to the African Americans at that time.

Dennis Brindell Fradin. *Bound for the North Star: True Stories of Fugitive Slaves.* Clarion, 2000. In 1850, the Fugitive Slave Act set free states against slave states because it compelled people to catch and return runaway slaves to their owners. Cover of this book shows a quilt representing the flight to freedom.

Deborah Hopkinson. *Sweet Clara and the Freedom Quilt.* Illustrated by James Ransome. Knopf, 1993. As a slave, Clara is not allowed to read or write, so she carefully stitches into the quilt the information she needs for her escape.

Alice McGill, coll. *In the Hollow of Your Hand: Slave Lullabies.* Illustrated by Michael Cummings. Houghton Mifflin, 2000. Despite their wretched conditions, slaves managed to express love for their children, through lullabies, for example. The quilt illustrations convey comfort. Includes a CD.

Quilts Today. Perhaps the most well-known quilt today is the AIDS quilt organized by the *Names Project.* Groups and individuals have made numerous panels in memory of people lost to this disease, stitching their feelings of loss into a quilt with words, designs, and familiar objects. Have students heard of this quilt or seen pictures of it? It has become so enormous that only portions of the quilt can be taken on tour. Read more about this interesting project that has brought people together.

Larry Dane Brimmer. *The Names Project: The AIDS Quilt.* Children's Press, 1999. Photo essay, with closeups and a panorama of the famous quilt.

Quilts are a perfect way to remember someone who is gone. The experience of planning and completing a quilt in someone's memory can provide important opportunities for grief and healing. The following book for primary students conveys the value of this process.

Jeannine Atkin. *A Name on the Quilt: A Story of Remembrance.* Illustrated by Tad Hill. Atheneum, 1999. A sister and brother realize they both have valuable memories of their uncle who has died. The quilt made in his memory represents their love for each other.

Following the model of the Names Project, many organizations have made similar group quilts, or Friendship Quilts, to raise awareness of issues such as breast cancer, for example.

The Meaning of Quilts. Quilts have developed meanings that go beyond the passing on of family history and memories. Because they are associated with women and the art of making do, quilts can also represent the changing social position of women. In addition, recognition of quilts as a significant art form can symbolize the participation of "ordinary" people in the production of "art." Above all, quilts make both the giver and the receiver feel good. Share some of these books with students and talk about the meaning of quilts.

Jeff Brumbeau. *The Quiltmaker's Gift.* Illustrated by Gail de Marcken. Pfeifer-Hamilton, 2000. Gloriously intricate illustrations support tale of greedy king who learns lesson about giving. Includes examples of many traditional quilt patterns and their colorful names. For all ages.

Anna Grosnickle Hines. *Pieces: A Year in Poems and Quilts.* Greenwillow, 2001. Twenty poems celebrate the seasons, accompanied by joyous quilts. Includes photos and stories behind the quilts.

Cynthia Rylant. *Poppleton Has Fun.* Illustrated by Mark Teague. Blue Sky Press, 2000. Making a quilt brings Poppleton and his friends together.

Gloria Whelan. *Homeless Bird.* HarperCollins, 2000. In this novel set in India, Koly finds herself doomed to a miserable life as a widow at 13. But dedication to her quilt embroidery opens unexpected possibilities.

Stories from around the World.   Quilts, or related textile art, appear in different forms in cultures around the world. Many children's picture books include aspects of these folk traditions as part of their illustrations, connecting the text to the underlying transmission of cultural heritage. Because the illustrations demand the reader's attention, these books can be appreciated at all grade levels.

Tanya Robyn Batt. *The Fabrics of Fairy Tale: Stories Spun from Far and Wide.* Illustrated by Rachel Griffin. Barefoot Books, 1999. Traditional tales that have fabric as a theme. Includes information about each region or country's particular textile—how it is made and what role it plays in society.

Clare Beaton. *Mother Goose Remembers.* Barefoot Books, 1999. The familiar verses accompanied by felt appliqué and a goose feather.

Lois Ehlert. *Market Day.* Harcourt Brace, 2000. Illustrations show how folk art, such as quilts and textiles, represents the power of cultural heritage.

Margaret Musgrove. *The Spider Weaver: A Legend of Kente Cloth.* Illustrated by Julia Cairns. Blue Sky Press, 1999. Tale from Ghana of how kente cloth was invented and came to represent African culture.

Adrienne Yorinks. *The Alphabet Atlas.* Winslow Press, 1999. Covers twenty-two countries, including a quilt/collage for each, such as "mud" cloth (kente) for Kenya.

Hmong Traditions.   Investigate other quilting-like traditions with students. Perhaps students know of the Hmong stitchery, called pa'ndau (story cloth). These intricate designs are passed on through generations. The Hmong come from Southeast Asia and are known for their colorful clothing. Show students examples in books such as:

Dia Cha. *Dia's Story Cloth: The Hmong People's Journey of Freedom.* Stitched by Chue and Nhia Thao Cha. Lee and Low, 1996. This story cloth, made by the author's aunt and uncle, chronicles Hmong life, past and present.

Pegi Deitz Shea. *The Whispering Cloth: A Refugee's Story.* Illustrated by Anita Riggio, stitched by Yon Yang. Boyds Mills, 1995. A Hmong family in a refugee camp in Thailand makes story cloths to earn money.

Amish Quilts.   The Amish, fleeing religious persecution and now living in small communities in Pennsylvania and other parts of the Midwest, are known for their quilts featuring solid colors and strong, simple, symmetrical designs. These quilts are representative of the Amish culture and beliefs, which include self-sufficiency, plain clothing, farming without machinery, and horse-driven buggies for transportation. Use a study of Amish quilts as a point of entry into this interesting culture and the choices that Amish people have made to live a simple life without modern technology.

Richard Ammon. *An Amish Year.* Illustrated by Pamela Patrick. Atheneum, 2000. Amish life through eyes of fourth-grader Anna.

Doris Faber. *The Amish.* Illustrated by Michael Erkel. Doubleday, 1991. Nonfiction.

Patricia Polacco. *Just Plain Fancy.* Bantam, 1990. A story about the Amish in Lancaster County, Pennsylvania.

Hawaiian Quilts.   Hawaiians are another group with a distinctive quilting tradition. The native Hawaiians sewed *tapa cloth* (made from bark) before the European arrival. When they began to make quilts, they adapted many of the same techniques to sewing cotton. Traditional Hawaiian quilts are made of a single large appliqué design (based on local flowers, trees, animals, or birds) sewn onto a solid background of a contrasting color. While in traditional European quilting everyone may use the same patterns to make very different quilts, Hawaiian quilters believe that every quilter should make her own pattern and not borrow another's without permission.

Students can experience the effect of a Hawaiian-style quilt by folding a square piece of paper into eighths (like a snowflake design). Cut out a design, making sure that they keep the paper connected along the folded side. Students may want to plan their design on paper first. They can draw designs based on animals, plants, or other familiar objects. When they unfold their design, notice how symmetrical it appears. Point out the axes of symmetry—vertical, horizontal, other.

Share the following book with students to introduce Hawaiian quilting.

Georgia Guback, *Luka's Quilt,* Greenwillow, 1994. Luka wants to make her own pattern, not the traditional Hawaiian one.

Quilt Quotes.   Include quotes about quilting as you discuss social studies, history, art, or other topics. Place quotes on the bulletin board for students to read. Students can write responses to these quotes. What do these quotes tell us about people's lives? About the importance of beauty in utilitarian objects? About our connection with the generations before us?

> My husband tells about the time he got sick with the measles. He was six years old. His mother set him to piecing a quilt and every other block he set in red polka-dot pattern. Said it was his measles quilt. (Patricia Cooper and Norma Bradley Allen. *The Quilters: Women and Domestic Art.* Anchor, 1989, p. 39)

> In the summers we'd put up the frame on the screened porch, and when the work was done, Mama would say, "O.K., girls, let's go to it." That was the signal for good times and laughin'. We'd pull up our chairs around the frame and anyone that dropped in would do the same, even if they couldn't stitch straight. Course we'd take out their stitches later if they was really bad. But it was for talking and visiting that we put in quilts in the summer. (Patricia Cooper and Norma Bradley Allen. *The Quilters: Women and Domestic Art.* Anchor, 1989, p. 76)

You can give the same kind of pieces to two persons, and one'll make a "nine-patch" and one'll make a "wild goose chase," and there'll be two quilts made out of the same kind of pieces, and just as different as they can be. And that's just the way with the living. The Lord sends us the pieces, but we can cut them out and put them together pretty much to suit ourselves, and there's a heap more in the cutting out and the sewing than there is in the calico. (*A Quilter's Wisdom: Conversations with Aunt Jane,* based on a text by Eliza Calvert Hall. Chronicle, 1994, pp. 37–38)

Everyone put their hand to piecing in the winter. All my boys pieced right along with the girls. It was work that had to be done. (Patricia Cooper and Norma Bradley Allen. *The Quilters: Women and Domestic Art.* Anchor, 1989, p. 154)

Nine-Patch Math. A nine-patch square is the basis for many quilt designs. Provide students with an 8- or 9-inch square. Have them divide it into thirds along each side, making nine equal spaces. Then ask them to divide some of those spaces in half. What are some different ways to do this? Can they divide the spaces into thirds or quarters? What different patterns can they make in their squares? Have students color in their designs. Show them how the same pattern can come out looking different depending on the arrangement of colors.

Figure 7.3 shows two examples of nine-patch patterns. Students can choose one to color. Assemble the student squares into a paper quilt. Are there alternative ways to put the quilt blocks together? Can students see larger patterns in the class quilt?

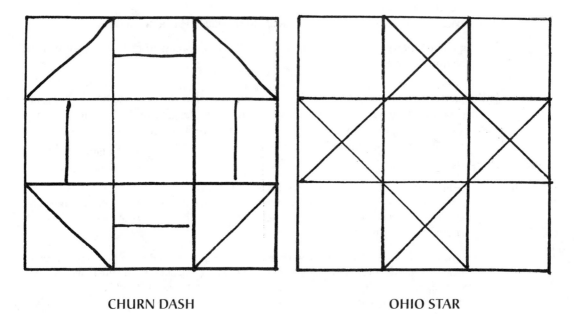

CHURN DASH   OHIO STAR

FIGURE 7.3   QUILT PATTERNS

Faith Ringgold's Story Quilts.   Sometimes quilts are used to tell a story. The story quilts of Faith Ringgold, an African American artist, are an example of stitched work based on a theme of pride in one's heritage. Her works assemble words and images in fabric in a revolutionary technique to create a narrative through a kind of collage. Investigate her work with students to show them how a person's own life and experience can be reflected in art. She has turned some of her quilts into children's picture books. Look at examples of her books and read about her life.

Faith Ringgold. *The Last Story Quilt.* Video, 1991. Ringgold talks about her life and shows her artwork.

Faith Ringgold. *Tar Beach.* Crown, 1991. This story of a girl's dreams as she lies on her city rooftop is framed by pieces of Ringgold's story quilts.

Faith Ringgold. *We Flew over the Bridge: The Memoirs of Faith Ringgold.* Little, Brown, 1995.

Robyn Montana Turner. *Faith Ringgold.* Little, Brown, 1993. From her childhood in Harlem in the 1930s to her status as an artist today, this detailed biography follows Ringgold's life and development, setting it in the context of African American experience.

Another famous story quilter is Harriet Powers, who worked in the nineteenth century. Her work links the quilting traditions of slaves with that of contemporary artists. Read about her surprisingly modern images in:

Mary E. Lyons. *Stitching the Stars: The Story Quilts of Harriet Powers.* Scribner's, 1993. African American artist's Bible-based quilts.

Students Make Friendship Quilts.   Students may be motivated to make quilts for many different reasons: to express their creativity, to distribute to the homeless, or to raise money. For example, they can select one of the many attractive Amish designs to cut out and sew, using solid colors. The drafting of the patterns for cutting will involve use of basic geometric shapes. Students in fourth grade and up can handle a sewing machine or a needle and thread with some adult assistance. Students can also make a crazy quilt, using donated scraps of fabric. Have each student assemble the odd-sized pieces on a foundation block of a fixed size so that the quilt can be assembled easily. Another popular theme for student quilts is "Our Neighborhood." Each student can make a block representing a house, embellishing each house differently with items such as trim and buttons. Or they can make individual blocks for particular features of the community—special buildings, sights, people. Students can also make an international quilt, showing children from many different countries and different backgrounds. In an *album* quilt, each student makes a block with his or her name in it, as a present for someone.

Primary students can draw on fabric with fabric crayons that become permanent after ironing. One kindergarten class made an alphabet quilt. For students who were unable to draw a letter, the teacher outlined large letters and the students colored them in. Later students pierced layers with yarn and tied knots to hold the quilt together.

Students can also adapt quilt techniques to paper. Collect supplies of colorful paper such as wrapping paper, magazines, or catalogs. Have students cut long strips of equal width. They can sew or glue these strips together lengthwise to make a band of 6 inches. Then cut across the strips every 6 inches so that you have squares. These squares can be assembled into the Rail Fence pattern. Encourage students to experiment with different possibilities for arranging their squares in a pleasing pattern.

Sources for Further Study

Raymond Bial. *With Needle and Thread: A Book about Quilts.* Houghton Mifflin, 1996. A social history of quilting.

Patricia Cooper and Norma Bradley Allen. *The Quilters: Women and Domestic Art, An Oral History.* Anchor, 1989. Collections of quilters' stories and memories. Also a play.

Roland Freeman. *A Communion of the Spirits: African American Quilters, Preservers, and Their Stories.* Rutledge Hill Press, 1996.

Eliza Calvert Hall. *A Quilter's Wisdom: Conversations with Aunt Jane.* Chronicle Books, 1994. Reprint of traditional comments, ascribed to "Aunt Jane."

Eli Leon. *Who'd a Thought It: Improvisation in African-American Quilting.* San Francisco Craft and Folk Museum, 1990. Shows the connections between contemporary quilting and African traditions.

Jacqueline L. Tobin and Raymond G. Dobard. *Hidden in Plain View: A Secret Story of Quilts and the Underground Railroad.* Anchor, 2000. Intriguing book makes argument that some quilt patterns served as codes for slaves to escape by the Underground Railroad.

FOCUSING ON TEACHING MUSIC MULTICULTURALLY

Music, too, enhances the curriculum, particularly at the elementary school level. Music offers a wide variety of possibilities—singing, dancing, playing an instrument. Here, again, we have an opportunity to reach a different form of intelligence and to expand students' multicultural understanding.

Effective Multicultural Music Strategies

Music is an important part of every culture. Students should experience a variety of music, either live or recorded—the blues, folk, classical—by members of many cultures. Introduce them to many fine musicians, singers, and songwriters who have contributed to the world's musical heritage, for example, Ravi Shankar, Duke Ellington, Kiri Te Kanawa, and Pete Seeger. Students are intrigued by the varied musical instruments used in different countries and less familiar musical scales. See also the special feature on jazz in Chapter 8.

Music should be an integral dimension of any unit of study that focuses on a group or country. Students should become aware of music as a universal language that all can share. They can create their own music to express their ideas and emotions.

Creating a Music Word Wall

Most of us enjoy music in one form or another. Students might brainstorm all the words and ideas they associate with music, just to assess what the class, as a group, knows about music. Write these words on a large sheet of paper to create a Music Word Wall, for example:

dancing	ballads	bagpipes
singing	country western	opera
notes	jazz	birds
lyrics	guitar	running water
piano	flamenco	samba
humming	church	symphony
rhythm	choir	

Keep adding words to this list as students think of other ideas—names of performers, titles of songs, kinds of dancing, and so on. You might link related words. Encourage students to bring in pictures to illustrate this wall as you create a collage of words and pictures. After the wall seems to be pretty well completed, ask students to study the collage and to state observations. They should note the great variety in the kinds of music and the groups of people represented. They might categorize the words. They might conclude that music is an important element of any culture. They could then study the music of specific cultures in cooperative learning groups.

Children's Books Depict Songs

Individual songs have often been presented with illustrations as picture books for children—for example, *She'll Be Comin' around the Mountain* and *Lift Ev'ry Voice and Sing*. Children will be interested in observing the artist's illustrations and may be motivated to create a book or a poster featuring a favorite folksong.

Reading about Music in the Lives of Young People

Students may be interested in reading stories that tell of young people who have musical talent. Some examples include:

Bruce Brooks. *Midnight Hour Encores.* Harper, 1986. Cellist.

Gillian Cross. *Chartbreaker.* Holiday House, 1987. Rock band.

Gavin Curtis. *The Bat Boy and His Violin.* Simon & Schuster, 1998.

Amy Littlesugar. *Marie in Fourth Position.* Philomel, 1996. Ballet.

Suzanne Newton. *I Will Call It Georgie's Blues.* Viking, 1983. Jazz piano.

Reading about Real Musicians

Students may select autobiographies, biographies, or fiction for reports required in the social studies, for example:

Pete Fornatale. *The Story of Rock 'n' Roll.* Morrow, 1987.

Robert Love. *Elvis Presley.* Watts, 1986.

Susan Saunders. *Dolly Parton: Country Goin' to Town.* Viking, 1985.

Catherine Scheader. *Contributions of Women: Music.* Dillon, 1985. Beverly Sills and four other women.

Jeanette Winter. *Sebastian, A Book about Bach.* Harcourt, 1999.

Challenge students to locate additional information about diverse persons who have made a contribution to the musical world.

An audio presentation, *Lives of the Musicians* (Audio Bookshelf, 1996), presents interesting facts about the lives of well-known musicians. Recommended for grades 4 through 8, the information is well-read and amusing.

Songbooks

The following collections of songs are particularly appropriate for supporting multicultural studies:

Lulu Delacre, ed. *Las Navidades: Popular Christmas Songs from Latin America.* Scholastic, 1990.

John Langstaff, ed. *What a Morning! The Christmas Story in Black Spirituals.* McElderry, 1987. Singing plus piano accompaniment.

Roland Vernon. *Introducing Gershwin.* Silver Burdett, 1996.

Nicki Weiss. *If You're Happy and You Know It.* Greenwillow, 1987. Picture book includes eighteen songs to sing together.

Folk Music from around the World

Folk songs from other countries offer immediate enjoyment through their patterned verses and easy-to-learn choruses.

Grace Hallworth. *Down by the River: AfroCaribbean Rhymes, Games, and Songs for Children.* Illustrated by Caroline Binch. Scholastic, 1996. Based on memories of growing up in Trinidad.

Kathleen Krull. *Gonna Sing My Head Off!* Knopf, 1992. Folk music accompanied by energetic artwork.

John and Nancy Langstaff, comp. *Sally Go Round the Mountain: Revels Songs and Singing Games for Young Children.* Revels, Inc., One Kendall Square, Building 600, Cambridge, MA 02139.

Nikki Siegen-Smith, comp. *Songs for Survival: Songs and Chants from Tribal Peoples around the World.* Dutton, 1995.

The following are some of the recordings available in different formats:

Alerta Sings Children's Songs in Spanish and English from Latin American, the Caribbean, and the United States. Folkways FH 7830.

Children's Songs and Games from Ecuador, Mexico, and Puerto Rico. Folkways FC 7854.

Ella Jenkins. *African American Folk Rhythms.* Smithsonian Folkways.

Lírica Infantil con José-Luís Orozco. Hispanic Children's Folklore. Arco Iris Records, P.O. Box 7428, Berkeley, CA 94707.

Sing Children Sing: Songs of Mexico. Caedmon TC 1654.

Songs for Singing Children with John Langstaff. CD/cassette.

Suni Paz. *Canciones para el recreo: Children's Songs for the Playground.* Smithsonian Folkways. Catalog from Folkways, Office of Folklife Programs, 955 L'Enfant Plaza, Suite 2600, Smithsonian Institution, Washington, DC 20560. Or order from Rounder Records, One Camp Street, Cambridge, MA 02140.

Music: A Universal Language

Brain research shows that music is truly universal. All humans seem to have music programmed in their brains just like language.

Savion Glover and Bruce Weber. *Savion! My Life in Tap.* Morrow, 2000. Biography of noted tap dance artist.

Matthew Gollub. *The Jazz Fly.* Illustrated by Karen Hanke. Tortuga Press, 2000. Experience the joy of improvisation, hear the "sound" of jazz, and learn to communicate in the "language" of music.

Nikki Grimes. *Jazmin's Notebook.* Dial, 1998. Jazmin confides her worries to her poetry journal.

Deborah Hopkinson. *A Band of Angels.* Illustrated by Raúl Colón. Atheneum, 1999. Fictionalized account of Jubilee Singers, keeping traditional black songs alive.

Toyomi Igus. *i see the rhythm.* Illustrated by Michele Wood. Children's Book Press, 1998. Poetry and images convey the history of black music, from forbidden drums to today.

Isaac Millman. *Moses Goes to a Concert.* Farrar, Straus & Giroux, 1998. Moses is deaf but he can "hear" the rhythm with his bare feet.

Ken Nordine. *Colors.* Illustrated by Henrik Drescher. Harcourt, 2000. Radio commentator's "word jazz" poems about colors.

Maria Diaz Strom. *Rainbow Joe and Me.* Lee & Low, 1999. Although Joe is blind, he portrays colors through music.

U.S. Folk Music from Every Region

Grades 3–8

Expected Outcomes
Learners will:

1. Identify folk songs representative of different regions in the United States.
2. Integrate music into social studies activities.
3. Present a program for other classes in the school.

Teaching/Learning Strategies

Resources Needed
This lesson ties in with studies of individual states and/or regions of the United States. It also fits with studies of different groups that live in this country, and it could be adapted to studies of other countries.

Check the catalogs of your school district or the public library to locate recordings of regional folk music. Songbooks may also include examples that you can use. Begin playing a song or two each day to students. Share the information provided about each song. Teach them the words to some of the songs to add to their singing repertoire.

Directions
Step 1:
Teach the class the following Pennsylvania Dutch folksong:

Johnny Schmoker

Pennsylvania Dutch Folk Song

John- ny   Schmo-ker,   John- ny   Schmo-ker

Can   you   sing?---   Can   you   play?----
Kannst du   sing- en? Kannst du   spiel- en?

I   can   play up-   on   my   drum-----
Ich kann spiel- en   auf mein trom- mel.

Rub- a-dub-a- dub, this   is   my   drum----
Rub- a-dub-a- dub, das   ist mein   trom- mel.

Explain that this song (with words in German) was sung by people of German ancestry who settled in what is now Pennsylvania. These people were called Pennsylvania Dutch because their name *Deutsch* (German) sounded like *Dutch*. You might also like to show students examples or pictures of their distinctive art. Then suggest that each group find a song that is typical of the state or region that they are researching. They should plan to incorporate the song into their report. They might plan to teach the song to the rest of the class.

Step 2:
Each group will plan to participate in an assembly to be attended by other classes. Each group will first point out on a large map the location of the area they studied. Group members will contribute to the presentation with information about the people who live there, how they live, and any distinctive contributions they have made.

Step 3:
Each group will submit a brief description of what they plan to contribute to the assembly. Two volunteers will prepare a printed program to send to the classes who are invited to attend their assembly. The groups will practice their presentations. The class will present the assembly.

Performance Assessment
The success of the total project will be assessed by each group. They will look at their individual presentations to decide what was particularly effective and also how it might have been improved. The responses from the other classes will add to the assessment process.

Infusing Multicultural Music Instruction across the Curriculum

Teaching Multiculturally around a Theme:
African Americans—Reclaiming Traditions

Africans brought to this country as slaves were deliberately torn from their cultural heritage, language, and traditions. They came here with nothing, unlike the historic waves of immigrants from Europe, who might have brought a few meaningful objects, or recent Latino immigrants, who can maintain family connections in another country. Today, African Americans need to learn a history in which they can take pride, rather than be portrayed as the passive victims of slavery. Students of all backgrounds can benefit from examples of the many African Americans who have fought for greater freedom for all people, particularly in the areas of education and civil rights.

Famous African Americans in History.   When students think of famous African Americans, the first names that come to mind are usually sports stars or music performers. But students need to hear about black men and women who have made contributions to our society in other areas. Challenge students to match these names with their contribution in Figure 7.4.

_____C_____	Matthew Henson	A.	astronomer
_____A_____	Benjamin Banneker	B.	first person killed in Boston Massacre (Revolutionary War)
_____D_____	Charles Drew	C.	went to North Pole with Admiral Peary
_____B_____	Crispus Attucks	D.	invented blood transfusions
_____G_____	Bill Pickett	E.	poet in colonial America
_____E_____	Phillis Wheatley	F.	led slaves to freedom
_____F_____	Harriet Tubman	G.	black cowboy

FIGURE 7.4   FAMOUS AFRICAN AMERICANS

Once students realize the number of blacks who have been recognized for their accomplishments, they will want to discover more names and find out more information about these people. Start a chart on the bulletin board where students can write the name of an achiever or someone they admire, and the reason. Students will be motivated to seek out names of historical figures, as well as people they know and respect today. *Come This Far to Freedom: A History of African Americans* by Angela Shelf Medearis and illustrated by Terea Shaffer is a collection of short sketches to start you off.

Special Days.   Several holidays provide reminders of African American accomplishments. Kwanzaa, celebrated in December, acknowledges African cultural roots. Feature books about Kwanzaa and about Africa.

Verna Aardema. *Misoso: Once Upon a Time: Tales from Africa.* Apple Soup, 1994. Collection of twelve fables and tales.

Ella Grier. *Seven Days of Kwanzaa.* Illustrated by John Ward. Viking, 1997. This special book features a kente-cloth border.

Angela Shelf Medearis. *The Seven Days of Kwanzaa; How to Celebrate Them.* Scholastic, 1994. An introduction to African American pride and culture. Includes ideas for gifts and food plus stories of seven African Americans to celebrate, from Fanny Lou Hamer to James Van Der Zee.

Another special day is Martin Luther King's birthday in January. On this day, provide opportunities to discuss King's work. What have we achieved in civil rights? How far do we still have to go?

Jean Marzollo. *Happy Birthday, Martin Luther King.* Illustrated by Brian Pinkney. Scholastic, 2000. A child asks his family why they celebrate King's birthday, and family members share their memories of King's accomplishments.

A significant date in African American history is Juneteenth (June 19), commemorating the day that the slaves in Texas finally learned about the Emancipation Proclamation. This would be a good time to focus on black history, particularly the period of slavery.

Jazz, A Unique Contribution.   Students can consult the encyclopedic *Jazz: A History of America's Music* by Geoffrey Ward and Ken Burns for more information about specific artists and the different influences on jazz. This series is unusually outspoken in locating the music in the social conditions of the time, such as poverty and lynchings.

Have students select an artist, an instrument, or an era to investigate. What did this person, object, or period contribute to the development of jazz? They can accompany the presentation with pictures and music. Here are some books to get them involved:

Ann Grifalconi. *Tiny's Hat.* HarperCollins, 1999. A young girl wears her father's hat to remind her of the musician father who is always on the road.

Andrea Davis Pinkney. *Duke Ellington: The Piano Prince and His Orchestra.* Illustrated by Brian Pinkney. Hyperion, 1998. Especially for primary students.

Fatima Shaik. *The Jazz of Our Street.* Illustrated by E. B. Lewis. Dial, 1998. The New Orleans Jazz Parade unites music, movement, and memories for the children who participate.

African American History.   The story of African Americans should be a part of the history that all of us learn. Unfortunately, presentations that focus on African Americans tend to occur in clumps in February and remain rare the rest of the year. Spread discussion of African American history throughout the curriculum with books that make black people more visible and help black students find their lives in history.

Michael L. Cooper. *The Double V Campaign: African Americans and World War II.* Lodestar, 1998. African Americans fought on two fronts—against Germans and against racism.

Jeri Ferris. *With Open Hands: A Story about Biddy Mason.* Lerner, 1999. Born a slave, she won her freedom and became one of the richest women in Los Angeles.

Ayanna Hart and Earl Spangler. *Africans in America.* Lerner, 1995. This history shows the continuity of African traditions and values.

James Haskins and Kathleen Benson. *Out of the Darkness: The Story of Blacks Moving North 1890–1940.* Benchmark, 2000. Uses two historical figures to explain this period.

Dorothy Hoobler and Thomas Hoobler. *The African American Family Album.* Oxford University Press, 1995. This social and cultural history, part of the *American Family Album* series, is full of project ideas.

Deborah Hopkinson. *A Band of Angels: A Story Inspired by the Jubilee Singers.* Illustrated by Raúl Colón. Atheneum, 1999. Ella Sheppard, born a slave, toured with the Jubilee Singers to raise money for Fisk University and keep the traditional songs alive.

Jacob Lawrence. *The Great Migration: An American Story.* HarperCollins, 1993. Sixty paintings by the famous artist Jacob Lawrence, accompanied by explanatory text, show the movement of blacks from the rural South to the urban North. Lawrence also painted sequences of the lives of Harriet Tubman and Frederick Douglass. The epilogue is a poem by Walter Dean Myers.

Osceola Mays. *Osceola: Memories of a Sharecropper's Daughter.* Disney Press, 2000. Outstanding oral history.

Walter Dean Myers. *Now Is Your Time: The African American Struggle for Freedom.* HarperCollins, 1991. The history of Africans in America starts in 1619 (before the Mayflower arrived) and continues today. This book is significant in showing African Americans not as victims but taking action on their own behalf.

Faith Ringgold. *Dinner at Aunt Connie's House.* Hyperion, 1993. Another book by distinguished artist Ringgold. When the children visit Aunt Connie, her paintings come to life and the women tell their stories. Voices of Mary McLeod Bethune, Madame Walker, and others will encourage readers to discover more about significant black women.

Slavery and the Civil War.   The history of African Americans in the United States is overshadowed by their involuntary presence as slaves. A common misconception is that the slaves accepted their condition passively until they were freed by Abraham Lincoln. In fact, free blacks worked unceasingly to abolish slavery, while enslaved blacks exercised what resistance they could. Correct student misconceptions by telling stories of African American resistance to slavery. When studying the history of the United States up to the Civil War, make sure that the story of slavery is included.

From the beginning of the slave trade in the early 1500s until it was outlawed by the French in 1848, 15 to 20 million Africans passed through the slave center on Goree Island in Senegal. By 1776, the black population in the United States was estimated at half a million. There were over 4 million blacks by the end of the Civil War.

Gwen Everett. *John Brown.* Paintings by Jacob Lawrence. Rizzoli, 1993. In this dramatic account, Annie Brown describes how her father led a "liberation army" in Virginia in 1859.

Tom Feelings. *The Middle Passage: White Ships, Black Cargo.* Dial, 1995. With no text, only paintings, this book communicates the experience of Africans crossing the ocean to slavery.

Virginia Hamilton. *Many Thousand Gone: African-Americans from Slavery to Freedom.* Illustrated by Leo and Diane Dillon. Knopf, 1992. The stories of the many brave blacks who struggled against slavery, from Harriet Tubman and Nat Turner to others less well known. Rich language lends itself to reading aloud.

James Haskins and Kathleen Benson. *Bound for America: The Forced Migration of Africans to the New World.* Illustrated by Floyd Cooper. Lee Lothrop & Shepard, 2000.

Julius Lester. *From Slave Ship to Freedom Road.* Illustrated by Rod Brown. Dial, 1998.

Linda Lowery. *Aunt Clara Brown: Official Pioneer.* Illustrated by Janice Lee Porter. Carolrhoda, 1999. Once freed, she made money in Colorado in order to help other former slaves.

Patricia C. McKissack and Frederick L. McKissack. *Rebels Against Slavery: American Slave Revolts.* Scholastic, 1996. Chronicles 250 years of anti-slavery movements, including the famous uprisings of Nat Turner (1831), Joseph Cinque (1839), Denmark Vesey (1822), and Gabriel Prosser (1800).

Walter Dean Myers. *Amistad: A Long Road to Freedom.* Illustrated by P. Lee. Dutton, 1998. Fascinating case of Africans, kidnapped in 1839, arguing for their freedom in court and being returned to Africa.

Doreen Rappaport. *Escape from Slavery: Five Journeys to Freedom.* Illustrated by Charles Lilly. HarperCollins, 1991. Relates the escape stories of courageous African Americans who found freedom in the years before the Civil War.

Read fictional accounts to feel what it was like to live as a slave. The following books help students understand how hard it was to maintain stable families, to remember previous lives in Africa, and to accomplish something as simple as learning to read and write.

Sara Harrell Banks. *Abraham's Battle: A Novel of Gettysburg.* Atheneum, 1999. An ex-slave's perspective on the Civil War, inspired by actual events.

James Berry. *Ajeemah and His Son.* HarperCollins, 1992. Ajeemah and his son, in Ghana on their way to celebrate his marriage, are kidnapped and sold as slaves in Jamaica. Atu, the son, kills himself, but Ajeemah doesn't give up hope. An excellent starting point for discussing the degradation of slavery and the different ways in which people responded to it.

Elisa Carbone. *Stealing Freedom.* Knopf, 1998. Based on true story of Ann Maria Weems, whose father was free but the rest of the family was broken up and sold.

Paula Fox. *The Slave Dancer.* Dell, 1973. Winner of the Newbery Award, this story tells of a boy who is forced to play his fife to make the slaves dance on the voyage from Africa to the United States to be sold. Recounts in vivid, gruesome detail a story of survival.

Walter Dean Myers. *The Journal of Joshua Loper: A Black Cowboy.* Scholastic, 1999. *My Name Is America* series. In 1871, a boy experiences prejudice but his hard work is also valued.

Kathryn Paterson. *Jip.* Lodestar, 1996. A boy in 1847 doesn't know his parents were slaves. Although free in the North, he can be taken back South and sold as a slave.

Gary Paulsen. *Nightjohn.* Delacorte, 1993. Sarny, a young female slave, risks her life in order to be taught to read and write by a mysterious escaped slave. Gripping short novel of the power of literacy and the drive to resist. *Sarny* (1997), the sequel, has her looking back on her 94 years of life.

Andrea Davis Pinkney. *Silent Thunder: A Civil War Story.* Hyperion, 1999. Two slaves, brother and sister, want to learn to read and write.

Michael J. Rosen. *A School for Pompey Walker.* Illustrated by Aminah Brenda Lynn Robinson. Harcourt Brace, 1995. Fiction based on true stories, the tale of a slave who, with the help of a white friend, had himself sold into slavery repeatedly and was able to save enough money to build a school for black children.

Mary Stolz. *Cezanne Pinto.* Knopf, 1994. Ex-slave Pinto, on his ninetieth birthday, looks back to his childhood on a Virginia plantation, his escape north, and his search for his mother.

The Underground Railroad.   Display a map of the United States to the class. Which were the slave states and which the free states? Have students trace the paths by which slaves could escape to freedom (to the North, frequently later to Canada, and also to the Bahamas, since they were British and, therefore, free). How far would slaves have to travel and how long would it take? What motivated people to risk such a long, difficult journey into unknown territory?

Research the history of the Underground Railroad in your area, if possible. Are there any remains or memories of stations where slaves were directed and hidden? Helping slaves escape was illegal and especially dangerous in the South, yet all kinds of people (northerners, southerners, Indians, Quakers, Canadians, British, free blacks, and other slaves) risked their own lives. Why would people do something for which they could be arrested or killed? Read biographies and historical accounts to understand the extraordinary people who fought against slavery.

Patricia Beatty. *Who Comes with Cannons?* Morrow, 1992. A young Quaker girl goes to live with her aunt, uncle, and cousins in North Carolina. Their home is also a station on the Underground Railroad. Explores why people risked their lives to help slaves reach freedom.

Virginia Hamilton. *The Mystery of Drear House.* Scholastic, 1997. Another story set in the house that was a stop on the Underground Railroad.

Kathryn Lasky. *True North: A Novel of the Underground Railroad.* Scholastic, 1996. In 1858, Afrika, a slave girl trying to escape, meets Lucy, a white Boston girl.

Gwyneth Swain. *President of the Underground Railroad: A Story about Levi Coffin.* Illustrated by Ralph L. Ramstad. Lerner, 2001.

Civil Rights Movement.   Sometimes students feel that all they hear about is African Americans and slavery. This focus can leave students feeling hopeless. Show students that there is more to the history of African Americans than slavery. The civil rights movement is important history in the immediate past, part of their parents' or relatives' memory.

Alice Faye Duncan. *The National Civil Rights Museum Celebrates Everyday People.* Bridgewater, 1995. Includes photos.

History of the Civil Rights Movement. Video, 1994. Includes historical base for civil rights.

Casey King and Linda Barrett Osborne. *Oh Freedom! Kids Talk about the Civil Rights Movement with the People Who Made It Happen.* Knopf, 1997. Includes 31 interviews that kids taped with family and friends, makes for a vivid documentary.

Ellen Levine. *Freedom's Children.* Putnam, 1993. Children share their experiences through stories and photos.

Amy Littlesugar. *Freedom School.* Philomel, 2001. Jolie in Mississippi is scared that her family will be in danger from hosting a white volunteer for the Freedom School.

Leon Walter Tillage. *Leon's Story.* Illustrated by Susan L. Roth. Farrar, 1997. Leon was born the son of a sharecropper and grew up in the segregated South but his family sustained him.

Deborah Wiles. *Freedom Summer.* Atheneum, 2001. Two boys are disappointed that anti-segregation laws don't bring change.

Jacqueline Woodson. *The Other Side.* Putnam, 2001. Two girls on opposite sides of the fence that divides the black and white sides of town.

Learning Pride in One's Culture.   African American children are surrounded by negative images of their race and culture. They need to have many opportunities to take pride in their history and heritage, their nappy hair, and African looks. Books can reach across time and space to supply what may be lacking in their own community. The following books give students something to hold on to, to help them counterbalance negative stereotyping. After reading these books, have students share examples of family stories and customs.

Bryan Collier. *Uptown.* Holt, 1999. Collage of today's Harlem.

Jay David. *Songs of Wisdom: Quotes from Great African Americans of the 20th Century.* Morrow, 2000. Inspiring quotations.

Elizabeth Fitzgerald Howard. *Aunt Flossie's Hats (and Crab Cakes Later).* Illustrated by James Ransome. Clarion, 1991. Two African American girls visit Great Aunt Flossie. She has a story to tell with each hat they try on.

Wade Hudson and Cheryl Hudson, sel. *How Sweet the Sound: African-American Songs for Children.* Illustrated by Floyd Cooper. Scholastic, 1996. From traditional songs and street cries to spirituals and protest songs.

Kathleen Krull. *Bridges to Change: How Kids Live on a South Carolina Sea Island.* Lodestar, 1995. Two descendants of Gullah speakers and their efforts to maintain their culture. From *A World of My Own* series.

Gail Carson Levine. *Dave at Night.* HarperCollins, 1999. Jewish orphan encounters world of Harlem Renaissance.

Amy Littlesugar. *Tree of Hope.* Illustrated by Floyd Cooper. Philomel, 1999. Orson Welles brought theater back to Harlem in the 1930s.

Belinda Rochelle. *Jewels.* Illustrated by Cornelius Van Wright and Ying-Hwa Hu. Lodestar, 1998. A girl's favorite time is spent with her grandparents as they tell stories about her ancestors, one freed by Harriet Tubman, another a Buffalo Soldier.

Anita Rodriquez. *Aunt Martha and the Golden Coin.* Clarkson-Potter, 1993. One of a series of books about Aunt Martha, who tells the children learning stories from her African American heritage. In this one, she has a magic coin that fends off a burglar. But is the coin really magic, or does Aunt Martha's own strength of mind save her?

Jacqueline Woodson. *We Had a Picnic This Sunday Past.* Illustrated by Diane Greenseid. Hyperion, 1998. Joys of a family picnic.

African American Folklore.   Some of the richest American folklore comes from the African American tradition. Read examples aloud to students to stimulate their interest in this oral tradition. Have students work in groups to present a tale to the class or for a school-wide program. Students who may not do as well with written work have a chance to shine as performers. And all students have the opportunity to develop their speaking skills as they concentrate on delivering their dialogue with appropriate emotions.

Oral performance provides a context in which to talk about different ways of speaking. Students can have some of the characters speak formal English and others speak so-called Black English. How will students distinguish these ways of speaking? Because students have had different amounts of experience with formal English, encourage them to share their knowledge as they work in groups to decide how each character will talk.

Virginia Hamilton. *The Girl Who Spun Gold*. Illustrated by Leo and Diane Dillon. Scholastic, 2000. African American version of Rumpelstiltskin story.

Julius Lester. *John Henry*. Dial, 1994. Can a steel-driving man work faster than a steam drill?

Patricia McKissack. *The Dark Thirty: Southern Tales of the Supernatural*. Illustrated by Brian Pinkney. Knopf, 1992. Favorite scary stories. Students will probably recognize familiar tales.

Robert San Souci. *The Talking Eggs*. Illustrated by Jerry Pinkney. Dial, 1989. This retelling of a Cinderella-like Creole folktale is set in the American South with African American characters.

Joyce Carol Thomas. *The Bowlegged Rooster and Other Tales That Signify*. Illustrated by Holly Berry. HarperCollins, 2000. Collection of stories that teach lessons in life.

Positive Images of Black Families in Literature.   Students need to see realistic yet positive images of the lives of people like themselves. Well-written children's books can give students a mirror against which to measure themselves as well as a chance to imagine a better world. The following books acknowledge the problems and conflicts typical of African American children's lives and at the same time offer hope. In addition, the quality of the writing ensures that children from other racial backgrounds will appreciate the stories, too.

Marie Bradby. *Momma, Where Are You From?* Illustrated by Chris K. Soentpiet. Orchard, 2000. Realistic pictures as girl's mother reminisces about her hard childhood.

Lucille Clifton. *Some of the Days of Everett Anderson*. Illustrated by Evaline Ness. Henry Holt, 1987. The famous black poet has written a series of picture books about lively Everett, with warm pictures of family life in an apartment in the city.

Monica Gunning. *Under the Breadfruit Tree*. Illustrated by Fabricio Ven den Broeck. Boyds Mills, 1998. Author's childhood in Jamaica.

Lorri Hewett. *Dancer*. Dutton, 1999. Black 16-year-old girl wonders whether to follow her dream to be a ballerina or go to college.

Mary Hoffman. *Amazing Grace*. Illustrated by Caroline Binch. Dial, 1991. Grace likes to act out characters from stories she reads. Her grandmother tells Grace she can be anyone she wants to be.

Elizabeth Fitzgerald Howard. *Virgie Goes to School with Us Boys*. Illustrated by E. B. Lewis. Simon & Schuster, 2000. Virginia wants to go to school to learn to read like her older brothers. Based on family's story.

Phil Mendez. *The Black Snowman.* Illustrated by Carole Byard. Scholastic, 1989. Jacob learns pride and bravery from a snowman that he builds with his younger brother.

Margaree King Mitchell. *Uncle Jed's Barbershop.* Illustrated by James Ransome. Simon & Schuster, 1993. A black man dreams of owning his own barbershop, not an easy goal in the 1920s.

Gloria Pinkney. *Back Home.* Illustrated by Jerry Pinkney. Dial, 1992. Eight-year-old Ernestine from the city visits relatives on a farm in North Carolina. She's eager to fit in, but the country ways are different. This story of a black family presents universal themes of home, family, and belonging.

Faith Ringgold. *Tar Beach.* Crown, 1991. Cassie and BeBe in Brooklyn dream of flying away from the pressures of the world.

Robert San Souci. *Sukey and the Mermaid.* Four Winds, 1992. Sukey finds comfort from a mermaid in her escape from her stepfather. Set in the Sea Islands, off the Carolina coast.

Mildred Taylor. *Roll of Thunder, Hear My Cry.* Phyllis Fogelson, 2001. Classic story of a southern black family maintaining its pride and its land despite the humiliations of racial prejudice. A Newbery Award winner, it is especially noteworthy for its acknowledgment of the complexity of black–white relations.

Sherley Williams. *Working Cotton.* Harcourt Brace Jovanovich, 1992. The story of an African American girl and her family's work in the cotton fields of central California.

Virginia Euwer Wolff. *True Believer.* Atheneum, 2001. In this novel, teenager LaVaughn struggles to achieve her goals despite the limitations of her situation.

Jacqueline Woodson. *Maizon at Blue Hill.* Delacorte, 1993. When Maizon is accepted at Blue Hill, an elite, mostly white boarding school, she has to leave behind her grandmother, her best friend, and her familiar neighborhood. She struggles to find her own place despite the barriers. Look for other stories about Maizon.

Black Voices in Poetry.   How many students know the names of any black poets? Students may be surprised to learn that there are famous male and female black poets. Share with the class poems such as "Motto" by Langston Hughes and "We Real Cool" by Gwendolyn Brooks. Both of these poems make especially effective use of "street" language.

As you discuss the poems, ask students why the poets chose to use this kind of language. The poems don't read like conventional poetry—can we still call them poems? Are they written to be read silently or aloud? Using these poems as models, students will be motivated to write poems based on their experience, with familiar words and rhythms.

Collections of poetry by African Americans for children include the following:

Davida Adedjouma, ed. *The Path of My Heart: Poetry by African American Children.* Illustrated by Gregory Christie. Lee and Low, 1996. Through writing workshops, inner-city children give voice to their concerns. These examples will motivate students to produce their own poetry.

Arnold Adoff, ed. *I Am the Darker Brother.* Simon & Schuster, 1997. A new edition of this book includes more recent poets, particularly women.

Catherine Clinton, sel. *I, Too, Sing America.* Illustrated by Stephen Alcorn. Houghton Mifflin, 1998. Three centuries of African American poetry, from Phyllis Wheatley to Rita Dove.

Paul Laurence Dunbar. *Jump Back, Honey: Poems Selected and with an Introduction by Andrea Davis Pinkney.* Illustrated by Ashley Bryan. Hyperion, 1999. Art by fourteen noted African American artists, such as Faith Ringgold.

Tom Feelings. *Soul Looks Back in Wonder.* Dial, 1993. Feelings illustrated the book, then selected poems by thirteen African American poets, past (Langston Hughes) and present (Maya Angelou), to accompany them. For older students.

Nikki Giovanni. *The Sun Is So Quiet.* Illustrated by Ashley Bryan. Holt, 1996. Short poems play with language in beautifully illustrated book for preschool to primary.

Eloise Greenfield. *Honey, I Love and Other Poems.* Illustrated by Jan Spivey Gilchrist. HarperFestival, 1995. Engaging poems to read aloud.

Nikki Grimes. *A Pocketful of Poems.* Illustrated by Javaka Steptoe. Clarion, 1999. Poems about a girl in Harlem, includes haiku and free verse.

Wade Hudson, ed. *Pass It On: African-American Poetry for Children.* Illustrated by Floyd Cooper. Scholastic, 1993. Poems by Gwendolyn Brooks, Paul Dunbar, Nikki Giovanni, Langston Hughes, and Eloise Greenfield, with information about the poets.

Javaka Steptoe, ed. *In Daddy's Arms I Am Tall: African American Celebrating Fathers.* Lee & Low, 1997. These poems about a range of fathers are illustrated by Steptoe's unusual collages.

Joyce Carol Thomas. *Brown Honey in Broomwheat Tea.* Illustrated by Floyd Cooper. HarperCollins, 1993. Poems that celebrate the color of one's skin.

Questions of Identity.   One of the issues confronting us as we teach multiculturally is how to define who is an African American. In the time of slavery, the answer was simple: People known to have even a drop of "African blood" were considered black, even if they came from primarily white ancestry. The label of African American has always included people of many different racial and ethnic backgrounds. Today, however, increasing attention has been drawn to the recognition of *multiracial* heritage. For the first time, respondents to the U.S. Census were allowed to identify themselves as members of more than one racial or ethnic group. One advantage to this change is that children who have parents from different racial groups are no longer forced to select an identity that excludes one parent. On the other hand, how do we count the African American population? From 29 million people in 1990, the number of blacks in 2000 has increased to 34 million (if you count the people who only checked one box) or 35 million (if you count the people who checked at least this race). The difference of one million people is a substantial one. In that case, what does it mean to be an African American? Should "multiracial" be considered a separate identity in the multicultural curriculum?

One person who has faced this question is the popular young golf star Tiger Woods. He has been called African American because his father is black, Afro-Asian because his mother is from Thailand, and simply multiracial in honor of his diverse heritage. Students can select one of the many biographies of this outstanding individual and then discuss the challenge of labeling people. What would they prefer to be called?

Carl Emerson. *Tiger Woods.* Child's World, 2000. Part of the *Sports Superstars* series. Good photographs.

Libby Hughes. *Tiger Woods: A Biography for Kids.* Genesis, 2000. For primary grades.

Paul Joseph. *Tiger Woods.* Abdo & Daughters, 2000. Part of the *Awesome Athletes* series.

Elizabeth Sirimarco. *Tiger Woods.* Capstone, 2001. Part of the *Sports Heroes* series, for intermediate grades.

Mark Stewart. *Tiger Woods: Drive to Greatness.* Millbrook, 2001. For intermediate grades.

Role Models.   Students need the benefit of examples of others who have faced similar hardships and obstacles of prejudice or poverty and overcome them to go on to lead positive lives. Provide students with many illustrations of people who have overcome adversity, freed themselves from a limited environment, contributed to the world, and inspired others. What can we learn from these people's lives? How did they cope with the problems that confront all of us?

The Spingarn Medal has been awarded by the NAACP since 1915 for high achievement by an African American. How many of these names do students know? How can we keep their memories alive and not tucked away in a dusty museum?

Mary McLeod Bethune (1935)	Alvin Ailey (1976)
Walter White (1937)	Coleman Young (1981)
Richard Wright (1941)	L. Douglas Wilder (1990)
A. Philip Randolph (1942)	Dorothy I. Height (1993)
Charles Drew (1944)	John Hope Franklin (1995)
Paul Robeson (1945)	A. Leon Higginbotham (1996)
Dr. Percy L. Julian (1947)	Myrlie Evers-Williams (1995)
Ralph J. Bunche (1949)	Carl Rowan (1997)
Edward Kennedy Ellington (1959)	Oprah Winfrey (2000)
Kenneth B. Clark (1961)	Vernon E. Jordan Jr. (2001)
Medgar W. Evers (1963)	John Lewis (2002)
Jacob Lawrence (1970)	Constance Baker Motley (2003)
Gordon Parks (1972)	

Biographies of African Americans.   Familiarize yourself with the enormous number of excellent biographies of African Americans, from the useful series books to books written by top children's authors. Groups of students can select a period (the Harlem Renaissance), a region (the West), or a field (science) to study. Help them collect biographies of people to study. Older students will benefit from comparing several biographies of the same person. There are many biographies of Harriet Tubman, for example. How do they differ in their approach to her life? Look carefully at what each writer chooses to include, what is not included, and how the writer presents the information. Are there disagreements about the facts of her history? Have students analyze critically the different interpretations in these historical accounts.

Here are a few biographies to feature including historical figures as well as modern ones.

Ellen R. Butts and Joyce R. Schwartz. *May Chinn: The Best Medicine.* Freeman/Scientific America Books for Young Readers, 1995. Born in 1896, she faced prejudice at every turn yet managed to establish a medical practice in Harlem.

Lesa Cline-Ransome. *Satchel Paige.* Illustrated by James Ransome. Simon & Schuster, 2000. Biography of baseball player.

Floyd Cooper. *Coming Home: From the Life of Langston Hughes.* Penguin, 1998. Touching picture book based on Hughes's lonely childhood with his grandmother in Kansas.

John Duggleby. *Story Painter: The Life of Jacob Lawrence.* Chronicle, 1998. Brief biography of narrative painter who won acclaim for his series of paintings reflecting the Black experience.

Ruth Tenzer Feldman. *Thurgood Marshall.* Lerner, 2001. From arguing before the Supreme Court to Supreme Court Justice.

Eloise Greenfield. *Mary McLeod Bethune.* Illustrated by Jerry Pinkney. HarperCollins, 1994. A picture book about the Great Educator.

Philip S. Hart. *Up in the Air: The Story of Bessie Coleman.* Carolrhoda, 1996. Coleman was the first African American to win a pilot's license. A book for middle school students. See also *Flying Free: America's First Black Aviators* by the same author.

Libby Hughes. *Colin Powell: A Man of Destiny.* Dillon Press, 1996. *People in Focus* series. Sets his life in the context of the closely knit West Indian community in Harlem. For older students.

Deloris and Roslyn Jordan. *Salt in His Shoes.* Simon & Schuster, 2000. Mother and sister tell of Michael Jordan's childhood when he worried he wouldn't be tall enough to play basketball.

Barbara Kramer. *Alice Walker: Author of* The Color Purple. Enslow, 1995. *People to Know* series. This biography for young adults describes hardships faced by Walker and analyzes the themes of her work—racism, feminism, rape.

Patricia McKissack and Frederick McKissack. *Red-Tail Angels.* Walker, 1995. The Tuskegee airmen persevered against racism and indignities in World War II and proved their heroism.

Walter Dean Myers. *The Greatest: Muhammed Ali.* Scholastic, 2001. Muhammed Ali is still respected as a boxing champion.

Andrea Davis Pinkney. *Duke Ellington: The Piano Prince and His Orchestra.* Illustrated by Brian Pinkney. Hyperion, 1998. Picture book biography of man who helped make jazz America's classical music.

Lawrence S. Ritter. *Leagues Apart: The Men and Times of the Negro Baseball Leagues.* Illustrated by Richard Merkin. Morrow, 1995. For the elementary student, an introduction to the baseball players and the hardships they faced in the days of segregated sport.

Jack L. Roberts. *Booker T. Washington: Educator and Leader.* Millbrook Press, 1995. *Gateway Civil Rights* series. Explains his debate with W. E. B. DuBois and his founding of the Tuskegee Institute, for the elementary student.

Kenneth Rudeen. *Jackie Robinson.* Illustrated by Michael Hays. HarperCollins, 1996. A chapter-book biography of the baseball player for elementary students.

Alan Schroeder. *Satchmo's Blues.* Illustrated by Floyd Cooper. Doubleday, 1996. A book to read aloud to primary students, based on the childhood of Louis Armstrong.

Victoria Sherrow. *Wilma Rudolph.* Illustrated by Larry Johnson. Lerner, 2000. Despite childhood weakness from polio, Rudolph earned several Olympic gold medals in running.

Maryann N. Weidt. *Voice of Freedom: A Story about Frederick Douglass.* Illustrated by Jeni Reeves. Lerner, 2001. Born a slave, he secretly learned to read and became an eloquent voice for abolitionism.

Videos are also available based on Chelsea House's *Black Americans of Achievement* series. Some titles include *Jesse Owens: Champion Athlete, Marcus Garvey: Black-Nationalist Leader,* and *Matthew Henson: Explorer.*

Featuring African American Authors for Children.   Talk about the authors of the books that you share with students. How many of them are African American? Make sure that students know who these people are, so that they recognize that African Americans can write books, too. Show them pictures of the authors and talk about the authors as real people. African American authors who have written many exceptional books for young people include Virginia Hamilton, Mildred Taylor, John Steptoe, and Julius Lester. Investigate books by some more recent authors, for example, Angela Johnson, Faith Ringgold, and Andrea Davis Pinkney.

Two major African American authors today are Patricia McKissack and Walter Dean Myers. Plan a special study around one of these authors. Have students analyze the author's style. What themes does this author prefer? Does the author use a particular style of language? What is the author's attitude toward his or her characters? Does the author favor a particular genre, or type of book, such as history or folklore? Find out more about the author's life. What led him or her to write for a young audience?

Patricia McKissack often writes books with her husband, Frederick McKissack. Here are some titles to look for:

Black Hands, White Sails: The Story of African American Whalers. Scholastic, 1999. (with Frederick McKissack)

Christmas in the Big House, Christmas in the Quarters. Scholastic, 1994. (with Frederick McKissack)

The Civil Rights Movement in America. Children's Press, 1991. (with Frederick McKissack)

The Honest-to-Goodness Truth. Illustrated by Giselle Potter. Atheneum, 2000.

Ida B. Wells-Barnett: A Voice against Violence. Enslow, 2001. *Great African Americans* series.

A Long Hard Journey: The Story of the Pullman Porter. Walker, 1989.

Ma Dear's Aprons. Simon & Schuster, 1997.

Mirandy and Brother Wind. Knopf, 1988.

Paul Robeson: A Voice to Remember. Enslow, 2001. *Great African Americans* series.

Rebels against Slavery: American Slave Revolts. Scholastic, 1996. (with Frederick McKissack)

Red-Tail Angels: Tuskegee Airmen. Walker, 1995. (with Frederick McKissack)

The Royal Kingdoms of Ghana, Mali, and Songhay. Holt, 1993. (with Frederick McKissack)

For more information about this author, see *Patricia McKissack: Can You Imagine?* (Richard C. Owen, 1997) in *Meet the Author* series.

An author who usually writes for a middle or high school audience is Walter Dean Myers, winner of the Newbery Honor Medal for *Scorpions* and the Coretta Scott King Award for *Fallen Angels.* In addition to these books about black teenagers, he has written poems, picture books, historical novels, and books about African American history and culture.

Amistad: A Long Road to Freedom. Dutton, 1997.

At Her Majesty's Request: An African American Princess in Victorian England. Scholastic, 1999.

Harlem. Illustrated by his son, Christopher Myers. Scholastic, 1997.

How Mr. Monkey Saw the Whole World. Doubleday, 1996.

The Journal of Scott Pendleton Collins: A World War II Soldier. Scholastic, 1999.

Malcolm X: By Any Means Necessary. Scholastic, 1994.

Now Is Your Time: The African American Struggle for Freedom. HarperCollins, 1991.

One More River to Cross: An African American Photograph Album. Harcourt Brace, 1995.

Righteous Revenge of Artemis Bonner. HarperCollins, 1992.

Somewhere in the Darkness. Scholastic, 1992.

Toussaint L'Ouverture: The Fight for Haiti's Freedom. Simon & Schuster, 1996.

Featuring African American Illustrators.   There are many excellent African American illustrators working in the field of children's literature. Encourage students to become more aware of the people who illustrate the books that they read. Provide information and talk about the artists as real people. Analyze the artist's style. Does this person use the same techniques in each book? What are the distinctive features of this artist's style? Students will notice artists such as Tom Feelings, Floyd Cooper, and James Ransome.

Two excellent artists who have been working in this field for a long time are the husband and wife team of Leo and Diane Dillon. They won the Caldecott Award for *Why Mos-*

quitoes Buzz in People's Ears (by Verna Aardema). This interracial couple is known for their atmospheric illustrations often accompanying folktales. Look for their work in these books:

Nancy White Carlstrom. *Northern Lullaby.* Philomel, 1992.

Virginia Hamilton. *The Girl Who Spun Gold.* Scholastic, 2000.

Virginia Hamilton. *Her Stories: African American Folktales, Fairy Tales, and True Tales.* Scholastic, 1995.

Virginia Hamilton. *Many Thousand Gone: African Americans from Slavery to Freedom.* Knopf, 1992.

Sharon Bell Mathis. *The Hundred Penny Box.* Viking, 1975.

Margaret Musgrove. *Ashanti to Zulu.* Dial, 1976.

Katherine Paterson. *The Tale of the Mandarin Ducks.* Lodestar, 1989.

Mildred Pitts Walker. *Brother to the Wind.* Lothrop, Lee, Shepard, 1985.

Students can see a video presentation of the Dillons' work for *Why Mosquitoes Buzz in People's Ears* in the collection *Emperor's New Clothes and Other Folktales* (Weston Woods Video, 1991). *The Art of Leo and Diane Dillon* edited by Byron Preiss (Ballantine, 1981) provides background for further study of these artists.

Another well-known illustrator is Jerry Pinkney. His work appears in these books:

Eloise Greenfield. *Mary McLeod Bethune.* HarperCollins, 1994.

Virginia Hamilton. *Drylongso.* Harcourt, 1992.

Julius Lester. *Black Cowboy, Wild Horses: A True Story.* Dial, 1998.

Gloria Pinkney. *Back Home.* Dial, 1992.

Robert San Souci. *The Talking Eggs.* Dial, 1989.

Alan Schroeder. *Minty: The Story of Young Harriet Tubman.* Dial, 1996.

A video is available of "A Visit with Jerry Pinkney" from Penguin USA Author Videos.

For more information about the life and work of Leo and Diane Dillon, Jerry Pinkney, and other artists, see Pat Cummings, ed., *Talking with Artists.* Includes conversations with fourteen children's illustrators.

Exploring Africa.   Africa still holds a special fascination due to its size, diversity, and long history. From Marcus Garvey to Nelson Mandela, Africa has exerted a powerful hold on the imaginations of American blacks. Bring Africa into the classroom through stories, music, games, and pictures.

Put a map of Africa on the board. Can students name any of the fifty-three countries? How big is it compared to the United States? To your state? What different languages are spoken on this continent? Why would some countries use English for their official language and others use French? These are languages they have to learn in school. Why don't they use the language they learn at home? Learn about Swahili, a language spoken in many countries.

Talk about the diversity of Africa. What do the people look like? Display pictures to show the population: Arabs, South African whites, Asians (Indians), different African tribes. Locate these groups on the map. A reference book that students can use is Yvonne Ayo, *Africa.* For intermediate students, this book covers the rich diversity of Africa, including topics such as houses, sports, religion, dress, and music.

Who is Nelson Mandela? Read about his life to find why he is an African leader respected around the world.

Floyd Cooper. *Mandela.* Philomel, 1997. A chronological overview of Mandela's life for primary students.

Benjamin Pogrund. *Nelson Mandela: Strength and Spirit of a Free South Africa.* Gareth Stevens, 1992.

Learn what life is like in the different countries by listening to music, playing games, and making crafts.

Carol Finley. *The Art of African Masks: Exploring Cultural Traditions.* Lerner, 1999.

Florence Temko. *Traditional Crafts from Africa.* Lerner, 1996. Using a variety of everyday materials, readers can make objects while learning about the role of crafts in African cultures.

Caedmon Records has collections of songs from different regions, such as *Songs of the Congo.*

Read stories about different tribes and countries in Africa to illustrate the diversity of this enormous continent (see Figure 7.5).

Robert Steven Bianchi. *The Nubians: People of the Ancient Nile.* Millbrook, 1994. These black Africans are less familiar than their neighbors the Egyptians. From *Beyond Museum Walls* series.

Jim Brandenburg. *Sand and Fog: Adventures in South Africa.* Walker, 1994. Set in Namibia, the most recently independent African country.

Jim Haskins and Joann Biondi. *From Afar to Zulu: A Dictionary of Cultures.* Walker, 1995. Explores thirty-two different groups with useful information for students.

Isimeme Ibazebo. *Exploration into Africa.* New Discovery Books, 1995. Includes information on geography, maps, and the current political situation.

Cristina Kessler. *My Great-Grandmother's Gourd.* Illustrated by Walter Lyon Krudop. Orchard, 2000. Trying to balance respect for tradition and technological progress in a village in Sudan.

Gregory Scott Kreikemeier. *Come with Me to Africa: A Photographic Journey.* Golden, 1993. This account of a trip through each country in Africa includes numerous photographs of people, animals, the countryside, and descriptions of how people live. Shows how the different African tribes vary in appearance and culture.

FIGURE 7.5   AFRICAN CONTINENT

Virginia Kroll. *Masai and I.* Illustrated by Nancy Carpenter. Four Winds, 1992. Linda, an African American city girl, learns about the Masai in East Africa. She wonders how her life would be different if she lived there.

Jane Kurtz. *Faraway Home.* Illustrated by E. B. Lewis. Harcourt, 2000. When a girl's father has to return home to Ethiopia, he shares memories of his childhood there. Home is where your family is.

Patricia and Fredrick McKissack. *The Royal Kingdoms of Ghana, Mali, and Songhay: Life in Medieval Africa.* Holt, 1993. The kingdoms of West Africa flourished from 500 A.D. to 1700. The great cities were centers for learning, medicine, and religion. Dispels the image of Africa as an empty, dark continent.

Margaret Sacks. *Themba.* Illustrated by Wil Clay. Dutton, 1992. Themba's father is expected home from working in the gold mines near Johannesburg. When he doesn't return, Themba leaves his Xhosa village to look for him.

Catherine Stock. *Where Are You Going, Manyoni?* Morrow, 1993. The spectacular, detailed watercolors evoke the African veldt of Zimbabwe showing a typical day in Manyoni's life as she gets up, walks through the countryside to the school, and plays with her friends. Illustrations have animals hidden in them to identify and show the homes, school, and children's games so that students can find similarities and differences.

African Tales.   All students will enjoy reading and acting out stories from various traditional African cultures. They will learn about the lives and values of the major African groups, from Ashanti to Zulu, and compare these cultures with their own.

Most short tales reflect common human problems and traits and are easily adapted to storytelling or creative dramatics. A typical story is *The Vingananee and the Tree Toad,* a Liberian tale retold by Verna Aardema.

Or you can read a story aloud and have students illustrate the characters and incidents. A good place to start is *The Crest and the Hide and Other African Stories* by Harold Courlander. The famed folklore collector not only includes a variety of stories but also offers important background on sources and related tales.

Students can also investigate a particular genre of folktale, for example, the trickster tales, exemplified by West African stories about Anansi the spider.

More African tales to read:

Verna Aardema, retold. *The Lonely Lioness and the Ostrich Chicks: A Masai Tale.* Illustrated by Yumi Heo. Knopf, 1996. A story from Aardema's classic *Tales for the Third Ear,* now out of print.

T. Obinharam Echewa. *The Magic Tree: A Folktale from Nigeria.* Illustrated by E. B. Lewis. Morrow, 1999. Literary folktale in the oral tradition provides realistic picture of village life.

Christopher Gregorowski. *Fly, Eagle, Fly! An African Tale.* Illustrated by Nikki Daly. Simon & Schuster, 2000. A tale told in Ghana, how an eagle raised among chickens finds his freedom.

Barbara Knutson. *How the Guinea Fowl Got Her Spots: A Swahili Tale of Friendship.* Carolrhoda, 1990. When a guinea fowl saves a cow from a lion, the cow reciprocates by giving her camouflage spots.

Gerald McDermott. *Zomo the Rabbit: A Trickster Tale from West Africa.* Harcourt Brace Jovanovich, 1992. The ancestor of Brer Rabbit, an African trickster tale.

Heather McNeil. *Hyena and the Moon: Stories to Tell from Kenya.* Libraries Unlimited, 1996. Representing the diverse ethnic groups of Kenya, this includes literal translations and versions for storytelling.

Angela Shelf Medearis. *Too Much Talk.* Illustrated by Stefano Vitale. Candlewick Press, 1995. This story from the Akan people (Ghana) is about a farmer who meets objects that talk.

Isaac O. Olaleye. *In the Rainfield: Who Is the Greatest?* Illustrated by Ann Grifalconi. Blue Sky, 2000.

John Steptoe. *Mufaro's Beautiful Daughters.* Lothrop, Lee, and Shepard, 1987. Based on a Shona folktale (Zimbabwe), this is a modern fable of two sisters, one proud and one humble.

Sheron Williams. *And in the Beginning.* Atheneum, 1992. Retelling of the myth of how the first man was created from the dark earth of Mount Kilimanjaro.

FOCUSING ON MOVEMENT AND DRAMA MULTICULTURALLY

Various forms of movement, including dance, offer an opportunity for many students to engage in a different way of expressing themselves. Drama, too, provides exciting possibilities for enhancing the standard curriculum. Both give students a chance to express their creativity as they interpret literature or emulate activities from different cultures. It is interesting to explore how movement and drama can become part of the mainline curriculum as we strive to educate children multiculturally.

Effective Multicultural Instructional Strategies

Following are a number of strategies that allow students to get out of their desks and to move around the room, perhaps even to move out onto the playground or into the multi-purpose room.

Improvisations

Have students prepare a series of cards, each of which bears five or six words, for example:

1. fox, rope, cabin, window, river
2. stone, candle, flashlight, pencil, telephone
3. fence, bell, chair, flowerpot, tree

Each student in turn draws a card. He or she then begins acting out an improvised story that incorporates the given words. Description and dialogue are included, as appropriate. Students can also engage in this activity in pairs or trios, but they will need a little time to confer before they perform.

Acting Out Vocabulary

Introduce students to varied synonyms for walking. Have students generate a long list of such words, for instance:

tramp	leap
stalk	creep
saunter	prance
stroll	strut

Then have one or more students demonstrate one way of walking while other members of the class guess which word is being illustrated, saying: "Kendra is demonstrating how she can stroll."

Acting Out Wordless Books

Bring in a number of picture books that contain few, if any, words. The pictures tell the story. Have one or more students act out the story that is depicted. Samples of wordless books that you might look for include:

T. C. Bartlett and Monique Felix. *Tuba Lessons.* Creative Press, 2004.

Bruce Macmillan. *Going on a Whale Watch.* Scholastic, 1992.

Mercer Mayer. *A Boy, A Dog and a Frog.* Puffin, 1979. (see other titles)

Peggy Rathman. *10 Minutes till Bedtime.* Putnam, 2001.

David Wiesner. *Sector 7.* Clarion, 1999.

Dance

Dance is also something that is shared and understood around the world. Demonstrate the universality of dance and its themes by showing videos of dancing performed by different cultures. Here are a few examples:

African Rhythms. 13 minutes, color. Associated Film, Inc., 1621 Dragon Street, Dallas, TX 75207.

Betty Casey. *International Folk Dancing.* Doubleday, 1992. Includes directions and pictures of costumes for students.

Dancer's World. 30 minutes. NET. Martha Graham discusses dancing as her students dance the emotions of hope, fear, joy, and love.

The Strollers. 6 minutes, color. The Moiseyev Dance Company in a Russian folk dance.

Students can learn some simple folk dances to perform.

Rhythms for Movement

Encourage students to move to various rhythms by playing recordings of music from different countries around the world. Representative records available include the following:

Authentic Afro-Rhythms. LP 6060, Kimbo Educational, P.O. Box 246, Deal, NJ 07723. Rhythms from Africa, Cuba, Haiti, Brazil, Trinidad, and Puerto Rico.

Authentic Indian Dances and Folklore. Kimbo Educational. Drumming and storytelling by Michigan Chippewa chiefs who narrate history of dances.

Authentic Music of the American Indians. 3 records. Everest. Chesterfield Music Shops, Inc., 12 Warren Street, New York, NY 10007.

Role Playing

Prepare a set of cards bearing this kind of information:

Setting:　Central Park in New York City

Characters:

　Joe: A 10-year old boy
　Marie: His 12-year-old sister
　Eduardo: The ice cream man

Situation:

　Joe and Marie want to buy some ice cream, but they have only enough money to buy one kind of ice cream.

Pull one card out of the pack of cards available. Call on students to play roles described on that card. Give them one minute to think about the situation before they act it out for the class. These performances are not expected to be polished.

Story Dramatizations

Read a story aloud to the class, for example, a folktale from Russia like "Baba Yaga." Then call on a set of students to act out the story. Encourage them to improvise dialogue, as appropriate.

　　After this set of students acts out the story, have students tell the actors what they especially liked about the performance. Then, have the first students choose other students to play their roles.

　　After working with a simple folktale, introduce the class to tales from other lands, perhaps a country they are studying in social studies, for example, Japan or Ghana. Many picture books present folktales with attractive illustrations that facilitate the dramatization. Blair Lent, for example, retold and illustrated an excellent version of *Baba Yaga.* Look for others in the children's section of the library under the nonfiction number 398.

Additional Useful Strategies

- Charades—titles, expressions, events
- Who Am I?—noted actors, national leaders
- Readers' Theater—combined with some actions
- Folkdancing
- Exercises
- Games with Motions—Simon Says, Squirrel-in-the-Cage

Infusing Multicultural Drama and Movement across the Curriculum

Drama and movement can enliven any thematic study. Dance is particularly appropriate to multicultural studies. Here are suggestions for relating drama and movement to other subjects in the curriculum.

Reading and Language Arts

- Read about performing artists, for example, dancer Alvin Ailey; actor Sidney Poitier; singer Lena Horne; or ballerina Maria Tallchief.
- Write responses to multicultural literature, for example, biographies of performing artists, poetry by Langston Hughes, a novel by Virginia Hamilton.
- Listen to the teacher's reading a story that could be acted out—*Amazing Grace; Let the Circle Be Unbroken; Bud, Not Buddy.*

Social Studies

- Folkdancing characteristic of different nationalities.
- Acting out folktales from different ethnic groups.
- Performing a play, for example, *Pushing Up the Sky: Seven Native American Plays for Children* by Joseph Bruchac. Illustrated by Teresa Flavin. Dial, 2000.

A THINKING + LESSON PLAN

Acting Out Scenes from *Morning Girl*

Expected Outcomes
The learners will:

1. Listen to the teacher's reading of a short book.
2. Identify important scenes in the book.
3. Act out these scenes for an audience.

Teaching/Learning Strategies

Resources Needed
Obtain a copy of *Morning Girl* by Michael Dorris. To encourage students to read, try to obtain multiple copies of this book.

Directions
Step 1: Read this short book aloud to the class, reading a chapter a day over a week's time. Take time to discuss the happenings in the story.

Step 2: Display a map of the southeastern portion of the United States. Locate the setting of this book.

Step 3: Assign two advanced students to research the Taino Indians and to report their findings to the class.

Step 4: Review the story. Have students identify significant scenes that tell the story. Choose students to play the roles of the boy and girl, other Indians, white explorers. Other students can assume various roles, for example, narrators, a chorus, a director and assistant, and so on.

Performance Assessment
Practice the performance. Invite another class to serve as the audience. Invite parents to come, too.

Developing a Thematic Study: Everyone Is Special

The integrated learning activities that are inherent in a thematic study allow for the full use of diverse intelligences. Activities that permit children to dramatize scenes from history or to create original songs to share the information they have gathered on the Internet will serve to make such a study exciting and involving. Following are resources to help you develop a study focusing on Everyone Is Special! The intent of the thematic studies included throughout this chapter is to infuse the performing arts into academic learning so that students experience a varied approach to education that is truly multicultural and engages multiple intelligences.

Each student brings a unique perspective to the classroom. Unfortunately, these differences can be experienced as problems rather than assets to benefit everyone. Focus on students as individuals who all have strengths and weaknesses. Show the students that they don't have to listen to people who make fun of them.

Special Days.   Students' birthdays offer an opportunity to recognize students as individuals. On your class calendar, list the birthdays that will occur each month. Let the birthday student do something special that day, for example:

- Wear a special hat.
- Choose a game for everyone to play.
- Teach the class a poem.
- Distribute papers or books for the teacher.
- Use a favorite color on the bulletin board.

Another way of recognizing a student is to have the rest of the class brainstorm what they like about that person. These comments can be written down and collected in a book for the student to take home. The students can also make up a song about that person and sing it, perhaps to the tune of "Happy Birthday."

Decide how to schedule celebrations for students with summer birthdays. You might ask students to select from open dates. An alternative would be to celebrate "unbirthdays."

Ask students how birthdays are celebrated in their families. Do they have any special customs or ceremonies? Suggest that there are many different ways to honor people on their special day.

Although many students enjoy being the center of attention for a day, others may be shy or embarrassed by the publicity. Monitor your birthday activities to make sure that the student feels like an important part of the class and not singled out for uncomfortable attention.

Some books to share about birthdays are:

Eve Feldman. *Birthdays, Birthdays, Birthdays! Celebrating Life around the World.* Bridgewater, 1996.

Elisa Kleven. *Hooray, a Piñata!* Dutton, 1996. Clara chooses a dog piñata for her birthday party but can't face breaking it. Her friend Samson helps solve the dilemma. Multiethnic neighborhood, detailed illustrations.

The "Me" Collage.   Collage comes from the French word *coller,* meaning "to stick together." When you make a collage, you assemble many different items, often overlapping, from different media, to create an image (see Figure 7.6).

Ask students to bring in materials for everyone to share as they make a collage. Have magazines, newspapers, pictures, paints, and pens on hand. Students can cut out pictures and words, illustrating their ideas through a variety of media, to prepare a collage poster that expresses who they are and what they are like. Talk about the topics they might include, for example:

- Hobbies.
- Birthplace—picture, part of a map.
- Baby pictures.
- Things they like—food, sports.
- Their family—people, pets.
- Where they have lived or traveled.

Provide large pieces of cardboard on which students can mount their collages. Display the collage posters for everyone to appreciate.

After they have thought about how to represent themselves through collage, ask the students to write something to accompany their work. They can write a short description or a series of phrases, perhaps a poem.

Students will be interested to see how illustrators of children's books have used the collage technique. Share books illustrated by collage artists/authors such as Ezra Jack Keats, Christopher Myers, and Simms Taback, as well as the following:

Andrew Clements. *Workshop.* Illustrated by David Wisniewski. Clarion, 1999. The collage illustrations of woodworking tools encourage a second look with their three-dimensional effect.

Steve Jenkins. *The Top of the World: Climbing Mount Everest.* Illustrated by the author. Houghton Mifflin, 1999. Cut and crushed paper collage adds a realistic effect to an informational book.

FIGURE 7.6   "ME" COLLAGE

Source: Tiedt, Tiedt, and Tiedt, *Language Arts Activities* (3rd ed.). Allyn and Bacon, 2001.

We All Belong to Many Groups.   Each student possesses multiple identities because each one belongs to many different groups. Discuss possible groupings with students and write their suggestions on the board. They might mention grouping by family background, language, country of origin, geography, religion, interests, and gender, for example. Point out that some of these are groups you are born into (gender and race), some you learn (language and culture), some you have chosen (education and activities), and some will change (age and interests).

After students have had the opportunity to share their ideas, have them make individual lists. They can draw a picture of themselves and write their lists alongside (see Figure 7.7).

I am. . .
a girl
a daughter
a member of the Wong family
a Californian
a member of this class
a twelve-year-old
a Chinese American
a U.S. citizen
an athlete

FIGURE 7.7   GROUPS I BELONG TO

Display these pictures on the wall. Later they can be bound as a class book: Room 15, the Class of 2004.

Not Like Everyone Else.   Everyone is familiar with the fear of standing out from others and the pressure to conform. Yet we need to help students recognize that each of them differs from every other student and provide safe places for the discussion of these differences. Open this sensitive topic by reading *The Straight Line Wonder* by Mem Fox, illustrated by Marc Rosenthal. This short book tells the story of a "straight line" whose desire to dance, jump, and twirl isn't understood by the other "straight lines." The humorous message will appeal to all students, from preschoolers to teenagers. Invite students to take different sides of the issue in role play, act or write out a different ending, or tell the story in the first person from the perspective of another character.

Other books you might use to address this concern are:

Katie Couric. *The Brand New Kid.* Illustrated by Marjorie Priceman. Doubleday, 2000. Lazlo's second grade classmates mock him because he speaks with an accent.

Pat Mora. *The Rainbow Tulip.* Illustrated by Elizabeth Sayles. Viking, 1999. Although Estrelita (called Stella in class) wishes her Mexican American family weren't so different from the other students' families, she learns that sometimes there are advantages in standing out from the others.

Christopher Myers. *Wings.* Scholastic, 2000. The new kid in school isn't accepted by the others because he has wings.

Journals for Personal Writing.   An excellent way to promote the kind of writing that supports students' self-esteem and self-discovery is to encourage students to write frequently in a journal. Journals can be spiral-bound notebooks or sheets of composition paper stapled together. Students can individualize the cover with drawings or a collage and also use simple binding techniques to make their own books.

Schedule a specific time for writing in students' journals, and continue this writing for at least three weeks. The journals should be kept in the classroom so that all students have their journals on hand at the scheduled time. We recommend that you, too, write in a journal, both to demonstrate the value of the activity and to share entries periodically. Personal writing should never be graded or corrected. Students may select an entry to share if they wish, but the students' privacy must be protected.

Stimulate student imagination by providing some examples of personal journals from children's literature, such as:

Marissa Moss. *The All-New Amelia Series.* Pleasant, 1999.

At all times, students should feel free to write about subjects important to them. However, you may want to provide a stimulus each day for those who need an idea. Select a quote, read a short poem, or use one of the following topics:

- Friends are important because . . .
- If I were a superhero, I would be able to . . .
- I felt sad when . . .
- The bravest thing I ever did was . . .
- One characteristic I would like to change about myself is . . .
- Some of my favorite activities are . . .

Before you embark on this activity, recognize that students may write about painful, intimate, or uncomfortable topics. Decide in advance how you will handle the vulnerabilities that students expose while acknowledging their concerns. If you share writing with the class or in small groups, talk with the students about treating each other's contributions with respect.

The following resources will help you set up a journal writing program.

Lucy Calkins and Shelley Harwayne. *Living between the Lines.* Heinemann, 1991.

Lorraine M. Dahlstrom. *Writing down the Days: 365 Creative Journaling Ideas for Young People.* Free Spirit, 1990.

Donald Murray. *Write to Learn,* 3rd ed. Holt, Rinehart, and Winston, 1990.

J. A. Senn. *325 Creative Prompts for Personal Journals.* Scholastic, 1992.

Death and Grieving.   Well-written literature can help children learn how to manage the emotional and practical aspects of loss. Reading about other children who have gone through similar experiences, from the upheaval of change to the loss of a loved one, will provide models of coping strategies, language to organize and process their experience, and a safe setting in which to express their emotions. Select stories that demonstrate the variety of approaches people have used to confront these problems.

Also note the cultural influences in attitudes towards death, grieving, and funerals.

T. A. Barron. *Where Is Grandpa?* Illustrated by Chris K. Soentpiet. Philomel, 2000. Members of a family try to make sense of their loss but a young boy just wants to know where Grandpa is.

Pat Brisson. *Sky Memories.* Illustrated by Wendell Minor. Delacorte, 1999. Girl and her mother prepare for the mother's death from cancer by developing a ritual to help her grieve.

Eve Bunting. *The Happy Funeral.* Illustrated by Mai Vo-Dinh. Harper and Row, 1982. Chinese American girl's grandfather dies.

Eve Bunting. *Rudi's Pond.* Illustrated by Ronald Himler. Clarion, 1999. When another child dies, a girl and her classmates create a special place where they can remember him and feel close to him.

Lucille Clifton. *Everett Anderson's Goodbye.* Holt, 1983. In one of many picture books about Everett Anderson, an African American boy, his father dies.

Audrey Couloumbis. *Getting Near to Baby.* Putnam, 1999. Relatives' misguided attempts to help family get over baby sister's death are countered by warmth and humor of two sisters.

Bruce Coville. *My Grandfather's House.* Illustrated by Henri Sorenson. Bridgewater, 1996. A boy can't understand where his grandfather has gone when he dies.

Paul Goble. *Beyond the Ridge.* Aladdin, 1993. This picture book shows an old woman confronting death according to the beliefs of the Plains Indians. Death may seem like an end but it is not.

Kevin Henkes. *Sun and Spoon.* Greenwillow, 1997. A 10-year-old boy lists fifty-two special things about his late grandmother.

Cynthia Rylant. *Missing May.* Orchard, 1992. In this extraordinarily sensitive novel, winner of the Newbery Award, 12-year-old Summer grieves for her Aunt May, who took her in when no one else in the family wanted her.

Personality Prints.   Another way to feature students as individuals in the primary grades is to make handprints. Have each student place his or her hand on a piece of paper and draw around it with a thick colored pen. Then each student writes something about him- or herself on each finger—for example, writing his or her name on the thumb, a descriptive adjective on the next finger, then a favorite activity, a favorite color, and finally a favorite book. Post these "prints" on the wall to affirm the students' diverse personalities.

My Lifeline.   Have students draw a series of mountain peaks across a sheet of paper (see Figure 7.8). Tell them that this line represents their life. What are the big peaks in their life? What are the smaller peaks? What are the valleys? Have them label the peaks and valleys that they have experienced in their lifetime so far.

Older students can make this a timeline by adding the years and sequencing the events in chronological order. This idea can be extended by describing their usual daily existence across the base of the mountains. A few fantasies can be added on clouds: "Someday I'd like to . . ."

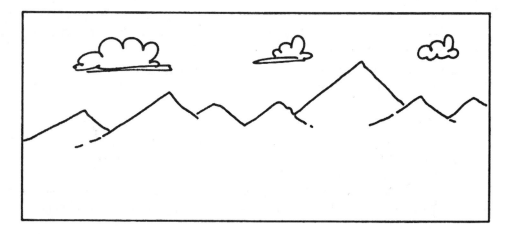

FIGURE 7.8   LIFELINE

The Color of One's Skin.   One of the most weighted ways we categorize ourselves is by skin color or race. Assemble a variety of pictures of people, showing the range of skin colors of human beings. Have students bring in examples as well. Create a display, All the Colors of the World, with these examples, illustrating the "human race." Use the pictures as a base for discussing physical differences among people. Primary students can talk about such elements as hair color and texture, facial features, and eye color.

Older students can develop the discussion further. Hold up objects that illustrate the colors "black," "brown," "yellow," "white," and "red." Do these words, conventionally used to describe the so-called races, really represent the human diversity depicted here? Ask students to brainstorm adjectives that could be used to describe the different colors of skin represented. Write these words in a circle around the display. Students will see that these "racial" categories cannot be mapped onto their examples of humans in the world.

Sandra L. Pinkney. *Shades of Black: A Celebration of Our Children.* Photos by Myles C. Pinkney. Scholastic, 1999.

Shelley Rotner and Ken Kreisler. *Faces.* Macmillan, 1994.

Everyone Has Fears.   Read aloud to the class a book such as *Ira Sleeps Over,* by Bernard Waber, to introduce the sensitive topic of fears. Ira is worried about going to a friend's house to sleep over for the first time. His older sister tells him that his friend will laugh at him if he brings his teddy bear to sleep with as he usually does. As you read, pause frequently to have students predict what will happen next. Afterwards, ask students what they would say to Ira. Would they laugh at him? Have them recommend strategies for Ira to handle the fearful situation.

When everyone has fears, sometimes it helps to talk about them or to discover that other people have the same fears. Talking with others may open up possible strategies for dealing with fears. Children's literature provides an excellent resource for raising these topics in the classroom. Use books such as the following to allay student anxieties.

Molly Bang. *When Sophie Gets Angry—Really, Really Angry.* Scholastic, 1999. Language and illustrations combine to show how Sophie loses her temper when asked to share a toy but later is able to calm down.

Julie Danneberg. *First Day Jitters.* Illustrated by Judy Leve. Whispering Coyote, 2000. In a twist on a first-day-of-school story, we find out only at the end—it's the *teacher* who is worried!

Saxton Freymann and Joost Elffers. *One Lonely Sea Horse.* Levine, 2000. In this colorful book especially for primary students, vegetable "sea creatures" such as banana octopi suggest ways to assuage Bea's sadness. She learns that friends can help if you tell them when you feel bad.

Florence Parry Heide. *Some Things Are Scary.* Illustrated by Jules Feiffer. Candlewick, 2000. What's scary for one person may not be scary for another. This edition has new illustrations.

If I Were in Charge of the World.   Read students' examples from *If I Were in Charge of the World and Other Worries* by Judith Viorst. Ask each student to complete the sentence:

> If I were in charge of the world, . . .

Have students share their suggestions. This would make an excellent bulletin board display. This activity could also be completed by several classes at different grade levels so that the responses could be compared.

Students can invent variations on this pattern:

> If I were in charge of this school, . . .
> If I were in charge of the universe, . . .

As a class project, have students collect their thoughts into a book. Responses can range from ridiculous to worldly. The following books will suggest more ideas.

Robert Bender. *Lima Beans Would Be Illegal: Children's Ideas of a Perfect World.* Dial, 2000. One hundred children's responses to "it would be a perfect world if . . ."

Dr. Seuss. *If I Ran the Zoo.* Random, 1977. Did you know that Dr. Seuss's father was a zookeeper?

Support for the Arts in Our Schools

Many educators recognize the need for continuing to offer strong programs in art, music, and drama as a way of stimulating student creativity. They realize also that given the varied kinds of intelligences represented in any single classroom we need to provide learning experiences that will reach the interests and abilities of all students. We really cannot expect that all students will excel in mathematics, nor will they all become excellent writers. Who can predict just wherein lies the ability of every student? Nonetheless, we must provide numerous opportunities for it to emerge.

An advertising executive who also teaches and writes about problems central to contemporary education writes:

> The arts offer people in society hope and promise, as well as the opportunity to dream of vistas not yet painted, sculpted, written, performed, or even imagined in the cold, hard world of data-driven logic. The beauty and power of artistic expression lie in its ability to transport the self beyond present circumstances to imagine what has not yet come to pass. Inspiration, hope, and promise are all part of a complex mix of emotions that can't be placed on a scale and weighed, or burned off as a byproduct in a chemistry lab.
>
> Rod Sims, author of *Middle School Mathematics: A Survival Guide to Improved Instruction,* Amazon.com, 2004

CONNECTIONS

Creativity is an essential aspect of each child's development. Art, music, and drama provide challenging outlets for children's energies, and they permit students of all ages to express their ideas and their response to life. These creative means of communicating also tie in with our study of multicultural education, for all cultures have engaged in such expressive arts over the ages.

FOLLOW-THROUGH

Expanding Your RTP

1. What is your response to these often quoted words from Albert Einstein?

    Imagination is more important than knowledge.

    First of all, who is Albert Einstein? Why has this Jewish man become one of the most famous citizens of the world? Why might these words sound strange coming from his mouth?

2. Locate one or more of the wordless books listed earlier in this chapter (or other ones a librarian might suggest). Write a plan for using this book with a group of students as a way of stimulating their multicultural understandings and providing experience with dramatizing a piece of literature.

Working with Your CLG

1. Choose one of the books listed as resources for the study Women: Searching for Equity that you can dramatize together. Follow the lesson plan for Morning Girl in this chapter, as you all read the book and then select the important scenes to dramatize. When your plan is complete, share your presentation with the rest of the class.

2. Read two additional books suggested for the other thematic studies. Report on these books to members of your group so that they, too, will know what the books have to

offer for teaching. Prepare a one-page summary for each book including the following information:

- Title, author, publisher, and publication year.
- Summary of the plot.
- Several suggestions for teaching, including a good quotation from the book.

If each of you duplicate these sheets for the whole group, you will all have a splendid addition for your resource file.

GROWING A PROFESSIONAL LIBRARY

Jan Greenberg. *Heart to Heart: New Poems Inspired by Twentieth-Century Art.* Henry Abrams, 2001.

George Littlechild. *This Land Is My Land.* Children's Book Press, 1993.

Chris Raschka. *John Coltrane's Giant Steps.* Atheneum, 2002.

Jacqueline Woodson. *Locomotion.* Putnam, 2003. Poetry, Winner of the Coretta Scott King Award.

ENDNOTE

1. Virginia Walker, "Digital Connections." *Booklinks* (November 1997): 64.

It takes
a whole village
to raise a child.

—African Proverb

Teaching Multiculturally around the Year

In this chapter we affirm multiculturalism every day of every month as we note events and the lives of people with particular multicultural connections. More than a "heroes and holidays" approach, these calendars provide the teacher with a powerful teaching tool. Students learn to inquire, using libraries and Internet resources; they learn to discuss the pros and cons of issues; and they learn persuasive devices to help them change the thinking of a fellow student. History is visibly alive!

Quotations and learning activities that accompany each calendar are designed to assist the teacher in engaging students in studies related to the happenings each month. Have a committee plan the calendar display each month, searching out appropriate pictures and words with which to frame the calendar, perhaps enlarged from this text. Other committees may choose to create an oversized calendar on a designated bulletin board with colored yarn outlining the spaces for each date. Students may create a learning activity to present to the class as a way of exploring a topic suggested by what is on a specific calendar. Thus, the curriculum is constantly changing as fresh ideas are encountered. The possibilities are endless!

This chapter is divided into three sections:

Using the Calendar
The Months of the Year
Movable Holidays

In addition, this chapter features the following multicultural units: (1) Time and (2) Jewish Americans: Living in a "Christian" Country.

USING THE CALENDAR

Have students choose an effective way to prepare the calendar for class display. They can brainstorm ideas for presenting the different months, perhaps working in teams to construct a display. While some students mount a frame for the calendar, others can research quotations, pictures, and other items to supply background information. Collect materials for each month in a class notebook that students can consult throughout the year.

The Multicultural Calendar should always be the result of the effort and interests of the whole class. Although you may be tempted to keep some of the materials that students have developed from year to year, remember that each class will need to create a personalized version, reflecting students' own concerns and current events.

Displaying the Calendar

You can install the calendar directly on a large bulletin board. Divide the display space into squares or rectangles using thick colored yarn or strips of colored paper. Students can select distinctive colors and pictures for each month.

Make the spaces as large as possible. Challenge several students to solve this measurement problem. Print large block letters for the days of the week and the names of the month. Also print a set of numbers from 1 to 31. Computer graphics will give students multiple options for font style and size. Print on colored paper for variety.

Developing the Calendar

Older students can write or print out events, names, and dates on slips of colored construction paper or unlined file cards to mount in the appropriate block for each month. Be sure that they check the current calendar so that the number 1 is placed under the correct day of the week; the rest of the dates will then fall in place accordingly. Add events that are celebrated locally or dates of personal interest to your students, such as birthdays. Include pictures and quotations wherever possible.

Quotations are of special interest for the multicultural calendar. Find as many as possible for people whose names appear for that month. Begin with the quotations presented throughout this book. Additional sources of quotations include:

Ella Mazel. *"And Don't Call Me a Racist!" A Treasury of Quotes on the Past, Present, and Future of the Color Line in America.* Argonaut Press, 1998.

Richard Newman. *African American Quotations.* Facts on File, 2000.

The Quotable Woman: The First 4000 Years. Facts on File, 2001.

J. A. Senn, comp. and ed. *Quotations for Kids.* Illustrated by Steve Pica. Millbrook Press, 1999. Includes the words of celebrities, historical figures, and fictional characters.

Pictures add a special dimension to the calendar. Have students search for varied multiethnic pictures for this purpose. If you have a large bulletin board on which to display the calendar, you might place a ring of pictures around the calendar. Ask students if they can identify the people and events pictured.

Encourage students to continue adding to the calendar. As they read, they can take notes on information to include in the calendar. They can search the Internet, newspapers, their textbooks, library reference books, and fiction. Students can become "investigators" as each one takes responsibility for exploring a specific topic.

Students can also decorate the bulletin board by adding seasonal designs, symbols, or illustrations. Snowflakes for the winter months, leaves for the fall, and flowers for the spring add interest and individuality to the calendar. Other possible motifs include pumpkins, kites, butterflies, and hearts. Avoid popular symbols that reinforce stereotypes, such as shamrocks or Indian headdresses.

Strategies for Using the Calendar

Often a more extensive unit of study is triggered by a single historical event or a series of dates on the calendar. Thematic units cross subject areas as well as periods of time and allow students to express their ideas in a variety of formats—spoken, written, drawn, performed, for example:

- Muslims in the United States
- Religions around the World
- Japanese Americans in Our Community
- Holidays and Celebrations
- Women in Sports

Almost any subject presented in the elementary and middle school classroom will lend itself to a multicultural approach. As you introduce each topic and discuss it with students, point to the contributions of various groups—ethnic, religious, racial, young and old, male and female—as an important thread woven into the quilt of our society.

Letters

Encourage students to express their ideas about people and issues in the form of letters. They can write letters to the local newspaper about an issue on which they have an opinion. They can also write letters to people from whom they would like information—members of Congress, authors of articles or books, leaders of groups or movements, and so on. Letters to parents can explain what the class is doing. Letters to different media can be used to inform the public of important events or activities.

Great Interviews

Students practice significant skills as they role play an interview of a personality from the past or present. Two or more students will need to develop this activity together as they plan the best questions and appropriate responses. Students can also interview several people, perhaps from different times. They will need to investigate a variety of sources to play these roles as realistically as possible.

Multimedia Presentation

Students select a person or topic from the calendar to research. They can present their findings in a speech to the class, using notes and appropriate visual and/or auditory aids, such as graphics imported from CD-ROMs or the Internet, pertinent newspaper items mounted on posters, audio or video recordings of speeches, overhead transparencies for new vocabulary, a time line displayed on the wall, and props or artifacts to share with the class. Older students can develop a Power Point presentation about the topic they choose.

The Time Machine

Ask students whom they would like to invite from the past to visit their community. For example, how would W. E. B. Dubois or Frederick Douglass respond to the problems of people today? What would they think of your town? Would they be impressed or disappointed? How might they react to meeting people such as U.S. Supreme Court Justices Clarence Thomas or Ruth Bader Ginsberg? Students can then write an imaginary diary for their visitor from the past, recording such reactions.

THE MONTHS OF THE YEAR

In this section we present ideas for celebrating multicultural understandings every day of the year. The activities in this section provide opportunities for students to ask and answer questions, to discuss fundamental issues such as race and identity, and to develop skills and information essential to living in a complex world.

Each calendar includes:

- Birthdays of historical and contemporary Americans from major ethnic groups.
- Important dates in the history of different groups.
- Religious and cultural holidays and festivals.

The individuals mentioned here are the exceptional few whose achievements have been recognized by history. We want to honor them without limiting ourselves to their example. In every community there are people who have made significant contributions to the welfare of society. One way to acknowledge and appreciate their efforts is to include them on the multicultural calendar as it is created by your class.

Following each month is a short list of suggested activities for incorporating the calendar information into your everyday teaching.

To facilitate presentation, we have not prepared the calendar for one specific year. You will need to make slight adaptations to correct the dates accordingly. For each month, too, there are certain special weeks or holidays that occur on variable dates. The months of

July and August are included so that you have the option of presenting this information at other times during the school year.

September Activities

Our calendar begins with September and the traditional opening of the school year. From September 15 to October 15 the contributions of Americans of Latino heritage are highlighted. What events occur during this time that are particularly associated with Latinos? Local celebrations will give you an excellent opportunity to collect ideas and materials that you can use in the classroom now and throughout the year, because your inclusion of Latinos will not be limited to this month. In addition, see the Thematic Study on Latinos in Chapter 2.

The fourth week of the month is Banned Book Week and Religious Freedom Week as well. The activities suggested for this section will enable students to explore issues of citizenship, literacy, and freedom of speech.

September 8

On International Literacy Day (sponsored by UNESCO since 1965), focus student attention on the importance of reading. Ask students if they have library cards. Have they ever been to the library? Provide information for students who aren't familiar with the library. For more information on this day, consult <*www.nifl.gov/celebrate*>.

Discuss "literacy" with students. What does it mean to be "literate"? Why is literacy important? Dictators traditionally control access to literacy for fear that knowing how to read and write will encourage people to seek their freedom. Share with students powerful tales of the importance of literacy. When blacks were enslaved, it was illegal to teach them to read and write. A fictional account, *Nightjohn* by Gary Paulsen (also available on video), describes the obstacles encountered by black slaves attempting to become literate. Read *Richard Wright and the Library Card* by William Miller, illustrated by Gregory Christie, to learn more about this writer and how he had to sneak books out of the library.

September 16

Prepare the class for Mexican Independence Day by featuring Mexico in the classroom. Use all available materials to create an atmosphere of Mexico. Travel posters, clothes, and objects from Mexico will contribute a festive appearance. Display books about Mexico. Older students can write reports on different aspects of Mexico to put around the room. Use a map of Mexico as a focus for featuring facts about Mexico. Have students research information to construct a time line of significant events in Mexican history. Why is Mexican Independence Day important? What are other historic dates celebrated in Mexico that are important to people living in the United States? Make cards such as the one shown in Figure 8.2 for individualized approaches.

Read students the Mexican tale *The Woman Who Outshone the Sun/La mujer que brillaba aún más que el sol,* from a poem by Alejandro Cruz Martínez. Provide colored pens

FIGURE 8.1 SEPTEMBER

1	2	3	4	5	6	7
International Literacy Day	Liliuokalani, 1838–1917, last sovereign of Hawaii	Prudence Crandall, 1803–?, first to admit black girls to her school	Richard Wright, 1908–1960, black author; Geronimo surrenders 1886	Harriet E. Wilson published first novel by black American		Artist Jacob Lawrence 1917–2000
8	**9**	**10**	**11**	**12**	**13**	**14**
	Ellis Island Museum of Immigration opened 1990; Sarah Douglass, 1806–1882, black teacher and abolitionist	Alice Davis, 1852–1935, Seminole tribal leader		Mae Jemison, first black woman in space, 1992	Maria Baldwin, 1856–1922, black educator and civic leader; Aloha Festivals, Hawaii	
15	**16**	**17**	**18**	**19**	**20**	**21**
Porfirio Díaz, President of Mexico, 1830–1915; Latin American Independence Day, 1821	Mexican Independence Day, 1821 (Pilgrims left England, 1620)	Citizenship Day; International Day of Peace	Québec surrendered to English, 1759	Lajos Kossuth, Hungarian patriot, 1802–1915; Booker T. Washington founded Tuskegee Institute, 1881		Sandra Day O'Connor, first women confirmed as Supreme Court Justice, 1981
22	**23**	**24**	**25**	**26**	**27**	**28**
Religious Freedom Week; Martha Corey hung as a witch, Salem, 1692; Banned Books Week		Francis Watkins Harper, 1825–1911, black author and reformer; Federal troops enforce desegregation Little Rock, 1957	Balboa "discovered" Pacific Ocean, 1513; Columbus began second trip to America, 1493; Howard University founded, 1867, first all-black university		Native American Day	Confucius' birthday (National holiday, Taiwan)
29	**30**					
Bryant Gumbel 1948–	Elie Wiesel 1928–					

Sept. 15–Oct. 15—Latino Heritage Month
4th week—Banned Books Week
4th week—Religious Freedom Week

. . . why I swore never to be silent whenever and wherever human beings endure suffering and humiliation. We must always take sides. Neutrality helps the oppressor, never the victim. Silence encourages the tormentor, never the tormented.

—*Elie Wiesel*

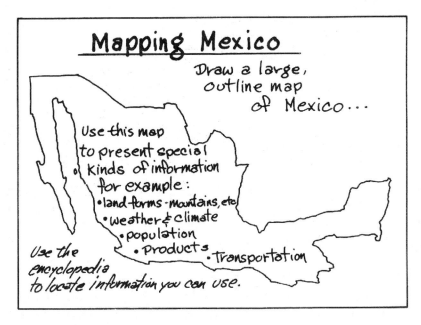

FIGURE 8.2   SAMPLE TASK CARD

for students to illustrate the story. Students can also compare the English and Spanish texts in this bilingual book. Perhaps a Spanish speaker can read the Spanish version aloud or on audiotape so that all students can hear how it sounds.

Other books to share with students include:

Antonio Hernández Madrigal. *Blanca's Feather.* Illustrated by Gerardo Suzán. Rising Moon, 2000. Simple story conveys the atmosphere of rural Mexico.

Naomi Shihab Nye, coll. *The Tree Is Older Than You Are: A Bilingual Gathering of Poems and Stories from Mexico.* Illustrated by various Mexican artists. Simon & Schuster, 1995. Includes works by children and adults, provides insight into contemporary Mexican cultures as well as universal concerns.

Jonah Winter. *Diego.* Illustrated by Jeannette Winter. Knopf, 1991. Biography of Diego Rivera, Mexican mural artist; for primary students.

September 17

The importance of citizenship is recognized on the anniversary of the signing of the Constitution (1787). Do students know what it means to be a citizen of a country? While people who are born in the United States are automatically U.S. citizens, legal immigrants must pass a test to become citizens. Once they are citizens they gain the right to vote, to hold public office, and to serve on juries. This process is called *naturalization.* About 1 million *aliens* (people from other countries) applied for citizenship in 1996. Conditions for naturalization are:

- Living in the United States for five years.
- No convictions for serious crimes.
- Ability to read, write, and speak basic English.
- Passing grade on U.S. history and civics test. (They have to be able to answer such questions as: How many stars are on the flag? What are the names of the first thirteen colonies?)

Discuss these requirements with students. Should all people who want to be citizens have to pass a test? Why do people want to become citizens? Invite an immigration lawyer or naturalization advisor to the class to explain the naturalization process. Discover what countries the new citizens come from.

Who Belongs Here: An Immigration Story, by Margy Burns Knight and Anne Sibley O'Brien, will spark student discussion of the issues of immigration and citizenship. A teacher's guide is also available. For more information see the sample Thematic Study on immigration in Chapter 2.

Fourth Week in September

Banned Books Week is sponsored by the American Library Association. The goal of the program is to highlight the importance of the First Amendment and the power of literature and to celebrate the freedom to read. Ask students what they would do if someone took their books away. Why is reading important? Have each student complete the sentence: Reading is important to me because . . .

For more information on censorship and challenges to books, contact the ALA, 50 E. Huron, Chicago, IL 60611 or *<www.ala.org/bbooks>*. They publish *The Banned Books Resource Guide.* The National Organization of Teachers of English (NCTE) also offers assistance to teachers concerned about issues of censorship. Contact them at SLATE, NCTE, 1111 W. Kenyon Road, Urbana, IL 61801-1096 or visit *<www.ncte.org/censorship/>*. See Chapter 11 for additional suggestions.

October Activities

October is National UNICEF Month. Latino Heritage Month also continues until October 15. The third week is Black Poetry Week, and the fourth is United Nations Week. In this month dominated by the presence of Christopher Columbus and the implications of his voyages, we must aim for a balanced perspective by pointing out the substantial presence of Native Americans and the impact his arrival had on them. The activities presented in this month (see Figure 8.3) will foster the development of multicultural understandings from Columbus Day to Halloween.

October 12

Columbus Day commemorates the landing of Christopher Columbus at San Sálvador in 1492. Locate San Sálvador on the map. Trace Columbus's journey from Spain to the "New World."

Columbus may not have been the first European to land on the continent. There is evidence of Viking settlements and perhaps other voyagers landed here. Should we celebrate

FIGURE 8.3   OCTOBER

1	2	3	4	5	6	7
Thurgood Marshall becomes first black Supreme Court Justice, 1967 International Day for the Elderly James Meredith became first black student at U Miss, 1962	Mohandas K. Gandhi, 1869–1948 First Pan American Conference—Washington, DC, 1889			Tecumseh (Shawnee) died, 1813	Author/artist Faith Ringgold, 1930– Fannie Lou Hamer 1917–1977, black Civil Rights leader	Imanu Amiri Baraka (LeRoi Jones), 1934– Marian Anderson, first black hired by Metropolitan Opera, 1954
8	9	10	11	12	13	14
Jesse Jackson, 1941–	Leif Erikson Day Mary Shadd Cary, 1823–1893, black teacher, journalist, lawyer	Shawnees defeated in Battle of Point Pleasant (WV), 1774, ends Lord Dunmore's War Chinese Revolution began, 1911	Eleanor Roosevelt, 1884–1962 Casimir Pulaski Memorial Day	Columbus lands at San Salvador, 1492 Día de la Raza (Latin America) Indigenous People Day		Eamon de Valera, Irish president, 1882–1975 William Penn, 1644–1718 National Children's Day
15	16	17	18	19	20	21
World Poetry Day	Sarah Winnemucca died, 1891, Paiute Indian leader Alaska Day Festival John Brown's Raid, 1859	Albert Einstein came to U.S., 1933	First Chinese opera performed in U.S.—San Francisco, 1852 Helen Hunt Jackson, 1831–1885, author of *Ramona*			Alfred Nobel, 1833–1896
22	23	24	25	26	27	28
	Hungarian Freedom Day, 1956 Pélé, Brazilian Soccer star, born, 1940	United Nations Day Kweisi Mfume, 1948–		Mahalia Jackson, 1911–1972	Ah Nam, first Chinese in California, baptized, 1815	Statue of Liberty Day, dedicated 1886
29	30	31				
		Black Hawk died, 1838, Sauk Indian leader Roberta Lawson, 1878–1940, Delaware civic leader				

National UNICEF Month

Sept. 15–Oct 15—Latino Heritage Month
3rd week—Black Poetry Week
4th week—United Nations Week

There is a sufficiency in the world for man's need but not for man's greed.
—*Mohandas Gandhi*

Viking Day instead? Discuss with students. Why has Columbus become the symbol of all European contact and colonization?

Encourage students to look at Columbus's voyages from different perspectives. How did the Native Americans perceive his arrival? Read *Encounter,* written by Jane Yolen and beautifully illustrated by David Shannon, a book for primary students. This encounter with Columbus is told from the point of view of a Taino boy on San Sálvador. An excellent book to read with older students is *Morning Girl* by Michael Dorris. A Taino boy and girl tell of their life in the West Indies, little dreaming of how it will change with the arrival of "strange visitors." After studying the many rich civilizations of the Native Americans before First Contact, students can write their own accounts of how they might have reacted upon first meeting the European explorers with their strange skin, language, clothing, and customs.

Students can also imagine what it was like to travel with Christopher Columbus. Share the excitement and adventure through the following books:

Pam Conrad. *Pedro's Journal: A Voyage with Christopher Columbus: August 3, 1492– February 14, 1493.* Illustrated by Peter Koeppen. St. Martin's, 1991.

Susan Martin. *I Sailed with Columbus: The Adventures of a Ship's Boy.* Overlook Press, 1991.

Miriam Schlein. *I Sailed with Columbus.* HarperCollins, 1991.

Have students work in CLGs as they prepare to accompany Columbus on his expedition. They will need to research the period in order to decide what to bring along and what to expect during the trip. How long will they be gone? How will they react to the people whom they encounter?

October 24

United Nations Day was first observed in 1948, three years after the creation of the United Nations. Fifty countries signed the charter in 1945. Large numbers of countries joined in the 1950s and 1960s as African colonies became independent and in the 1980s and 1990s as the Soviet Union broke up. Have students look into the history of the United Nations and the League of Nations that preceded it. What are the advantages and disadvantages of such an organization? What power does the UN actually have? How are UN peacekeeping forces constituted and where are they sent? For more information, write the United Nations Information Center, 1889 F Street NW, Washington, DC 20006 or visit <*www.un.org*>.

October 31—Halloween

Popular customs for this time of year draw on many of the world's cultures. In ancient Egypt they used to set out oil lamps and delicacies in honor of Osiris, the god of the dead. The Romans established November 1 and 2 for similar rituals. October 31, All Hallows Eve, became a Christian holiday in 1006. In the British Isles, Samhain (the Celtic festival of the dead) meant candles lit in carved turnips. For the autumn festival of Bon, the Japanese dress up in disguise and hang paper lanterns to guide the spirits of their ancestors home. In Mexico, November 2, El día de los muertos (the Day of the Dead) is celebrated with special sweets to feed the spirits and with masks and skeletons to scare them away.

How is Halloween celebrated in different communities in the United States? Read about the Day of the Dead in George Ancona's *Fiesta USA* (also available in Spanish). His photos document the inclusive spirit of the ritual as celebrated by a Latino community in San Francisco. *Day of the Dead* by Diane Hoyt-Goldsmith, with photographs by Lawrence Migdale, shows a Mexican American family in Sacramento, California. How does this celebration compare with the one in your community?

Have students prepare favorite mysterious stories for reader's theater or storytelling to present to other classes. (Check the index for folklore resources.) Independent readers will enjoy Brian Selznick's *The Boy of a Thousand Faces,* a scary story about Alonzo King, born on Halloween, who loves monsters. Or share a read-aloud such as *Celie and the Harvest Fiddler,* by Vanessa and Valerie Flournoy, illustrated by James Ransome, set in the 1870s in the South. *The Halloween Book,* from DK Ink, offers a guide to varied projects students can make for this holiday.

National UNICEF Month

Previously UNICEF Day, the U.S. Committee for UNICEF (now called the United Nations Children's Fund) has expanded its focus, working in partnership with schools and communities in order to understand global diversity better. For more information, write UNICEF, 331 East 38th Street, New York, NY 10016 or visit <*www.unicef.org*>.

An excellent resource for introducing global diversity is *Children Just Like Me: A Unique Celebration of Children around the World,* by Barnabas and Anabel Kindersley. Included are pictures and information about individual children, ages 6 to 12, from a variety of backgrounds. Representing the United States are an Acoma Pueblo boy and a Yu'pik Eskimo boy. How are these children like the ones your students know? How are they different? What more would students like to know about these children? Information about a penpal club is provided if students want to explore further.

November Activities

In November we celebrate Native American Heritage Month (see Figure 8.4). (Chapter 5 includes a unit on Native Americans that you can consult for suggestions.) Watch for new and interesting material about Native Americans, historic and current, that you will be able to use throughout the year to appear during this month. In addition to the seasonal focus on Indians and Pilgrims, the activities in this section also look at the position of African Americans and whether it has changed much since slavery.

November 5 and 8

Edward Brooke was elected to the Senate in 1966 and Shirley Chisholm to the House of Representatives in 1968. They were the first blacks in Congress since Reconstruction. Have students investigate and discuss these questions. How many African American men and women serve in the U.S. Congress now? How many African Americans (or women or people from other historically underrepresented groups) are in your state legislature? What about city mayors or state governors? What factors, such as racial prejudice or lack of financial support, affect the presence of African Americans in politics today? Why should

FIGURE 8.4 NOVEMBER

1	2	3	4	5	6	7
National Family Literacy Day; Sholem Asch, 1880–1957; Seminole War began FL, 1835; El Día del Todos los Santos (All Saint's Day)	Haile Selassie crowned Emperor of Ethiopia, 1930; El Día de los Muertos (Day of the Dead)			Shirley Chisholm, first black woman elected to House of Representatives (NY), 1968; Guy Fawkes Day (Canada)		L. Douglas Wilder, 1st black governor since Reconstruction (VA) elected 1989; Alabama repeals anti-miscegenation law, 2000
8	**9**	**10**	**11**	**12**	**13**	**14**
Edward Brooke, first black U.S. senator, elected (MA), 1966; First Women's College, Mt. Holyoke, 1837	Kristallnacht, 1938; W. C. Handy, 1873–1958; Benjamin Banneker, 1731–1806; Berlin Wall torn down, 1989		Remembrance Day (Canada)	Dr. Sun Yat-sen, 1866–1925; Baha'u'llah birthday, 1817, founder of Baha'i faith	Supreme Court upheld segregated buses illegal, 1956	Freedom for Philippines, 1935; Jawaharlal Nehru, 1889–1964
15	**16**	**17**	**18**	**19**	**20**	**21**
	Louis Riel hanged (Canada) 1885; Chinua Achebe, 1930– Brother and Sister Day (India, Nepal); W. C. Handy, father of the blues, 1873–1958		First Thanksgiving, Pilgrims and Massasoit, chief of Wampanoags, 1777	Indira Gandhi, 1917–1984; Christopher Columbus landed, Puerto Rico, 1493; Día del Descubrimiento (Puerto Rico)	Atahualpa, Inca of Peru, filled room with gold for Pizarro, 1532	
22	**23**	**24**	**25**	**26**	**27**	**28**
Nation of Islam (U.S.) founded, 1930			St. Catherine's Day (Canada); Religious Liberty Day	Sojourner Truth died, 1883		
29	**30**					
	Shirley Chisholm, 1924–2005					

Native American Heritage Month

To understand is hard. Once one understands, action is easy.
—*Sun Yat-sen*

minority groups be represented among our lawmakers? Shirley Chisholm ran for the presidential nomination in 1972. Discuss the following quote:

> I don't want to be remembered necessarily as the first black woman to have made a bid for the presidency. Or even the first black woman elected to the U.S. Congress. I would rather be remembered as a daring, determined woman who happened to be black and was a catalyst for change in the 20th century.

Thanksgiving

While November has traditionally been the month for activities featuring Pilgrims (hats) and Indians (headdresses), we can help students comprehend the one-sidedness of that perspective. From the perspective of Native Americans, Thanksgiving is a national day of mourning. Make it possible for students to understand this point of view by sharing several books such as the following:

Joseph Bruchac. *Squanto's Journey: The Story of the First Thanksgiving.* Illustrated by Greg Shed. Harcourt, 2000. Historically accurate, Squanto tells his version of helping the Plymouth colony survive and the circumstances of the Thanksgiving feast.

Michael Dorris. *Guests.* Hyperion, 1994. Moss is confused by the strange white visitors his father has invited to the feast.

Marcia Sewall. *People of the Breaking Day.* Atheneum, 1990. The Wampanoag were a tribe in what is now Massachusetts when the Pilgrims arrived.

Instead of reinforcing the stereotype of the first Thanksgiving, consider ways to promote multicultural understanding. Celebrate the season with a harvest festival, featuring the food of cultures from around the world, to learn about the sources of our food as well as issues of hunger and famine. For example, why do we have turkey at this time of year? Do other people eat turkey as well? The turkey we eat comes originally from Mexico, where the Aztecs called it *uexolotl,* and it was brought to Europe in the 1500s. What are some of the dishes at your holiday feast? Where do they come from? (For a thematic unit on food, see Chapter 5.) Discuss differences in family rituals. Students can write short poems, modeled on *Thanksgiving Day at Our House* by Nancy White Carlstom and illustrated by R. W. Alley, about their favorite activities. This collection of poetry can also be used to motivate oral presentations.

A Holiday of Arrival. Because we all, including Native Americans, came from some other place, make Thanksgiving a holiday of arrival, a day to honor the many immigrants to this country. How and why did the students, their parents, or their ancestors come to this country? By choice, by force, or by migration? To seek better jobs, to flee religious or political persecution, for educational opportunities? How has each group of newcomers been treated by the previous inhabitants of this country?

Read *Coming to America,* by Eve Bunting, a book for primary-grade children about a family forced to flee their country for the United States and freedom. When they arrive, they find that everyone is celebrating Thanksgiving and they join in gratefully. As the author notes, whether you arrive by boat or by airplane, you share the pain of leaving the familiar and the challenge of making a home in the new land.

Molly's Pilgrim by Barbara Cohen, a book for intermediate-level students, teaches everyone a lesson about diversity when a simple assignment to dress a doll like a Pilgrim has unexpected consequences. Molly's mother doesn't know the story of the Pilgrims, but she does understand religious freedom. As a result, she dresses the doll to represent herself, a Russian Jewish immigrant woman. Molly is embarrassed in front of her classmates because her doll looks "different." But the teacher explains how Molly's "Pilgrim" fits the true spirit of Thanksgiving.

November 26

In 1851, Sojourner Truth said:

> The man over there says women need to be helped into carriages and lifted over ditches, and to have the best place everywhere. Nobody ever helps me into carriages or over puddles or gives me the best place . . . ain't I a woman? Look at my arm! I have ploughed and planted and gathered into barns and no man could head me—ain't I a woman? I could work as much and eat as much as a man—when I could get it—and bear the lash as well! And ain't I a woman? I have born 13 children and seen most of 'em sold into slavery, and when I cried out with my mother's grief, none but Jesus heard me . . . and ain't I a woman?

Who was Sojourner Truth? Investigate her life with the class. She was born a slave in the late 1790s and won her freedom in 1827 when all the slaves in New York were freed. Look for information on the life of women and of African Americans at that time. Why did Sojourner Truth, a black woman, fight for the women's movement and women's right to vote? What might she say to women today? A biography for young students is *A Picture Book of Sojourner Truth* by David Adler and illustrated by Gershom Griffith. Older students will appreciate *Sojourner Truth: Ain't I a Woman* by the award-winning African American author, Patricia McKissack.

December Activities

Many cultures, ancient and modern, celebrate the end of darkness and the return of the sun, or the winter solstice, on December 21. Instead of restricting December festivities to Christmas and Santa Claus, which can exclude many students, a multicultural approach to this month would be to study the variety of winter celebrations around the world and the cultural origin of specific customs such as lighting candles, burning the Yule log, and decorating a tree (see Figure 8.5). Students can learn the Hanukkah dreidl song, reenact the Posadas, interpret the seven principles of Kwanzaa, make snowflakes, and write their updated version of *'Twas the Night before Christmas.* (See *'Twas the Night b'fore Christmas,* by Melodye Rosales, for a Southern African American retelling.)

Include books in your classroom that reflect diverse perspectives on this time of year, such as the following:

Marc Brown. *Arthur's Perfect Christmas.* Little, Brown, 1999. Arthur's expectations of a perfect holiday are all broken.

Lulu Delacre. *Las Navidades: Popular Christmas Songs from Latin America.* Scholastic, 1990. This collection of songs and music for Christmas to Epiphany includes information on the origins of the songs and descriptions of the traditions.

FIGURE 8.5   DECEMBER

1	2	3	4	5	6	7
Rosa Parks arrested, 1955, refused to give up seat on bus	Monroe Doctrine, 1823	Myrtilla Miner opened first Colored Girls School, Washington DC, 1851 International Day of Disabled Persons		Phillis Wheatley died, 1784, black poet	Feast of St. Nicholas Columbus landed, Haiti, 1492	Bombing of Pearl Harbor by Japanese, 1941 La Gritería (Nicaragua)
8	**9**	**10**	**11**	**12**	**13**	**14**
Diego Rivera, 1886–1957		Red Cloud died, 1909 U.S. acquired Cuba, Guam, Puerto Rico, Philippines, 1898 Human Rights Day, Universal Declaration of Human Rights ratified, 1948	Aleksandr Solzhenitsyn, 1918–	Día de la Virgen de Guadalupe	Yehudi Menuhin makes NY debut, 1927	
15	**16**	**17**	**18**	**19**	**20**	**21**
Bill of Rights Day, Bill of Rights ratified, 1791 Sitting Bull killed, 1890	Las Posadas begin	Maria Stewart died, 1879, black teacher and lecturer	Ratification of 13th Amendment ended slavery, 1865	Bernice Pauahi Bishop, 1831–1884, Hawaiian leader	Cherokees forced off their land in Georgia because of gold strike, 1835 Sacajawea died, 1812, Shoshoni interpreter	María Cadilla de Martinez, 1886–?, early Puerto Rican feminist Pilgrims landed at Plymouth (MA), 1620
22	**23**	**24**	**25**	**26**	**27**	**28**
Teresa Carreño, 1853–1917, Venezuelan American concert pianist	First Chinese theater built, San Francisco, 1852 Madame C. J. Walker, 1867–1919, black businesswoman	Nochebuena	Christmas Day	Kwanzaa begins		
29	**30**	**31**				
Wounded Knee massacre 1890	Pocahontas rescued Captain John Smith, 1607 Gadsden Purchase signed with Mexico, 1853	2nd week—Human Rights Week				

We didn't have any of what they called Civil Rights back then. It was just a matter of survival—existing from day to day.

—*Rosa Parks*

Gail Gibbons. *Santa Who?* Morrow, 1999. History of the famous symbol, from an original bishop who gave to the poor to today's bringer of gifts.

Mary Hoffman. *An Angel Just Like Me.* Illustrated by Cornelius Van Wright and Ying-Hwa Hu. Dial, 1997. Tyler's African American family looks for an angel that represents them.

Cynthia Rylant. *Silver Packages.* Illustrated by Chris K. Soentpiet. Orchard, 1997. A rich man tosses packages to poor children in Appalachia for Christmas.

December 10 and 15

Human Rights Day celebrates the proclamation of the Universal Declaration of Human Rights by the United Nations (1948). Ask each student to complete this sentence: Every human being has the right to . . .

Related to human rights is the Bill of Rights, the first ten amendments to the U.S. Constitution (see Figure 8.6). Groups of students can present the Bill of Rights as a series of short skits, acting out the meaning of each amendment. Enlarge the copy of the Bill of Rights in Figure 8.6 to display on a bulletin board. Copy it on a transparency for use in classroom discusssions.

December 16

Latino communities hold several distinctive celebrations at this time of year. Las Posadas, a nine-day ritual commemorating the journey of the Holy Family in search of lodging, and the lighting of luminarias are customs characteristic in New Mexico. Students can decorate the classroom with "papel picado," as shown in Chapter 7. Two books to share with the class are:

Rudolfo Anaya. *Farolitos for Abuelo.* Illustrated by Edward Gonzales. Hyperion, 1998.

Diane Hoyt-Goldsmith. *Las Posadas: An Hispanic Christmas Celebration.* Holiday, 1999.

In Spanish Catholic tradition, children receive their gifts from the Three Kings on January 6, El Día de los Reyes, or Epiphany. This custom is maintained in communities such as Puerto Ricans in New York City. George Ancona's book *Fiesta USA* includes photographs of the festive Puerto Rican parade as well as Las Posadas in Albuquerque, New Mexico.

December 18

The ratification of the Thirteenth Amendment meant the official end of slavery. Begin reading a book such as *The Slave Dancer* by Paula Fox, which won the Newbery Award in 1974, an excellent historical novel for grades 5–9.

> Neither slavery nor involuntary servitude, except as a punishment for crime whereof the party shall have been duly convicted, shall exist within the United States, or any place subject to their jurisdiction.

A book for younger students, *The Freedom Riddle* by Angela Shelf Medearis and illustrated by John Ward, tells the story of a slave named Jim who composes a riddle in order to win his freedom one Christmas.

FIGURE 8.6   UNITED STATES BILL OF RIGHTS

Amendment 1
Congress shall make no law respecting an establishment of religion, or prohibiting the free exercise thereof; or abridging the freedom of speech, or of the press; or the right of the people peaceably to assemble, and to petition the government for a redress of grievances.

Amendment 2
A well-regulated militia being necessary to the security of a free State, the right of the people to keep and bear arms shall not be infringed.

Amendment 3
No soldier shall, in time of peace, be quartered in any house without the consent of the owner; nor in time of war but in a manner to be prescribed by law.

Amendment 4
The right of the people to be secure in their persons, houses, papers and effects, against unreasonable searches and seizures, shall not be violated, and no warrants shall issue but upon probable cause, supported by oath or affirmation, and particularly described the place to be searched, and the persons or things to be seized.

Amendment 5
No person shall be held to answer for a capital or otherwise infamous crime, unless on a presentment or indictment of a grand jury, except in cases arising in the land or naval forces, or in the militia, when in actual service in time of war or public danger; nor shall any person be subject for the same offense to be twice put in jeopardy of life or limb; nor shall be compelled in any criminal case to be witness against himself, nor be deprived of life, liberty, or property, without due process of law; nor shall private property be taken for public use, without just compensation.

Amendment 6
In all criminal prosecutions the accused shall enjoy the right to a speedy and public trial, by an impartial jury of the State and district wherein the crime shall have been committed, which district shall have been previously ascertained by law, and to be informed of the nature and cause of the accusation; to be confronted with the witnesses against him; to have compulsory process for obtaining witnesses in his favor, and to have the assistance of counsel for his defense.

Amendment 7
In suits at common law, where the value in controversy shall exceed twenty dollars, the right of trial by jury shall be preserved, and no fact tried by a jury shall be otherwise reexamined in any court of the United States than according to the rules of the common law.

Amendment 8
Excessive bail shall not be required, nor excessive fines imposed, nor cruel and unusual punishments inflicted.

Amendment 9
The enumeration in the Constitution of certain rights shall not be construed to deny or disparage others retained by the people.

Amendment 10
The powers not delegated to the United States by the Constitution, nor prohibited by it to the States, are reserved to the States respectively, or to the people.

> Mr. Lincoln had told our race we were free, but mentally we were still enslaved.
> —*Mary McLeod Bethune*

Discuss this quote. What does *mentally enslaved* mean? Is it possible to change people's thinking by passing a law? What factors made it difficult to change? (education, jobs)

December 26–January 1

Begun in 1966, Kwanzaa (Swahili for "first fruits of the harvest") is a nonreligious celebration of African American culture, community, and family that lasts seven days. Each day participants light a candle and discuss one of the seven principles to live by all year: Umoja (unity), Kujichagulia (self-determination), Ujima (collective work and responsibility), Ujamma (cooperative economics), Nia (purpose), Kuumba (creativity), and Imani (faith).

The Seven Days of Kwanzaa: How to Celebrate Them, by Angela Shelf Medearis, includes all the instructions students need for this holiday, such as ideas for gifts to make, African foods, and stories of inspirational African Americans. Another rich source of information is *Celebrating Kwanzaa* by Diane Hoyt-Goldsmith, with photographs and text showing how 13-year-old Andey's family celebrates African American history and traditions.

Books for primary students include:

Denise Burden-Patmon. *Imani's Gift at Kwanzaa.* Illustrated by Floyd Cooper. Simon & Schuster, 1992.

Andrea Davis Pinkney. *Seven Candles for Kwanzaa.* Illustrated by Brian Pinkney. Dial, 1993.

Donna L. Washington. *The Story of Kwanzaa.* Illustrated by Stephen Taylor. HarperCollins, 1996.

January Activities

The name of this month comes from the Roman god Janus, who had two faces and looked back into the past and forward into the future. Janus was the spirit of doorways and the god of beginnings, also represented as two sides of the same coin. It is very appropriate, therefore, to take time now to consider where we have been and where we are going (see Figure 8.8). Talk with the class about the history of this country. Have them list ways in which the country has changed: inventions, attitudes, and people. Then ask them to face forward and think about what might change in the future. What would they like to see happen in their lifetime? Use the excitement of speculating about the future to show the importance of finding the roots of the future in the past.

January 1

Although the Emancipation Proclamation was supposed to free the slaves, it had little impact in the South since the Confederate States would not be bound by it until the war was over. It did, however, enable blacks to join the Union forces. The Massachusetts 54th Colored Infantry was the first officially sanctioned regiment of black soldiers. These heroic

FIGURE 8.7 JANUARY

1	2	3	4	5	6	7
Emancipation Proclamation, 1863; Commonwealth of Australia established, 1901; Ellis Island opened, 1892	Emma, 1836–1885, Queen of Hawaii		Louis Braille, 1809–1852; Selena Sloan Butler, 1872, founded first black PTA in country	Sissieretta Jones, 1869–1933, black singer	Celebration of King's Day—Pueblo Dances; Lucy Laney, school for Negro children, 1886; Día de los Reyes (Epiphany)	Harlem Globetrotters played first game (Illinois), 1927
8	**9**	**10**	**11**	**12**	**13**	**14**
	Joan Baez, 1941–, Latina singer	League of Nations founded, 1920, Geneva; George Washington Carver, 1864–1943, black scientist	Eugenio de Hostos, 1839–1903, Puerto Rican patriot	Adah Thomas, 1863–1943, black nursing leader	Charlotte Ray, 1850–1911, first black woman lawyer; First black Cabinet member, Robert Weaver, becomes Secretary of HUD, 1966	Carlos Romulo, Philippine leader, 1901–?; Albert Schweitzer, 1875–1965
15	**16**	**17**	**18**	**19**	**20**	**21**
Martin Luther King, Jr., 1929–1968, black minister and civil rights leader; Human Relations Day	Religious Freedom Day				Martin Luther King holiday began 1986	Fanny Jackson-Coppin died, 1913, black educator; Eliza Snow (Smith), 1804–1887, "Mother of Mormonism"
22	**23**	**24**	**25**	**26**	**27**	**28**
Sam Cooke, 1932–1964	24th Amendment barred poll tax in federal elections, 1964; Amanda Smith, 1837–1915, black evangelist; Elizabeth Blackwell, first woman to receive U.S. medical degree, 1849	Eva del Vakis Bowles, 1875–1943, black youth group leader	Florence Mills, 1895–1927, black singer and dancer	Bessie Coleman, 1892–1926, black aviator; Republic Day (India); Liberation of Auschwitz	Vietnam War ended, 1973	Louis Brandeis, first appointment of American Jew for U.S. Supreme Court, 1916; Zora Neal Hurston died, 1960
29	**30**	**31**				
	Mohandas Gandhi (India) assassinated, 1948	Jackie Robinson, 1919–1972				

It may be true that the law cannot make a man love me, but it can keep him from lynching me, and I think that's pretty important....

—*Martin Luther King, Jr.*

Past ←——————   ——————→ Future

FIGURE 8.8   LOOKING TO THE PAST AND FUTURE

soldiers fought in the front lines despite knowing that, if captured by the Confederate forces, they would be treated as slaves and not military prisoners. Have students investigate the word "emancipation." What does it mean? What other words contain the root word "manu"? How many synonyms for "emancipation" can students list?

January 15

Discuss with students the quotation by Martin Luther King, Jr., featured on the calendar. What does lynching mean? Martin Luther King, Jr., is known as a leader in the civil rights movement for African Americans. What are civil rights? In 1964, he received the Nobel Prize for Peace, an international award in recognition of his work for human relations. Why would people in other countries think that his work was important?

Happy Birthday, Dr. King, written by Kathryn Jones and illustrated by Floyd Cooper, features a boy puzzled by a school assignment to celebrate King's birthday. But after talking with his family, he learns about the civil rights movement and King's achievements.

Ask students what they would do if they wanted to change someone's behavior or opinion. What methods work best, and when? Do any laws protect them from other people? What about classroom rules—do they protect anyone? Discuss problems the students might have with a bully or a liar. Have them write and act out possible strategies to resolve the conflict.

Students can find out more about the life of Martin Luther King, Jr., and his most famous speech, "I Have a Dream," in these books:

Rosemary Bray. *Martin Luther King, Jr.* Greenwillow, 1995.

Margaret Davidson. *I Have a Dream, the Story of Martin Luther King.* Scholastic, 1991.

King was only 39 when he was assassinated in 1968, yet he continues to be a hero to many people. His birthday became a national holiday in 1986. Martin Luther King, Jr.'s vision of an inclusive society is an inspiration for all Americans, not only African Americans. How should we celebrate this holiday? Involve students in planning and carrying out an appropriate celebration. They might read excerpts from his speeches or prepare a skit dramatizing an important event in his life. Check your library for audio or videotapes to illustrate the power of King's words. Other resources are:

I Have a Dream: Dr. Martin Luther King. An Illustrated Edition. Scholastic, 1997. The text of King's speech, given August 28, 1963, in Washington, DC, is accompanied by paintings from noted black children's book artists such as Leo and Diane Dillon, Floyd Cooper, James Ransome, Jan Spivey Gilchrist, Brian Pinkney, Jerry Pinkney, and Tom Feelings.

Martin Luther King, Jr. *Wisdom of Martin Luther King, Jr.* Meridian, 1993.

January 30

Although Gandhi lived in India, his successful use of nonviolent protest to overthrow the British imperial rule has had a major impact on many people throughout the world, from Martin Luther King, Jr., in the United States to Nelson Mandela in South Africa. Feature several quotations from this influential philosopher/activist.

Ahimsa ("harmlessness" or nonviolence) means the largest love. It is the supreme law. By it alone can mankind be saved. He who believes in nonviolence believes in a living God.

All humanity is one undivided and indivisible family, and each one of us is responsible for the misdeeds of all the others. I cannot detach myself from the wickedest soul.

All amassing of wealth or hoarding of wealth above and beyond one's legitimate needs is theft. There would be no occasion for theft and no thieves if there were wise regulations of wealth and social justice.

My nationalism is intense internationalism. I am sick of the strife between nations or religions.

A biography to share with students is John Severance's *Gandhi: Great Soul.*

February Activities

February is African American History Month so you can look forward to programs, articles, speeches, and discussions about the history and current status of African Americans (see Figure 8.9). Formerly Negro History Week, this celebration is sponsored by the Association for the Study of AfroAmerican Life and History, founded by historian Carter G. Woodson. The week was first observed in 1926 and it included the birthdays of Abraham Lincoln (12th) and Frederick Douglass (14th). However, the celebration was expanded in 1976, in honor of the bicentennial, because the whole month is rich in the birthdays of exceptional African Americans. Request from the association a publication list of materials to be used

FIGURE 8.9   FEBRUARY

1	2	3	4	5	6	7
Langston Hughes, 1902–1967 National Freedom Day Treaty of Guadalupe Hidalgo, 1848	Día de la Candelaria	15th Amendment (right to vote) ratified, 1870	Liberia founded, 1822 home for freed slaves Apache Wars begin, 1861 Rosa Parks, 1913–	Constitution Day (Mexico)	Senate ratified treaty ending Spanish-American War, 1899	
8 Alice Walker, 1944–	**9**	**10** Leontyne Price, 1927– End of French and Indian War, 1763	**11** Nelson Mandela released from prison, 1990 Vermont abolished slavery, 1777	**12** NAACP begun, 1909 Fannie Williams, 1855–1944, black lecturer, civic leader Thaddeus Kosciusko, Polish patriot, 1746–1817 Abraham Lincoln, 1809–1865 Chinese Republic, 1912	**13**	**14** Frederick Douglass, 1817–1895 Valentine's Day
15 Galileo Galilei, 1564–1642 Susan B. Anthony, 1820–1906	**16**	**17** Chaim Potok, 1929–	**18** Toni Morrison, 1931–	**19** Amy Tan, 1952– Executive Order signed, 1942, Japanese-Americans sent to camps	**20** Buffy Saint-Marie, 1942–	**21** Malcolm X Day, assassinated, 1925–1965 Barbara Jordan, 1931–1996
22 Gertrude Bonnin, 1876–1938, Sioux author and reformer Ishmael Reed, 1938–	**23** W. E. B. Du Bois, 1868–1963	**24**	**25** First black in Congress, Hiram Revels (MS), 1870 José de San Martín (the great liberator), 1778–1850	**26**	**27** Marian Anderson, 1902–1993	**28**
29 Emmeline Wells, 1828–1921, Mormon leader and feminist Mother Ann Lee, 1736–1784, founder of the Shakers	African American History Month Week of 3rd Monday: Brotherhood/Sisterhood Week			If a race has no history, if it has no worthwhile tradition, it becomes a negligible factor in the thoughts of the world and it stands in danger of being exterminated. —*Carter G. Woodson*		

at this time: Mrs. Irena Webster, Executive Director, 7961 Eastern Avenue, Suite 301, Silver Springs MD 20910 or at <*www.artnoir.com/.*

As the calendar quotation illustrates, Carter G. Woodson was concerned about promoting the history of underrepresented groups. The National Council for the Social Studies presents the Carter G. Woodson Book Award annually for the most distinguished social studies book for young readers that depicts ethnicity in the United States, to encourage writers and readers of literature that treats multicultural subjects sensitively and accurately. The winners for 2000 were (elementary) Ruby Bridges, *Through My Eyes,* and (secondary) Sharon Linnea, *Princess Ka'iulani: Hope of a Nation, Heart of a People.* Honors went to Carmen Lopez Garza, *Magic Windows,* and Frank Staub, *Children of the Tlingit* (for elementary), Richard Wormser, *The Rise and Fall of Jim Crow: The African American Struggle against Discrimination 1865–1954,* and Patricia and Frederick McKissack, *Black Hands, White Sails: The Story of African American Whalers* (for secondary). For more information, contact the Council at <*www.ncss.org/awards*>.

Students can learn the lyrics of James Weldon Johnson's song, also known as the African American National Anthem, presented in *Lift Ev'ry Voice and Sing* (Scholastic, 1995), illustrated by Jan Spivey Gilchrist. James Weldon Johnson, a school principal, wrote the poem and his brother, J. Rosamond Johnson, composed the music in 1900 to celebrate Abraham Lincoln's birthday. James Weldon Johnson also became the first African American director of the NAACP, in 1920.

> Lift every voice and sing
> Till earth and heaven ring.
> Ring with the harmonies of Liberty;
> Let our rejoicing rise
> High as the listening skies,
> Let it resound loud as the rolling seas.
> Sing a song full of the faith that the dark past has taught us,
> Sing a song full of the hope that the present has brought us,
> Facing the rising sun of our new day begun,
> Let us march on 'til victory is won.

Students can also prepare their own book of illustrations and writing about this song as a special project for African American History Month.

Another activity for this month is to feature "Celebrating African Americans" as shown in Figure 8.10. You can challenge students to create their own acrostics using the names of historic or contemporary African Americans.

African American Read-In Chain

In 2000, the eleventh year of this international celebration promoting literacy, it is estimated that more than 1 million people participated. As part of Black History Month, this read-in brings schools, libraries, and communities as well as students and parents together with the goal of reading books by African American writers. To find out more about creating or joining African American Read-In events in your community, contact

Fill in the last names of these famous twentieth-century African Americans to solve this puzzle. Their occupations are given as clues.

_ _ B _ _ _ _ _	baseball player
_ _ _ _ L _	Secretary of State
_ _ _ _ _ _ A _	children's advocate
_ _ C _ _ _ _	ran for president
_ _ _ K _ _	author, poet
H _ _ _ _ _	poet, leader in Harlem Renaissance
_ I _ _ _ _ _	talk show/book club host
_ S _ _	tennis champion
_ _ T _ _ _ _	educator
_ _ _ _ _ O _ _	artist, quilter
_ _ R _ _ _ _ _	former Supreme Court justice
_ _ _ _ Y	comedian, actor
M _ _ _ _ _ _ _	won Nobel Literature Prize
_ _ _ _ O _ _	astronaut
_ N _ _ _ _ _	writer, poet, dancer
_ _ _ _ T _ _	writer, folklorist
_ _ _ _ _ _ H	Olympic star runner

1. Choose one name and find out why that person is famous.
2. List five other famous African Americans in the same field.

Answers to "Celebrating African Americans": Jackie Robinson, Colin Powell, Marian Wright Edelman, Jesse Jackson, Alice Walker, Langston Hughes, Oprah Winfrey, Arthur Ashe, Mary McLeod Bethune, Faith Ringgold, Thurgood Marshall, Bill Cosby, Toni Morrison, Guion Bluford, Maya Angelou, Zora Neale Hurston, Wilma Rudolph.

FIGURE 8.10 CELEBRATING AFRICAN AMERICANS

NCTE, 1111 W. Kenyon Drive, Urbana, IL 61801-1096 or at *<www.ncte.org/special/aa-read-in.shtml>*.

February 1

Introduce students to the poetry of Langston Hughes. An attractive collection is *The Dream-keepers and Other Poems,* illustrated by Brian Pinkney. Langston Hughes's poetry lends itself to graphic presentation. Have students create posters featuring a selection from a poem.

Encourage them to use calligraphy and art on the poster in order to celebrate the poem. *The Collected Poems of Langston Hughes* is available from Knopf. Play the recording *Langston Hughes Reads and Talks about His Poems* for students or read aloud Floyd Cooper's biography for younger students, *Coming Home: From the Life of Langston Hughes.*

Students can learn a poem or tell a story. "Thank You, Ma'am," a short story by Langston Hughes, is included in *Jump up and Say! A Collection of Black Storytelling* (Linda Goss and Clay Goss). *The Sweet and Sour Animal Book* is an alphabet book of poems by Langston Hughes illustrated by students from the Harlem School of the Arts. Students will enjoy these humorous poems that offer playful language.

February 12

Have students prepare a bulletin board display about Abraham Lincoln, a president who has become a folk hero. He symbolizes the poor boy who rose to leadership, the president who freed the slaves. Feature quotations by Lincoln around his picture, for instance:

> The ballot is stronger than the bullet.

> Any people anywhere, being inclined and having the power, have the right to rise up and shake off the existing government, and form a new one that suits them better. This is the most valuable, a most sacred right—a right which we hope and believe is to liberate the world.

> A house divided against itself cannot stand. I believe this government cannot endure, permanently half *slave* and half *free.*

> As I would not be a *slave,* so I would not be a *master.* This expresses my idea of democracy. Whatever differs from this, to the extent of the difference, is no democracy.

A group of students can prepare "The Gettysburg Address" for choric speaking. Plan a short program using this address, quotations, and poetry about Lincoln. One or two students might tell a story about Abe.

The following books illustrate a range of approaches to this man who is everyone's hero.

Harold Holzer. *Abraham Lincoln the Writer: A Treasury of His Greatest Speeches and Letters.* Boyds Mills, 2000. Examples of his powerful writing put in historical context, with time line and photographs.

Elizabeth Van Steenwyk. *When Abraham Talked to the Trees.* Illustrated by Bill Farnsworth. Eerdmans, 2000. Fictionalized account of young Abraham practicing his speaking where no one could hear him.

Presidents Day

The creation of the Presidents Day holiday as a replacement for Lincoln's and Washington's birthdays provides an opportunity for students to look more closely at those who have been president in the past and perhaps speculate on possible presidents of the future. What are the qualifications for President? Can anyone grow up to be President? Have students discuss the following comment:

The time has come to change America. Someday, somewhere, somehow, someone other than a white male could be President.
—Shirley Chisholm

What might be obstacles to someone other than a white male becoming President?

These books will answer students' questions and encourage them to explore the topic further.

Kathleen Karr. *It Happened in the White House.* Illustrated by Paul Meisel. Hyperion, 2000. A humorous look at the White House from a child's point of view, including such information as presidential pets.

Judith St. George. *So You Want to be President?* Illustrated by David Small. Philomel, 2000. Rather than follow the typical time line or repeat the tired stories, this book addresses what being president is really like. The presidents are shown as similar in many ways and yet diverse.

George Washington. *George-isms.* Atheneum, 2000. When he was young, Washington copied out a series of maxims to live by. Students will enjoy comparing their paraphrase of the original words that Washington wanted to remember with the translation that accompanies them.

March Activities

Women's history is celebrated this month on March 8 (see Figure 8.11), along with International Women's Day. This holiday commemorates the beginning of a strike by women garment workers in New York City in 1908, which resulted in the eight-hour work day.

As you collect materials for use in the classroom this month and throughout the year, aim for a diverse perspective: women of the past and women of today, women who represent different ethnic and other groups, stories of both women and men who have actively combated stereotypes about both sexes. The National Women's History Project (7738 Bell Road, Windsor, CA 95492-8518) offers books, posters, and other resources for the classroom. (Also see Chapter 4 for activities and information to feature this month.)

March 10

Harriet Tubman led an active and dangerous life. Despite not knowing how to read or write, she was able to escape slavery and flee to the North where she was free. Instead of remaining safe in the North, however, she returned to slave-holding territory many times to guide other slaves to freedom. Read about her exploits and have students choose several crucial events to dramatize. They can prepare a play by writing dialogue and narration and using a few props. This play can be presented for other classes to watch. There are many biographies of Harriet Tubman. A book for primary students is *Minty: The Story of Young Harriet Tubman* by Alan Schroeder and illustrated by Jerry Pinkney. This fictionalized account focuses on her childhood.

Harriet Tubman is not just a figure from the past but has come to symbolize freedom and strength for today. For example, in Faith Ringgold's book *Aunt Harriet's Underground Railroad in the Sky,* Harriet is the "conductor" for a modern, liberating trip through the

FIGURE 8.11 MARCH

1	2	3	4	5	6	7
Ralph Ellison, 1914–1994, black author Peace Corps est., 1961 St. David's Day (Wales)	Texas declares independence from Mexico, 1836 Puerto Rico became territory, 1917	Doll Festival (Japan) Indian Appropriations Act, 1885	Knute Rockne, 1888–1931	Crispus Attucks Day	Fall of the Alamo, 1836	Thomás Masaryk (Czech patriot), 1850–1937 First Selma (Alabama) civil rights march, 1965—Bloody Sunday
8	**9**	**10**	**11**	**12**	**13**	**14**
International Women's Day Women garment workers began strike, New York, 1908	Amerigo Vespucci, 1451–1512, Italian navigator Antonia Novello, first woman, first Latina surgeon general, 1990	Harriet Tubman's death, 1913 Hallie Q. Brown, 1850–1949, black teacher and women's leader		Gabriele d'Annunzio, 1863–1938		Albert Einstein, 1879–1955
15	**16**	**17**	**18**	**19**	**20**	**21**
Eugene Marino, first black Archbishop, appointed 1988 Ruth Bader Ginsburg 1933–	*Freedom's Journal*, first black newspaper in United States, 1827	St. Patrick's Day Myrlie Evers-Williams, 1933–	Hawaii admitted to Union, 1959 (50th state)	St. Joseph's Day (Italy)	Harriet Beecher Stowe's *Uncle Tom's Cabin* published, 1852 Spike Lee, 1957–	Benito Juárez, Mexican leader, 1806–1872 Namibia became independent, 1990 New Year (India)
22	**23**	**24**	**25**	**26**	**27**	**28**
Emancipation Day (Puerto Rico)		Canada gives blacks right to vote, 1837	Seward's Day (Alaska)	Kuhio Day (Hawaii)	Marconi sends first international wireless message, 1899 First Mormon temple dedicated, 1836	
29	**30**	**31**				
	U.S. purchased Alaska from Russia, 1867	First treaty U.S.–Japan, 1854 U.S. took possession of Virgin Islands from Denmark, 1917 César Chávez, 1927–1993				

Women's History Month
Irish American Heritage Month
3rd Saturday—Día de los Compadres (Mexico)

My spirit was never in jail.
—*César Chávez*

273

skies of New York. Talk with students about the importance of symbols. Why was the organization that helped slaves to freedom called the "underground railroad"? Slaves were "packages," helped from "station" to "station" by "conductors."

March 17

March is also Irish American Heritage Month. Although highly stereotyped because of the association with shamrocks and leprechauns, St. Patrick's Day offers an opportunity to recognize Irish Americans and their history. Two books provide accurate information on Ireland and the Irish immigrants.

Eve Bunting. *St. Patrick's Day in the Morning.* Clarion, 1993. Set in Ireland, a boy wants to prove he is big enough to march in the parade.

Steven Kroll. *Mary McLean and the St. Patrick's Day Parade.* Illustrated by Michael Dooling. Scholastic, 1991. Story of Irish immigrants in New York in 1850. Includes information on Irish traditions and St. Patrick.

Ask students what they think of when they hear the word *Ireland.* If a shamrock or a leprechaun is all they know, have students look into Irish folklore and historical traditions. They can report their findings to the class.

Read aloud Irish tales such as the following:

Sheila MacGill-Callahan. *The Last Snake in Ireland.* Illustrated by Will Hillenbrand. Holiday House, 1999. Retelling of legend of St. Patrick and the snake with a surprise ending.

Some students will be aware of the ongoing conflict in Northern Ireland. Older students can discuss how they might feel if they lived under those conditions. Share books such as the following to give them a clear picture of that world.

Patricia McMahon. *One Belfast Boy.* Houghton Mifflin, 1999. Photos show life of an 11-year-old Catholic boy in Northern Ireland.

March 22

Emancipation Day. Puerto Rico is a part of the United States but it is not a state. As a result, Puerto Ricans cannot vote for representation in Congress. Have students investigate the history of Puerto Rico's relationship to the United States. What is Puerto Rico like? One way to explore Puerto Rico is through its traditional folklore.

Jan Mike. *Juan Bobo and the Horse of Seven Colors: A Puerto Rican Legend.* Troll, 1995. A traditional tale with a foolish folk hero; includes information about Puerto Rico.

Nicholasa Mohr. *Old Letivia and the Mountain of Sorrows.* Illustrated by Rudy Gutierrez. Viking Penguin, 1996. This tale, meant to be read aloud, features a curandera (healer) in the Puerto Rican rain forest.

Nicholasa Mohr and Antonio Martorell. *The Song of El Coquí: And Other Tales of Puerto Rico.* Viking, 1995. This collection includes stories from the three strands of Puerto Rican heritage—Taino (native), African, and Spanish. A good resource for storytelling, it includes Spanish vocabulary in context and a glossary.

April Activities

Because April includes many birthdays of jazz (and blues) musicians such as Duke Ellington and Ella Fitzgerald, you might choose to focus this month on jazz, America's "classical" music. Jazz, with its roots in African rhythms and the black church and interwoven with Latin traditions, has become an international language (see Figure 8.12). Introduce students to the special magic of jazz through these books, suitable for a variety of grade levels:

Debbi Chocolate. *The Piano Man.* Illustrated by Eric Velasquez. Walker, 1998. A young African American girl recalls the life of her grandfather in vaudeville.

Linda England. *The Old Cotton Blues.* Illustrated by Teresa Flavin. McElderry, 1998. A city boy living with his mother wants to play the clarinet but has no money for an instrument.

Matthew Gollub. *The Jazz Fly.* Illustrated by Karen Hanke. Tortuga Press, 2000. Introducing students to the art of improvisation, it includes CD.

National Poetry Month

April is also National Poetry Month. Post the following quote as a theme for this month and invite students to respond:

> It is difficult
> to get the news from poems
> yet men die miserably every day
> for lack
> of what is found there.
> —William Carlos Williams

Keep a collection of poetry beside you so that you can easily read a short poem when you have the chance. In addition, provide a variety of poetry collections in the classroom for students to investigate. They are often drawn in by the beautiful illustrations. Make sure that students see poetry that is written by and about people just like them, such as:

Davida Adedjouma, ed. *The Palm of My Heart: Poetry by African American Children.* Illustrated by Gregorie Christie. Lee & Low, 1997. Coretta Scott King Honor book for illustration.

Nikki Grimes. *Shoe Magic.* Illustrated by Terry Widener. Orchard, 2000. Sixteen poems in which different kinds of shoes spark kids' imaginations.

Neil Philip, ed. *It's a Woman's World: A Century of Women's Voices in Poetry.* Dutton, 2000.

For more information about poetry-related activities in April, visit the Children's Book Council website <*www.cbcbooks.org*> or the Academy of American Poets website <*www.poets.org*>.

FIGURE 8.12 APRIL

1	2	3	4	5	6	7
Spring Corn Dances (Pueblos) Telugu New Year (India)	Ponce de León landed in Florida, 1513 International Children's Book Day Hans Christian Andersen, born 1805, Denmark		Martin Luther King, Jr., assassinated, 1968 Henry Cisneros elected mayor of San Antonio, 1981, first Hispanic mayor of a large city	Booker T. Washington, 1856–1915 Pocahontas married John Rolfe, 1614 Colin Powell, 1937–	Peary and Henson reached North Pole, 1909 John Smith founded Mormon Church, 1830 Alexander Herzen, 1812–1870	Billie Holiday, 1915–1959
8 First synagogue in America founded in NYC, 1730 Buddha's birthday (Japan), 563–483 BC	**9** Civil War ended, Treaty of Appomattox, 1865 African Methodist Episcopal Church established, 1816	**10** Joseph Pulitzer, 1847–1911 Dolores Huerta, 1930– Buchenwald Liberation Day, 1945	**11**	**12** Civil War began, 1861, Ft. Sumter Yuri Gargarin, cosmonaut, became first person to orbit earth, 1961	**13** Lucy Laney, 1854–1933, black educator Tamil New Year	**14** Pan American Day Abraham Lincoln assassinated, 1865 Carlos Romulo, Philippine leader, 1899–1985 First U.S. abolition society (PA), 1775
15 Bessie Smith, 1894–1937, black blues singer Jackie Robinson signed by Brooklyn Dodgers, 1947	**16** Mary Eliza Mahoney, 1845–1926, first black nurse	**17** World Health Day Giovanni Verrazano entered NY harbor, 1524	**18**	**19** Revolutionary War began, 1775	**20**	**21** Spanish-American War began, 1898
22 Earth Day U.S. Holocaust Memorial Museum opened, 1993	**23**	**24**	**25** Ella Fitzgerald, 1918–1996 UN founded, 1945	**26** Gertrude (Ma) Rainey, 1886–1939, black blues singer Syngman Rhee, 1875–1965 First democratic elections South Africa, 1994	**27** Coretta Scott King, 1927– Eritrea becomes independent from Ethiopia, 1993 August Wilson, 1945–	**28** Canada/U.S. Goodwill treaty signed, 1817
29 Emperor's birthday (Japan) Duke Ellington, 1899–1974 St. Catherine (Italy)	**30** Louisiana Territory purchased, 1803 Loyalists and blacks attacked Shrewsbury, NJ, 1780 Día del Niño (Day of the Children)					

National Poetry Month

You can't hold a man down without staying down with him.

—Booker T. Washington

April 14—Pan American Day

On this day, we remember that "America" includes many countries besides the United States. James Blaine, the U.S. Secretary of State under President Benjamin Harrison, called for an international conference of North and South American countries. The group met April 14, 1890, to form the Pan American Union, now the Organization of American States. In recognition, President Hoover established Pan American Day in 1931.

Display a map of North, Central, and South America, showing the names of the countries and their capitals. Illustrate it with the flags of the different countries. Discuss what these countries have in common. For example, all the countries of the Americas have great ethnic, linguistic, and racial diversity, as well as substantial immigrant populations. What are the major languages spoken in each country? Note that the people in these countries are "Americans" too.

April 15

On this date in 1947, Jackie Robinson broke the colorline. He became the first black big league baseball player. Before this date, blacks played in the Negro Baseball League and only whites could play in the major leagues. Why was Jackie Robinson's achievement significant? Have racial barriers to equitable treatment in sports been eliminated?

Students can investigate the position of black athletes then and now. Read about Jackie Robinson, the problems he faced, and how he handled them.

Peter Golenbock. *Teammates.* Harcourt Brace Jovanovich, 1990. Racial prejudice experienced by Jackie Robinson, first black player in major league baseball.

Kenneth Rudeen. *Jackie Robinson.* HarperCollins, 1996. Easy-to-read biography.

Interview adults who remember Jackie Robinson's career. How did they feel about his success? Compare Jackie Robinson to the black athletes of today. How do they continue to struggle against racial stereotypes and prejudice?

After learning about Jackie Robinson's experience, students will be able to formulate more complex questions about the historical context for his achievements. Have them brainstorm a list of questions raised by their study, such as:

- What was it like playing in the segregated leagues?
- Were there other players as good as Jackie Robinson?
- Would black players prefer to play in the major leagues?
- Who supported these changes?

They can find out more about the Negro Baseball Leagues in the following books.

Patricia McKissack and Frederick McKissack. *Black Diamond: The Story of the Negro Baseball Leagues.* Scholastic, 1994.

Jonah Winter. *FairBall! Fourteen Great Stars from Baseball's Negro Leagues.* Scholastic, 1999.

April 22

The U.S. Holocaust Memorial Museum in Washington, DC, opened on this date in 1993, keeps alive public awareness of the immensity of this tragedy in which 6 million men, women, and children were killed simply because they were Jewish. What does the word *holocaust* mean? Talk about *genocide*. Analyze the parts of this word. Can students apply this understanding to similar words such as suicide, patricide, fratricide, homicide? What other words does the morpheme *gen-* appear in?

Many people believe that this tragedy could never happen again. Yet large groups of people around the world are still being killed because of their religion, ethnic background, or race. What lesson does the Holocaust have for those of us living today? How can students respond to the genocide occurring even now around the world? Discuss the following quotes:

> Forgiveness is the key to action and freedom.
> —Hannah Arendt

> The motto should not be: Forgive one another; rather, Understand one another.
> —Emma Goldman

The Holocaust Day of Remembrance (Yom Hashoah) is celebrated on the 27th day of Nissan according to the Jewish calendar and falls in March, April, or May.

April 26

In 1994, the black population in South Africa, long a majority in the country, was finally allowed to vote. Locate South Africa on the map. Who lives here? The population includes colonial groups of English and Boer (Dutch) settlers and varied African tribal groups such as Xhosa. Sanctions, or penalties, by many nations against the white government for its system of *apartheid* (racial separation) helped force South Africa to hold democratic elections.

Who is Nelson Mandela, the former political prisoner who was elected president in this first free election? Share a biography with students, such as Jack L. Roberts's *Nelson Mandela: Determined to Be Free.*

How did it feel to be able to vote? Find out by reading:

Elinor Batezat Sisulu. *The Day Gogo Went to Vote: South Africa, April 1994.* Illustrated by Sharon Wilson. Little, Brown, 1996. A 6-year-old Thembi girl accompanies her 100-year-old grandmother who is determined to vote for the first time.

How would students feel if their families were not allowed to vote? Why is being able to vote important, especially for groups that have experienced discrimination? When did African Americans receive the right to vote? When were women allowed to vote? Compare these dates to 1924, when Native Americans were granted citizenship. What is required in order to vote in the United States today? The last major change in voting requirements was the lowering of the age limit from 21 to 18. Students can debate the question: Should teenagers be allowed to vote?

May Activities

This month has been selected to recognize the contributions made by people of Asian and Pacific Islander heritage. During this month, we can acknowledge the diversity of Asian and Pacific Island immigrants, and the rich cultural and linguistic heritage that they hope to maintain (see Figure 8.13).

How many groups of Asian and Pacific Islanders can students name? Which groups are represented in your class? In your community? Locate their place of origin on the map. Note that this category includes such diverse groups as Koreans, Hmong, Pakistanis, Samoans, and Filipinos.

May 5

This day is the Children's Festival in Japan and Japanese children fly carp kites. Students can make their own gaily decorated fish to hang like streamers. Students can draw their own, or you can provide one for everyone to trace onto construction paper. (Enlarge model below.) They should have two fish shapes, one right side and one reversed. After the children color and cut out the fish, they glue the two pieces together around the edges (except for the mouth) and gently stuff with tissue paper for a three-dimensional effect. These fish can be hung around the room with thread tied to the back, or attached to a stick (fishing pole) by the mouth. If you have Japanese-speaking children in the class, this is a good opportunity to have them teach the class how to count in Japanese.

ichi—one	san—three	go—five	shichi—seven	ku—nine
ni—two	shi—four	roku—six	hachi—eight	ju—ten

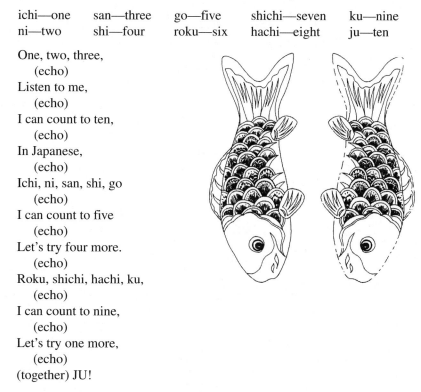

One, two, three,
   (echo)
Listen to me,
   (echo)
I can count to ten,
   (echo)
In Japanese,
   (echo)
Ichi, ni, san, shi, go
   (echo)
I can count to five
   (echo)
Let's try four more.
   (echo)
Roku, shichi, hachi, ku,
   (echo)
I can count to nine,
   (echo)
Let's try one more,
   (echo)
(together) JU!

FIGURE 8.13   MAY

1	2	3	4	5	6	7
Lei Day (Hawaii) Agrippa Hull, free black, began six years of army service, 1777		Golda Meir, 1898–1978 World Press Freedom Day		Children's Festival (Japan) Gwendolyn Brooks won Pulitzer Prize for Poetry, 1950 Cinco de Mayo	Chinese Exclusion Act passed, 1882 Rudolph Valentino, 1895–1926	Rabindranath Tagore, 1861–1941
8	**9**	**10**	**11**	**12**	**13**	**14**
Joan of Arc Day (France) Teacher's Day (U.S.)		Chinese labor helped complete Transcontinental Railroad, Utah, 1869 Nelson Mandela inaugurated president of South Africa, 1994			Joe Louis, 1914–1972 Congress declared war on Mexico, 1846	Jamestown established, 1607
15	**16**	**17**	**18**	**19**	**20**	**21**
Día del Maestro (Mexico)		Supreme Court declared racial segregation in schools unconstitutional, 1954, *Brown v. Topeka*	Hispanic Society of America founded, 1904 Supreme Court affirmed separate but equal laws, 1896, *Plessy v. Ferguson*	Malcolm X, 1925–1965 Lorraine Hansberry, 1930–1965	Cher, 1946–	Amelia Earhart completed solo flight across Atlantic, 1932
22	**23**	**24**	**25**	**26**	**27**	**28**
	Emilio Aguinaldo, Philippine independence leader, captured, 1901	Ynés Mexia, 1870–1938, Mexican American botanical explorer	African Freedom Day	Susette LaFlesche Tibbles died, 1903, Omaha Indian rights advocate	Victoria Matthews 1861–1907, black author and social worker Buddha's birthday (China)	Jim Thorpe, 1888–1953
29	**30**					
Baha'u'llah Ascension Day	Hernando de Soto landed in Florida, 1539 Countee Cullen, 1903–1946	Asian and Pacific Islander Heritage Month				

I have fought against white domination, and I have fought against black domination. I have cherished the ideal of a democratic and free society in which all persons live together in harmony and with equal opportunities. It is an ideal which I hope to live for and to achieve. But if needs be, it is an ideal for which I am prepared to die.

—*Nelson Mandela*

Count Your Way through Japan by Jim Haskins is a good book for primary students, with numbers in Japanese accompanied by pictures of the country. Provide a variety of other books on Japan so that students can explore this country.

John Langone. *In the Shogun's Shadow: Understanding a Changing Japan.* Little, Brown, 1994. Covers history and culture, including information on United States–Japan relations.

Richard Tames. *Exploration into Japan.* New Discovery Books, 1995.

May 5

Cinco de Mayo marks the victory of Mexican forces over the French at Puebla, Mexico, on May 5, 1862. While not a major holiday in Mexico, it is celebrated today in Latino communities in the United States as the occasion for a fiesta, with a parade, dancing, and other activities. You can plan a fiesta in your room. Bring recordings of Mexican popular music, folk songs, or Mexican Indian music. Let the students prepare food such as tortillas, guacamole, or buñelos. Students can decorate the room appropriately by using poster paint or felt pens to create murals that evoke Mexico and Mexican American life. Possible subjects include food, sports, clothing, arts and crafts, and historical figures.

Create a learning center on Mexico. Have students contribute ideas. Explore your library for nonfiction and fiction about Mexico as well as stories about Mexican Americans/Chicanos. Develop activity cards that focus on Mexico for reading in the content areas. Use a biography such as *¡Viva México! A Story of Benito Juárez* and *Cinco de Mayo* by Argentina Palacios and illustrated by Howard Berelson. This volume in the *Stones of America* series tells of the Mexican hero of the battle of Puebla. Although born a poor Zapotec Indian in Oaxaca, he grew up to be compared to Abraham Lincoln.

May 25

African Freedom Day offers an opportunity to present information about the great cultural and racial diversity of Africa as well as to discuss the origins of African Americans. Explore books such as the following:

Picture Books

Muriel Feelings. *Jambo Means Hello; A Swahili Alphabet Book.* Dial, 1974.

Xan Hopcraft and Carol C. Hopcraft. *How It Was with Dooms: A True Story of Africa.* McElderry, 1997. A boy and his pet cheetah in Kenya.

Ifeoma Onyefulu. *A Triangle for Adaora: An African Book of Shapes.* Penguin, 1999. Fascinating search for shapes in an African village.

For Independent Readers

Ashley Bryan. *Lion and the Ostrich Chicks, and Other African Tales.* Atheneum, 1986.

Eric Campbell. *The Story of the Leopard Song.* Harcourt, 1992. Animal life on the Serengeti Plain in Africa.

Jason Lauré. *Botswana.* Children's Press, 1993. *Enchantment of the World* series. Describes country and people of Botswana.

Beverly Naidoo. *No Turning Back.* Harper, 1997. Sipho's life with a gang in urban Johannesburg.

June Activities

See calendar of activities and events in Figure 8.14.

June 11

Discover Hawai'i, the fiftieth state, with your students. One of the state's assets is its multicultural, multilingual heritage. Investigate the history of Hawai'i. How and when did it become a state? People from many different countries are represented in Hawai'i. What are some of them? Who are the native Hawaiians? Point out the different spellings for this state: *Hawaii* and *Hawai'i.* Many people prefer the form *Hawai'i* because it reflects the native pronunciation. The apostrophe represents a sound (called a "glottal stop") in the Hawaiian language and so this form is considered more respectful.

Ask students to find examples of unusual facts about Hawai'i, for example, words for different foods. Here are a few words used commonly in Hawai'i:

ae	(eye)	yes
aloha	(ah *loh* hah)	hello/goodbye
haole	(*how* lay)	foreigner (white person)
hula	(*hoo* lah)	dance
lani	(*lah* nee)	sky
lei	(lay)	wreath
luau	(loo ah oo)	feast
mahalo	(mah *hah* loh)	thanks
mauna	(*mou* nah)	mountain
moana	(moh *ah* nah)	ocean

Following are examples of books about the multicultural heritage of Hawai'i:

Roy Kakulu Alameida. *Stories of Old Hawai'i.* The Bess Press, 1997.

Sharon Linnea. *Princess Ka'iulani: Hope of a Nation, Heart of a People.* Eerdmans, 1999. Biography of a princess.

Emily McAuliffe. *Hawai'i Facts and Symbols.* Capstone, 2000.

June 14—Flag Day

On this day in 1777, the U.S. flag was adopted. In 1877, Congress declared the flag should be flown on this day. In 1916, President Woodrow Wilson proclaimed Flag Day. The first flag, "Old Glory," had thirteen stars and thirteen stripes. How is today's flag different? A flag is a symbol. Ask students what symbols represent the United States to them. What would they put on an American flag if they designed a new one? Students can discuss

FIGURE 8.14   JUNE

1	2	3	4	5	6	7
Brigham Young, 1801–1877 International Children's Day	Congress granted American Indians citizenship, 1924	DeSoto claimed Florida for Spain, 1539 Roland Hayes, 1887–1977		English colonists massacre Pequot village in Pequot War, 1637 Kaahumanu died, 1832, Hawaiian ruler	Marian Wright Edelman, 1939– Evacuation of Japanese Americans into concentration camps completed, 1942 Sarah Remond, 1826–1887?, black lecturer and physician	Gwendolyn Brooks, 1917–, black poet Nikki Giovanni, 1943–
8	**9**	**10**	**11**	**12**	**13**	**14**
			Kamehameha Day (Hawai'i) Addie W. Hunton, 1875–1943, black youth group leader Henry Cisneros, 1947–	Philippine Independence Day Anne Frank Day Girls allowed to play Little League baseball, 1974	St. Anthony (Portugal, Brazil)	Hawaii organized as territory, 1900 Harriet Beecher Stowe, 1811–1896 Flag Day
15	**16**	**17**	**18**	**19**	**20**	**21**
	Flight of Valentina Tereshkova (first woman in space), 1963 Soweto Day	Susan LaFlesche Picotte, 1865–1915, Omaha physician James Weldon Johnson, 1871–1938 Sweden-America Day	War of 1812 declared against Great Britain, 1812 Sally Ride, first U.S. woman in space, 1983	Statue of Liberty arrived in New York Harbor, 1885 Juneteenth— Emancipation reaches Texas, 1865	Start of French Revolution, 1789 Announced purchase of Alaska from Russia, 1867	
22	**23**	**24**	**25**	**26**	**27**	**28**
Slavery abolished in Great Britain, 1772 Joe Louis (Brown Bomber) defeated Max Schmeling, 1938	William Penn signed treaty with Indians, 1683 Wilma Rudolph, 1940–1994	San Juan Day (Puerto Rico)	Crazy Horse (Sioux) defeated Custer— Battle of the Little Bighorn, 1876	Pearl S. Buck, 1892–1973 UN Charter signed, 1945	Paul Dunbar, 1872–1906, black writer Joseph Smith, Mormon prophet, killed, 1844 Helen Keller, 1880–1968	Treaty of Versailles ended World War I
29	**30**					
First African church in the U.S. (Philadelphia), 1794 Azalia Hackley, 1867–1922, black singer José Rizal, 1861–1896	Korean War began 1950					

… We could never learn to be brave and patient, if there were only joy in the world.
—*Helen Keller*

283

different kinds of flags and banners—for countries, states, organizations—and work together on creating a banner to represent their classroom or school.

June 19—Juneteenth

News of the 1863 Emancipation Proclamation freeing the slaves did not reach African Americans in Texas until June 1865, more than two months after the end of the Civil War. As a result, *Juneteenth* (June 19) has become a community celebration of African American heritage, featuring picnics and music.

In Carole Boston Weatherford's *Juneteenth Jamboree,* illustrated by Yvonne Buchanan, Cassandra, who has just moved to Texas, learns about the history of this celebration and the end of slavery.

June 20

Investigate Alaska, the forty-ninth state. Only a little more than half a million people (619,500 estimated in 1999) inhabit this huge area (656,424 square miles). That's about one person for every square mile. Alaska is the first of the fifty states in size but forty-eighth in population. (Only Vermont and Wyoming have fewer inhabitants.) Compare Alaska's population and area to that of Hawai'i, which had 1,185,497 people in 1999 (estimate) in only 10,932 square miles. How do these figures compare with your state? Have students calculate how many times their state would fit inside Alaska's area. How many times would Alaska's population fit into their state's population?

Who lives in Alaska? Read about this unusual land in the following books:

Ruth Crisman. *Racing the Iditarod Trail.* Silver Burdett, 1993. The famous Alaska dogsled race.

Jean Craighead George. *Snow Bear.* Illustrated by Wendell Minor. Hyperion, 1999. Polar bear cub and Eskimo child play together briefly.

Carolyn Meyer. *In a Different Light: Growing Up in a Yu'pik Eskimo Village in Alaska.* Simon & Schuster, 1996.

Debbie S. Miller. *A Caribou Journey.* Illustrated by Jon Van Zyle. Turtleback Books, 2000. Nonfiction, shows life of caribou mother and her calf, in-depth coverage in a picture book.

Debbie S. Miller. *River of Life.* Illustrated by Jon Van Zyle. Clarion, 2000. How an Alaskan river changes through the seasons.

Claire Rudolf Murphy. *A Child's Alaska.* Alaska Northwest Press, 1994. Many different people live in Alaska, including Eskimos, Indians, and Aleuts.

Lori Yanuchi. *Running with the Big Dogs: A Sled Dog Puppy Grows up in Denali National Park Alaska.* Illustrated by Wendy Brown. Ridge Rock Press, 1999. First year of training for puppy to work with rangers in park.

July Activities

See Figure 8.15 for this month's events and activities.

FIGURE 8.15   JULY

1	2	3	4	5	6	7
Canada Day	Thurgood Marshall, 1908–1993 Civil Rights Act of 1964 Voting Rights Act became law, 1964	Champlain founded Québec, 1608	Edmonia Lewis, 1845–?, black-Cherokee sculptor Lucy Stowe, 1885–1937, black teacher and administrator Giuseppe Garibaldi, 1807–1882		Cecil Poole, first black U.S. attorney, 1961	
8	**9**	**10**	**11**	**12**	**13**	**14**
	Dr. Daniel Hale Williams, black doctor, performed first open heart surgery, 1893	Mary McLeod Bethune, 1875–1955 Arthur Ashe, 1943–1993, black tennis star			Wole Soyinka, 1934–	Bastille Day (France), 1789 George Washington Carver monument dedicated, 1951
15	**16**	**17**	**18**	**19**	**20**	**21**
Maggie Walker, 1867–1934, black insurance and banking executive Ch'iu Chin, 1875–1907	Ida Wells-Barnett, 1862–1931, black journalist and civic leader Mary Baker Eddy, 1821–1910, founder, Christian Science	Spain transferred Florida to U.S., 1821 S. Y. Agnon, 1888–1970	Miguel Hidalgo, 1753–1811, Father of Mexican independence	Alice Dunbar Nelson, 1875–1935, black author; teacher	Seneca Falls Convention (NY) launched women's suffrage movement, 1848	First daily black newspaper, New Orleans Tribune, 1864 National Women's Hall of Fame dedicated, 1979
22	**23**	**24**	**25**	**26**	**27**	**28**
	Pham Tuan, first non-Caucasian in space, 1980	Simón Bolívar, 1783–1830 Mormons settled Salt Lake City, 1847 Pioneer Day	Puerto Rico became a commonwealth, 1952 (Constitution Day) Saint James (Spain)	Americans with Disabilities Act signed, 1990	Korean War ended, 1953	Senator Hiram Fong (HI) and Rep. Daniel Inouye (HI) first Asian Americans in Congress, 1959
29	**30**	**31**				
		Sarah Garnet, 1831–1911, black educator and civic worker				

I did not equate my self-worth with my wins and losses.
—*Arthur Ashe*

July 1 and 3

Recognize Canada on Canada Day, celebrating the Confederation in 1867. Display its symbol, the maple leaf, with pictures of Canada from travel folders. Can students name some famous Canadians? Display a map of Canada. Look at the names of the provinces. What do they indicate about the ethnic influences in Canada and where the early settlers came from? How is the history of Canada different from that of the United States? How is it similar?

Ted Harrison. *O Canada.* Tickner and Fields, 1993. Book by noted Canadian artist, based on national anthem.

Lawrence Jackson. *Newfoundland & Labrador.* Fitzhenry, 1999. Part of *Hello Canada* series.

Bobbie Kalman. *Canada: The Culture.* Crabtree, 1993. Part of the *Lands, Peoples, and Cultures* series.

Include books set in Canada in your library such as the following:

Dave Bouchard. *If You're Not from the Prairie . . .* Illustrated by Henry Ripplinger. Aladdin, 1998. A poem describing the world of children who live on the Canadian prairie.

Jonathan London. *The Sugaring-Off Party.* Illustrated by Gilles Pelletier. Dutton, 1995. Paul's Grandmère describes the French-Canadian custom.

Gary Paulsen. *Hatchet.* Aladdin, 1999. Thirteen-year-old Brian must learn how to survive alone when his plane crashes in Canadian wilderness.

July 4—Independence Day

Independence Day for the United States can be recognized in many ways. Prepare a program that includes poetry and prose representing the many voices of America—people of different colors, languages, and religions united in their celebration of U.S. independence. *Celebrating America: A Collection of Poems and Images of the American Spirit,* poetry compiled by Laura Whipple with art from the Art Institute of Chicago, is an excellent example of a multicultural sampler.

A book to share with students is *Celebration!* by Jane Resh Thomas, illustrated by Raúl Colón, about an African American extended family gathered for the Fourth of July. Rich with description of food and games, this story will stimulate student discussion of their family get-togethers. They can compare the foods they eat and the activities they engage in with those described in this book.

Younger students can talk about words associated with the Fourth of July, such as democracy, independence, equality, liberty, and fraternity.

July 10

Mary McLeod Bethune, known as The Great Educator, was born in South Carolina and grew up working in the cotton fields. In an age when the education of black children was not considered terribly important, she graduated from college and became a teacher. When she heard that the town of Daytona Beach in Florida didn't have a school for blacks, she established one for young black women that is now the Bethune-Cookman College. She also founded the National Council of Negro Women. In 1935, President Franklin Roosevelt appointed her administrator of the new Office of Minority Affairs.

Challenge students to find out more about this amazing woman. Read a biography such as *Mary McLeod Bethune* by noted poet Eloise Greenfield, illustrated by Jerry Pinkney or *Mary McLeod Bethune* by Patricia McKissack.

Provide the following quote for discussion:

> I am my mother's daughter, and the drums of Africa still beat in my heart. They will not let me rest while there is a single Negro boy or girl without a chance to prove his worth.
> —Mary McLeod Bethune

August Activities

In this month that includes the bombing of Hiroshima and Nagasaki, the fall of the Aztec Empire to the Spanish conquerors, and the violence accompanying Indian and Pakistani independence, we focus on the need for world peace and justice (see Figure 8.16). Talk with students about the need to resolve differences peacefully, without resorting to violence, on a personal level as well as an international level.

First Sunday in August—Celebration of Peace Day

How can we help students appreciate peace without their having to endure the horrors of war? Stories of what people have experienced in war and how they survived offer students an opportunity to empathize yet not be overwhelmed. Two books for young children tell of life in times of war:

Haemi Balgassi. *Peacebound Trains.* Illustrated by Chris K. Soentpiet. Clarion, 1996. A young girl's grandmother tells her of life during the Korean War. Although she was forced to flee Seoul by train with her children, someday the trains will bring people home from war.

Rosemary Breckler. *Sweet Dried Apples: A Vietnamese Wartime Childhood.* Illustrated by Deborah Kogan Ray. Houghton Mifflin, 1996. Two children living in the countryside are forced out of their village by the war.

August 6—Hiroshima Day

Hiroshima Day marks the anniversary of the dropping of the atomic bomb on Japan, resulting in Japan's surrender, ending World War II. Although the war was over, the effects of radiation from the bomb lingered long afterward. Explore the impact of the bomb on the Japanese people and the implications of this event for world peace.

Eleanor Coerr's *Sadako,* illlustrated by Ed Young, is a picture book suitable for younger students; it's a rewrite of the author's famous earlier book *Sadako and the Thousand Cranes,* the true story of a Japanese girl who suffered from radiation poisoning. Sadako attempted to ward off death by folding a thousand origami cranes. Although she was not successful, Japanese schoolchildren still fold paper cranes in her memory, united

FIGURE 8.16   AUGUST

1	2	3	4	5	6	7
Maria Mitchell, 1818–1889, astronomer	James Baldwin, 1924–1987	Columbus started first voyage, 1492	Anne Frank captured, 1944; Freedom of the Press Day; Zwenger acquitted, 1735	Friendship Day	Hiroshima Day (U.S. bombed Hiroshima, Japan, 1945); President Johnson signed Voting Rights Act, 1965	Ralph Bunche, 1904–1971; Congress authorized Vietnam War, 1964

8	9	10	11	12	13	14
Roberto Clemente, 1934–1973	Janie Porter Barrett, 1865–1948, black social welfare leader; U.S. bombed Nagasaki, Japan, 1945		Alex Haley, 1921–1992; Watts Riots (CA), 1965	U.S. annexed Hawai'i, 1898; King Philip's War ended, first Indian War, 1676	Cortez conquered Aztecs, 1521	Japan surrendered, World War II, 1945; Pakistan became independent, 1947

15	16	17	18	19	20	21
India became independent, 1947	Carol Moseley-Braun, 1947–	Charlotte Forten (Grimke), 1837–1914, black teacher and author; V. S. Naipaul, 1932–	19th Amendment ratified 1920, women's right to vote	Mammy Pleasant, 1814–1904, black California pioneer	Bernardo O'Higgins Chilean patriot, 1778–1842; First African slaves arrived in U.S., 1619	

22	23	24	25	26	27	28
	Pharsi New Year; Sacco and Vanzetti electrocuted, 1927	Lucy Moten died, 1933, black educator; Amelia Earhart flew nonstop across U.S., 1932		Women's Equality Day; Women's Suffrage 19th Amendment certified, 1920	Rose McClendon, 1884–1936, black actress	Martin Luther King, Jr., gave "I Have a Dream" speech, Washington, DC, 1963

29	30	31				
	Guion Bluford, first black astronaut, flew 1983; Saint Rose of Lima (Americas)	Josephine Ruffin, 1842–1924, black leader				

The wonder is not that so many Negro boys and girls are ruined but that so many survive.

—*James Baldwin*

in their desire for world peace. Today a statue of Sadako holding a golden crane in outstretched hands stands in Hiroshima Peace Park. Inscribed below are the words: "This is our cry, this is our prayer: Peace in the world."

Other books to support student study of this period are:

Tatsuharu Kodama. *Shin's Tricycle*. Illustrated by Noriyuki Ando. Translated by Kazuko Hokumen-Jones. Walker, 1995. Shin dreamed of having a tricycle but the war meant that metal was scarce. He never had the chance to enjoy the tricycle he received for his fourth birthday because he was killed in Hiroshima. His tricycle is displayed at the Hiroshima Peace Museum.

Laurence Yep. *Hiroshima*. Scholastic, 1995. This book juxtaposes the flight of the *Enola Gay,* the airplane delivering the bomb, with the story of two Japanese sisters taking a walk in their city. Includes accounts of survivors.

August 7

> I was offered the ambassadorship of Liberia once, when the post was earmarked for a Negro. I told them I wouldn't take a Jim Crow job.
> —Ralph Bunche

Ralph Bunche was a famous diplomat and the first African American to win the Nobel Peace Prize in 1950, in recognition of his role as United Nations mediator in the Palestine armistice. Ask students whether they know what a "Jim Crow" job is. Can they guess? Why would the ambassador to a country such as Liberia be expected to be black? Find out more about this early peacemaker in a biography:

Anne E. Schraff. *Ralph Bunche: Winner of the Nobel Peace Prize.* Enslow, 1999.

Martin Luther King, Jr., is another African American who was awarded a Nobel Peace Prize. What other famous people have received this award? How are the recipients chosen? Students can investigate the lives and achievements of the following men and women from diverse backgrounds who have won this international recognition for their efforts on behalf of peace and justice.

2002	Jimmy Carter (United States)
2001	Kofi Annan (Ghana), UN
2000	President Kin Dae Jung (South Korea)
1999	Doctors without Borders
1998	John Hume and David Trimble (for Northern Ireland)
1997	Jody Williams, U.S.-International Campaign to Ban Land Mines
1996	Bishop Carlos Ximenes and Jose Ramos-Horta (Timor)
1994	Yasir Arafat (Palestine), Shimon Peres, and Yitzhak Rabin (Israel)
1993	Frederik de Klerk, Nelson Mandela (South Africa)
1992	Rigoberta Menchú (Guatemala)
1991	Aung San Suu Kyi (Myanmar, formerly Burma)

Read a biography to students such as the following:

Caroline Lazo. *Rigoberta Menchú*. Dillon, 1994. Tells how a poor Mayan Indian woman from Guatemala came to world attention for her philosophy of nonviolence and her ability to bring groups together. Part of the *Peacemakers* series.

August 13

Who were the Aztecs and how did the Spanish conquer them? Pose such questions to the students and have them search for the answers. The Aztec civilization is particularly interesting because it was so advanced, and yet we know very little about it because the Spanish destroyed most of the records. Investigate the Spanish treatment of the Aztecs. (See information on the Aztec calendar later in this chapter.)

The following books are a starting point for student research.

John Bierhorst. *The Hungry Woman: Myths and Legends of the Aztecs*. Morrow, 1993.

Johanna Defrates. *What Do We Know about the Aztecs?* Bedrick Books, 1993.

Andrea Guardiano. *Azteca: The Story of a Jaguar Warrior*. Rinehart, 1992.

MOVABLE HOLIDAYS

Listed here are holidays or events that fall on different dates each year. Students can determine the particular dates and add them to the calendar.

United States Holidays or Special Days

Note that many holidays are celebrated on a Monday or Friday to provide a holiday weekend.

Commonwealth Day (Canada)	second Monday in March
Memorial Day	last Monday in May
Labor Day	first Monday in September
Canadian Thanksgiving	second Monday in October
Election Day	first Tuesday after first Monday in November
Veterans' Day	fourth Monday in October
Thanksgiving Day	fourth Thursday in November

Jewish Feasts and Festivals

Because the Jewish calendar (described later in this chapter) is lunar (based on the moon's cycles), the (Gregorian) dates that Jewish holidays fall on will vary each year. Figure 8.17 gives the names and dates for the holidays by year and shows the corresponding Jewish calendar year under Rosh Hashanah, when the new year begins. Note that each holiday actually begins at sundown on the preceding day.

Islamic Holidays

Figure 8.18 shows the dates of the major Islamic celebrations. See more information on the Islamic calendar later in this chapter.

FIGURE 8.17   JEWISH HOLIDAYS

(Gregorian) Year	Purim (Feast of Lots)	Pesach (Festival of Freedom)	Shavuot (Feast of Weeks)	Rosh Hashanah (New Year)	Yom Kippur (Day of Atonement)	Succot (Feast of Tabernacles)	Hanukkah (Feast of Dedication)
2004–5	Mar. 7	Apr. 6	May 26	Sept. 16 (5765)	Sept. 25	Sept. 30	Dec. 8
2005–6	Mar. 25	Apr. 24	June 13	Oct. 4 (5766)	Oct. 13	Oct. 16	Dec. 26
2006–7	Mar. 14	Apr. 13	June 2	Sept. 23 (5767)	Oct. 2	Oct. 7	Dec. 16
2007–8	Mar. 21	Apr. 20	May 9	Sept. 13 (5768)	Sept. 22	Sept. 27	Dec. 5

VARIABLE HOLIDAYS AND ACTIVITIES

Divali

Divali, the Hindu New Year celebration in October or November, lasts five days. Like Hanukkah, Divali is known as the Festival of Lights, because South Asians light oil lamps and set off fireworks, symbolizing the triumph of good over evil. Divali has become a chance to celebrate Hindu culture as well as religion. At this time of year, Hindus give thanks for life's bounty with special foods, gifts, and cleaning the house. The holiday commemorates the return of Lord Rama after fourteen years of exile and his victory over Ravan, the demon king. See the following books:

Rachna Gilmore. *Lights for Gita.* Illustrated by Alice Priestley. Tilbury House, 1995. Gita, a recent immigrant from New Delhi, is looking forward to celebrating Divali in Canada, her new country. At first disappointed because the weather is not like at home, she learns the true meaning of the holiday.

Dilip Kadodwala. *Divali.* SteckVaughn, 1998. Describes the activities of each day in detail, including the third day, the last day of the old year, and the fourth day, the first day of the new year. The fifth day is known as Sister's Day. (*A World of Holidays* series)

Dianne M. MacMillan. *Divali: Hindu Festival of Lights.* Enslow, 1997. Shows celebrations of South Asians in United States and Canada with photographs. Includes a glossary.

FIGURE 8.18   ISLAMIC CELEBRATIONS

New Year: Muharram 1	Ashura: Muharram 10	Mawlid: Rabi'l 12	Ramadan: Ramadan 1	Eid al-Fitr: Shawwal	al-Adha: Zulhijjan 10
2004–5 March 4 (1425)	Mar. 31	May 13	Oct. 26	Nov. 25	Feb. 1
2005–6 Feb. 20 (1426)	Feb. 19	Apr. 21	Oct. 4	Nov. 3	Jan. 10
2006–7 Jan. 30 (1427)	Feb. 8	Apr. 10	Sept. 23	Oct. 23	Dec. 30
2007–8 Jan. 20 (1428)	Jan. 29	Mar. 31	Sept. 12	Oct. 12	Dec. 20

Asian New Year

According to the lunar calendar used by Chinese, Koreans, Vietnamese, Tibetans, and Hmong, the New Year falls in January or February. For many Asian Americans, this is the biggest holiday of the year (see Figure 8.19). Chinese American families give children red (lucky) envelopes containing money and hold large family banquets. Firecrackers and a parade also herald the New Year. Korean Americans pay homage to their ancestors and feast on special dishes. The Vietnamese Americans celebrate with firecrackers, incense, food, and an exchange of gifts. Tet, the Vietnamese New Year, is also the advent of spring. Ask Asian American students in your class to describe how their families plan to celebrate the holiday. Share the following books with your students to dispel misinformation and introduce students to the Chinese New Year celebrations:

Karen Chinn. *Sam and the Lucky Money.* Illustrated by Cornelius Van Wright. Lee & Low, 1995. After receiving his lucky money envelope, Sam and his mother go to Chinatown (New York) to spend it. The book shows Chinatown alive with preparations for the holidays—the reader sees firecrackers, red lanterns, bakery tarts, and a Chinese lion dancing in the street.

Demi. *Happy New Year: Kung-Hsi Fa-Ts'Ai!* Dragonfly, 1999. How the New Year is celebrated in China.

Diane Hoyt-Goldsmith. *Celebrating Chinese New Year.* Illustrated by Lawrence Migdale. Holiday House, 1998. Photos of community enjoying parade, food, music.

Ramadan

Muslims throughout the world celebrate God's delivery of the Koran, Islam's holy book, to Muhammed by fasting for the month of Ramadan. For 29 or 30 days, Muslims are forbid-

FIGURE 8.19   HAPPY NEW YEAR (CHINESE)

den to eat, drink, or smoke from sunrise to sunset. The fast ends with the three-day feast of Eid al-Fitr. Because many students are unaware of Muslim observances or have stereotyped preconceptions, share books such as the following:

Suhaib Hamid Ghazi. *Ramadan.* Illustrated by Omar Rayyan. Holiday House, 1996. Hakeem, an elementary school student, shows how Muslims celebrate Ramadan. Includes information on Islamic history and customs.

Mary Matthews. *Magid Fasts for Ramadan.* Illustrated by E. B. Lewis. Houghton Mifflin, 2000. Eight-year-old Muslim wants to celebrate Ramadan by fasting.

Hanukkah—The Festival of Lights

On this eight-night Jewish holiday, candles are lit in a menorah to commemorate the survival of the Jews in the second century B.C. Non-Jewish students may have heard about Hanukkah but be confused about the meaning of this holiday. Books to help primary students understand the holiday are:

Linda Glaser. *The Borrowed Hanukkah Latkes.* Illustrated by Nancy Cole. Whitman, 1997. Rachel solves the problem of getting an elderly neighbor to join the celebration.

Fran Manushkin. *Latkes and Applesauce: A Hanukkah Story.* Illustrated by Robin Spowart. Scholastic, 1990. A poor family saves a starving cat and dog, which then help the family find food.

Intermediate students will appreciate *Celebrating Hanukkah* by Diane Hoyt-Goldsmith, with photos by Lawrence Migdale. This book explains and illustrates the distinctive features of the holiday. It also includes instructions for playing the dreidl (a top to spin), a recipe for making latkes (potato pancakes), and information about the Hebrew calendar.

TEACHING MULTICULTURALLY AROUND A THEME: TIME

The study of time is fascinating to students. They are often surprised to find all the different ways that humans have counted time, in the past as well as today, because they tend to assume that "time" is a fixed concept that can be viewed in only one way. In addition, different cultures have contributed to our understanding and measurement of time, leading students to observe that even a "scientific" topic such as time is subject to social forces and political considerations. This unit suggests activities that unite the study of time with the language arts, social studies, math, science, and the arts.

Marking Time

What is a day? One idea of day is a 24-hour period that includes both light and darkness. Is it not strange that we count a day from the middle of a night to the middle of the next night?

In some cultures there is no word that means just that. Many ancient cultures recognized a single event such as dawn, the rising of the sun, and spoke of so many dawns or suns. Other cultures used the night and spoke of "sleeps." Gradually the light period was broken up with terms related to the sun: daybreak, sunrise, noon, afternoon, twilight, and sunset. The crowing of cocks, the yoking of oxen, and the siesta are other examples of ways of marking the time of day. Italians in the seventeenth century counted the hours from 1 to 24, beginning at sunset, so that the hours of the day varied according to the season. For some peoples day begins with dawn, but, for example, Hebrew days begin at sundown. Dividing the day into equal hours is a modern concept brought about by industrialization.

Folklore provides a wealth of information related to these concepts of time. Encourage students to search out such ideas. They might begin with expressions or beliefs related to time; for example, Friday is a bad day, and Friday the thirteenth is the worst of all days! *Blue Monday and Friday the Thirteenth* by Lila Perl explores the origins of many beliefs. Students can pursue the study of cultural beliefs and superstitions in such books as *Cross Your Fingers, Spit in Your Hat* by Alvin Schwartz.

How Calendars Developed

Encourage students to investigate the history of calendars. They can learn, for example, the origins of the word, which goes back to the Latin *calendarium,* which means *account book.* Calendars are associated, therefore, with the payment of debts, marking times when payments were due. A calendar, as generally used, is a system for recording the passage of time. Congress, for example, has a calendar, or schedule of events.

The first calendars, created by the Babylonians, were based on moons. Twelve moons make a 354-day year. When it was observed that every four years the year needed an adjustment to make the calendar fit the seasons, the Babylonians added another moon, or month. This calendar was adapted by the Egyptians, Semites, and Greeks.

The Egyptians modified this calendar by basing their calculations on the regular rising of the Nile River, which occurred each year just after Sirius, the Dog Star, appeared. They developed a calendar that more nearly matched the solar year, using 365 days, which was still a little off from the 365¼ days we now consider accurate. Considering that they created this system around 4000 B.C., however, they were amazingly exact. They worked with 12 months of 30 days each and simply added 5 days at the end of the year.

Plot some of these different calendars on a time line. Show students what calendars (Julian, Gregorian) were in use in different parts of the world at the same time.

The Christian Church Calendar

On this calendar there are certain fixed dates, such as December 25, Christmas, based on the solar year. Movable feast days include Easter and Palm Sunday, based on the lunar calendar (see Figure 8.20).

Orthodox Christians—such as Greeks, Syrians, Ethiopians, Eritreans, Bulgarians, Russians, and Serbs—celebrate Easter and other holidays according to a different formula.

FIGURE 8.20   CHRISTIAN HOLIDAYS

	Ash Wednesday	*Easter Sunday*
2004	February 25	April 11
2005	February 5	March 27
2006	March 1	April 16
2007	February 7	April 8
2008	February 8	March 23
2009	February 9	April 12
2010	February 17	April 4

The Hebrew Calendar

Another calendar that is widely used today is the Hebrew, or Jewish, calendar, based on the Creation, which preceded the birth of Christ by 3760 years and 3 months. The Hebrew year begins in September rather than January. From the fall of 2002 to the fall of 2003, therefore, the Hebrew year was 5763.

Based on the moon, the Hebrew year usually contains 12 months, alternately 30 and 29 days long. Seven times during every 19-year period, an extra month of 29 days is inserted to adjust this calendar, as shown in Figure 8.21.

The Jewish New Year, Rosh Hashanah, begins on the first day of Tishri. Students can learn more about the Jewish calendar from books like *Annie's Shabbat* by Sarah Marwil Lamstein, illustrated by Cecily Lang, and *Milk and Honey: A Year of Jewish Holidays* by Jane Yolen, illustrated by Louise Anjust.

FIGURE 8.21   MONTHS IN THE HEBREW CALENDAR

Tishri	Nisan
Heshvan	Iyar
Kislev	Sivan
Tevet	Tammuz
Shevat	Av
Adar	Elul

Note: Veadar added in leap years and one day added to Adar.

The Islamic Calendar

Also based on the moon, the Islamic calendar dates from Mohammed's flight from Mecca, the Hegira, in 622 A.D. The year has only 354 days so that its New Year moves with respect to the seasons. It makes a full cycle every 32½ years. The twelve Islamic months are:

Muharram	Rabi II	Rajab	Shawwal
Safar	Jumada I	Shaban	Zulkadah
Rabi I	Jumada II	Ramadan	Zulhijjah

Muharram 1 is the New Year. The months begin with the sighting of the new moon. A book such as *Id-Ul-Fitr* by Kerena Marchant will help students appreciate the Islamic calendar.

The Chinese Calendar

One of the oldest calendars still used, the Chinese lunar calendar is said to have been invented by Emperor Huangdi in 2637 B.C. By 350 B.C., the Chinese were able to calculate the solar year. Years are counted in cycles of 60. The years within each cycle are divided into repeating 12-year cycles. Each of these 12 years is named after an animal. The year 2002 in the Gregorian calendar was the year of the horse, the 19th year in the 78th cycle. The Chinese New Year starts at the second new moon after the beginning of winter. Another important celebration in the Chinese calendar is the Moon Festival in mid-autumn. Share *Moon Festival* by Ching Yeung Russell, illustrated by Christopher Zhong-Yuan Zhang, in which she recalls the joys of family and tradition when she was a child in China.

The Aztec Calendar

The Aztecs flourished in the Valley of Mexico from 1215 to 1521. Although they had no horses and no wheels, they possessed sophisticated astronomical knowledge and built a vast, powerful nation. Because the Spanish conquest destroyed most of their culture, we know very little about them. They counted using a base 20 system. The Aztecs had two calendars, adopted from the Mayans. One was for sacred or ritual purposes and had 20 days that combined with the numbers 1 to 13 to yield 260 days. The day names and numbers told a person's fortune (see Figure 8.22).

The other calendar represented the solar year and had 18 months of 20 days each to make 360 days. To this were added five empty or unlucky days to complete the year. Children born during this time received names meaning "worthless." The two calendars meshed every 52 years, which was a time of celebration.

How Music Came to the World, retold by Hal Ober and illustrated by Carol Ober is a source of pictures and other information on the Aztecs and their calendar.

Sources for Further Study

Franklyn M. Branley. *Keeping Time: From the Beginning and into the 21st Century.* Illustrated by Jill Weber. Houghton Mifflin, 1993. Clock time and calendar time.

David Ewing Duncan. *Calendar: Humanity's Epic Struggle to Determine a True and Accurate Year.* Avon Books, 1998.

Leonard Everett Fisher. *Calendar Art: Thirteen Days, Weeks, Months, and Years from around the World.* Four Winds Press, 1987. How various civilizations have measured time, including Aztec, Babylonian, and Roman.

FIGURE 8.22 THE AZTEC DAY SIGNS

Betsy Maestro. *The Story of Clocks and Calendars: Marking a Millennium.* Illustrated by Giulio Maestro. Lothrop, Lee, Shepherd, 1999. From prehistory to the atomic clock, shows sociocultural influences on calendar.

E. G. Richards. *Mapping Time: The Calendar and Its History.* Oxford University Press, 1999. Theory of clocks, calendars, and numbers.

MULTICULTURAL FOCUS ON A GROUP— JEWISH AMERICANS: LIVING IN A "CHRISTIAN" COUNTRY

Since the time of Thomas Jefferson, the separation of church and state has been acknowledged as one of our fundamental principles. But from the perspective of non-Christians living in this country, there is no question that Americans are assumed to be Christians. "In

God We Trust" says our money and we pledge allegiance to "one nation, under God." We even follow a calendar that, no matter how secularized it appears to be now, counts from the "birth of Jesus" and was organized to predict the important Catholic holidays. Jewish Americans (and other non-Christians such as Muslims, Buddhists, Sikhs, and followers of Santería) find themselves in a position of belonging, only up to the point at which they are suddenly excluded or made to feel outside the expected range of "normal" behavior. In a moment, you can change from "one of us" to "one of them." Community debates over the celebration of Christmas in school, taxpayer support for a city-run Nativity creche, or prayers before an athletic event illustrate the extent to which (many Christian) people are unaware of the effect that this exclusion must have on people such as Jewish Americans. In addition, although people may try to justify prejudice against Jews because of religious belief, physical features, occupational tendencies, or fear of hidden influences, in fact this anti-Semitism is just one more way to wall off a group of people. A multicultural approach to teaching about Jewish Americans would include:

- Overcoming stereotypes such as "victims of the Holocaust" or "all Jews are rich and powerful."
- Presenting Jews as participants throughout U.S. history.
- Assembling information about the diversity of Jewish life, culture, and customs.
- Understanding how religious discrimination and anti-Semitic prejudice hurts all of us.

The Jewish Immigration to the United States

Jews formed a significant percentage of the immigrants that poured into the United States through the holding station at Ellis Island, fleeing prejudice, poverty, and pogroms (mass killings) for a new start. When you talk about immigration, have students compare and contrast the immigrants of the last century with the immigrants or refugees of today. What was it like to go through the inspections at Ellis Island? How did it feel to leave family and memories behind? The following books will give all students insight into the universalities of the immigrant experience as well as the specific obstacles facing the Jewish immigrants.

Carol Bierman with Barbara Hehner. *Journey to Ellis Island: How My Father Came to America.* Illustrated by L. McGaw. Hyperion, 1998. Life in Russia was hard and so was trying to get past Ellis Island.

Joanne Rocklin. *Strudel Stories.* Delacorte, 1999. Follows generations of Jews as they move from Odessa, Russia, to New York and Los Angeles.

Rosemary Wells. *Streets of Gold.* Illustrated by Dan Andreasen. Dial, 1999. Picture book biography based on Mary Antin's account of her life in Russia and her family's immigration to the United States.

Jewish Life and Customs

Many foods once associated only with Jews have spread to other groups and regions of the country, such as bagels and lox. The Jews themselves brought different traditional foods depending on where they came from: Germany, Poland, or Russia, for example. Foods aren't the only characteristic that distinguishes Jewish life. Many students may know about Jewish holidays, such as Hanukkah, the Festival of Lights, and the latkes (potato pancakes) that are associated with this festival. But most people would say that being Jewish is more than eating special foods (or keeping *kosher,* observing religious restrictions regarding food preparation); it's an ethnic identity. Use the following books to introduce the concept of Jewish identity and encourage Jewish children to share their own experiences.

Gilda Berger. *Celebrate: Stories of the Jewish Holidays.* Illustrated by Peter Catalanotto. Scholastic, 1998.

Naomi Howland. *Latkes, Latkes, Good to Eat.* Clarion, 1999. In a Russian village, a magic pan makes endless latkes.

Eric Kimmel, ed. *A Hanukkah Treasury.* Illustrated by Emily Lisker. Holt, 1998. Many activities to share with all students.

Jane Breskin Zalben. *Beni's Family Cookbook for the Jewish Holidays.* Holt, 1996. Presents recipes arranged around twelve Jewish holy days, with background information and anecdotes from the author's Beni stories.

Invisible to History

Like members of other minority groups, Jews have been left out of most accounts of U.S. history. Yet it is the varied strands of these different experiences that make up the American multiculture today. Students can learn more about our history than the traditional "mainstream" accounts that gloss over differences in the way certain groups were affected by historical events. Use examples of Jewish Americans to encourage students to ask questions such as, "Was the Revolutionary War/Civil War/settling of the West/fight for civil rights a different experience for this group?" The following books will get you started.

Philip Brooks. *Extraordinary Jewish Americans.* Children's Press, 1998. Short biographies of more than sixty Jewish Americans, past and present.

Jerry Stanley. *Frontier Merchants: Lionel and Barron Jacobs and the Jewish Pioneers Who Settled the West.* Crown, 1998. A different perspective, brothers who sold food to the early settlers in the West.

The Holocaust

The memory of the Holocaust continues to overshadow the world today. The fact that more than 6 million Jews—men, women, and children—were rounded up, taken to concentration camps, and killed in mass executions under Nazi orders, without substantial outcry and with the support of many other governments, is still difficult to grasp. However, too often the Jews are portrayed as passive victims of this atrocity, as were the African American slaves. Even young children can learn something about the horrors of this time and still understand how people fought to stay alive.

Charles Anflick. *Resistance: Teen Partisans and Resisters Who Fought Nazi Tyranny.* Rosen, 1999. Three methods of resisting presented.

Livia Bitton-Jackson. *I Have Lived a Thousand Years.* Simon and Schuster, 1997. A memoir of the Hungarian ghetto and concentration camp.

Sandra Giddens. *Escape: Teens Who Escaped from the Holocaust to Freedom.* Rosen, 1999.

Anne Isaacs. *Torn Thread.* Scholastic, 1999. Two sisters are taken from the Warsaw ghetto to a forced labor camp in Czechoslovakia.

Anita Lobel. *No Pretty Pictures: A Child of War.* Greenwillow, 1998. A child of 5, she struggled to survive on the streeets in Poland, in prison, and at Auschwitz.

Uri Orlev. *Run, Boy, Run.* Boston: Houghton, 2003.

Patricia Polacco. *The Butterfly.* Philomel, 2000. Girl in Nazi-occupied Paris discovers Jewish family hiding in basement.

Naomi Samson. *Hide: A Child's View of the Holocaust.* University of Nebraska Press, 2000. A child in Poland.

Jerry Spinelli. *Milkweed.* Knopf, 2003.

Talk with students about the word "Holocaust" and what it means. Originally applied by Elie Wiesel to the Jewish experience, it has been used to describe other periods of mass murder/genocide/ethnic cleansing such as the African slave trade and civil war in Rwanda.

Norma Fox Mazer. *Goodnight, Maman.* Harcourt Brace, 1999. After fleeing from Nazis, 12-year-old Karen Levy and brother find refuge in New York.

Frank Dabba Smith. *The Secret Camera: Life in the Lodz Ghetto.* Photos by Mendel Grossman. Harcourt, 2000. Photos taken secretly in Polish ghetto provide record of life.

The Life and Diary of Anne Frank

Young Anne Frank, of Amsterdam, has come to be a symbol of the Holocaust. Yet we know very little about her since only her writing survives, and it can be easy to distance ourselves from this real person. Provide a larger context for students as they read about Anne Frank and her short life. There are a number of resources available in addition to different editions of her diary. Students will be interested to learn that her father, Otto Frank, who found the diary, suppressed many parts of it for years. Do any students keep a diary? If someone read their diary fifty years later, what kind of picture of life would they get?

Otto H. Frank and Mirjam Pressler. *Anne Frank: The Diary of a Young Girl, the Definitive Edition.* Anchor, 1995. Anne Frank and her family hid in a small room in an Amsterdam apartment.

Alison Leslie Gold. *Memories of Anne Frank.* Scholastic, 1997. A friend of Anne's recalls that time. Nonfiction.

Mirjam Pressler. *Anne Frank: A Hidden Life.* Dutton, 2000.

Rian Verhoeven and Ruud van der Rol. *Anne Frank.* Viking, 1993. A photographic remembrance of the family shows they weren't just passive victims.

IDEAS IN ACTION!

Sharing a Rainbow

"There's nothing sweeter than a rainbow shared by Jewish and Palestinian kids," says Abdessalam Najjar, mayor of an experiment in getting along, a village where both Jewish and Palestinian families live. Created in 1972, Neve Shalom/Wahat-al-Salam (Oasis of Peace) continues to serve as an example of the possibility for Jews and Palestinians living together in peace. The children of the cooperatively governed village attend a Hebrew-Arabic primary school along with children from neighboring communities. The villagers hope that, as the children grow up playing together, they will become leaders in the struggle for peace.

Are there divisions in your school between groups? How can you bring these groups together to talk and get to know each other? Perhaps the children come from different neighborhoods or have learned to hate another group. Discuss "What good does hate do?"

Never Forget

Students may feel that the Holocaust happened a long time ago (before they were born) and ask why they should care about what happened to Jews, especially if they are not Jewish. But the Holocaust wasn't just about the Jews. Many other groups of people were included in the category of "undesirable," such as Gypsies, homosexuals, and Slavs. In addition, we must remember what happened to the Jews so that it can never happen again, to anyone. Display the following quote for students to read and discuss:

> (I would like people to know) that I have tried to keep memory alive, that I have tried to fight those who would forget. Because if we forget, we are guilty, we are accomplices. . . .
>
> When human lives are endangered, when human dignity is in jeopardy, national borders and sensitivities become irrelevant. Wherever men or women are persecuted because of their race, religion or political views, that place must—at that moment—become the center of the universe.
>
> —Elie Wiesel, from his Nobel Peace Prize acceptance speech, 1986

Do students agree with his argument that, if we forget, we are all guilty? Have them write their response to this quote.

Find out more about Elie Wiesel, his life and work. Why did he receive the Nobel Peace Prize?

What Would You Do?

Many people cooperated with the authorities in the plan to exterminate the Jews, sometimes out of fear, and others simply looked the other way. Yet, a few people stood up to prejudice and helped Jewish people, friends or strangers, survive. What kind of people would risk their lives to help others? Talk with students about how they would feel if they took a stand for what they thought was right. Students can learn more about people who stood up to help the Jews in the following books:

Anne L. Fox and Eva Abraham-Podietz. *Ten Thousand Children: True Stories Told by Children Who Escaped the Holocaust on the Kindertransport.* Behrman House, 1999. Many children were able to escape thanks to efforts by concerned British citizens. (Accompanied by teaching guide.)

Jo Hoestlandt. *Star of Fear, Star of Hope.* Illustrated by Johanna Kang. Walker, 1995. Helen grew up with Lydia, a Jewish girl, in France and now regrets her lack of understanding when Lydia's family faced arrest.

Ken Mochizuki. *Passage to Freedom: The Sugihara Story.* Lee & Low, 1997. The Japanese consul to Lithuania defied his own government and issued visas to Jewish refugees. Up to 10,000 people survived as a result of his work.

Maxine Rosenberg. *Hiding to Survive: Stories of Jewish Children Rescued from the Holocaust.* Clarion, 1994.

Hudson Talbott. *Forging Freedom: A True Story of Heroism during the Holocaust.* Putnam, 2000. Jaap Penraat, a printer in Amsterdam, risked his life when he forged papers that helped the Jews escape the Nazis.

The "Problem" of Christmas

For teachers in many schools, December has become a month to dread, a time of awkwardly balancing the competing claims of Christmas, Hanukkah, Kwanzaa (and Paganism, perhaps). But from the point of view of Jewish children, it is even more confusing. Hanukkah, which is not a major holiday on the Jewish calendar, has become "Christmasized," with "Hanukkah bushes" and other oddities. Yet Christmas is hardly a purely "Christian" holiday, with its pagan-derived customs of Santa Claus, Christmas tree, mistletoe, and yule log. In addition, as intermarriage between Christians and Jews increases, more children face the dilemma of reconciling these differences in their own families. The goal of multicultural teaching, under these circumstances, is to support students' understanding of each other through presenting facts, sharing experiences, and acknowledging both commonalities and differences.

Janice Cohn. *The Christmas Menorahs: How a Town Fought Hate.* Illustrated by Bill Farnsworth. Whitman, 1996. Christians join with Jews to fight anti-Semitism.

Effin Older. *My Two Grandmothers.* Illustrated by Nancy Hayashi. Harcourt Brace, 2000. A child is finding new ways to combine two religious traditions at Christmas.

Joanne Rocklin. *The Very Best Hannukah Gift.* Illustrated by Catharine O'Neill. Delacorte, 1999. When the relatives can't make it because of the weather, family invites neighbors to share their latkes (made with zucchini).

Michael Rosen. *Elijah's Angel: A Story for Chanukah and Christmas.* Illustrated by Aminah Brenda Lynn Robinson. Harcourt Brace, 1992. An elderly Christian barber and a Jewish boy are friends.

Jewish Folklore

There is a rich tradition of Jewish folklore, mostly poking fun at the frailties of humanity. In addition to the familiar patterns of wishes, magic pots, and Cinderella tales, Jewish folklore includes a variety of specific types. Many tales involve the rabbi, who is the respected scholar and source of wisdom on all things. Others depend on the presence of demons, imps, and other monsters who naturally torment humans in creative ways. Finally, there is the village of Chelm, inhabited by people who are either very silly or very wise, depending on your point of view. The following books will start you off with examples for reading aloud, storytelling, or dramatization:

Eric Kimmel, retold. *Gershon's Monster.* Illustrated by Jon J. Muth. Scholastic, 2000. Demons threaten the baker Gershon unless he takes responsibility for his misdeeds.

Eric Kimmel. *The Jar of Rocks.* Illustrated by Mordecai Gerstein. Holiday, 2000. Tales from the village of Chelm.

Francine Prose. *The Demons' Mistake.* Illustrated by Mark Podwal. Greenwillow, 2000. Problems arise when demons accidentally wake up fifty years later, in today's world.

Howard Schwartz and Barbara Rush, sel. *A Coat for the Moon and Other Jewish Tales.* Illustrated by Michael Iofin. Jewish Publication Society, 1999. Tales of magic to the bizarre from around the world.

Erica Silverman. *Raisel's Riddle.* Illustrated by Susan Gaber. Farrar, Straus & Giroux, 1999. Raisel, left on her own after her grandfather, a Talmudic scholar, dies, wins recognition for her learning.

Simms Taback. *Joseph Had a Little Overcoat.* Viking, 1999. Adapted from a Yiddish folksong (included in the book); lesson is that you can always make something out of nothing.

Stories within Stories

Simms Taback won the Caldecott Medal in 2000 for *Joseph Had a Little Overcoat.* Although the text is a simple tale based on a Yiddish (language spoken by many Jews) folk song, he has used background illustrations of collage and diecuts to tell a story *around* the story. Read the story aloud and then invite students to explore the book itself more deeply. What kinds of objects has Taback included in the background (photos, newspaper clippings)? Do some of the same people appear more than once? Read the words that you can see on the walls. What does all of this extra information contribute to your understanding of the story? Students will have to look closely—Taback used this book to integrate aspects of his own family life with Jewish history and culture.

Discuss the following quote with students. Do they agree with the author that one's ethnicity doesn't matter in U.S. culture?

> This book may fill a gap for many people whose Jewish immigrant families spoke Yiddish, but very little of the real history or real culture got transmitted to them. I hope it will also introduce more people to a wonderful culture and a rich history that shouldn't only be known by Jews. I don't think it matters what your ethnicity is because our American culture has adopted a lot of Jewish sayings and Jewish words. There are 500 Yiddish words in the American dictionary.
>
> —Simms Taback, from his Caldecott acceptance speech, 2000.

Sources of Information for Teaching about Jewish Americans: Living in a "Christian" Country

David Adler. *Child of the Warsaw Ghetto.* Holiday House, 1995. What happened to millions of Jews under the Nazis; a personal biography.

Leonard Everett Fisher. *To Bigotry, No Sanction: The Story of the Oldest Synagogue in America.* Holiday House, 1998. The building of the Touro Synagogue in Newport, Rhode Island.

Leslie Kimmelman. *Dance, Sing, Remember: A Celebration of Jewish Holidays.* Illustrated by Ora Eltan. HarperCollins, 2000.

Light unto the Nations. A video from the Jewish Television Network and Blast-Off Productions. Phil Baron, Michelle Baron, and Len Levitt. Jewish Media Fund, 1998. Two children (puppets) don't want to share with a stranger until Emma Lazarus reminds them of her poem on the Statue of Liberty, welcoming everyone.

Lila Perl and Marian Lagan. *Four Perfect Pebbles: A Holocaust Story.* Greenwillow, 1996. The experiences of Marion and her family during Hitler's persecution of the Jews; for advanced students.

Howard Schwartz, retold. *The Day the Rabbi Disappeared: Jewish Holiday Tales of Magic.* Viking, 1998.

Edith Tarbescu. *Annushka's Voyage.* Illustrated by Lydia Dabcovich. Clarion, 1998. Two Russian girls on a crowded ship finally reach Ellis Island.

CONNECTIONS

Through using the multicultural calendars every day in every classroom, students will experience diverse points of view and practice looking at the world through the eyes of others. *Esteem, Empathy,* and *Equity* are promoted when students feel represented and the presence of alternative interpretations is acknowledged.

FOLLOW-THROUGH

Expanding Your RTP

1. Many people find the designation of February as "African American History Month" a degrading practice. Others argue that at least we do recognize the contributions of black Americans at that special time. How can we keep from reducing multicultural education to the simplest of "heroes and holidays" levels? In your journal respond to this issue. What do you think and why? How would you answer critics of using the calendar as presented in this chapter?

2. Make a list of learning activities that you might use as a way of introducing information presented on the calendar each month. Review the calendars from September through June for ideas.

Working with Your CLG

1. Discuss the different ethnic/religious/racial groups who live in your community or your part of the country. Select one of these groups and plan for your CLG to become "experts" on that group. Collect such information as important celebrations or facts about the group's history, and influential leaders, past or present, who represent that culture. Plan a presentation for parents or another class that will enable you to share the information you have gathered. Each CLG will make a presentation.

2. Following the Jigsaw learning model, have all CLGs break up and regroup so that each group is comprised of persons from each CLG. Discuss the following questions:
   * How do the different groups in your community get along?
   * What opportunities are there for interaction?
   * How can teachers promote greater empathy among these groups?
   * Are there additional questions you should address?
   * Return to your original groups and go over the same questions, sharing what you learned from other groups.

3. April 2, 2005 marks the 200th anniversary of the birthdate of Hans Christian Andersen whom many consider the originator of the fairy tale, which all of us have enjoyed through the years. Check the Internet to find out what you can about this famous Dane. You will find the following books particularly informative and entertaining as you learn about this man's childhood and his later accomplishments:

   Andersen, H. C. *The Fairy Tale of My Life: An Autobiography.* Reissued. New York: Cooper Square, 2000. Originally published in 1871, this readable story of his life reveals interesting understandings about this writer's life and how such stories as "The Princess and the Pea" came to be written.

Wullschlager, Jackie. *Hans Christian Andersen: The Life of a Storyteller.* Knopf, 2000. A well-documented biography.

Andersen is said to have written more than 150 fairytales. Look for some of these picture books that can be used with any age level:

Thumbelina. Retold and illustrated by Brad Sneed. Dial, 2004. (Compare other presentations of this story.)

The Emperor's New Clothes. Retold by Marcus Sedgwick and illustrated by Alison Jay. Chronicle, 2004.

The Wild Swans. Translated by Naomi Lewis and illustrated by Anne Yvonne Gilbert. Barefoot, 2005.

Brainstorm how you can present these tales in a classroom activity.

GROWING A PROFESSIONAL LIBRARY

Byrd Baylor. *I'm in Charge of Celebrations!* Illustrated by Peter Parnell. Scribner's, 1986. Useful for initiating discussion and writing, also for introducing a thematic study: Celebrations! available in paperback.

Jane Yolen. *The Perfect Wizard: Hans Christian Andersen.* Dutton, 2005.

Jane Breskin Zalben. *To Every Season: A Family Holiday Cookbook.* Simon & Schuster, 1999.

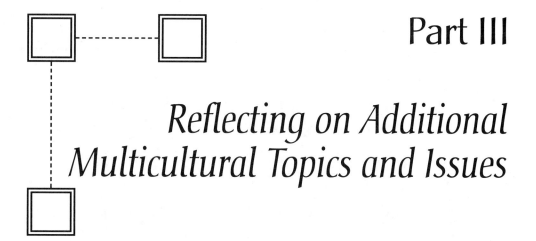

Part III

Reflecting on Additional Multicultural Topics and Issues

History is being made around us as we live each day. We need to remain conscious of the many issues and concerns that continue to face us as we strive to improve the welfare of all children, the future citizens of our great country.

In the previous section, we focused on ideas, activities, resources, strategies, and concepts that help make multicultural education seem doable for every teacher in every classroom. As a result of this work, you will be able to create the inclusive community of learners necessary for multicultural education to touch all children.

Now we turn to look at the great challenges that lie between us and our goals, forces from the outside that affect our chances to plan and deliver a multicultural curriculum effectively, forces that we may not be able to control or change—issues such as language use in society, the achievement gap—and to recognize that the process of becoming a culturally sensitive teacher does not end here, with this book or this course. Just as you hope that your students will become "learners for a lifetime," we hope that you will continue in your quest to be the best teacher possible.

Remember the words of the "Great Law" of the Iroquois Confederacy:

> In our every deliberation, we must consider the impact of our decisions on the next seven generations.

We shall overcome
We shall overcome
We shall overcome
    some day
Oh, deep in my heart
 I do believe
We shall overcome
    some day

Adapted from an
early gospel song.

Examining the Achievement Gap: Definitions, Causes, and Cures

Education has long been considered the key to advancement in the United States. An educated citizenry, furthermore, is also seen as necessary for carrying out a sound democracy. Throughout our history, therefore, efforts have consistently been made to improve the K–12 public schools and the curriculum offered across the nation. Schools have always changed to meet the goals of our nation.

Slowly progress has been made over the years. The number of students attending school and the number who graduate from high school have steadily increased. Teacher preparation and teacher pay have improved. The curriculum has also become more demanding. The quality of education is better today than it was more than fifty years ago when *Brown v. Board of Education* was decided by the U.S. Supreme Court.

However, as we study the results of our efforts, we find that there is still a need for major improvement. Not all education is equal. Nor is all student achievement equal. Testing reveals serious achievement gaps, for example, between children of color and those students who have white skins. Why have there been achievement gaps? What has been done about it? What remains to be done? That is the subject we will discuss in this chapter.

DEFINING THE ACHIEVEMENT GAP

No one thought much about achievement gaps until the end of the twentieth century. Prior to 1950 all white children were encouraged to attend school and to do their best. Black American children attended separate schools, which were assumed to be good enough compared to those attended by white children. Immigration and the influx of Latinos and Asian immigrants and its impact on the public schools was yet to come.

Toward the middle of the century, however, concerned activists began to question whether the schools provided for black children really were "separate, but equal." A number of lawsuits were filed in an endeavor to permit black children to attend the same schools that white children did. Grouped together, these cases were heard by the Supreme Court as *Brown v. Board of Education.* The court's decision in 1954 that separate schools were not equal for a number of reasons changed the public schools forever; but the change, that was so slow in coming, is still ongoing.

Following this important Civil Rights decision, which literally outlawed segregated schools, the expectation was that all children would have an equitable education, and therefore, they would learn more. And, African American children did make noticeable gains in achievement in the 1970s and 1980s after they were able to attend better schools with better qualified teachers.

Then came the development of education research and an emphasis on testing. As education researchers began studying students' achievement at state and national levels as part of accountability efforts, it was natural that sooner or later someone would compare the achievement levels of different groups of students. Gaps between students of different genders were noted, particularly in specific subject areas. And, despite the gains noted earlier, children of color—namely, African American students—failed to achieve as highly as did non-Hispanic white students. This disparity in achievement was also observed for children from low-income homes compared to those from families that are relatively well-to-do.

According to the records of the National Assessment of Educational Progress, there remains a serious achievement gap between African American, Latino, and Native American children and their white, non-Hispanic, peers. All minority children, particularly those who live in poverty conditions, are at risk. Note, however, that Asian American children are not a concern as we discuss this issue because, with the help of their parents, they did very well.

Thus, we come to the recognition of what has become a major concern: The Achievement Gap, which is defined as follows:

> An achievement gap exists when groups of students with relatively equal ability don't achieve in school at the same levels—in fact, one group often far exceeds the achievement of the other. There are gaps between girls and boys, gaps between poor and wealthy students, and gaps between urban and suburban students, just to name a few. But the most glaring gap, nationally and locally, is between races: African-Americans, Latinos, and Whites.
> —Dr. Joseph Johnson, Ohio Department of Education[1]

The data are plentiful to substantiate the presence of this gap. It occurs in any community that includes a diversity of students—that is, every school in the United States.

Comparing the Achievement of White Students and Students of Color

Testing has now been done extensively over a period of years. How does the achievement of different students compare? Although it is of interest, we are not discussing gender gaps at this time. When educators discuss the achievement gap today, the chief concern is determining why there is such a disparity between the achievement of students of color and white, non-Hispanic children in general.

Although the National Assessment of Educational Progress (NAEP) notes that progress was made in narrowing the gap between whites and students of color, this progress appeared virtually to stop past the mid-1980s. The U.S. Department of Education reports, for example, that in 2003, 39 percent of white students scored at the proficient level or beyond on fourth grade reading examinations, whereas just 12 percent of black students and 14 percent of Latino children attained proficient scores. Similarly, 42 percent of white youngsters scored at a proficient level in mathematics compared to the achievement of only 10 percent of black students and 15 percent of Latinos.

This gap shows up early as children enter school. The National Black Caucus of State Legislators, for example, reported in 2001 that only 16 percent of black kindergarten children can be expected to earn a bachelor's degree in college compared to 30 percent of white children who will graduate from college. Furthermore, the U. S. Department of Education provided data in 2000 revealing that both black and Latino kindergarteners already trail their white peers on tests of general knowledge as well as reading and mathematics readiness skills.

These data represent just the tip of the iceberg, so to speak. Students who are far behind in achievement at the elementary school level, as indicated by the testing results cited, continue to fall further behind as they move through middle school and into high school. This effect is noted in the grades they earn for coursework and in all standardized test scores in later years. It also affects the kinds of courses they choose to take in high school and in student drop-out rates before completing high school. Obviously, students who are lagging behind in the K–12 schools will not enter college to prepare for valuable lifetime careers.

These data expose a serious problem for the schools and for society in general. Polls conducted by Phi Delta Kappa and Gallup in 2003 indicate that the public is strongly behind efforts to close this achievement gap. Although many people feel that this problem is highly complex, going beyond teaching in the public schools, more than 50 percent of Americans think that the schools must make an effort to alleviate this disparity between what children of diverse races and ethnic groups can achieve. Therefore, we need to work toward identifying possible causes of the achievement gap and then endeavor to provide solutions to this serious societal problem.

IDENTIFYING CAUSES OF THE ACHIEVEMENT GAP

What causes this achievement gap? Many people are happy to provide simplistic answers: The schools are failing their job. Black American children are less intelligent than children of white parentage. We don't spend enough money on education. Studies show, however, that the causes for this persistent achievement gap are far more complex than any single answer would indicate.

Research tells us that there are numerous factors involved in creating this achievement gap. A 2003 report from the Educational Testing Service in Princeton, New Jersey, for example, identifies fourteen societal and education factors that are relevant to the study of what causes this gap.[2]

ETS categorizes these core factors as attributable to the following: (1) early development, (2) school environment, and (3) home learning environment, as shown in Table 9.1.

As the author of the report, Paul Barton, notes:

> The results are unambiguous. In all 14 correlates of achievement, there were gaps between the minority and majority student populations. Eleven of those also showed clear gaps between students from low-income families and higher income families. The gaps in student achievement mirror inequalities in those aspects of school, early life, and home circumstances that research has linked to achievement.

Sharon Robinson, President of ETS's Educational Policy Leadership Institute, states: "This research shows that the achievement gap is not only about what goes on once kids get into the classroom; it's also about what happens to them before and after school."

The Northwest Regional Educational Laboratory has also researched the achievement gap, making an effort to address the problems involved. They summarize the essential causes along more general lines, as follows:[3]

- Family involvement
- Cultural differences
- Expectations
- Grouping arrangements
- English language acquisition

Let's examine these topics in more detail. How does each of these factors affect the achievement of children in school?

Family Influences and Involvement

Children of color who often come from families in the lower socioeconomic ranges particularly need the schools to provide the best possible learning opportunities. Unfortunately, their neighborhood schools tend to offer less in terms of resources, the quality of instruction, and a demanding curriculum. Nor are the teachers in these schools especially well prepared to meet the needs of culturally diverse students.

TABLE 9.1   CORE FACTORS CAUSING THE ACHIEVEMENT GAP

Early Development	School Environment	Home Learning Environment
• Weight at birth	• Rigor of the school curriculum	• Reading to young children
• Lead poisoning	• Teacher preparation	• TV watching
• Hunger and nutrition	• Teacher experience and attendance	• Parent availability and support
	• Class size	• Student mobility
	• Availability of appropriate classroom technology	• Parent participation
	• School safety	

IDEAS IN ACTION!

Speaking to Parents

Comedian Bill Cosby startled a largely black audience at Howard University in 2004, telling college students and their parents bluntly that they needed to work to pull their children out of the illiteracy hole into which too many young black Americans have fallen. He made it clear that parents could make the difference and literally chastised them for not doing their part. His remarks made the *New York Times* and were carried in most other newspapers across the country. Seldom has a black American of such stature spoken out so directly about the achievement gap as it continues to affect black youngsters.

Of course, black parents need to hear Cosby's words. On the other hand, we all need to recognize realistically that many poor parents are not capable of providing the necessary help for their children. In Washington, DC, for example, there is a 38 percent illiteracy rate among adults. But, they can still do much to support what the schools are trying to do for their children by simply seeing that their children get to school, fed, clean, ready to learn. They can also make it clear to their children that, as parents, they value an education, the schooling that they may not have received themselves.

This is the message we educators need to share with all poor parents, particularly parents of children of color. Our problem is to devise an effective way to communicate our message. Can you and your colleagues write a Letter to Parents that is informative, compassionate, yet not patronizing? What would you say to parents about how you and they can work together to provide the best schooling for their child? This will take a bit of effort and much revising to set just the right tone.

And, the children's families are not prepared to supplement what the schools fail to offer. Commonly both parents work hard to make a living for the family. They usually don't have high levels of educational achievement themselves, and their homes are not filled with books or other reading material. Although television is present in almost all homes, it does not provide the source of enrichment that it might.

These parents may also feel uncomfortable dealing with teachers and hesitate to enter the school itself. They are seldom in a position to help their children learn, for example, guiding their performance of homework, and the home probably does not provide the best environment for studying. Children who live in such homes enter school with limited experiential backgrounds, a factor that affects their ability to learn at any level.

Cultural Differences

Many students of color have trouble fitting into the school culture. African American students, for example, tend to be more interactive in a social setting than are their white peers.

Teachers are often ill-prepared to build on the abilities of these children, seeing them as disruptive compared to white children. Nor are teachers apt to allow for the variety of learning styles present in a classroom with children from diverse backgrounds. Furthermore, teachers frequently come from a culture far different from that of their students, so there is a teacher–student cultural gap.

Expectations

Research also reveals that teachers' expectations of how children will perform in school often influences students' actual performance. Teachers who are not experienced and/or well informed may have stereotyped ideas about what children can be expected to do. They may, for example, assume that African American, American Indian, or Latino children, particularly those from poorer homes, will not succeed to a high degree. On the other hand, they will expect that white children from middle-class homes will do rather well. The students, not surprisingly, tend to perform as expected.

Grouping Arrangements

There is a question of whether grouping according to ability levels and/or tracking might be a detriment to the achievement level of children from minority groups. Once labeled "remedial," they have trouble moving out of that track. There is also the consideration of whether the same methods and materials can or should be used for all students in a class. Again, teachers commonly are not well prepared to deal with the many problems they face in teaching a class of such diverse learners.

English Language Acquisition

Since most instruction in U.S. schools is conducted in English, the level and quality of students' ability to speak and write English is another important factor influencing their achievement levels. Here, again, the home is also involved as many students use languages other than English at home. Even African American students, who would most likely speak English at home, may lack an extensive vocabulary and fluency in educated English. We need to consider Black English and other dialects as part of this discussion. See Chapter 10 for additional information.

The controversy about bilingual education also continues. Many educators still regard knowledge of a second or third language as a handicap rather than an asset. And, few teachers are equipped to teach bilingually. Thus, the increasing number of native speakers of Spanish, for example, are at a disadvantage in our schools. So also, are other immigrant children from homes that speak languages other than English.

Here, then, are major factors that impede high levels of achievement of large groups of students who attend our public schools. Overcoming the achievement gap that has been clearly identified is a challenge for our schools and for the public in general, raising numerous questions:

- Do we care enough to try to alleviate this gap?

- What difference does it make to the welfare of our country?
- What should or can we do to improve the achievement of minority children?

NARROWING/CLOSING THE ACHIEVEMENT GAP

Americans have never hesitated to rise to any challenge that faces the populace. A review of Civil Rights legislation over the years (see Chapter 1) makes that clear.

We cannot afford to ignore this serious flaw in the education of children in the United States that exists today. As has often been stated: "Our children are our future." If we truly believe that, we must move quickly to assure that all children are fully educated in order to achieve to their fullest potentials. We need to enable all of them to perform as well-educated adult citizens who can make wise decisions for the good of our country and for the world.

Educators and legislators across the country are endeavoring to narrow the achievement gap with the intent of eventually closing it completely. Let's examine some of these efforts, for example:

- Evaluating Assessment Methods in Education
- Headstart Legislation and Funding
- No Child Left Behind Legislation
- Communities and Schools Working Together

As teachers, we must participate actively in this endeavor. We all need to address the complex problem that we have identified as we work together to seek solutions.

Evaluating Assessment Methods in Education

Before we accept the results of any bank of tests used to assess the achievement of students in the schools, we need to examine the tests to determine the efficacy of each test, its reliability and validity. Is there bias in the test items, for example? How is the test administered? In other words, just how is achievement in school measured? We might, for example, consider the following:

- How are all students assessed?
- Why should we be concerned about it?
- Are examination writers operating from a deficit model?
- Does the exam emphasize the strengths of each child?

As we plan for assessment of children who are entering our schools, we may run into a number of potential problems, for example:

1. Evangeline H. Stafanakis questions whether we are seeking to identify the strengths of young immigrant students as we assess them for placement in the school system. In testing non-English speakers, she notes that 85 percent of the children are referred to Special Education classes. It may take a child six years to get out of Special Education once that placement is made. This could be quite a handicap for a bright child who immigrates from Latvia, Venezuela, or Iran.

2. The Boston School District has been using an Early Screening Test Instrument (ESTI), which was developed on 700 middle-class children from Rhode Island. No minorities were included in the sample as the test was developed. The reliability and validity of the test was last checked in 1972.
3. In discussing the results of testing, examiners typically suggest that any deficit is in the child. Research tells us that educators must "look not only at what is 'wrong' with the child but also what is 'wrong' about what *they* know about language and culture, as well as the learning environment itself (the school, the classroom, or the curriculum)."
4. Understanding the difference, not the deficit, is the true role of education assessment.[4]

Contrast the deficit model with a sociocultural approach that assumes each child is a unique example of difference and complexity. Consider how we might assess students' knowledge of language following this model.

We know, for example, that children learn language in real-life situations. Therefore, we would expect them to display different knowledge and language uses depending on the social contexts in which they are learning and living. We would operate following these three premises:

1. Bilingualism is a cognitive asset that enhances thinking and learning.
2. Assuming that sociocultural factors affect learning, and the context or learning environment, is the key to understanding language use.
3. Language proficiency and individual learning abilities should be assessed in context and over time.

Improving Methods of Assessment

We know enough about teaching and learning, including testing, to know that how, where, and by whom a test is administered makes a difference. Therefore, we need to look carefully at the interaction between the teacher who is administering an examination and the student who is being tested. It is essential, for example, that all tests be administered in a child's preferred language. For this purpose, we will often need to bring in qualified speakers of English and the other language in question. We also need to clarify the purposes, formats, and processes associated with assessment of diverse learners. Testing processes need to be equitable in all respects.

Tips for Assessing Language-Minority Students: A Sociocultural Approach
- Assess your own knowledge, then research the child's language and culture.
- Assess the language demands of the classroom.
- Probe for the child's individual strengths.
- Gather data on the child by monitoring his or her daily interactions in various groups within the classroom (and at home).

Although, admittedly it requires more time than paper and pencil screening, the most accurate and fair assessment of a child's abilities is made by Portfolio Assessment, which involves the following components:

- Observation of play behavior by two or three teachers and/or other personnel.
- Observation of group interaction using a formal checklist.
- A preschool screening or testing instrument.
- A parent questionnaire and followup interview.
- Research on the child's culture of origin.

In addition to such data collected, we need to consider the many other factors that may affect the assessment process and the child's performance in school, for example:

- Health and nutrition
- Parents' education
- Language spoken in the home
- Socioeconomic status of family

At all times with assessment processes, we must bear clearly in mind that our goal should always be to "find the best in all children who attend our schools."

Headstart Legislation and Funding

Headstart is an outstanding example of a successful federal endeavor that provides enrichment experiences for preschool children. It was designed to enhance the experiential level with which children from low socioeconomic homes enter kindergarten in the public schools.

Headstart schools across the nation receive federal funding that has been slowly increased over the years. These schools may be located in churches, in elementary schools, or in any other suitable available space. The curriculum addresses the needs of the whole child, emphasizing emotional and social development, motor skills, and an appropriate academic program.

This program was created especially to help 4- and 5-year-old children in lower socioeconomic neighborhoods by providing learning experiences beyond what the home can provide. Typical learning activities might include:

- Listening to books read aloud by the teacher.
- Singing and playing games.
- Counting and math manipulative activities.
- Taking a fieldtrip to the library.

Emphasis is on language and concept development. Children are learning to adjust to the school culture, working together with other students, acquiring the habit of learning and performing successfully. Millions of black and Latino children have benefited from this program over a period of some forty years.

Assessment of Headstart and its results is an important aspect of this program. In 2004, a proposed new test, Head Start National Reporting System, was criticized by such organizations as the National Black Child Development Institute and the National Council of La Raza. These organizations were concerned that assessment was being too narrowly defined, focusing only on the children's language and mathematical ability rather than looking at the broader educational aims for which Headstart is noted, as outlined above. Early childhood educators will be keeping their eye on how the assessment of Headstart progresses in the future.

NO CHILD LEFT BEHIND LEGISLATION

Passed in 2001, the No Child Left Behind Act represents federal legislation designed to alleviate the achievement gap that we have been discussing in this chapter. The act aims to improve education for all students. It appears to be a very positive effort, but as we will see, there is growing controversy regarding the implementation of this act.

This legislation is strongly supported by President George W. Bush, who stated:

> These historic reforms will improve our public schools by creating an environment where every child can learn through real accountability, unprecedented flexibility for states and school districts, greater local control, more options for parents, and more funding for what works.

The U.S. Department of Education has published a full set of transparencies online to support a presentation about the No Child Left Behind (NCLB) legislation from which we draw the following description of what this act entails.[5] For example, the four guiding principles of the No Child Left Behind Act include:

1. Accountability for student performance
2. Focus on what works
3. Reduced bureaucracy and increased flexibility
4. Empowerment of parents

To achieve these four guiding principles, the NCLB Act calls for:

- Annual testing of all public school students in reading and math, grades 3–8 and high school, by the 2005–2006 school year.
- Annual report cards on school performance for parents, voters, and taxpayers.
- Ensuring that every child reads by the third grade.
- A highly qualified teacher in every public school classroom by 2005.

The need for accountability, the first guiding principle, is based on the following reasons:

- A significant gap exists between disadvantaged students and their more affluent peers, despite billions in federal spending since 1965.
- Sixty percent of poor fourth graders cannot read at a basic level.
- U.S. students lag behind their international peers in key subjects.
- Past federal education policy has lacked focus and has never insisted on results.

The NCLB also calls for the establishment of standards to provide a "Road Map to Reform." The standards are expected to "provide guideposts for academic achievement, clearly telling teachers, students, and parents where they are going." The challenge is "to establish clear expectations of what students should know and be able to do for schools, teachers, and students." The solution is "to require each state to establish its own standards in the core content areas of reading, math, and science."

The emphasis must also be on what really works based on education research, illustrated by "What Works in Reading Instruction," which is based on a report of the National Reading Panel *Teaching Children to Read.*[6] For example, this report identifies five essential components of reading instruction, as follows:

- Phonemic awareness
- Phonics
- Fluency
- Vocabulary
- Comprehension

The NCLB Act calls for "qualified teachers" in every classroom, and it defines "qualified" as having the characteristics shown in Figure 9.1.

FIGURE 9.1 WHAT IS A "HIGHLY QUALIFIED TEACHER"?

Elementary School Teacher	*Middle or High School Teacher*
• Holds a bachelor's degree.	• Holds a bachelor's degree.
• Has demonstrated mastery by passing a rigorous test in reading, writing, math, and other areas of the curriculum.	• Has demonstrated competency in subject area taught by passing a rigorous state test, or through completion of an academic major, graduate degree, or comparable coursework.

As you review this overview of what the NCLB Act entails, it is likely that you will find little to object to with the intent of the No Child Left Behind Act. On the surface it sounds good. However, as schools began implementing the requirements expected of every school district in the fifty states, as spelled out in the NCLB Act, problems arose. Many educators have spoken out against aspects of this legislation. We, for example, question the stated expectations for the preparation of teachers like yourselves who remain a crucial element in alleviating the achievement gap.

Controversy Regarding Implementation of This Legislation

In 2002, Gene Carter, Executive Director of the Association for Supervision and Curriculum Development, an influential professional group of educators at the K–12 levels, spoke out, thus:

> Education policies such as No Child Left Behind demonstrate Americans' conviction that all children are entitled to a quality education. It is not enough, however, to give students the academic knowledge to be successful workers. We also need to import the skills and understandings necessary for young people to participate actively in a democratic society. The

broader notions of citizenship and service are too often lost in the quagmire of nationally mandated testing, sanctions, and incentives focused on core academic subjects, such as math and reading.[7]

The first real analysis and evaluation of this legislation appeared in 2003 under the title *No Child Left Behind? The Politics and Practice of School Accountability,* edited by Paul E. Peterson and Martin R. West and published by the Brookings Institution Press. These authors examine the law's origins and the political and social forces that have shaped it. They also comment on some possible effects of its implementation and the legislation's impact on U.S. education.

Available online is a 170-page report, *Failing Our Children: How No Child Left Behind Undermines Quality and Equity in Education, and an Accountability Model That Supports School Improvement,* prepared by the National Center for Fair and Open Testing, or FairTest (<*www.fairtest.org*>). It criticizes implementation of NCLB based on:

- Flawed requirements for identifying schools in need.
- Heavy reliance on standardized tests.
- Requirements leading to narrowed curriculum.
- Lack of adequate funding to provide for welfare of children.
- Intensive teaching to the test.
- Intensification of problems for poor and minority students.

Published in 2003, this report by what is termed a "watchdog group" concludes that NCLB aggravates rather than "solving the real problems that cause many children to be left behind."

In 2004 Margaret DeLacy, board member of the Oregon Association for Talented and Gifted Students, writes in *Education Week* (June 23) that talented and gifted students are actually victims of the NCLB Act. She argues that the special needs of bright students are largely forgotten in our eagerness to improve the learning of those in the lowest quartile.

She questions, furthermore, using the report from the National Research Council, which did not include experts on education of the gifted. This report ignored significant research, recommending instead instructional strategies that have long been discarded. For example, bright students do not benefit from being in mixed-ability groups of learners as do some of the lowest achievers. Rather than moving ahead at an appropriate pace for them, the talented kids spend time reviewing material intended to meet standards that they have already met. No wonder they are bored, often depressed, and vulnerable to attempted suicide. Few teachers are adequately prepared to engage the gifted students in extending their learning, although these students do need supportive instruction in order to progress appropriately.

Superintendent of Schools in Brandon, Vermont, William J. Mathis, also writing in *Education Week* (April 21, 2004), notes the lack of federal funding provided for carrying out the added requirements of NCLB. In a time of decreased funding for schools in most states, the federal government is imposing further demands on schools without providing appropriate funding to support these additional costs. A number of states are rebelling against these mandates, which they are unable to carry out. As Mathis points out: "Assuming that schools can simply buy an inexpensive and 'proven' teaching program runs counter to the dismal record of 'one size fits all' reforms." He notes, furthermore:

> Among those who say the No Child Left Behind Act is adequately funded, the most troubling shortcoming of their analyses is the lack of attention they give to children's needs. A poor, hungry, and abused child does not learn arithmetic simply because we improve the teaching methods. These studies also ignore the huge and increasing inequities in wealth and educational spending between our poorer and richer schools.

In addition, as a number of experts have noted, No Child Left Behind is unrealistic because it requires a rate of improvement that is far too demanding for most schools to accomplish. It is especially scary because our knowledge is so weak. It tries to force educators to produce results akin to medicine's development during the past century, which would be a truly rapid pace.

Communities and Schools Working Together

Many elements make a difference in the effort to alleviate this achievement gap that affects us all. Wendy Schwartz prepared an excellent summary published in *ERIC Digest* of what each of the following components of the education system need to contribute:

State and School District
Development and implementation of shared education goals
Development and implementation of rigorous standards that provide a basis for strong curriculum, practice, and performance
Development of accountability standards
Dissemination of research-based instructional programs
Provision of resources needed for successful student learning
Provision of opportunities to share findings across levels

Early Childhood Initiatives
Provision of high-quality preschool programs to promote readiness
Provision of parent education and social services
Provision of family literacy programs

School Climate
Expectation that all students can succeed, assistance in doing so
Giving students a sense of efficacy and drive toward excellence
Individualized assessments to determine potential, appropriate placement
Recognition of diverse cultures as part of mainstream leading to success
Safe, orderly school; clear code of conduct enforced

School Organization
Full desegregation of all school activities
Smaller classes, particularly in early grades
Equitable grouping of students of color at all levels

Teaching and Learning

Increased teaching time on reading, math, and other basic skills
Challenging curriculum and instructional strategies
Provision of learning resources—teachers, library books, technology, texts
Magnet schools and special programs to promote student interest
Individualized learning supports, tutoring, extra classes
Professionals as mentors and models
In-depth, appropriate assessments for individual support as needed

School Management

Experienced, well-qualified teachers, accountable for student performance
Able administrators providing pedagogical leadership, accountability
Professional development for new curricula, including multiculturalism
Standards applied to curriculum and instruction, assessment, and teaching
Data collection to compare performance and to guide decision making

Family Supports

Encourage parents to have high expectations for children
Encourage parent participation in school events
Provision of education, health, and social services for families

Community Involvement

School culture that values learning and achievement
Provision of libraries, museums, and other cultural institutions
Provision of support services, that is, health, adult education, finance
Active school partnerships to support families
Leisure activities with academic focus[8]

Education Research

A number of education researchers have noted the need to expand the goals and objectives for education in the twenty-first century to include more than simple basic literacy and computational skills. Particularly in this age of terrorism and the world leadership position that the United States must assume, they stress the need for students to understand the requirements of involvement in a democracy including fighting for the freedom that we expect to have in our country.

The National Assessment of Educational Progress notes, for example:

Disturbing gaps in students' civic knowledge.
Young people less involved in civic life, 57 percent totally disengaged—15- to 25-year-olds

This report emphasizes the following needs:

Improving instruction in history and civics.
Engaging students in opportunities for Service Learning.

Building and nurturing a school culture that provides opportunities to practice being an engaged citizen.[9]

Experimental Efforts in the Schools

Most educators are aware of the need to improve education with the intent of helping all students achieve at the highest possible level. School district personnel are experimenting with a variety of strategies that have yet to be fully studied, for example:

Reducing class sizes, for example, reduction of enrollment in grades 1 to 3 to twenty children per classroom

Creating smaller schools, for example, high schools

Expanding early childhood education, for example, full-day kindergartens

Raising academic standards, for example, increasing graduation requirements

Improving the quality of teacher education, for example, increasing multicultural education coursework and experience

Improving the quality of teaching in low socioeconomic neighborhoods, for example, offering pay incentives to teachers in urban schools

Although such efforts promise to improve the quality of schooling offered all children, they do not address the totality of concerns related to the achievement gap. Education researchers need to continue examining causes of this gap in an effort to improve the learning of students of color.

Helping Families Help Their Children

Some aspects of this problem related directly to the family may be largely beyond the scope of the school, for example:

- Socioeconomic status of the family.
- Education level achieved by parents.

On the other hand, the schools and the community can make an effort to alleviate the negative aspects of such influences.

Schools and community members can offer further support for all parents and children by increasing library facilities. Not only do libraries provide books and other literacy materials, they also offer story hours for children and parents and assistance with choosing suitable books to share. They may offer multicultural programs that include local parents and children who share their culture with the community. As community centers, they can present support for parents, such as literacy instruction or English language classes.

Teachers need to learn ways of reaching out to parents of the diverse children in their classrooms with the intent of breaking down barriers between the home and school. They can, for example, entice parents into the classrooms to observe what their child experiences in school by having a Party for Parents at which the children share what they are doing and serve light refreshments they have made. Messages to the home describing periodically what each student has achieved can be written in whatever language is appropriate. Students can be included in parent conferences that are nonthreatening and friendly.

IDEAS IN ACTION!

Appreciating Our Folkways

In 1966, in northeastern Georgia, a schoolteacher named Eliot Wigginton began to publish a little magazine with his students called *Foxfire*. They were inspired by the need to preserve on paper the old folkways they saw around them before the knowledge was lost and to show other students the value of their heritage. *Foxfire* included techniques such as pickling vegetables and salting a freshly butchered hog, recipes for local specialities, and traditional herbal lore. No one thought that anyone who lived outside of the area would be interested, but this small project became so popular that the material was collected into a series of books and published for a wider audience.

Encourage your students to see their local community and their own culture as resources worthy of preserving and sharing with others. Depending on the ability and interests of your students, collect examples of traditional recipes to publish as a book, learn a folk song that has been passed down for a number of generations, or interview elders in the community about their memories and how life has changed.

Schools can offer such programs as Reading Is Fundamental, which provides books for children. The local PTA or Home and School Club might support Book Fairs or activities that give books to children, perhaps as holiday gifts. Getting books into all homes could well be an objective for the organization.

Workshops for parents might focus on Learning English in a sociable setting. Others might focus on providing information about any important topic, for example, Recommended Foods for Children, Information about Good Health for All of Us, or Free Fun for Families.

The teachers in a single school should brainstorm possible ways to reach out to parents. They might include selected parents in a planning group as they could contribute considerable insight into what is entailed.

Considering "What Works in Education"

On April 12, 2004, Karin Chenoweth, *Washington Post* columnist, wrote in her syndicated column:

> We adults are supposed to be teaching children BUT do we know what works? We must understand education in order to revolutionize it! We need to know what methods work for which kids under what circumstances!

We might well begin this study by identifying questions to which we need to know possible answers, for example:

- What is the best way to ensure that ESL students learn English efficiently as well as the other academic subjects?
- Did we achieve the stated goal of seeing that every child learns to read by the end of third grade before 2005? What has been accomplished?

One question that remains is "Are the schools doing the best possible job?" Additional problems that need to be addressed include:

- Recognizing the effect of poverty on learning.
- Broadening experiential backgrounds for preschool children.
- Expanding experiential and knowledge bases in school.
- Providing enriching afterschool programs.
- Working with parents.
- Creating a community of learners.

The achievement gap will not disappear without the input of much effort from all persons concerned: K–12 teachers, parents, other community members, legislators, and teacher educators. Such efforts require time, but the rewards will be worth it.

CONNECTIONS

A serious achievement gap in education has been identified among students of color and non-Hispanic white students. Now that this gap has been identified, we also need to determine the multiple causes that produce the gap. Then, we need to seek strategies that will gradually narrow this gap and ultimately close it. Solving this problem in education is essential to the well-being of our entire country.

FOLLOW-THROUGH

Expanding Your RTP

1. Write several paragraphs that you could use to introduce a group of parents to the achievement gap and its implications for their children's schooling. Include at least one paragraph that outlines what they, as parents, can do to help their children learn successfully.

2. Review the description of a "well-qualified teacher" included in the No Child Left Behind Act earlier in this chapter. As a person planning to be a teacher, what would you add to this description? What more do you need to know to become a well-qualified teacher? What do you need to know to help alleviate the achievement gap for the diverse students that you will teach?

Working with Your CLG

Imagine yourselves as teachers in an urban school where many of the children come from poor homes.

1. Discuss how you can:
   - Support the self-esteem of a shy young girl who has been abused.
   - Help several 10-year-old African American boys who are slow readers.
   - Deal with bullying that you observe on the playground.

2. Discuss methods you might use to establish rapport with the parents of the children you teach. How would you communicate with these parents? Share your ideas with the larger group.

3. Research the following topics on the Internet:
   - Rosenwald Schools (historically black schools funded by Julius Rosenwald to improve the education of African American children)
   - "Black, White, and Brown: Latino School Desegregation Efforts in the Pre- and Post- *Brown v. Board of Education* Era" (see <*www.maldef.org*>).

   Search for information on any other relevant topic that interests your group. Share your findings with the class.

GROWING A PROFESSIONAL LIBRARY

William Ayers. *Teaching toward Freedom: Moral Commitment and Ethical Action in the Classroom.* Beacon Press, 2004. Teacher encourages teaching that has meaning for children as well as for the teacher.

Sam Swope. *I Am a Pencil: A Teacher, His Kids, and Their World of Stories*. Holt, 2004. A children's literature author relates his experiences with immigrant urban elementary school students as he engages them in writing.

ENDNOTES

1. Joseph Johnson. Ohio Department of Education *Newsletter* (September 14, 2004): 1.
2. Educational Testing Service, *Report on Core Factors Causing the Achievement Gap* (November 2003).
3. Northwest Regional Educational Laboratory, *Report on Causes of the Achievement Gap.* U.S. Department of Education, October 2003.
4. Evangeline H. Stafanakis, "The Assessment of Children Entering School." *Education Week* (November 15, 2004).
5. No Child Left Behind (NCLB). Accessed from <*www.ed.gov/nclb*>

6. National Reading Panel, *Teaching Children to Read.* U.S. Department of Education, April 2003.
7. Gene Carter, "Examining Education Policies." *Education Week.* October 25, 2002.
8. Wendy Schwartz, "Alleviating the Achievement Gap." *ERIC Digest.* October 15, 2003.
9. National Assessment of Educational Progress, "Gaps in Students' Civic Knowledge." *Education Week.* October 24, 2004.

The limits of my language
Are the limits
of my world.

Ludwig
Wittgenstein

C H A P T E R

Language: A Key Component of Multicultural Education

Language is an essential part of one's culture and the language that students bring to school is as significant as any other aspect of their culture to their identity. Says the Chicana poet Gloria Anzaldúa: "If you want to really hurt me, talk badly about my language. Ethnic identity is twin skin to linguistic identity—I am my language."[1] In addition, language is an important part of the way we categorize other people as "like us" or "not like us." We can also look at language as an example of social behavior as we use language to persuade others, to socialize children through stories, and to explain our inner selves to other people. Multicultural education must include language in its discussions of identity and getting along with others. The language component of our multicultural curriculum will include such concepts as:

- Many languages are spoken in the United States and in the world.
- Multilingualism is the normal condition in communities.
- Students have the right to maintain their own language while learning that of others.
- "Standard" English is a special form of English that is the result of regional conventions that change over time.

STUDENTS AND LANGUAGE

One of the most important components of multicultural education is the teacher's knowledge of and attitude toward students' language. Each child comes eagerly to school using a particular language, an integral part of his or her personal identity. We need to see this language ability as an asset and begin building from that base.

Language has been a major stumbling block for many monolingual teachers who have only limited experience with different languages. It is time to realize that these limitations, including negative attitudes toward languages other than English, may seriously damage students' self-esteem and thereby severely limit their chances of success in school. All teachers must, therefore, become informed about language in general and learn at least

```
┌─────────────────────────────────────────────────────────────┐
│                      QUOTE FOR THE DAY                        │
├─────────────────────────────────────────────────────────────┤
│                    Wonderful Language                         │
│                                                               │
│  Language–using controls the rest;                            │
│  Wonderful is language!                                       │
│  Wondrous the English language, language of live men,         │
│  Language of ensemble, powerful language of resistance,       │
│  Language of a proud and melancholy stock, and of all who aspire... │
│                                                               │
│  Language to well-nigh express the inexpressible,             │
│  Language for the modern, language for America.               │
│                       Walt Whitman                            │
└─────────────────────────────────────────────────────────────┘
```

a modicum about languages other than English. Knowing more than one language needs to become a standard expected for all educated Americans if we are truly to be world leaders.

Students' Right to Their Own Language

Any instructional program that gives students the idea that they will have to forget their home languages in order to be accepted into the English-speaking classroom cuts at the heart of student identity and motivation to learn. For this reason, teachers need to know more about the languages of their students and about language in general.

By making our value for students' languages clear, we are consciously building each individual student's sense of *Esteem*. Speakers of every language have a contribution to make to the classroom. As we talk about language diversity, and have students give examples of words from the languages they know, such as Amharic, Spanish, Gujarati, or Russian, we are helping all students develop their *Empathy* for others. We can introduce the major languages spoken in the world and in the countries of origin for many students who may come to be U.S. citizens. By offering positive feedback and assistance to students who are learning English as an additional language instead of regarding them as deficient, we strive to create *Equity* in the classroom.

In 1972, when questions about students' native languages were first seriously discussed, the National Council of Teachers of English passed a resolution on "students' rights to their own patterns and varieties of language," and they published a position paper, "Students' Right to Their Own Language," spelling out the implications of this resolution. In 2003, after reviewing this statement, NCTE reaffirmed their agreement with this position and encouraged "its members, other educators, and all people interested in education to become familiar with the document" (see Figure 10.1).

Teaching Multicultural/Multilingual Children

By 2030 demographic experts predict that 40 percent of the enrollment in our country's schools will be working with English as a second language. Yet research shows that teach-

FIGURE 10.1 STUDENTS' RIGHT TO THEIR OWN LANGUAGE

Background

Members of NCTE and its constituent group, the Conference on College Composition and Communication (CCCC), became concerned in the early 1970s about a tendency in American society to categorize nonstandard dialects as corrupt, inferior, or distorted forms of standard English, rather than as distinct linguistic systems, and the prejudicial labeling of students that resulted from this view. Be it therefore

Resolution

Resolved, that the National Council of Teachers of English affirm the students' right to their own language—to the dialect that expresses their family and community identity, the idiolect that expresses their unique personal identity;

that NCTE affirm the responsibility of all teachers of English to assist all students in the development of their ability to speak and write better whatever their dialects;

that NCTE affirm the responsibility of all teachers to provide opportunities for clear and cogent expression of ideas in writing, and to provide the opportunity for students to learn the conventions of what has been called written edited American English; and

that NCTE affirm strongly that teachers must have the experiences and training that will enable them to understand and respect diversity of dialects.

Be it further Resolved, that, to this end,

that NCTE make available to other professional organizations this resolution as well as suggestions for ways of dealing with linguistic variety, as expressed in the CCCC background statement on students' right to their own language; and

that NCTE promote classroom practices to expose students to the variety of dialects that comprise our multiregional, multiethnic, and multicultural society, so that they too will understand the nature of American English and come to respect all its dialects.

---

ers in general feel unable to cope with the multicultural, multilingual students that are typical in most classrooms.

Roland G. Tharp and other researchers at the Center for Research on Education, Diversity, and Excellence at the University of California in Santa Cruz have found that most students respond to a classroom that provides interaction with adults as well as peer groups.[2] Because of the diverse cultures represented by students in, for example, inner-city schools, these researchers determined that teachers need to create a new inclusive classroom culture to which all students could learn to respond. The five critical standards they identified as essential to success for diverse students include:

- Teachers and students "producing" together, whether they are producing knowledge or some tangible product.
- Developing students' language and literacy competence in all subjects.
- Connecting school and learning to students' lives, or "contextualizing" knowledge.
- Teaching complex thinking and problem solving.
- Teaching through an instructional conversation or dialogue rather than relying almost exclusively on lectures.

Although a *monolingual* teacher cannot actually "teach" students' native languages, that teacher can foster *multiliteracy* in the classroom. Some of the ways that teachers may address language in the classroom include:

- Forbid native languages.
- Allow native languages.
- Maintain native languages.
- Foster native languages.

Forbidding use of children's home languages denies the children the opportunity to learn their native languages well. Allowing the home language usually means restricting usage to specific times or settings, such as recess or after school. This option reinforces the subordinate position of the child's home language. The third option, maintenance, is associated with weekend schools or extracurricular programs, often taught by native speakers but not professional teachers. Fostering multiliteracy in the school setting, on the other hand, seems to be a radical alternative. This either takes the form of the dual language/bilingual programs and/or monolingual teachers fostering multiliteracy within any regular classroom. Because a bilingual program produces the highest levels of oral and written proficiency in both languages, it is the preferred choice. However, in classes where there is a diversity of languages, the following practices can still promote multiliteracy to meet the needs of all children:

- Create a multiliterate print environment.
- Use literature in students' native languages.
- Invite community members to share their native languages.
- Create curricular language centers with the help of community members.
- Assess students' literacy in their first languages.
- Start learning some words in the students' languages as well as your own heritage language.
- Create audiotape cassettes for a Listening Center.
- Involve community members as active participants in the class.
- Translate environmental print as well as letters sent to parents so that students see purposeful and authentic uses of their native languages.
- Use the students' culture and background as a resource, inviting students to share their knowledge with others.

Bilingual Books

Include examples of books in different languages in your classroom library. Bilingual books allow students to compare languages and diverse writing systems directly. What can students learn about other languages from these books?

Lee Merrill Byrd. *The Treasure on Gold Street/El Tesoro en la Calle Oro.* Cinco Puntos Press, 2004. In Spanish and English.

Charlotte Pomerantz. *If I Had a Paka.* Mulberry, 1998. Collection of poetry includes examples of words from many different languages.

Chamroeun Yin. *In My Heart I Am a Dancer.* Philadephia Folklore Project, 1996. In Cambodian and English.

Bilingual books can be accompanied by audiocassettes in languages other than English so that all students can hear a different language. Enlist community members who speak other languages to assist you in preparing these materials.

DIALECTS AND LANGUAGES

What's a dialect? How does it differ from a language? The study of dialects can be fascinating for both teacher and student. Most languages are made up of many dialects, including English. As with languages, teachers need to learn a positive attitude toward dialects that may be spoken by children entering the classroom. And, the teacher's own dialect may become the subject of an enlightening study, especially if it differs from the dialect used by the students.

When we talk about different forms of spoken English, we usually call them dialects, as opposed to "standard" English, which can leave the impression that standard English is inherently better than the others. But when we look at how English has changed we see that different varieties of speech have gained or lost prestige over time. The form of English that is accepted as the current standard is not actually better, or more effective at communicating ideas, than any other dialect. Linguists often define language as a dialect with an army and a navy, indicating that what we call a language is simply one dialect among many, but one that has become associated with power and prestige.

Standard English

Speaking "standard" English rather than another regional or social dialect has become associated with intelligence and level of education. But, in fact, the best argument for learning the so-called standard, or most prestigious form of a language, is to enable the speaker to reach the largest audience. On the other hand, there are advantages to speaking other dialects. In many contexts, use of regionally identified speech, such as Texas English when speaking to Texans, will give the speaker a greater edge by positioning him or her as one of the locals. Speaking Standard English would, instead, be interpreted as "putting on airs" and sounding like an outsider.

The more we communicate with others around the world, the more we are concerned to make sure that ALL students, no matter what dialect of English or other language they speak, have equal access to learning the language forms that will provide the greatest access to the most opportunities. Whatever variety of English these students have learned at home, they are just as capable of learning the variety that is considered more prestigious. Our goal is to develop their language competence, which we define as the ability to use diverse forms of language as appropriate for specific settings.

The Language in the Dictionary

If we all speak different varieties of English, whose variety is the one we put in dictionaries? Students may look on dictionaries as the ultimate authority on language, not realizing that the editors of dictionaries have to select carefully which words and specific pronunciations are included in their pages. As students might predict, some dialects are more likely to be represented than others. How is this decided? Are the most prestigious dialects the most likely to be included? (What are "the most prestigious" dialects?) Can you tell how to pronounce a word by looking it up in the dictionary? Should dictionary entries include regional variations in word pronunciation? Ask students to propose arguments on both sides.

Before the 1960s, dictionaries generally professed to set an example of "good" English, so they did not include slang, swear words, or "street" (informal) vocabulary. Modern dictionaries illustrate a more inclusive definition of language, aiming to describe English as it is actually used. Test this goal by having students suggest words and look them up in different dictionaries. Do the entries match how they themselves pronounce these words? They can also look up slang words. What is the difference between *slang* and standard English? Have students discuss when and why the use of slang is appropriate. Do all dictionaries include slang words? Are there words that might not be included? Should dictionaries include all the words in English? After discussion, students will realize that it is impossible to collect *all* the words in English.

An excellent library resource for further investigation is the 1993 *New Shorter Oxford English Dictionary* (2 vols), a new edition of the famous guide to the English language. This edition includes new words from fields such as computers (laptop), physics (quark), politics (political correctness), music (grunge), and the street (dweeb). Have students brainstorm a list of contemporary words that should be in the dictionary. They can research these words and report back to the class. Have them argue in favor of including these words in the dictionary.

Black English Vernacular (BEV)

A dialect that has special interest for educators in the United States is Black English Vernacular (BEV), a form of English that has developed from the languages used by the African American slaves. Again, information and attitude are important in dealing with this aspect of student language.

Black English Vernacular (BEV) is a dialect of English (sometimes referred to as *ebonics*) spoken by many people in the United States, primarily African Americans. It has many distinctive features of grammar and vocabulary, and it serves as a significant marker of African American identity. As with all dialects, speakers vary in the ease with which they can switch to more standard dialects of English. The Oakland, California, school board brought public attention to BEV as an educational issue in 1997 when they declared *ebonics* a separate language suitable for bilingual education programs. Although the structure of BEV as a legitimate variant to English has been known for many years, some people still wrongly associate it with poor grammar and lack of learning skills.

Speaking Black English Vernacular doesn't prevent students from being able to learn in school. At the same time, students who come to school speaking only BEV will benefit from access to the language of wider communication, in this case, Standard English. Reassure students that they can learn to use Standard English without losing their familiar language that connects them to family and community.

Varied models for the teaching of Standard English to speakers of black vernacular have been based on bilingual education or the teaching of (Standard) English as a second language. We would like to suggest a model of "code switching." All speakers switch among various "codes" of their language (or languages), using specific forms for different purposes and in different contexts. To be an effective communicator, a speaker of black vernacular needs to be able to use that form in casual talk, perhaps with peers in the African American community, and at the same time be able to switch to a more formal style when needed, as when applying for a job.

What can teachers and students do to learn more about Standard English and to master the skill of code switching between different forms as appropriate?

Teachers can:

- Model Standard English as part of formal speech in the classroom.
- Switch into BEV in specific situations or informal discussion.
- Point out and discuss specific features that differ in BEV and Standard English.

Students can:

- Create a list of BEV expressions and translate them into Standard English.
- Translate common phrases in Standard English into BEV.
- Develop role-play exercises, setting up different situations that might require using different speech forms.
- Analyze the way black characters deliberately vary speech patterns on television programs or other media.
- Read and retell stories in both BEV and Standard English.

Throughout these activities, establish shared goals with students. Your aim is to increase their exposure to Standard English, to permit them to practice using Standard English in safe, playful environments, and to direct their conscious attention to the differences between BEV and Standard English.

Many well-respected contemporary writers have attempted to reproduce the sound of BEV in their books. Some just include black slang and others incorporate both vocabulary and grammatical features of BEV. Unfortunately, no written version can accurately portray spoken BEV, just as standard spoken English is very different from written English. However, these books have the advantage of sounding more familiar to speakers of BEV and may be easier for black students to read than Standard English. They also are important for introducing other students to BEV, because the context makes the meaning of unfamiliar words and constructions clear.

Read passages from some of the following books to the class and discuss the language used. How do students feel? Does it sound realistic or familiar? Do they understand what the people are saying? What effect does it have when someone tries to write the way people actually talk?

Picture Books

Eloise Greenfield. *There She Come Bringing Me That Little Baby Girl.* Harper, 1993.

Patricia McKissack. *Mirandy and Brother Wind.* Knopf, 1998.

Tony Medina. *Love to Langston.* Lee & Low, 2002.

For Independent Readers

Christopher Paul Curtis. *Bud, Not Buddy.* Delacorte, 2003.

Virginia Hamilton. *Sweet Whispers, Brother Rush.* Putnam, 1982.

Walter Dean Myers. *Fast Sam, Cool Clyde, and Stuff.* Viking, 1988.

THE STORY OF ENGLISH

Where and how did the English language begin? How has it changed over the centuries? Knowing how English developed as a language explains, for example, some of our peculiar spellings. The study of how English developed after it arrived in North America should be of special interest because our language is still changing "as we speak"!

The Indo-European Language Tree

Prepare a bulletin board to provide information about the family of Indo-European languages, spoken by half the world's population, and the relationship of English to other languages. Construct a large tree out of construction paper, with eight branches representing the main groups (see Figure 10.2):

* Albanian
* Armenian
* Balto-Slavic: Russian, Polish, Serbian, Croatian, Czech, Ukrainian, Bulgarian, Lithuanian
* Celtic: Irish, Scots, Gaelic, Welsh, Breton
* Greek
* Indo-Iranian: Hindi, Urdu, Bengali, Persian
* Romance: French, Italian, Spanish, Portuguese, Romanian
* Germanic: German, English, Dutch, Danish, Norwegian, Swedish

Have students research what languages belong to each branch. Where does English fit in? Which are the most populous branches? In what countries are these languages spoken?

When the language tree is constructed and the branches labeled with the major languages, have students add life to the tree by discovering words in these different languages. Students can look up words or use words they have found in books. Provide "leaves" cut out of construction paper on which to write words to place on the tree according to the "branch" they belong to.

Exercises such as looking up the word for *ten* in many languages will help demonstrate to students the relationship among these languages, as well as their similarities and differences. Here are some examples to begin with:

English	ten	German	zehn
French	dix	Dutch	tien
Italian	dieci	Swedish	tio
Spanish	diez	Danish	ti
Portuguese	dez	Norwegian	ti
Romanian	zece		

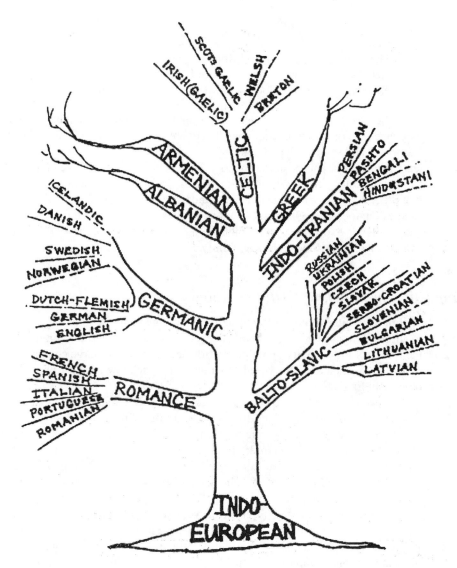

FIGURE 10.2   THE LANGUAGE TREE

Other Language Families

Can students name languages that do not belong to the Indo-European language family? (Check names against the Indo-European family tree you constructed.) They may suggest some of the following names:

Language	Family
Chinese	Sino-Tibetan
Japanese	Japanese and Korean
Hebrew	Semitic (includes Arabic and Aramaic)
Hungarian	Ural-Altaic (includes Turkish and Finnish)

After the class has accumulated a list, have students look up the languages to find out which languages are related to one another. There are many language families besides the Indo-European, and some include languages with many speakers. Students may be surprised to learn that Chinese and Japanese are not related but belong to separate families. What we call Chinese is really a group of distinct languages. Speakers of one language, such as Mandarin (the official language of China), cannot understand speakers of any other Chinese language such as Cantonese, the language of many Chinese Americans. Many Native American languages belong to distinctly different language families as well. Few of these families are as well studied as the Indo-European family.

Linguistic Diversity in the United States

Within the United States, many, usually monolingual, speakers of English decry the need to address languages in our schools. They see no need for learning *foreign languages.* Yet, the reality of the diversity in our population and the trend for large companies and our government to work around the world demands that we acknowledge the presence of languages other than English.

Encourage students to begin a collection of different languages that they see in print. The newspapers and magazines often have examples of the languages in local communities. Companies that serve the public frequently publish instructions in the languages people use in their service area. Figure 10.3, mailed in February 1997 to users of the local telephone services in a large California city, reveals some interesting language characteristics. Students will note that the phone numbers are written the same way in all these languages.

While languages may differ in vocabulary for cultural and historical reasons, all languages have the same expressive potential. There is no such thing as a primitive language, just as there is no such thing as a primitive people. All human languages and all human cultures are rich and complex and capable of adapting to different circumstances. A language may not express some concepts that are considered important in our society, but it can develop the vocabulary to express any of them if the speakers of the language consider it necessary. The use of formerly unwritten African languages to conduct all the affairs of law, government, and education is an example of the flexibility of language. Another example is Hebrew, an ancient language that was revived for use as a national language in modern Israel. All languages possess the capacity to adapt to such new uses.

The 2000 census figures, still being analyzed, will provide us with an up-to-date picture of language diversity in the United States. Meanwhile, the 1990 results still give us a good idea of the languages around the United States. For example, one in every fourteen

Para obtener más información sobre los dos cargos adicionales nuevos en su factura, por favor llame al 1-800-573-7847 y oprima el número 1 en su teléfono de botones.

Muốn biết chi tiết về hai khoản bội phí mới trong hóa đơn của quý vị, xin gọi số 1-800-573-8828 và bấm số 1 trên điện thoại bấm số của quý vị.

有關您的帳單上兩項新的附加費之資料，請電1-800-570-8868 （粵語），或1-800-303-8788（國語），並請在您的按鍵式電話上按1。

귀하의 전화 요금 청구서에 있는 두 가지의 새로운 부과세에 관한 정보를 원하시면 1-800-560-8878로 전화를 거신 다음, 터치톤 전화기 번호판에서 1번을 누르십시오.

Para sa impormasyon tungkol sa mga bagong surcharges sa inyong bill, tumawag sa 1-800-404-1212, pagkatapos ay pindutin ang number 1 sa inyong touch-tone phone.

FIGURE 10.3   EXCERPT FROM LOCAL TELEPHONE INSTRUCTIONS

U.S. residents over the age of 5 spoke a language other than English at home in 1990. This represented a 35 percent increase over the figures for the 1980 census. Contrary to popular perception, however, 80 percent of these people spoke English fluently as well. Not surprisingly, Spanish was the most common language next to English; 17.3 million people reported that they speak Spanish at home (see Tables 10.1 and 10.2).

Determine what languages are represented in your classroom. Ask students not only what languages they speak but what languages their ancestors spoke. Students can learn about the history of this country as they find out what languages their families

TABLE 10.1   LANGUAGE DIVERSITY IN THE UNITED STATES

Spanish	17,339,172
French	1,702,176
German	1,547,099
Italian	1,308,648
Chinese	1,249,213
Tagalog	843,251
Polish	723,483
Korean	626,478
Vietnamese	507,069
Portuguese	429,860
Total	31,844,979

Source: Modern Language Association, accessed from www.mla.org

TABLE 10.2   TEN STATES
WITH GREATEST DIVERSITY

All languages, other than English, combined

State	Total
California	12,401,756
Texas	6,010,753
New York	4,962,921
Florida	3,473,864
The Commonwealth of Puerto Rico	3,008,567
Illinois	2,220,719
New Jersey	2,001,690
Arizona	1,29,237
Massachusetts	1,115,570
Pennsylvania	972,484

Source: Modern Language Association, accessed from www.mla.org

spoke before coming here and when their family started speaking English. Make a list of the languages represented and show on a map where they are spoken. Students can better understand the concept of ethnic diversity when they see how many of their parents and grandparents (and their friends' parents and grandparents) came from another country and had to learn to speak English when they arrived. Students will also identify more with the problems of recent immigrants when they realize how recently their own families arrived.

A Fable

In a house there was a cat, always ready to run after a mouse, but with no luck at all.

One day, in the usual chase the mouse found its way into a little hole and the cat was left with no alternative than to wait hopefully outside.

A few moments later the mouse heard a dog barking and automatically came to the conclusion that if there was a dog in the house, the cat would have to go. So he came out, only to fall in the cat's grasp.

"But where is the dog?"—asked the trembling mouse.

"There isn't any dog—it was only me imitating a barking dog," explained the happy cat, and after a pause added, "My dear fellow, if you don't speak at least two languages, you can't get anywhere nowadays."

Source: Reprinted from *BBC Modern English* 2 (10) (December 1976): 34.

English in the World

Why do many children who speak other languages than English learn English as a foreign language in school? As a leader in the world community, what is our responsibility in terms of language? Ask students if they know which language has the most speakers in the world (see Table 10.3). Write several guesses on the board. Have students research how many people speak each language. They can prepare a chart of the most widely spoken languages in the world. Figures can be obtained by counting the populations of countries that speak a particular language, or you can use information on what languages people learn as a second language. Check figures in almanacs and encyclopedias. Because the population of China is large, more people grow up speaking Chinese than any other language. Cantonese, the form of Chinese most common in the United States, is sixteenth on this list, with 66 million speakers.

Compare how many people in the world speak English and how many speak Spanish. Which languages in the world would be the most useful to learn as second or third languages? Why?

English is likely to maintain its position as one of the world's most important second languages. However, speakers of English will be at a disadvantage in tomorrow's world if they assume that everyone else knows how to speak English. Gradually, students in the United States are going to have to become multilingual in order to operate successfully outside their immediate area.

Influences from Other Languages

Americans came from many lands, and they brought their languages with them. And, Americans have been great travelers, bumping against many other languages as they go. They,

TABLE 10.3   THE TEN TOP LANGUAGES OF THE WORLD (IN MILLIONS, 1998)

(Mandarin) Chinese	885.0
Spanish	332.0
English	322.0
Bengali	189.0
Hindi	182.0
Portuguese	170.0
Russian	170.0
Japanese	125.0
German	98.0
(Wu) Chinese	77.2

Source: Statistical Abstract of the United States, 1999.

too, have brought language back with them. American English has become an eager borrower of words and ideas, continuing to be enriched from many sources.

The language that we speak today is a mixture of many languages. Although English is historically related to German (see the Language Tree in Figure 10.2), it has been heavily influenced by contact with the French language and has borrowed words from many other languages. Words that were borrowed a long time ago are now treated as a part of English, while words borrowed more recently usually show their foreign origins. For example, discuss with students why *massage* isn't pronounced like *message*.

List a number of borrowed words for students (see Table 10.4). How many of the words do they know? Can they guess the language each word came from?

Prepare a display showing the origins of the words. Use a map of the world pinned to the bulletin board with the words printed on cards placed near their country of origin. Or mount the Indo-European tree on the bulletin board and place the borrowed words on leaf shapes attached to the proper branches. Have we borrowed words from any non-Indo-European languages? Discuss how the display shows which languages have contributed most to the English language. Why are some languages represented more than others? Speculate on why these words might have been borrowed.

TABLE 10.4   BORROWED WORDS

Language	Word
Malay	ketchup, batik, orangutan
Arabic	alcohol, syrup, algebra
German	kindergarten, sauerkraut
French	souvenir, menu, encore
Hindi	shampoo, khaki
Spanish	bonanza, mosquito, tamale, cargo, alligator
Dutch	cole slaw, sleigh, boss, yacht, cruise
Tagalog	boondocks
Italian	macaroni, piano, crescendo, cello
Yiddish	kosher
Japanese	kimono, bonsai
Bantu	tote

LEARNING ENGLISH AS AN ADDITIONAL LANGUAGE

The number of students who are learning English in addition to the language or languages they already speak, is steadily growing. Again, an informed teacher who values the child's language is essential to providing for the acquisition of yet another way of speaking.

The instructional choices we make reflect our knowledge that children acquire a first language by being biologically attuned to language as a system. By the age of 6 or 7, children already possess a fundamental knowledge of the grammar of their childhood language. Children who have grown up with two languages will have the basics of both languages on which to build, as they increase their knowledge of vocabulary and sentence structure. But the framework is already in place. Now imagine these children attending school for the first time. The experience of school is a new one for everyone, but the degree of unfamiliarity can vary radically. Some children have attended preschool or day care where they have encountered lessons and other school-like patterns. Other children may have trouble adjusting to the taking turns, listening to the teacher, and raising a hand when you wish to speak expectations of a typical classroom. Still other students may lack any bridge to comprehending this new experience because they do not speak the language used in school by the teachers and others. However, students of all ages and backgrounds benefit from this kind of instructional support—providing English labels for objects in the classroom, teaching English through content such as science experiments, and rewarding students for recognizing words and letters in different contexts, for example. Older students learning English as an additional language learn best when they have good reasons to communicate. Pairing a student with an English-speaking buddy will ensure that explanations of classwork will occur, through some combination of words and acting out. And teaching routines such as passing in assignments or organized playground games will enable the student to find his or her place in the group.

Language learning is facilitated by providing oral practice, developing a literacy base, and teaching vocabulary in context as needed.

As you prepare your lessons for students learning English as a second language, keep the following points in mind:

1. Proficiency in English does not develop automatically.
2. Primary language literacy facilitates literacy development in English.
3. Oral language development is the foundation for literacy development.
4. The primary purpose for assessing the language and literacy development of English language learners is to inform instruction.
5. No single instructional approach will meet the needs of all English language learners.
6. Meaningful reading instruction should integrate thinking, listening, speaking, reading, and writing.
7. Students should have access to literacy that includes a variety of genres, interests, levels, and cultural perspectives.[3]

Oral Practice

Many students learning English as a second language (ESL) respond well to choral activities because they are not singled out or embarrassed by their mistakes. The class can learn a short piece to recite together, or a group of students can prepare a passage to present to the class. Different parts can be spoken by different groups or parts of the class. Poems and prose with a strong rhyme and rhythm are easier to learn and more fun to recite. ESL students will learn oral skills such as pronunciation and intonation by participating.

In the following example, divide the class in half and ask each group to alternate lines.

> If all the seas were one sea,
> What a *great* sea that would be!
> If all the trees were one tree,
> What a *great* tree that would be!
> And if all the axes were one ax,
> What a *great* ax that would be!
> And if all the men were one man,
> What a *great* man that would be!
> And if the *great* man took the *great* ax,
> And cut down the *great* tree,
> And let it fall into the *great* sea,
> What a splish-splash that would be!
>
> *(Old Nursery Rhyme)*

Young students with limited English skills can participate in class activities when you sing songs together. Simple tunes and repeated patterns make learning songs a positive experience. Here are some examples for primary students:

Eensy-Weensy Spider. Little, Brown, 2000. Familiar song with accompanying hand movements.

Little White Duck. Little, Brown, 2000. Simple words for group sing-along.

For more examples, see Chapter 4.

Developing Fluency

Tape-record several stories from a class reading textbook or other literature book. Enlist parents, aides, or older students to help you with this, providing a variety of voices. ESL students can listen to the stories on cassette as they follow along in the book. If you use multiple headsets, a group of students can listen and read at the same time. They will enjoy listening to these stories over and over again, and in the process, they will begin to make the connection between sound and symbol.

The following books provide models for developing oral language fluency, appropriate for all levels of English language learning, including native speakers. Repeated phrases and rhyming structure hold student interest, while illustrations provide the context for understanding vocabulary. Students can respond as a group at first and then individually or in writing.

Eloise Greenfield. *Honey I Love.* Illustrated by Jan Spivey Gilchrist. HarperFestival, 1995. Poet lists things she loves.

IDEAS IN ACTION!

Making Positive Choices

"Most people join gangs to have a family. . . . Sometimes the only way to get out is death," says one 13-year-old. In Oakland, California, kids who have known violence are studying how to end it. In a new program that looks at positive ways to effect social chance, twenty-four students—black, white, and Latino, many of whom live in very poor neighborhoods and have seen firsthand the violence that often plagues their communities, have begun by studying the causes of violence and racism as well as nonviolent ways to effect change and handle conflict. As one of the leaders stated: "There are so many young people who can't control their tempers. Our kids don't have enough to do, places to go." The program is like an intense summer camp that included a canoe trip to a local marsh, a tour of historic sites in the Black Panther movement, and discussions of topics ranging from unhealthy eating habits to racial epithets. Christina, a 15-year-old girl who witnessed a shooting, said: "Sometimes it's not safe to go to the store or sit on your porch. You don't know what's going to happen. . . . All you see now is young people dying." Inspired by a speaker who talked about prison and losing a nephew, one boy commented, "Oh, I do not want to go to jail. I got cousins, they're in a gang. . . . I thought about joining gangs, too. Hearing it from him, he spoke in true words. . . . I'm going to try to stay in school and go to college."[4]

Talk with your students about the violence that they have experienced and the racism in their lives. Brainstorm ways that they can break out of this cycle. Invite community members to class to listen to what the students have to say. Plan a program of audio and visual presentations to support your points.

Alison Jackson. *I Know an Old Lady Who Swallowed a Pie.* Illustrated by Judith Byron Schachner. Dutton, 1997. This version of the familiar humorous verse tells of a woman who ate too much at Thanksgiving dinner—"perhaps she'll die."

Anne Miranda. *To Market, to Market.* Illustrated by Janet Stevens. Harcourt, 1997. Animals run wild in this updated rhyming tale of chaos at home.

ESL students of any age can learn about English grammar by reading primary/picture books that establish a syntactic pattern and then repeat it through many variations. For example, Wanda Gag's *Millions of Cats* provides excellent practice with number words and the plural ending. After the first couple of pages, students will have no trouble filling in the refrain: "Millions and millions of cats." *The Judge,* by Margot Zemach, focuses attention on the -*s* ending as it repeats verbs in the third person singular. And Marjorie Flack's *Ask Mr. Bear* is an excellent exercise for pronouns, especially the possessive adjective.

These books achieve their appeal through repetition, making them easy to memorize. Students learn the patterns quickly and practice important grammatical elements painlessly. Students will be motivated to "read" these books that they have memorized.

Look for additional examples such as the following.

Jan Brett. *The Gingerbread Baby.* Putnam, 1999. New version of old tale features familiar refrain "Catch me if you can!"

Laura Numeroff. *If You Take a Mouse to the Movies.* Illustrated by Felicia Bond. Harper-Collins, 2000. One thing leads to another in this circular plot.

Philemon Sturges. *The Little Red Hen (Makes a Pizza).* Dutton, 1999. Struggles of hen to make pizza invite students' predictions at each stage.

Advanced students can write down their examples and create their own books based on these structures.

Developing a Literacy Base

Students who come to school with little or no English-speaking proficiency need a solid foundation in basic areas to achieve literacy in either or both of their languages. In any program that starts with the student's first language and gradually introduces English in order to develop literacy skills, the following points are fundamental to success.

1. *Read aloud to students.* Students need to hear the special kind of language used in books. Have them respond by writing in the language they choose.
2. *Give students time to write everyday.* Beginning writers need frequent practice to develop fluency. "Invented" spelling and grammatical mistakes are evidence that students are applying hypotheses about how each language works.
3. *Publish some student writing.* This gives students an incentive to polish some of their pieces. As they revise and edit, they learn the conventions of written language. Use teacher-student writing conferences to focus attention on aspects of form and content.
4. *Provide many books and printed materials, particularly in the language other than English.* Students can transfer their literacy skills from one language to another. The more they read, the more they will learn about language.

Remember that students who don't know any English still want to communicate. Provide them with varied media and nonjudgmental opportunities to express themselves.

With this technique, even students with limited English vocabulary can write their own stories. Introduce students to the language experience approach (LEA) by composing a story as a group. After an experience shared by the class, begin writing about it on a chart. As students make comments, write down the sentences they contribute. Prompt them to include more information if necessary. After the story is completed, read it back to the class so that they can see it is *their* story. Create a class collection of Big Books that students can read later. Or students can copy the class story and read it themselves.

The same technique can be used for individuals. Students can dictate a story to the teacher or an aide, or write it themselves, in their own fashion, to read back later. ESL students can dictate stories into a tape recorder. After these stories are transcribed and typed, they can be read back to the students, showing the relation between the spoken and written language.

Another technique to provide practice in reading and writing stories is the use of books with illustrations but no words. Wordless books can be used with students of all ages. Students can ask each other questions, describe the action taking place, and make predictions about what will happen. Because each student can create a text at his or her own level, these books can be used again and again.

Lewis Trendheim. *Happy Halloween.* Scholastic, 2003. Halloween monsters create havoc for everyone.

Gabrielle Vincent. *A Day, a Dog.* Front Street, 2000. Minimal illustrations of eventful day in the life of a dog allow space for multiple interpretations.

David Wiesner. *Sector 7.* Clarion, 1999. On class field trip to Empire State Building, a boy is carried off by a cloud and becomes a "cloud architect."

Encourage students to participate in their own language learning by making their own books. They can control the content, the level of vocabulary, and the purpose. Here are some books that can serve as models for students to emulate, from a simple collection of words for objects to more demanding content-area comprehension activities.

Steve Jenkins. *Hottest, Coldest, Highest, Deepest.* Houghton Mifflin, 1998. Statements such as "The Nile River is the longest river in the world" are the building blocks for interesting information, maps, and diagrams about geography around the world.

Mandy Stanley. *First Word Book.* Kingfisher, 1999. Labels for collection of everyday objects.

Recording Class Activities

All students can participate in recording class activities and other information on a daily basis. They can make weather observations, write about special events, and note birthdays and other news. Students can take turns being secretary, making entries in a class log or diary by copying information off the board or from weather instruments. This is useful to refer to later and it is interesting to show to visitors as a record of the class year.

October 3

It was 76 degrees outside and partly cloudy at 10 A.M. Today a woman from the Police Department came to talk to us about bicycle safety. She gave us a list of rules and taught us how to lock up our bikes. We saw a film about life in the ocean. My favorite part was how the hermit crab lives in other shells.

Older students can benefit from the challenge of producing a "newspaper" for the class or school. The variety of language activities required (writing short fiction, interviewing, persuasive advertising, argument, expository writing, and editing) is especially appropriate for a class with mixed English language abilities.

Andrews Clements. *The Landry News.* Simon & Schuster, 1999. Fifth graders learn the power of the printed word.

Vocabulary Development

Have primary-grade ESL students develop their own picture dictionaries. They can cut out or draw illustrations of all the new objects they encounter and copy the English word next to each one. Then students can refer to these dictionaries in class and even take them home for extra practice. Some older students may benefit from recording the pronunciation phonetically in their own language.

Intermediate and upper-grade students could construct a dictionary/notebook that focuses on signs and symbols. They could include examples such as these shown in Figure 10.4.

FIGURE 10.4   PICTURE DICTIONARY

Another vocabulary game that helps ESL students is the familiar "Categories." Most often used as a unit review, it consists of a word (the topic) written down the left side of a sheet and several categories across the top (see Table 10.5). Students fill in words under each category that begin with the letters of the topic word. For example, after discussing the subject of "space" for several days, give students this challenging exercise.

This game works best if there is more than one possible answer. If you want to make it more difficult, you can give points for each letter and reward students who have the longest entries.

TABLE 10.5   CATEGORIES

	Heavenly Bodies	*Colors*	*People/Professions*
S	Saturn	silver	scientist
P	Pluto	purple	pilot
A	Asteroid	azure	astronaut
C	Ceres	cocoa	chemist
E	Earth	emerald	engineer

Welcoming Limited-English-Speaking Students

Your English-speaking students can help you enormously to integrate the student with limited English skills into the class. Assign a "buddy" to each student. This buddy can show the student where to go and what to do, as well as help explain what the teacher wants. Most significantly, the buddy, by speaking lots of English, provides important vocabulary and grammar input for the English language learner. And both participants in the pair receive rewards.

Peer tutoring, using a student in the same class, and cross-age tutoring, when a student in the upper grades helps a student in the lower grades, have proved helpful for language development of ESL students.

Encourage older ESL students to prepare a guide to the school. It could include information useful for other ESL students as well as any new students. Have students take pictures of classrooms, student activities, and other important elements of school life. They can prepare captions ranging from a few words to a longer description of what is expected of a student. If you work with one particular language group, you might consider having the guide translated and sent out to incoming families as a bilingual introduction to the U.S. school system.

Older students can extend this project by preparing a guide to the community. It might include information about important resources for non-English-speaking families.

CONNECTIONS

In this chapter we continue the *Esteem, Empathy,* and *Equity* model through acceptance of the language students bring to the classroom. First comes interest in students' language and cultural backgrounds as they develop empathy for each other and learn about language in the world setting. Throughout the emphasis on language we provide equitable treatment to meet the individual differences and needs of our students.

FOLLOW-THROUGH

Expanding Your RTP

1. Write a few paragraphs about your own language background and experiences that you may have had with language in school. What language(s) were spoken in your home? How many generations do you have to go back to find non-English speakers?
2. Read the following quote and write a response. Share your comments with your CLG.

    The English language has developed standards in pronunciation just as it has in spelling. These pronunciations are recorded in dictionaries and do a great service to us all. They help to keep us from fragmenting into dialects that cannot be understood by other Americans. Of the regions in the United States, Midwesterners pronounce words closest to the dictionary standard, so these people have the least accent. The reason accents cause problems is that most have negative connotations. By disregarding the dictionary pronunciation, a person with an accent may be perceived as pretentious, uneducated, or even dull-witted. (Marilyn vos Savant, *Parade Magazine,* April 11, 2004)

Working with Your CLG

1. As you read multicultural literature, note those that include examples of different languages. Bring these books in to share. Discuss Black English Vernacular, regional variations in languages, or words from other languages that they include and how you might incorporate this in classroom instruction.
2. Review the policy statement from the National Council of Teachers of English presented at the beginning of this chapter.

    Do you believe that some forms of English are more prestigious than others? Investigate this issue. Listen to different people speaking on television and radio. Can you hear regional dialect differences or different accents? Talk about stereotypes (positive or negative attitudes) people might have about the language others speak.

GROWING A PROFESSIONAL LIBRARY

Robert McNeil. *Do You Speak American?* PBS Video Series, 2005.

Allan Metcalf. *The World in So Many Words: A Country-by-Country Tour of Words That Have Shaped Our Language.* Houghton Mifflin, 1999.

ENDNOTES

1. Annie Nakao, "Remembrance of a Chicana Poet." *San Francisco Chronicle,* June 20, 2004.
2. Roland Tharp, paper presented at the Holmes Partnership Conference, January 2001.
3. Roland Tharp, et al. Center for Research on Education, Diversity, and Excellence. *Center Report #10,* UCSC, 2004.
4. Carrie Sturrock, "Kids Who Have Known Violence Study How to End It." *San Francisco Chronicle,* August 28, 2004.

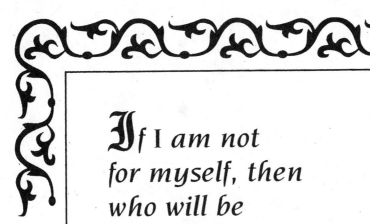

If I am not
for myself, then
who will be
for me?

And if
I am only
for myself,
then,
what am I?

And
if
not now,
when?

—Rabbi Hillel
Mishnah c. 190 C.E.

Investigating Additional Issues and Concerns Related to Multicultural Education

As we begin a new century, we can see the United States in the process of redefining itself. Immigration, relations with the United Nations and other countries, our role as defender of democracy and human rights—all are areas of current concern. Gone are some of the familiar moorings, such as the Cold War and the industrial economy. Instead, we find ourselves forced to adapt to the possibilities of terrorist attacks on our own soil, "outsourcing," and high prices at the gas station, due to our dependence on other countries for oil.

Such fundamental changes require a rethinking of all of our assumptions and approaches to teaching traditional topics. In fact, our constantly shifting culture needs multicultural education in the schools now more than ever. The ability to work well with diverse people in diverse settings has become one of the most important and valuable skills in the world today. In this chapter, we address issues and concerns related to multicultural education that have not been discussed elsewhere in the book.

THINK GLOBALLY, ACT LOCALLY

Many events in other countries have had repercussions in even the smallest communities across America, illustrating vividly the extent of global interdependence. Political unrest and economic hardship drive immigrants and refugees to the United States, and they may end up in small towns far from the border as well as in urban areas more often associated with these groups. For example, many communities today are facing a problem of what to do with Spanish-speaking young men who congregate on street corners, waiting for someone to drive by and offer them work. The presence of these day laborers (or "jornaleros") causes neighborhoods to confront some difficult decisions: whether to accept their existence and work with it or to try to make them go away.

When we look at these neighborhood concerns from the perspective of multicultural education, we recognize the familiar patterns of the "Not in My Backyard" (NIMBY) approach to problems from communities with the political influence that means they are listened to as well as the isolationism that has often plagued American thinking. With little or no information about the conditions in other countries, people can perhaps be excused for their lack of understanding of why their particular community suffers from this problem or their lack of awareness of its connection to larger world issues. Remarks such as, "I'd rather not have them in my neighborhood," "My wife doesn't feel safe walking by them," and "I'm not being racist, but—" reflect the quickly growing frustration of residents at the lack of an easy solution and the attempt to separate themselves from these "others." Multicultural consciousness helps us to see the underlying racist assumptions in these attitudes because the presence of these migrant workers is related to economic conditions in the areas they come from, as well as the employment conditions that make cheap labor desirable in the areas where they congregate.

Teaching multiculturally means teaching students to understand the relationship between what they see around them and conditions in distant places that may appear to have no connection to their lives. When students investigate the concerns of their own communities, they quickly begin to see that possible solutions are complex and effective responses are tied to larger social forces than just the conditions in their own commuities. Multicultural education requires that teachers encourage students to look closely at their community while providing a global context for local issues.

Suggested Resources:

Global Teach Net News, National Peace Corps Association. *<www.globalteachnet.org>*

Mary Pipher. *The Middle of Everywhere: The World's Refugees Come to Our Town.* Harcourt, 2002.

WHEN CRIMES BECOME *HATE* CRIMES

In just one case in 2003, fifteen to twenty white youths allegedly yelled racial slurs and kicked and punched five Asian American teenagers in San Francisco, leaving them with severe injuries. "There's no doubt this was a hate crime, motivated by racial prejudice," Superior Court Judge Kevin McCarthy told the courtroom. Malcolm Yeung, attorney at the Asian Law Caucus, a San Francisco group, said that this case highlighted the importance of reporting hate crimes.

In the United States hate crime incidents had dropped by about 10 percent in 2003 from the previous year. There was an increase in 2001, mostly due to anti-Arab assaults after the September 11th terrorist attack. But hate crimes against blacks have remained the major motivator of cases based on race, ethnicity, or national origin. National figures show about four hate crimes every day and, because not everyone reports a hate crime, there are probably more. As we become more multiculturally conscious, we become more aware of the added burden carried by those who belong to a stigmatized group, whether black, gay, or Arab, the insecurity of fearing a possible attack at any time, by any person.

A classroom of students from diverse races, ethnicities, or national origins includes students who carry this burden of fear. They know that something like this could happen to them and that they would not necessarily be able to rely on the full protection of the law. Teaching multiculturally means acknowledging this reasonable fear while attempting to create a safe environment in the classroom for everyone. And multicultural education means teaching students from more privileged groups how it feels to be someone who might be attacked just for belonging to the wrong group and being in the wrong place at the wrong time.

Selected Resources:

Judith Butler. *Precarious Life: The Power of Mourning and Violence.* Harper, 2004.

Katherine S. Newman. *Rampage: The Social Roots of School Shootings.* Basic Books, 2004.

GAY MARRIAGE: THE PROS AND CONS

San Francisco was accused of igniting a "wildfire" of same-sex marriages across the country as the U.S. Senate prepared for a hearing to amend the Constitution in order to prevent the fire from spreading. Despite the defeat of the Senate's same-sex marriage ban, the idea of lesbians and gays marrying remained controversial enough to become a major factor, at least for religious conservatives, in the 2004 election. Polls showed a majority of voters consistently oppose gay marriage. However, the oldest generation shows the greatest antipathy, leading us to think that this may be an issue resolved by waiting.

Opponents of same-sex marriage cite the work of Stanley Kurtz, research fellow at the Hoover Institution at Stanford University, who claims that gay marriage is detrimental to society because it kills off heterosexual marriages.[1] In addition, Kurtz argues that registering partnerships drives an irreparable wedge between parenthood and marriage. Others contest his interpretation of marriage statistics, asserting that many factors may be causing the rate of family dissolution to increase.

Meanwhile, the state of Massachusetts has licensed same-sex marriages and Washington may do the same. In support, the American Anthropological Association released a statement, saying:

> The results of more than a century of anthropological research . . . provide no support whatsoever for the view that either civilized or viable social orders depend upon marriage as an exclusively heterosexual institution. . . . Rather, anthropological research supports the conclusion that a vast array of family types, including families built up in same-sex partnerships, contribute to stable and humane societies.[2]

The Human Rights Campaign, which led the effort to defeat the anti-same-sex marriage ban in the Senate, is fighting ballot initiatives to change state constitutions in Georgia, Kentucky, Mississippi, Louisiana, Missouri, Oregon, Montana, Utah, Michigan, Oklahoma, and

Arkansas. Meanwhile, conservatives rely on the 1996 Defense of Marriage Act, which gives states the right to deny recognition of same-sex marriages from other states, despite rulings against this in federal courts.

What does this mean for the students we encounter every day? First, we need to be conscious of our own assumptions. We know that our students are being raised in a number of different family arrangements. We shouldn't expect that a child with two parents necessarily has different-sex parents. Second, we need to recognize that many students may know people who are gay or have family members who are gay. Third, we must acknowledged the deep-seated homophobia that surrounds us. As our students struggle with their own male and female identities, we can support them by providing teaching materials that promote diverse families and by talking through male and female stereotyping.

Suggested Resources:

American Anthropological Association. *<www.aaanet.org>*

Susan Dominus. "Got a Problem with My Mothers? Coming of Age with Same Sex Parents." *The New York Times Magazine,* October 24, 2004.

Nancy Garden. *Molly's Family.* Farrar, 2004. Picture book in which child draws a picture of her family, but is told she can't have two moms.

"Focus On: Gays, Lesbians, Bisexuals, and Transgendered Persons." National Education Association, 1201 16th Street NW, Washington, DC.

THE DIGITAL DIVIDE

A household income of $50,000 or above is a key predictor of Internet use, according to a Pew study called "Internet and the American Life" in 2003.[3] That puts families below the poverty line at a disadvantage. Statistics from the Department of Education confirm this, showing that 77 percent of whites used computers at home in 2001, compared to 41 percent blacks and Hispanics.[4] Although research shows that this digital divide between rich and poor children over access to key computer skills may be shrinking, "the kids who are left behind are in even deeper trouble than those in previous years. Their lack of knowledge is almost akin to not knowing how to use the telephone." "Their peers are absolutely surrounded by digital media. It's one of the basic ways in which kids communicate and find out about the outside world, form community and engage in social relationships."

"Literacy alone is no longer our business. Literacy and technology are," says Cynthia Selfe of her work on computers and education. She claims that we have to pay attention to the technology that the students are picking up and learning to use so that we can help them direct their attention to critical thinking and exploring the world.[5] However, we can't help them become literate in the Internet unless we have some experience ourselves. Then we can show students how to navigate the Internet, how to evaluate the information they obtain, and what to do with the information once they've retrieved it. The understandings involved are not so far removed from those we are familiar with from teaching reading comprehension and reading in the content areas—critical analysis, paraphrasing, summarizing, separating fact from opinion.

Selected Resources:

Lauren Myracle. *ttyl.* A novel in text message from <*www.ncte.org/collections/weblit/ strategies*>

Nancy Patterson. "Becoming Literate in the Ways of the Web: Evaluating Internet Resources." *Voices in the Middle,* March 2003.

Cynthia Selfe. *Technology and Literacy in the Twenty-First Century.* Southern Illinois University Press, 1999.

ENFRANCHISEMENT FOR ALL

One group that is eager to be able to participate in the democratic process is the immigrants. Undocumented immigrants cannot vote, yet their children are in school and they are affected by the decisions made by such elected officials as the local school board. "These issues—whether immigrants should be allowed to participate in the democratic process—are fundamental questions for this country, whether it's drivers' licenses or noncitizens voting in local elections," says Marcelo Suarez-Orozco, a professor at New York University. "These are very important questions at the heart of a democracy. . . . One hundred years ago, the question of the day was—are Italians and eastern European Jews and Irish going to be contributing citizens to our culture of democracy? . . . Today it's the same question, but this time it's Mexicans, Chinese, and Haitians. We love immigrants looking backward, talking about our travails and the fabulous contributions of our great-grandparents. It's always in the here and now there is ambivalence and anxiety."[6]

Latinos are already one-third of California's population of 35 million. They are expected to become the largest population group by 2025 and the new majority by 2040. But there are two different Californias—the resident population (increasingly Latino) and the voting population (still non-Hispanic white). Many Latinos, regardless of their green card status, want government services and a say in how they are delivered. In fact, in four states, local governments have granted noncitizens voting rights in some municipal elections. "By and large, most politicians realize they're not going to win by making enemies out of immigrants," says Viviana Andrade, vice president of public policy at Mexican American Legal Defense Fund (MALDEF). "Parties on both sides of the aisle recognize the Latino vote could be pivotal in some battleground states."[7]

RESISTANCE TO MULTICULTURAL EDUCATION

Many individuals and groups resist or actively combat multicultural education, because they do not believe that this emphasis is appropriate in our schools. They argue for assimilation into the so-called majority culture and the use of English as the only language in the

United States. They bemoan the use of culturally sensitive terminology for groups and tag such efforts as "political correctness," a term that has acquired strong negative connotations in the media.

Daniel Boorstin, Pulitzer Prize–winning historian and former librarian of Congress, states: "The menace to America today is in the emphasis on what separates us rather than on what brings us together—the separations of race, or religious practice, of origins, of language."[8] He sees the idea of a "hyphenated American" as "un-American" and will not use such terms as African American, stating that we are all Americans. He does not support bilingual teaching, citing his own Jewish heritage as an example of appropriate assimilation in the new world. He advocates an emphasis on community rather than diversity. If such a respected, prominent writer and thinker speaks against multicultural approaches in education and the celebration of diversity, just think of the numbers of lesser-known people who share this viewpoint!

As teachers, you must be aware of such opposing viewpoints and prepare to combat criticism of sound theories and practices that the schools are trying to implement. You need to have a clear understanding of your stance and the rationale for including multicultural education in the schools in order to argue persuasively.

Selected Resources:

Jared Diamond. *Guns, Germs, and Steel: The Fates of Human Societies.* Norton, 1999.

Joseph Ellis. *Founding Brothers: The Revolutionary Generation.* Random House, 2002.

Herbert Zinn. *A People's History of the United States: 1492–Present.* Harper, 2003.

POVERTY AND THE WORKING POOR

There were 35.9 million Americans living in poverty in 2004, representing a 1.3 million increase over the previous year. One in ten U.S. households experienced hunger or the risk of hunger. Over the past twenty years, the poverty rate among working families has increased by almost 50 percent. In addition, nearly one in five of all Americans 65 and older live in poverty or near poverty. In such states as California, the cost of living is so high that even families that earn more than the poverty rate have trouble paying their rent, buying food, and obtaining health insurance. "Diabetes is increasing in all populations within the the the United States, and American Indians have been hit hardest of all populations in this country," says Donald Warne, a Native American and a doctor.[9] This increase has taken place over the last 100 years, as the native diet of natural foods has been replaced by government handouts loaded with sugar and lacking in nutrition. Lack of money to spend on healthy food may also have detrimental effects on the population.

Poverty, poor health, disease, death around the world—the facts appear daily in our newspapers. Access to safe drinking water and sanitation are important worldwide concerns and a top priority for the United Nations. "The hardest hit by bad sanitation are the rural poor and the residents of slums in fast-growing cities, mostly in Africa and Asia, but the quality of drinking water and sanitation facilities also has dropped in some industrialized nations, particularly the former Soviet republics," according to a 2004 UNICEF report.[10]

"About 2.4 billion people are likely to face the risk of needless disease and death by 2015." Leaders at a 2000 summit adopted the Millennium Goals and pledged to:

- Cut in half the number of people living on less than $1 a day.
- Reduce child mortality.
- Provide universal primary school education by 2015.
- Promote gender equality and empowerment of women.
- Improve the lives of slum dwellers.
- Improve maternal health.
- Halt or reverse the spread of HIV-AIDS, malaria, and other diseases.
- Close the so-called digital divide between the poor and the wealthy.
- Work to improve environmental sustainability.
- Establish a global partnership for development.[11]

Mark Malloch Brown, Head of the UN Development Program said: "The world is doing so poorly in meeting the poverty-reduction targets that it will take African countries almost 150 years to achieve them."[12]

No wonder so many persons want to emigrate to the United States where they are happy to work in low-paying sweatshops in Los Angeles or as farm workers in North Carolina. Once in the United States, however, they find themselves in a vicious cycle of poverty again where "Poverty leads to health and housing problems. Poor health and housing lead to cognitive deficiencies and school problems. Educational failure leads to poverty," as David Shipler states in his 2004 book, *The Working Poor.*[13] The wealthy continue to acquire wealth on the backs of the poor. Is there any way out?

Selected Resources:

Barbara Ehrenreich. *Nickel and Dimed.* Holt, 2002.

Sharon Hays. *Flat Broke with Children: Women in the Age of Welfare Reform.* Oxford University Press, 2004.

Mike Rose. *The Mind at Work: Valuing the Intelligence of the American Worker.* Viking, 2004.

David K. Shipler. *The Working Poor: Invisible in America.* Knopf, 2004.

SLAVERY IN THE TWENTY-FIRST CENTURY

We think of slavery as something that is over and done with. The word *slavery* calls to mind images from the nineteenth century, such as African Americans working in cotton fields. In those days, slavery thrived on a shortage of person power. Slavery was big business when the average slave in 1850 sold for around $40,000 in today's money.

But slavery still exists, even in the twenty-first century. In 2003, an estimated 27 million men, women, and children worldwide were physically confined or restrained and forced to work, controlled through violence, or in some way treated like property.

Today vulnerable people are lured into slavery in expectation of a better life. Because there are so many desperate people in the world, we see forced labor in West Africa, 5- and 6-year-old Pakistani children delivered to the Persian Gulf to serve as jockeys on racing camels, Thai child prostitutes, Brazilian slave gangs hacking at the Amazon rain forest, farm laborers in India bound to landlords by debt inherited from parents and passed on to children.

The buying and selling of people is still a profitable business and globalization has made it easier to move people and money around the world. People who want to move where the jobs are face more stringent regulations on legal immigration. As a result, those who can't move legally or pay for smuggling often end up in the hands of illegal traffickers.

There are no countries where slavery is legal, but there are at least 104 countries where more than a hundred human beings are known to have been trafficked in 2003, ranging from Austria to Japan, and Ethiopia to the United States.

Modern slavery is a mix of total domination and economic exploitation. Slaves are controlled not by legal ownership but by violence. Only twenty-five countries actively prosecute trafficking in human beings as a serious crime. "There's a tacit acceptance of slavery here," says the director of SOS Slaves, an anti-slavery group in Mauritania. "A society that cannot look itself in the face cannot advance."[14]

Recent cases in the United States include:

- Luring a 14-year-old girl from Cameroon with promises of schooling, then isolating her in a Maryland home, raping her, and forcing her to work as a servant for three years.
- Recruiting women from Uzbekistan with promises of jobs, seizing their passports, and forcing them to work in strip clubs and bars in Texas.
- Forcing children into prostitution in Georgia, where they were tortured for disobedience.
- Transporting Mexicans to Florida and forcing them to work as fruit pickers. In addition, local people were brutally beaten for trying to help the Mexicans escape.

Selected Resource:
Andrew Cockburn. "21st Century Slavery." *National Geographic,* September 2003.

STILL A QUESTION OF ACCESS FOR PEOPLE WITH DISABILITIES

Noreen Grice, astronomer, was working as an intern while at Boston University when students from nearby Perkins School for the Blind were visiting and she helped them to seats in the planetarium. Afterwards, she asked how they liked the show. "That stunk!" said one.

Like most planetarium shows, it had been a visual show of the night sky with no explanation to help those who couldn't see it for themselves to know what it was all about. Grice asked, "Why does it have to be that way?" Writing a brochure in Braille wasn't the answer; what was missing were the pictures. So she went to Perkins and looked at their astronomy books. There were no pictures because the only tactile illustrations available were made by an expensive labor-intensive process.

Finally, technology caught up and she could use a VersaPoint machine to make bas-relief pictures to hand to visually impaired visitors—constellations and phases of the moon. She published a book of astronomical diagrams *Touch the Stars.*

Bernhard Beck-Winchatz, astronomer and associate director of NASA Space Science Center for Education, proposed a similar book of tactile Hubble Space Telescope images. *Touch the Universe* (Joseph Henry Press, 2002) was tested on astronomy students at the Colorado School for the Deaf and Blind in Colorado Springs. The book includes fourteen pictures taken by Hubble—images of planets, stars and galaxies—in full color for sighted, but with contours of Saturn's rings, the swirl of Jupiter's red spot, brilliant color of interstellar gas clouds conveyed by ridges and bumps embossed on images for the visually impaired.

Is there any point to giving this information to people who will never see the sky? Ask Kent Cullers, radio astronomer with SETI (Search for Extraterrestrial Intelligence) who is totally blind. Blindness doesn't inhibit his ability to handle information. Although he lacked the ability to see the constellations, he could still read the scientific data off the computer.

Learning disabilities raise other problems of access. When the mayor of San Francisco, Gavin Newsom, came out about his dyslexia, it was front page news in the local newspaper. This often misunderstood disability appears to be at least twice as common in boys as in girls, claims Dr. Michael Rutter, of King's College, London.[15] However, others suggest that girl's reading problems are more likely to go unnoticed by teachers.

Nearly 3 million children in the United States have learning disabilities, and about 80 percent of them are dyslexic. Their dyslexia does not affect their intelligence, only their ability to read and identify words, numbers and sounds. More than a half a million 3- to 5-year-olds received special education services in 2003, and that number may grow as toddlers are diagnosed even earlier.

A public preschool in New Jersey designed for the benefit of special education students that invites children of typical abilities to attend is currently overwhelmed by applications from parents of non-special education children. This "reverse mainstreaming" approach is proving popular because it provides a rich setting in which all can learn. The advantage of the special education focus is a "very individualized education that looks at a child from many points of view, delivered by a team in a familiar and supportive environment," says Rick De Matteo, director of personnel and special services in Waterford, Connecticut. In addition, the teachers use different strategies and techniques to reach different students in different ways.[16] This kind of education is not only appropriate for those students who need special services, but for all students, and is a model for multicultural education.

Selected Resources:

Susan Burch. *Signs of Resistance: American Deaf Cultural History 1900–World War II.* New York University Press, 2004.

David Chandler. "To Touch the Heavens." *Smithsonian Magazine,* August 2003.

Paul Longmore and Lauri Umansky, eds. *The New Disability History: American Perspectives.* New York University Press, 2003.

Steven Noll and James W. Trent, Jr., eds. *Mental Retardation in America.* New York University Press, 2004.

WHEN BOOKS ARE BANNED

As author Judy Blume states: "It's not just the books under fire now that worry me. It is the books that will never be written. The books that will never be read. And all due to the fear of censorship. As always, young readers will be the real losers."[17]

The American Library Association has compiled a list of "The 100 Most Frequently Challenged Books of 1990–2000." The top ten titles are:

Scary Stories (series) by Alvin Schwartz
Daddy's Roommate by Michael Wilhoite
I Know Why the Caged Bird Sings by Maya Angelou
The Chocolate War by Robert Cormier
The Adventures of Huckleberry Finn by Mark Twain
Of Mice and Men by John Steinbeck
Harry Potter (series) by J. K. Rowling
Forever by Judy Blume
Bridge to Terabithia by Katherine Paterson
Alice (series) by Phylis Reynolds Naylor

The American Library Association received 6,364 challenges, which were used in compiling this list. However, they note that "Research suggests that for each challenge reported there are as many as four or five which go unreported." A teacher in New York found herself embroiled in a yearlong battle to defend her right to teach and her students' right to learn. Instead of being excited about teaching a challenging book, *Bless Me Ultima* by Rudolfo Anaya, to her ninth graders, she had to fight a parent who wanted the book removed from the entire district.[18]

Censorship is such a complex and frequent concern that it deserves special attention. This topic could well be the subject of staff development within your district or a discussion for your school staff, including the principal. For example, you can determine together just how to handle requests to eliminate books from a reading list or from the school library. Having a procedure in place is very helpful for all staff members.

You might begin by obtaining material from various professional organizations. Such information also provides the authority of a large, respected professional group to support your school practices. For example, the National Council of Teachers of English (NCTE) will give you one free copy of its position statement *Censorship: Don't Let It Become an Issue in Your Schools,* written by its Committee on Bias and Censorship in the Elementary School. It will also provide one free copy of a statement related to nonprint media, *Guidelines for Dealing with Censorship of Nonprint Materials.* Address requests to NCTE, 1111 Kenyon Road, Urbana, IL 61801.

A subtler kind of censorship is the result of teachers' prioritization of what is presented in the curriculum. Teachers often appear uninterested in multicultural education.

Given a choice in selecting workshops at a conference, they tend to choose topics that fit the mainline curriculum—for example, ideas for teaching reading or motivating student writing. It is difficult to know how to overcome this passive resistance.

Selected Resources:

American Library Association. <*www.ala.org*>

National Coalition against Censorship. <*www.ncac.org*>

John Simmons and Eliza Dresang. *School Censorship in the 21st Century: A Guide for Teachers and Library Media Specialists.* International Reading Association, 2001.

GENDER-FAIR EDUCATION

The Bush administration announced plans in March 2004 to allow public schools to educate boys and girls separately, a loosening of restrictions that could lead to the most dramatic shakeup of the coed system in more than thirty years. The proposed changes would let school districts offer classes, grade levels, or entire schools to just boys or girls. Federal regulations currently prohibit single-sex education in public schools except in sex education classes and PE classes involving body contact. Single-sex schools or classes would rely on voluntary enrollment and could be offered only if "opportunities for both sexes are substantially equal," according to the U.S. Department of Education. The proposal—backed by a bipartisan group of female senators—met with tepid reaction in much of the country.[19] However, we already know that separate but equal rarely winds up fair.

Title IX of the Education Amendments of 1972 prohibits sexual discrimination in schools that receive federal funding in order to assure that girls and boys get equal resources both in the classroom and on the athletic field. But as girls have narrowed the achievement gap—even outpacing boys in some areas—political opposition to single-sex education has dwindled. Democratic senators such as Hillary Clinton, D-NY, and Barbara Mikulski, D-MD, joined Republicans such as Kay Bailey Hutchison of Texas in calling for greater options. The Bush administration believes that loosening the regulations will give teachers, parents, and kids a broader choice in education. "I think this move is really turning back the clock to equal educational opportunities for girls." The National Coalition of Girls' Schools states: "This is no experiment. Single-sex schooling is a time-tested means of helping today's children become tomorrow's leaders, and we applaud efforts to make this option available to all families."[20]

How can we reduce sexism and promote gender equity in our classrooms? A gender-fair curriculum, claims Gretchen Wilbur, quoted in the AAUW report *How Schools Shortchange Girls* would:

- Acknowledge and affirm variation among students.
- Be inclusive of all students.
- Present accurate information.
- Affirm differences in values.

- Represent multiple perspectives.
- Be integrated, weaving in males and females.[21]

In your selection of materials, in your discussions, in your responses to students, you can communicate the message that both boys and girls should speak up, that all students need to learn how to work together, and that girls are just as capable in math and science as boys.

A gender-fair curriculum will promote self-esteem in all students, develop their ability to empathize with others in different positions, and contribute to equitable treatment for every student, regardless of gender.

ENGLISH AS THE OFFICIAL LANGUAGE OF THE UNITED STATES

Should we designate English, by law or by amendment, as the official language of the United States (or of individual states)? Perhaps this question appears superfluous because, as we all know, English has been assumed to be the language of commerce, and it is used for all official purposes. However, the question is more complex than it would first appear because it raises a number of related issues, for example:

- Should English be the *only* language permitted in the United States?
- Does English as the official language mean English *only*?
- Is education considered an official use of language?
- Is the nurturing of a child's home language permissible in public schools?
- Are fully bilingual programs to be promoted?
- Should we promote the learning of additional languages in schools?

The National Council of Teachers of English passed the following resolution in 1986 stating its position on "English as the 'Official Language.'"

> **Background:** The proposers of this resolution voiced concern about the current movement in some states to establish English as the official language. Such efforts, successful in one instance so far, can include removal of the native languages of many Americans from official documents, they noted, and called such actions potentially discriminatory.
>
> The proposers commended the recent Public Broadcasting System TV series "The Story of English" for illustrating the capacity of English to accommodate and incorporate the linguistic characteristics of many people and cultures.
>
> **RESOLVED,** that the National Council of Teachers of English condemn any attempts to render invisible the native languages of any Americans or to deprive English of the rich influences of the languages and cultures of any of the people of America;
>
> that NCTE urge legislators, other public officials and citizens to oppose actively any actions intended to mandate or declare English as an official language or to "preserve," "purify,"

or "enhance" the language. Any such action will not only stunt the vitality of the language, but also ensure its erosion and in effect create hostility toward English, making it more difficult to teach and learn. . . .[22]

Selected Resources:

John McWhorter. *Doing Our Own Thing: The Degradation of Language and Music and Why We Should, Like, Care.* Gotham, 2003.

The National Council of Teachers of English. Support for the Learning and Teaching of English (SLATE) website. *<www.ncte>*

STUDENTS AT RISK

Many children are at risk of not succeeding in the schools today. We recognize that "school people did not create or cause most of the problems that confront young people today, nor can they solve the problems by themselves." On the other hand, educators have a responsibility for not only alleviating but actively counteracting the conditions that place some students at risk and helping them overcome obstacles that impede successful achievement in school. For too long we have failed to solve the problem of reaching diverse students, intervening in the early years, providing models with whom they can identify. For example, our teaching has often failed to recognize that "at-risk students need to learn higher order thinking such as problem solving, not just basic skills that may keep them dependent thinkers all their lives." Multicultural approaches to education may offer all students something special as we deliberately select literature with which they can find a common bond and make a sincere effort to provide equitable opportunities for successful learning experiences, beginning in the primary grades.

Phi Delta Kappa, an educational honor society, sponsored extensive research of at-risk students. Begun in 1988, the study was based on reports from almost 22,000 elementary, middle school, and high school students, including about 30 percent African American, Latino, Native American, and Asian students. Researchers identified thirty-four indicators of risk, which were grouped into the following five categories or factors:

- Personal pain (drugs, abuse, suspension, suicide)
- Academic failure (low grades, failure, absences, low self-esteem)
- Family tragedy (parent illness or death, health problems)
- Family socioeconomic situation (low-level income, negativism, lack of education)
- Family instability (moving, divorce)

Notice that these factors are not limited to so-called minority students or students from low-income families, but appear across the whole group of students.

Researchers addressed four major questions:

- Who is at risk? Only one in five of students interviewed had no risk factors; one out of four had three or more risk items evident. Older students are more at risk than younger; African Americans are more at risk than whites; Latinos are more at risk than Asians; and boys are more at risk than girls.

- What factors put them at risk? "Most of the risk factors are beyond the sphere of influence of the school." If one risk factor is present, usually there are others. More than half of students who were retained came from broken homes. One-third of them had low grades and 17 percent had fathers who had not graduated from high school.

- What are schools doing to help these students? Nearly one-fourth of the 9700 teachers interviewed say they spend more than 50 percent of their time with at-risk students. Strategies used by more than 75 percent of teachers include individualized scheduling, conferences with parents, more time on basic skills, emphasis on thinking skills, and notification of parents.

  The following practices were judged to be at least 75 percent effective: special teachers, smaller classes, special education, individualized scheduling, conferences with parents, more time on basic skills, peer tutoring, vocational courses (in high school), special study skills, emphasis on coping skills, emphasis on thinking skills, notification of parents, and teacher aides. In addition, "teachers and principals provide students who are at-risk with more instructional efforts than students who are not at-risk, and teachers are committed to and are concerned with helping students who have special problems, whatever those problems might be."

- How effective are the schools' efforts? Although teachers and principals considered their efforts only 71 to 75 percent productive, principals reported that their schools had a great deal of influence over students' reading comprehension, math, writing, and listening skills; daily attendance, general behavior, and attitude toward school; completion of homework, attention in class, and higher order thinking skills.[23]

Yale professor James Comer, author of *Beyond Black and White,* supports these recommendations, noting: "Black children need somebody to care about them, first of all. They need somebody who wants them to learn, who believes they can learn, and who gives them the kind of experiences that enable them to learn. That's what all children need."[24] Comer also stresses the importance of emphasizing relationship issues and the social condition—"interaction between teacher and student, between parent and student, between parent and teacher." In carrying out his School Development Program, he argues for providing support for "the kind of development that all children need."

Selected Resources:

Association for Supervision and Curriculum Development, 1250 N. Pitt Street, Alexandria, VA 22314. Audiocassette series; five tapes by educators from large urban school districts describing how they are handling the problem of at-risk students.

Robert D. Barr and William H. Parrett. *Hope at Last for At-Risk Youth.* Allyn and Bacon, 1995.

David L. Marcus. *What It Takes to Pull Me Through.* Houghton, 2005.

IDEAS IN ACTION!

Teaching for Tolerance

When Matthew Shepard, a young gay man, was brutally beaten and killed in Laramie, Wyoming, in 1998 because of his homosexuality, his mother decided to get involved. She set up the Matthew Shepard Foundation and began to accept speaking engagements around the country. Her message was always the same: tolerance. All of the people who had been outraged by the story of Matthew's death and engaged in national soul-searching and discussion of homophobia and anti-gay violence now had a focus for their energies.

Below is a selection of ideas from the pamphlet "101 Tools for Tolerance" <*www.tolerance.org*>, 400 Washington Avenue, Montgomery, AL 36104.

- Help an adult learn to read.
- Speak up when you hear slurs.
- Participate in a diversity program different from your own.
- Learn sign language.
- Go to an ethnic restaurant. Learn about more than the food.
- Donate acceptance-related books, films, magazines, and other materials to local and school libraries.
- Organize a book drive.
- Ask school counselors what resources they have for supporting gay and lesbian youth. Offer additional materials if necessary.
- Partner with a local school and encourage your colleagues to serve as tutors or mentors.
- Seek out co-workers from different backgrounds, different departments, and at different levels in the company. (Seek out students of backgrounds, cliques, social-economic groups, or interest groups different from your own.)
- Advocate for domestic partnership benefits.
- Provide employees with paid leave to participate in volunteer projects.
- Frequent minority-owned businesses and get to know the proprietors.
- Make sure that anti-discrimination protection in your community extends to gay and lesbian people.
- Be an educated voter. Know who your representatives are and where they stand on issues important to you—and VOTE. It is your privilege and your responsibility.

What can you do in your community to foster tolerance? What groups are victims of intolerance in your area—how could you find out? Invite students to prepare a handout for other people of the same age. What activities can they suggest to help spread an attitude of tolerance? What strategies can they pursue when they come across an example of intolerance?

BULLYING AND HARASSMENT

At all grade levels students may encounter a "bully," the kid who needs to feel powerful, often a boy, but not always. Bullying is defined as "systematically and chronically inflicting physical hurt and/or psychological distress on one or more students."[24] Often, in the elementary school, bullying takes the form of excessive teasing or "making fun of" another person. Boys more often apply physical abuse, while girls tend to use social ostracism or psychological abuse. According to the National Association of School Psychologists (NASP), approximately one in seven children practices or is a victim of bullying behavior. It is estimated that some 5 million elementary and junior high school students are directly affected by bullying in the United States, which about one-fourth of the time affects their school performance. If bullying behaviors are allowed to continue, the bullies may go on to increasingly serious violence as adults.

Far from a new problem, bullying affects more than the immediate victim. Children usually are afraid to tell adults about such behavior. Even those who only observe the bullying may be afraid of retaliation. Bullying is a serious problem that must be dealt with in the classroom. Discuss this problem in general in every class, giving students an opportunity to write about possible experiences they may have had. Students who are the targets of repeated bullying behavior often show signs of fear and stress, such as:

> Fear of going to school
> Fear of going to the bathroom
> Fear of riding to and from school on the bus
> Physical symptoms of illness
> Diminished ability to learn

Teach students effective strategies for coping with bullying or potentially threatening situations. The following are some strategies that you can discuss and practice:

> Learning to control anger or cool off
> Collaborative problem solving
> Active listening
> Seeking a mediator

Following the Esteem/Empathy/Equity Model will lead to less need for students to bully others. As a teacher, you need to be present, to observe, and to listen to what is going on as students interact. Communicate clearly a Zero-Tolerance Policy for bullying in your classroom.

Selected Resources:

Allan L. Beane. *The Bully-Free Classroom: Over 100 Tips and Strategies for Teachers K–8.* Free Spirit Publishing, 1999.

Let's Get Real, documentary film by Debra Chasnoff, Helen S. Cohen, and Kate Stilley. New Day Films. 190 Route 17M, P.O. Box 1084, Harriman NY 10926.

National Bullying Awareness Campaign, National Education Association. 1201 16th Street NW, Washington DC 20036.

Not in Our Town I and *Not in Our Town II,* PBS specials. NIOT Campaign/The Working Group. P.O. Box 70232, Oakland CA 94612-0232. <*www.pbs.org/niot*> Patrice O'Neill and Rhian Miller, producers. video.

Nan Stein. *Secrets in Public: Sexual Harrassment in Our Schools.* Harcourt, 2001.

AFFIRMING MULTIRACIAL IDENTITY

The stories of resistance to biracial marriages and multiracial children go back a long way in the history of the United States. They touch on white plantation owners and their black female slaves—for example, Thomas Jefferson and Sally Hemmings. They touch on antimiscegenation laws such as that of 1880 in California that "prohibited the marriage between a white person and a Negro, mulatto, or Mongolian." Representing the feelings of the day, John Miller, who was later a U.S. Senator, stated: "Were the Chinese to amalgamate at all with our people . . . the result of that amalgamation would be . . . a mongrel of the most detestable that has ever afflicted the earth." Social change was slow in coming. In 1958, for example, the first Gallup poll on interracial marriages reported that 94 percent of white people opposed such marriages.

Willy Wilkinson tells of his Chinese mother's experience in applying for a teaching job in 1959 in California: The principal said, "Wilkinson is not a Chinese name. Do you have any difficulties in your marriage?" His mother replied, "My husband doesn't have a problem being of another race." Fortunately, the principal laughed wholeheartedly and offered her a job. Her son notes that his parents have celebrated their fifty-third wedding anniversary after raising four children. He sees them as "our role models for the freedom to love and create family."[25]

In 2003, Essie-Mae Washington-Williams revealed her identity as the daughter of Senator Strom Thurmond after his death at the age of 100. A 78-year-old retired schoolteacher in Los Angeles, she had a long-distance relationship with her father. Interestingly, Strom Thurmond was known as a strong segregationist. His daughter is now in contact with the other members of her family, and plans "to join the United Daughters of the Confederacy to explore her heritage and encourage other African Americans to fully understand their bloodlines."[26]

Selected Resource:

Cooperative Children's Book Center. School of Education, University of Wisconsin-Madison, 2000.

FOLLOW-THROUGH

Expanding Your RTP

1. Select one of the topics presented in this chapter and prepare to become an "expert" on it. Collect materials that you would use to teach students and develop activities to support their learning. Present your information to the class.

2. Scan your local newspaper for topics of concern relating schools and society. Clip articles that you find and bring them in to share with the class. Reflect on the way the issue was presented in the newspaper. Was the coverage fair? Did you feel that more information was needed in order to understand what was going on? Write a response to these questions in your RTP.

Working with Your CLG

1. Have each group choose a topic that is not covered in this chapter, such as the teaching of evolution (separation of church and state) or high-stakes testing (No Child Left Behind). As a group, develop a list of questions outlining what you would like to know. Investigate resources for teachers and students on this topic. Prepare a presentation for the class, including a packet of material summarizing what you have learned.

2. As a group, select and explore the resources available on the Internet from various professional organizations such as National Council of Teachers of English, International Reading Association, National Association for the Education of Young Children, National Council for the Social Studies, and National Association for Multicultural Education. Develop a directory of useful information.

ENDNOTES

1. Stanley Kurtz. "The End of Marriage in Scandinavia: The Conservative Case for Same Sex Marriage Collapses," in *The Weekly Standard,* February 2, 2004.
2. American Anthropological Association Policy Statement, quoted in the *San Francisco Chronicle,* February 27, 2004.
3. *Internet and the American Life.* Pew Center for the Study of American Life, 2003.
4. U.S. Department of Education Report, 2002.
5. Cynthia Selfe, *Technology and Literacy in the Twenty-first Century.*
6. Marcelo Suarez-Orozco, quoted in *San Francisco Chronicle,* March 3, 2003.
7. Viviana Andrade, quoted in *San Francisco Chronicle,* March 3, 2003.
8. Daniel Boorstin, Speech at Moorhead State University, April 17, 1993.
9. Donald Warne, quoted in Jason B. Johnson, "Concern Grows in Diabetes in Indians." *San Francisco Chronicle,* July 6, 2004.
10. *World Health Organization and UNICEF Joint Report,* quoted by Jonathan Fowler, "UN World Health Goals in Limbo." *San Francisco Chronicle,* May 20, 2004.
11. Mary Robinson, "Sociology Meets Human Rights: The UN Millennium Goals." *San Francisco Chronicle,* August 15, 2004.
12. WHO and UNICEF op. cit.
13. David Shipler, *The Working Poor: Invisible in America.* Knopf, 2004.
14. Elizabeth Bryant, "Despite Official Ban, Slavery Lives on in Mauritania." *San Francisco Chronicle,* August 29, 2004.
15. Dr. Michael Rutter, quoted in *San Francisco Chronicle,* April 28, 2004.
16. Susan Brenna, "Very Special Education." *Education Week,* November 9, 2003.
17. Judy Blume, quoted in <*www.ala.org*>, "Most Frequently Challenged Books of 1990–2000."

18. "Defending the Right to Read: Librarians, Teachers Navigate the Chilly Waters of Censorship." *New York Teacher, <www.nysut.org>*. Downloaded October 6, 2003.

19. Ruth Rosen, "Where the Girls Are." *San Francisco Chronicle,* March 11, 2003.

20. Heather Knight, *San Francisco Chronicle,* March 4, 2004.

21. AAUW and NEA, *How Schools Shortchange Girls.* American Association of University Women Report, 1992.

22. *English as the Official Language.* National Council of Teachers of English. 1986.

23. Jack Frymier, "Growing Up Is Risky Business, and Schools Are Not to Blame." *Phi Delta Kappan,* 1992.

24. James Comer, "Dr. James Comer's Plan for Ensuring the Future." *Black Issues* 10 (May 20, 1993).

25. *National Bullying Awareness Campaign.* National Education Association.

26. Willy Wilkinson, "A Marriage Taboo." *San Francisco Chronicle,* August 24, 2004.

27. Jason B. Johnson, "What Strom Thurmond's Illegitimate Daughter Wants." *San Francisco Chronicle,* August 9, 2004.

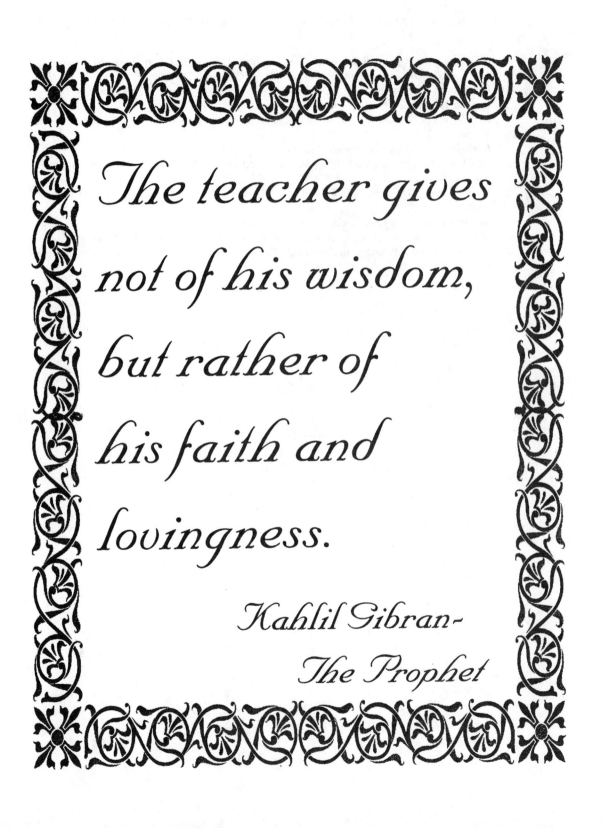

The teacher gives
not of his wisdom,
but rather of
his faith and
lovingness.

Kahlil Gibran-
The Prophet

Continued Professional Growth

In this final chapter we invite you to reflect on what you have learned about multicultural education so far. First, we review just when educators began to advocate multicultural education in our schools. Second, we guide you to assess where you are today as individual teachers who believe in developing *Esteem, Empathy,* and *Equity* in the schools. Then, we suggest a few professional organizations and publications that will assist you as beginning teachers in continuing to grow professionally. Finally, we share a number of additional literature titles designed to assist you in developing thematic studies

Following this chapter is an Afterword from the authors to you who will carry out multicultural education for our children.

REFLECTION: WHAT HAVE YOU LEARNED?

Continued professional growth is essential if teachers are to lead the way in offering multicultural education. All teachers need to be familiar with the latest research that supports specific teaching strategies. They also need to know a wide variety of resources that will enhance their teaching and enable them to reach the diverse student population in our classrooms today. Teacher training does not end with the college classroom. It must be self-motivated, continuing as lifelong learning throughout a teacher's career. We hope that you will be able to carry out the vision expressed by Kahlil Gibran.

As you reflect now on this study of multicultural education in which you have engaged, it is appropriate to reflect on the journey just completed. We invite you to share the words of the noted author Aldous Huxley, which appeared in an interview in the *New York Times* in 1926:

> So the journey is over and I am back again, richer by much experience and poorer by many exploded convictions, many perished certainties, for conviction and certainties are too often the concomitants of ignorance. I set out on my travels knowing, or thinking I knew, how men should live, how be governed, how educated, what they should believe. I had my views

on every activity of life. Now, on my return, I find myself without any of these pleasing certainties . . . The better you understand the significance of any question, the more difficult it becomes to answer it. Those who attach a high importance to their own opinion should stay at home. When one is traveling, convictions are mislaid as easily as spectacles, but unlike spectacles, they are not easily replaced.

As we reflect on our journey, consider how your thinking has changed. What convictions have you lost along the way?

The Roots of Multicultural Education

Multicultural education is a recent development. Prior to 1978, *multicultural education* was not even listed as a category in the *Education Index,* which indicates that few articles were being written in pedagogical journals about this topic. An entry using the term *Mexican Americans* first appeared in the 1963–1964 volume of this index. At that time multiethnic topics were referred to as *Intergroup Education.* All references to blacks were entered under *Negroes* until 1978. References to Asian Americans were listed under *Orientals* until 1980. Only within the past decade do we find a substantial number of books and articles on multicultural education. *Multicultural Teaching* was the first text to address the topic. First published in 1979, this text provided a unique overview of diversity and its impact on teaching and learning in the schools.

Given the lag that typically occurs between the development of a theory and its impact on practice, these findings make it clear that we have not yet sufficiently emphasized teaching about cultural diversity in teacher education programs. Few classroom teachers and professors of teacher education teaching today were educated to teach multicultural concepts. Members of the public educated years ago, too, still frequently use the melting-pot metaphor with well-meaning, but mistaken, intent and effects; and such terms as *culture* are often misused in textbooks and public dialogue.

Standards listed in 1987 by the National Council for Accreditation of Teacher Education (NCATE) were the first to include multicultural education. Teacher education programs are therefore now examined to see that multicultural concepts are present in class syllabi. The expected "multicultural perspective" is defined as

> . . . a recognition of (1) the social, political, and economic realities that individuals experience in culturally diverse and complex human encounters and (2) the importance of culture, race, sex and gender, ethnicity, religion, socioeconomic status, and exceptionalities in the education process.[1]

Teachers need to know accurate definitions, terminology, and concepts that can be shared with students at all levels of instruction. They need to know literature that will inform such instruction. They also need to accept the responsibility for teaching to enhance empathy in all classrooms.

The solution to this problem lies in both preservice and inservice staff development. *Multicultural Teaching* is designed to add to the knowledge base for future teachers as well as those already in the field. Throughout this text we have presented numerous up-to-date references that you can explore to extend your knowledge base. We have also recommended experiences and activities that will enhance your ability to teach for diversity as you work with young learners.

The Professionalization of Teaching

Increasingly, attention is being placed on the quality of teaching and the professionalization of teaching as a respected career. A 1988 nationwide study by the Association of Supervision and Curriculum Development identified the following teacher-related issues as being of concern:

1. Inconsistency of teacher certification requirements and the overuse of "alternative" or "emergency" teaching certificates.
2. Limited criteria for teacher evaluation.
3. Loss of self-esteem for teachers leading to low morale.
4. Low salaries negating efforts to attract best teachers.
5. Lack of preparation in instructional skills and classroom management.
6. Shortage of highly skilled teachers and gradual reduction of persons choosing teaching as a career.
7. Inadequate staff development for teaching roles and responsibilities.
8. Lack of preparation time to handle numerous tasks required of teachers.

Respondents to the same survey recommended emphasis on the following to improve the quality of instruction and to provide a more professional role for teachers at all levels:

- Empowerment: Teachers need more control and autonomy in the classroom and in determining what is taught in general.
- Recruitment: We need to work to attract top-quality people to teaching as a career.
- Retention: We also need to work to retain top-quality teachers in the field.
- Roles: Teachers need support as they assume new roles, for example, in management of the inclusive classroom.
- Training: Teachers need more professional staff development opportunities.[2]

The establishment of The National Board of Teaching represents a positive effort to upgrade the status and ability of teachers in the field. Funded by the Carnegie Foundation and grounded in the work of Lee Shulman, the board provides a performance-based test as a basis for national certification as a master teacher. It is expected that many top teachers will opt to acquire this national recognition.

Site-based management is another positive approach to involving teachers in decision making about how education is carried out at the local level. Although not an easy process to initiate, some principals and their staffs are committed to the necessary study and effort required. The emphasis is on collaboration rather than top-down direction; everyone needs to be informed. Such promising practices add to a sense of empowerment for teachers involved.

Activism results from teacher empowerment as teachers become advocates for school change. Informed teachers are needed to take a position and speak on children's behalf. Ask yourself what you truly believe about teaching. What do you have to say about teaching to provide equity for diverse learners?

True empowerment of the teacher comes from within. It is not something that an external task force can fund or a legislature can enforce. We all, however, have a responsibility to nurture this sense of empowerment, which is akin to self-esteem and self-confidence. The teacher who has this sense of power is best able to teach multiculturally, addressing controversy with equanimity and sharing leadership with young learners in the classroom.

Teacher education can empower novice teachers by providing them with basic knowledge in the foundations, liberal studies, and pedagogy, including multicultural education. Such teachers have confidence in their knowledge base, but above all they know how to apply this knowledge in the classroom. Furthermore, the teacher who possesses a sense of empowerment is best able to nurture that same feeling in students.

You may wish to explore this topic further in the following resources:

James A. Banks and Cherry Banks. *Multicultural Education: Issues and Perspectives,* 2nd ed. Allyn and Bacon, 1997.

Bruce Joyce et al. *The Self-Renewing School.* Association of Supervision and Curriculum Development, 1993.

Seymour B. Sarason. *The Case for Change: Rethinking the Preparation of Educators.* Jossey-Bass, 1993.

Schools as Centers of Inquiry

Gradually, teachers are recognizing that direct, teacher-dominated instruction is not as effective as discovery methods that engage students in inquiry. We need to consider the goals of education in terms of student learning, the expected outcomes that we identify. The testing of student achievement should then reflect what we really mean to teach. The evaluation of teacher performance should in turn reflect our expectations for student learning.

In direct instruction the teacher typically lectures, perhaps addressing questions to individual students one by one; only a small percentage of students are actively involved at any one time, and there is little student interaction. This is the quiet, orderly classroom; learning follows predictable lines and is easily evaluated. In this type of teaching, the teacher generates the questions, and the kind of question asked usually has one correct answer, which of course the teacher knows. This has been the traditional mode of instruction for many years.

When inquiry approaches are used, however, the students generate questions to which they need to know the answers. There is self-motivation as each one works 100 percent of the class time on a self-selected problem or project. Metacognitive approaches guide students to awareness of the thinking processes in which they are engaged. They talk and write to express thinking and test their ideas against the thinking of other students in pairs or small groups. They accept ownership for the learning that is going on because they selected a topic in which they have an interest. Far from abdicating their role, teachers plan extensively in order to set up discovery learning situations; often they plan directly with students. They facilitate and support the learning process and serve as resource persons.

Evaluation of progress is part of the inquiry—a process shared by teacher and student. In this kind of classroom students have an opportunity to learn more than is presented in a single textbook, and they naturally develop self-esteem. Thus, what they learn is both cognitive and affective, but it may not always be easily measured by tests used by school districts. Because such approaches are more sensitive to individual student needs, they fit with the outcomes we have identified for multicultural education. They also show promise in supporting the at-risk students, an identified group that needs special attention in our schools.

Explore this topic further through the following resources:

Kenneth Goodman et al. *Report Card on Basal Readers.* National Council of Teachers of English, 1988.

Robert J. Marzano et al., eds. *Dimensions of Thinking: A Framework for Curriculum and Instruction.* Association for Supervision and Curriculum Development, 1988.

James Moffett and Betty Jean Wagner. *The Student-Centered Curriculum,* 3rd ed. Houghton Mifflin, 1996.

Self-Assessment: How Am I Doing?

Multicultural teaching is a broad topic that cannot be taught in one single course. Therefore, we have presented multicultural studies as a spiraling curriculum comprising concepts and understandings that evolve over years of schooling. Threading its way through all instruction, multicultural education is a lifelong endeavor. For the purposes of review and self-assessment, we state in Table 12.1 a dozen summary conclusions describing the theory and practice of multicultural education as presented in *Multicultural Teaching.* Use this list as a self-assessment as you plan for your continued professional development as a multicultural teacher.

Where are you in your development as a multicultural teacher? In which areas do you feel the most need for additional study? It is important to remember that multicultural education will continue for all of us throughout our lives. We all have much to learn about "getting along" with others.

TABLE 12.1   SUMMARY CONCLUSIONS FROM *MULTICULTURAL TEACHING*

Multicultural Education: Theory and Practice

Well prepared	Adequate	Needs study	
			1. The United States is a multiculture, a society comprising many diverse cultures. All of living, including schooling, involves contact between different cultures and is, therefore, multicultural. No one culture can be considered more American than any other.
			2. The United States is gradually moving away from the goal of assimilation or making everyone alike (the melting-pot metaphor) toward recognizing and appreciating the diversity in our society (the "tossed salad," or mosaic, metaphor).

(continued)

Well prepared	Adequate	Needs study	
			3. Multicultural education is too complex and pervasive a topic to be encompassed in a single course for teacher educators. All of education must reflect multicultural awareness. Curricula for grades K–8 must be designed to teach content about our multiculture and to provide equity for all learners in all subjects.
			4. We should not pretend or even aim to be creating teaching materials that are bias-free. Instead, we should guide students to recognize the biases from which they and all people operate.
			5. We need to clarify our use of such terms as *culture, ethnicity,* and *race*. We also need to be aware of accepted labels for groups of people within our population, speaking out against insensitive usage whenever appropriate.
			6. Although every child grows up within a given culture, he or she is shaped over the years by additional influences, such as education and personal interactions with others. Education can guide students to become more aware of and appreciative of their individual cultures, their heritage. Children can also learn to avoid ethnocentrism by being open to the cultural ideas of others.
			7. All children enter school with a store of prior knowledge, closely aligned with their individual identities or cultural backgrounds, on which teachers can build. Their native languages are valued and nurtured as they learn English and other new content.
			8. The K–8 curriculum must be student centered and designed to promote *Esteem, Empathy,* and *Equity* for all children. Goals must be both affective and cognitive. Multicultural teaching enables all students to achieve their greatest potential.
			9. Teachers need to be aware of their own cultural backgrounds and biases. They need to be aware of how these biases might influence their expectations of students and how they interact with others. Open dialogue with students will acknowledge these cultural influences as common to us all. Both teachers and students can learn together about different ideas and ways of thinking.
			10. Multicultural teaching is exciting because it is grounded in reality. Through active, constructivist learning strategies, students become directly involved in their learning. At the same time, teachers may find such multicultural approaches more difficult because they may include controversy and emotion.
			11. Multicultural education, global studies, and internationalization of the curriculum are related in their focus on human concerns. Thus, a study of universal needs suggests topics that overlap so that the three are not completely separate areas to be added to the school curriculum.

Well prepared	Adequate	Needs study	
			12. Multicultural education deals with values and attitudes as well as knowledge. We can guide students to be aware of their own thinking and that of others. We guide them to make choices based on expressed reasoning, problem solving, and decision making. Because changes in values and attitudes and the development of empathy take time, assessing such changes quickly is not possible.

What other conclusions would you add to this summary list?

HOW CAN WE GROW PROFESSIONALLY?

Every teacher will benefit from belonging to a professional educators' organization that offers annual conferences and publications. Membership in these organizations includes a professional journal. Following are a few that you might consider:

- The International Reading Association, 800 Barksdale Road, Newark, DE 19714.
  Journals: *The Reading Teacher* (elementary/middle school)
  > *Journal of Adolescent to Adult Literacy* (middle school/secondary)
  > *<www.reading.org>*
- The National Association of Multicultural Education (NAME), 733 15th Street NW, Suite 430, Washington, DC 20005.
  Journal: *Multicultural Perspectives* (all levels)
- The National Council of Teachers of English, 1111 W. Kenyon Road, Urbana, IL 61801.
  Journals: *Language Arts* (elementary/middle school)
  > *English Journal* (middle school/secondary) *<www.ncte.org>*

Other professional journals that review literature suitable for multicultural education (not connected with membership):

- *Book Links.* Published by the American Library Association, 50 Huron Street, Chicago, IL 60611. Information: *<www.ala.org/Booklinks>*. Subscription; published bimonthly.
- The American Library Association also publishes lists of awards given books for children annually: Caldecott (for illustrations), Coretta Scott King (for African American authors and illustrators), and Newbery awards (author). Print out from the Internet. *<www.ala.org/awards>*.

Become a Reader

We often hear teachers state that they never read the newspaper. And, they don't have time to read magazines and books. If teachers don't read, how can they expect their students to read? Reading not only accesses information, it stimulates your thinking and creativity.

Read the Newspaper

Multiculturalism permeates your newspaper. Almost daily you will find fascinating information about different ethnic groups; perhaps the Koreans are celebrating New Year's Day or the Greek Americans are having a festival to which the public is invited—good food and lively dancing that everyone can enjoy. Here is information you can share with your students. You might even engage your students with reading the daily newspaper. Check with your local newspaper about getting class sets of papers and enlist their help in presenting a unit of study on the newspaper.

Multicultural education is a subject very much in flux, and it is clearly a current concern as we all learn to deal with the increasing diversity of the U.S. population. Newspapers reflect what people are talking about: What is the new president going to do about funding for bilingual education? What is the breakdown of the current census figures? Which African Americans are we honoring during Black History Month? The newspaper answers such questions. Almost every day it offers us something we can use in teaching.

Get to Know Multicultural Literature

Begin to read the work of authors whose books you might select for class study. Fine writers are creating outstanding books for K–8 students. You might explore recognized authors who have written for different levels. Cynthia Rylant, for example, wrote *When I Was Young in the Mountains,* a fine picture book that tells of her own experiences living in Appalachia. You might find reading this book aloud to fifth and sixth graders a wonderful way to introduce them to her award-winning novel, *Missing May,* which deals with how we handle our grief when someone dies. You might want to know an intriguing picture book about searching for self-identity, *The Big Box,* which Toni Morrison co-authored with her son, Slade Morrison. This challenging book might lead gifted eighth graders to explore her adult novels.

Biographies about authors are not only interesting but also supply information to share with students. Often your students might also read these biographies. Ezra Jack Keats, author/illustrator of *The Snowy Day,* which was one of the early picture books about African American characters, won the Caldecott Award for outstanding art. It is interesting that this Jewish man saw the need for books that had black characters. Dean Engel and Florence Freedman wrote an excellent biography about him titled *Ezra Jack Keats: A Biography with Illustrations.* A very talented African American artist, Faith Ringgold, who creates huge story quilts, developed one of her works into a fine children's book, *Tar Beach.* Examples of her art are presented in *Faith Ringgold* by Robyn Montana Turner.

Select literature that your students might enjoy. Literature is a particularly fine resource for the development of a multicultural thematic study. Talented authors write literature that:

communicates the universality of human emotions,

models prosocial behavior,

gives children pride in their ethnic heritage,

introduces children to contemporary families both alike and different from their own,

reveals to children how it feels to be different,

enables children to participate in another social era,

shows a wide range of human characteristics and aspirations, and

immerses children in another culture.[3]

Choosing multicultural literature that supports instruction in different subjects you are teaching adds the opportunity to deal with breaking down stereotypes and adding to student knowledge of people from diverse cultures. The following are representative of the multicultural fiction and nonfiction you might choose to read aloud and to talk about:

Picture Books

Rosa Guy. *Billy the Great.* Delacorte, 1992. Perspective on prejudice; friendship.

William Miller. *The Piano.* Lee & Lou, 2000. Race, class, intergenerational friendship.

Gary Paulsen. *The Tortilla Factory.* Harcourt, 1995. How tortillas are made from corn.

Taro Yashima. *Crow Boy.* Viking, 1955. A boy who is different comes to be accepted.

Novels

Robert Cruise. *Fiona's Private Pages.* Harcourt, 2000. Diary entries reveal problems of friendship and secrets.

Malka Drucker. *Grandma's Latkes.* Harcourt, 1992. Grandmother passes the Jewish family's traditions to Molly.

Ofelia Lachtman. *The Girl from Playa Blanca.* Piñata Books, 1995. Children from Mexican village come to Los Angeles to search for their father.

Mary E. Lyons. *Letters from a Slave Girl: The Story of Harriet Jacobs.* Scribner, 1992. Historical fiction told through letters from a woman abolitionist.

Megan McDonald. *Judy Moody Was in a Mood: Not a Good Mood, A Bad Mood.* Candlewick, 2000. Unique funny solutions to problems.

Harriette Robinet. *Washington Is Burning.* Holt, 1997. U.S. history from a slave's viewpoint.

Brenda Seabrooke. *The Bridges of Summer.* Cobblehill, 1992. Friendship between two girls across racial divisions in South Carolina.

Gary Soto. *The Skirt.* Delacorte, 1992. A picture of a Mexican American family in California.

Frances Temple. *Tonight by the Sea.* Orchard, 1995. A Haitian girl escapes military dictatorship.

Laurence Yep. *Dragonwings.* Harper, 1976. Historical novel about the Chinese in early California.

Read for Pleasure

Keep a book beside your bed—fiction, poetry, essay, autobiography, nonfiction—whatever appeals to you. Ask your friends what they are reading. Here is a sampling of fiction by excellent writers that we can recommend:

Barbara Kingsolver. *The Poisonwood Bible.* Harper, 1998. A missionary and his family move to the Belgian Congo in 1959. Novel.

Susan Sontag. *In America.* Farrar, Straus, 2000. A Polish actress emigrates to California to establish a utopian community. Novel.

Wallace Stegner. *Beyond the Hundredth Meridian: John Wesley Powell and the Second Opening of the West.* Houghton, 1953. Historical fiction about the Grand Canyon.

If you enjoy reading mysteries, that's a place to start. Explore nonfiction, too; offerings take varied forms. Find a subject that interests you, for example:.

Robert Bly. *What Have I Ever Lost by Dying?* Harper, 1992. Lovely prose poems.

Jill Kerr Conway. *When Memory Speaks; Reflections on Autobiography.* Knopf, 1998. Essays.

Sue Hubbell. *Waiting for Aphrodite: Journeys into the Time before Bones.* Houghton Mifflin, 1999. Nonfiction by a fine writer. The evolution of life on this planet and the world of little things.

Ursula LeGuin. *Dancing at the Edge of the World: Thoughts on Words, Women, Place.* Harper, 1990. Fascinating commentary by a noted author who writes for children and adults. Talks and essays.

Read Stories of Real Teachers Working with Diverse Students

Are you concerned about actually facing a classroom full of students? Are you a young white teacher having doubts about your ability to work with students of color? At this time you might find it very helpful to read some of the books that have been published about real teachers who worked successfully with children who came from cultures very different from their own.

Sylvia Ashton-Warner was one of the first, writing about her work with Maori children in New Zealand. Later, Jonathan Kozol and Herbert Kohl wrote of teaching in urban schools in Boston and New York City. More recently, a Pulitzer-prize-winning author, Tracy Kidder, wrote an engaging case study, speaking for Mrs. Zajac, a teacher in Holyoke, Massachusetts, who worked with fifth graders, half of whom were Puerto Rican. All of these teachers' stories are interesting; all are inspiring. Following are more detailed descriptions of the books that relate their experiences. Look for them in your local used-book store.

Sylvia Ashton Warner: Teaching Maori Children in New Zealand

Sylvia Ashton Warner wrote of her work with Maori children in an amazing book, *Teacher* (1963, 1986), which American teachers quite literally gobbled up. She introduces us to organic reading instruction as she helps children in her infant school make the "bridge from the known to the unknown; from a native culture to a new; and, universally speaking, from the inner man out."

She describes her work with 5-year-olds. Based on a "key vocabulary," words that she draws from each child first thing every morning, words that have personal dynamic meaning, the children begin to read. Each child has his or her own pile of cards bearing words printed by the teacher. They read their cards, read them again, and read them again. They draw pictures to go with their word captions, and gradually they create their own books which they can read. As this teacher says:

> It may sound hard, but it's the easiest way I have ever begun reading. There's no driving to it. I don't teach at all. There is no work to put up on the blackboard, no charts to make and no force to marshal the children into a teachable and attentive group. The teaching is done among themselves, mixed up with all the natural concomitants of relationship. I just make sure of my cards nearby and my big black crayon and look forward to the game with myself of seeing how nearly I hit the mark. And the revelation of character is a thing that no one can ever find boring.

Teacher was first published in 1963, years after this enthusiastic young teacher worked with the Maoris. After her death in 1984, the book was reissued in 1986 with a foreword by Maxine Hong Kingston. Sylvia Ashton Warner also wrote a best-selling novel, *Spinster* (1968), as well as a number of other less-noted works.

Vivian Gussin Paley: A Jewish White Kindergarten Teacher Works with Diverse Children

Vivian Paley has taught kindergarten for many years in the Midwest, and she has written a number of books about what she, as a teacher-researcher, has learned about teaching young children. All of them have something to offer our work with multicultural education. In *You Can't Say, "You Can't Play,"* (1982) for example, she teaches children how to get along together. In *The Kindness of Children* (1986) she focuses on teaching children how and why to be kind to one another. In *White Teacher* (2004), which we will discuss in more detail here, she provides insight into her own concerns about a white Jewish teacher's ability to guide the learning of black youngsters.

In *White Teacher,* a panel of black parents is invited for the first time to discuss their children's learning experiences with the faculty in a midwestern school. Not uneducated, the parents speak frankly revealing their perception of the prejudice and unfairness that they observe in the school where Vivian Paley teaches kindergarten. The teachers in this relatively liberal school are surprised and somewhat defensive. But this incident leads Vivian to begin taking notes about her interaction with the black students (about one-third of the class) in her room. She asks herself:

Do I respond to each child in a similar manner?
Am I fair to the black children?

Vivian Paley introduces us to the children she teaches through describing pertinent events that she observes—friendships, free discussion about such ideas as skin color, sharing favorite family songs, inviting parents to bring a family food to share in the classroom, and so on. And, a blessing for this liberal teacher comes in the form of a talented, older student teacher who happens to be black. Together, they work to assist the learning of the children in the room.

As a teacher-researcher, Vivian Paley is eager to investigate the hidden curriculum and to discover something of her own identity in the process. As she observes what is happening in her classroom, she comes to the following conclusion:

> The black child is Every Child. There is no activity useful only for the black child; there is no manner of speaking or unique approach or special environment required only for black children. There are only certain words and actions that cause all of us to cover up, and there are other words and actions that help us reveal ourselves to one another. The challenge in teaching is to find a way of communicating to each child the idea that his or her special quality is understood, is valued, and can be talked about. It is not easy, because we are influenced by the fears and prejudices, apprehensions and expectations, which have become a carefully hidden part of every one of us.

Thus, Vivian Paley ends the forward to the study of her teaching in her own classroom. This philosophy, we might add, reflects a key understanding that we present in the introductory chapters of *Multicultural Teaching*. Teaching *multiculturally* means enabling every child to reach his or her greatest potential using whatever methods and materials are most appropriate.

Herbert Kohl: Teaching Sixth Grade in Harlem

Herbert Kohl describes his exhausting first days as a beginning teacher working with (not teaching) 36 sixth-grade black children in Harlem. The classroom is ugly; he has no books. His chief goal in those first days is to remain in control, moving methodically through his lesson plan—reading, arithmetic, social studies. One young girl inquires plaintively:

> "You like it here, Mr. Kohl?"
> I looked up into a lovely sad face.
> "What do you mean?"
> "I mean do you like it here, Mr. Kohl, what are you teaching us for?"

After several miserable days plugging through the inadequate books that finally arrived, interspersed with periods of chaos, this Harvard graduate begins to "see" the kids as individuals. At last he comes to this momentous conclusion:

> I am convinced that the teacher must be an observer of his class as well as a member of it. He must look at the children, discover how they relate to each other and the room around them. There must be enough free time and activity for the teacher to discover the children's human preferences. Observing children at play and mischief is an invaluable source of knowledge about them—about leaders and groups, fear, courage, warmth, isolation.

He notes, furthermore, that never in his year of teacher training did he hear anyone talk about how to observe children or even suggest that this might be valuable. With that self-enlightment, the doors open for Kohl and his students as they talk about what is important in their lives and write stories of events that are real. Many of these stories are reproduced in Kohl's book *36 Children,* which was published in 1967. This book shocked the American public with its honest revelation of one teacher's endeavors to set children free from the traditional controlled inadequate education that was commonly offered in urban ghetto schools. Herbert Kohl followed this first book with others as he continued to endeavor to improve the education of children in poor urban areas.

Jonathan Kozol: Teaching Fourth Grade in a "Compensatory Program" in Boston

Jonathan Kozol, an untrained teacher, is hired in the 1964–1965 school year as a long-term substitute to work with 35 "bewildered-looking" fourth-grade children, most of whom are black. His class shares an auditorium with another fourth-grade class, the glee club, play rehearsals, special reading, special arithmetic, at times a phonics class, and occasionally, a sewing class. At one time Kozol counts 120 people attempting to learn something in this overloaded, inadequate space. The teachers accept what is given, but Kozol notes:

> One of the most grim things about teaching in such a school and such a system is that you do not like to be an incessant barb and irritation to everybody else, so you come under a rather strong compulsion to keep quiet. But after you have been quiet for a while there is an equally strong temptation to begin to accept the conditions of your work or of the children's plight as natural.

A friend accuses Jonathan of "quietly colluding," but Kozol takes notes and eventually describes his experiences in the Boston ghetto schools in *Death at an Early Age,* which was published in 1967.

Ten years after the Brown decision he describes methods, teacher attitudes, and such textbook content as this:

> The people of the British Isles are, like our own, a mixed people. Their ancestors were the sturdy races of northern Europe, such as Celts, Angles, Saxons, Danes, and Normans, whose energy and abilities still appear in their descendants. With such a splendid inheritance what could be more natural than that the British should explore and settle many parts of the world, and, in time, build up the world's greatest colonial empire?

> The people of South Africa have one of the most democratic governments now in existence in any country.

> The white men who have entered Africa are teaching the natives how to live.

Kozol also notes the lack of literature with black characters and the reading books, *Streets and Roads,* with stories about such characters as little white girls like Betty Jane Burns and Sarah Best, Miss Molly and Fluffy Tail, and Miss Valentine of Maple Grove School—completely foreign to the children of South Boston. Finally, Kozol dares to share a poem by Langston Hughes with his students, and he is immediately fired because "that poem is not in the official Boston Course of Study."

Despite a large turnout of Negro parents, a sit-in, and wide media coverage the administration does not reinstate him. Kozol includes a copy of the poem he shared with his students, "Ballad of the Landlord," at the end of *Death at an Early Age.*

Jonathan Kozol did teach in other schools. Following the publication of *Death at an Early Age,* which was widely used in teacher education courses, he has been a much sought-after speaker at education conferences and parent groups. He wrote other books intended to expose the conditions in city schools, particularly the inequality of the education offered children of color in urban schools. Among them are *Who Rules America?* (1987), and perhaps, the most important recent publication, *Savage Inequalities* (2001). His work clearly demonstrates the power of critical thinking and honest, informed writing.

Tracy Kidder: A Case Study of a Fifth-Grade Teacher in Holyoke, Massachusetts

Skilled author Tracy Kidder was once a teacher of high school English, but it is not his own teaching that he chooses to write about. Rather, he relates the story of Chris Zajac's year with a troupe of fifth graders who live in the poorest section of one of our smaller industrial cities. Clearly, Kidder has observed and listened with understanding in order to produce his publication, *Among Schoolchildren,* published in 1989. Although he changed the names of the children and the student teacher, this case study describes the work of a real teacher with all her doubts as she attempts to help individual pupils, half of whom are Puerto Rican.

We come to know to know Clarence, for example, "a small, lithe, brown-skinned boy with large eyes and deep dimples." Clarence made frequent journeys to the pencil sharpener, taking "the longest possible route around the room, walking heel-to-toe and brushing the back of one leg within the shin of the other at every step—a cheerful little dance across the blue carpet, around the perimeter of desks, and along the back wall, passing under the American flag, which didn't quite brush his head."

Clarence's cumulative record (*cume file*) is as thick as the Boston phone book, but Chris is not interested in reading it. She keeps him after school, which only punishes her because Clarence refuses to write. As he leaves the classroom after the second detention, he calls back, "I hate Mrs. Zajac!" and Chris is left with her feelings of guilt. But Mrs. Zajac doesn't give up.

We come to know Chris Zajac intimately, sharing her innermost thoughts, her reluctance to let the student teacher take over "her" classroom, her worries about what will happen to Judith, a bright child who has great potential, and, of course, Clarence, who is still angry at the end of the year. The dialogue is real; the situations typical of poor urban schools, the interactions with principal and other teachers, human. It's nonfiction, but it reads like a novel punctuated with humor and pathos.

Through *Among Schoolchildren* we also come to know Tracy Kidder, a Pulitzer Prize–winning author. You may be interested in exploring his other works: *The Road to Yuba City* (1989), *The Soul of a New Machine* (1999), and *House* (2002).

Share Reading with Your Students

Occasionally, tell your students about something you are reading. Read a segment aloud. (You're providing a good role model!) Engage your students in a recommended strategy for stimulating reading: Sustained Silent Reading. Set aside a given time when everyone reads, including the teacher! Bring in a cart of multicultural literature so all students have something to read. Then, read, read, read without interruption for perhaps twenty minutes. Students who become accustomed to this regular reading time really enjoy it. Schedule a time for talking in small groups about what each person is reading. (You join a group, too.) Such talk motivates interest in reading and introduces students to different books they might enjoy.

Arrange to take your students to the library so that they get library cards, too, or give older students points if they show you that they have obtained a card (let them tell others how they got the card).

Just as with your students, once you get hooked on reading, you will continue. Make going to the library a habit for yourself.

CONNECTIONS

As a result of the mobility within our society, the student mix in most classrooms in K–8 schools throughout the United States has changed perceptibly in the past twenty to thirty years. Increasingly, even rural and small-town classrooms in the Midwest more closely reflect the diversity of the total population in the United States. Frequently, the cultural roots of the teacher and the children she or he teaches are very different. Therefore, all teachers must know how to provide an equitable education for students from a wide variety of cultural backgrounds. Moreover, teachers must lead the way in promoting multiculturalism at the local and state levels.

FOLLOW-THROUGH

Reviewing Your RTP

1. Review your Reflective Teaching Portfolio to see how your thinking has evolved during this course. Observe the kinds of comments you made as you completed each chapter's focus. Write a one-page summary of your preparation as a multicultural teacher. Answer some of these questions as you write:

   - How has your thinking changed from the beginning of this course to the end?
   - What ideas do you think will be most helpful to you as a classroom teacher?
   - What do you plan to do now to make sure that you continue to grow as an outstanding teacher of multicultural concepts and understandings?

2. Prepare to share your portfolio with your instructor. Mark those items that you would especially like him or her to read or to be aware of. Naturally, you will select those things in which you take most pride.

Sharing Conclusions in Your CLG

1. In your CLG plan to interview local educators to identify one exemplary practice related to multicultural education in your area. Write a review of this idea or program and attempt to obtain newspaper coverage for this outstanding instructional practice.
2. Write a letter together to the editor of your local newspaper, pointing out the accomplishments of one minority group in your community.

GROWING A PROFESSIONAL LIBRARY

Barbara Feinberg. *Welcome to Lizard Motel: Children, Stories, and the Mystery of Making Things Up.* Beacon, 2004.

Deborah Meier, Theodore P. Sizer, and Nancy F. Sizer, eds. *Keeping School: Letters to Families from Principals of Two Small Schools.* Beacon, 2004. Principals write to families about four themes: authority, community, learning, and standards.

ENDNOTES

1. National Council for Accreditation of Teacher Education, *Standards.* NCATE, 1987.
2. Association of Supervision and Curriculum Development, *Survey on Teacher Education.* ASCD, 1992.
3. Mary Jalongo. In Edwina B. Vold, *Multicultural Education in Early Education Classrooms,* 6th ed. National Education Association, 1992, pp. 62–3.

AN AFTERWORD

Now we have come full circle with you in our study of multicultural education and our focus on *Multicultural Teaching*. We have shared our model focusing on *Esteem, Empathy, and Equity* and its implications for instruction in all classrooms. As authors, we know that our words will never be heard by all the students in K–8 classrooms. We cannot reach each child for whom these words are truly intended.

We must trust you as teachers to be our emmissaries, to go forth into the schools as teachers dedicated toward making a difference in the lives of children. We trust you to establish a classroom climate in which all children have a sense of belonging. And we trust you to smile at those diverse faces, even though some may scowl in return.

Furthermore, we hope you will address children with respect and caring and get to know each one as an individual who needs you desperately as an adult guide and advocate at this crucial stage of their lives. Keep in mind the words of the famous educator, John Dewey, who wrote in 1902:

> Education enables all individuals to come into full possession of all their powers.

That, then, is our expectation for you and for our schools. You are one of the educators who will make it possible for children to reach their fullest potentials. What you do in one year with a single child may make the difference between success and failure in achieving this goal.

What you do also in speaking out about curriculum development and how teachers can collaborate to make our schools outstanding is essential.

Go forth with aim and purpose. We wish you well.

We are always glad to hear from our readers who have ideas to share. Contact us at *tiedtp@aol.com* or *irist@cwo.com*.

Pamela and Iris Tiedt

MULTICULTURAL TEACHING

INDEX

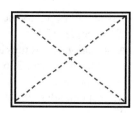